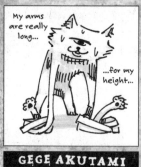

My arms
are really
long...

...for my
height...

GEGE AKUTAMI

Here's the prequel to *Jujutsu Kaisen*,
serialized in *Weekly Shonen Jump*.
Good things are sure to come to
those who read this!

GEGE AKUTAMI published a few short
works before starting *Jujutsu Kaisen*, which began
serialization in *Weekly Shonen Jump* in 2018.

JUJUTSU KAISEN

VOLUME 0
SHONEN JUMP MANGA EDITION

BY GEGE AKUTAMI

TRANSLATION **Stefan Koza**
TOUCH-UP ART & LETTERING **Snir Aharon**
DESIGN **Joy Zhang**
EDITOR **John Bae**

Published by VIZ Media, LLC
P.O. Box 77010
San Francisco, CA 94107

10 9 8 7 6 5 4 3 2 1
First printing, January 2021

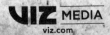

viz.com

JUJUTSU KAISEN

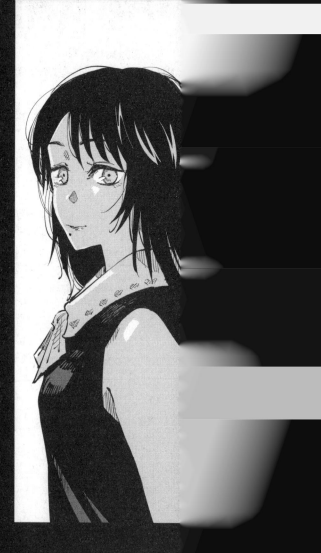

STORY AND ART BY GEGE AKUTAMI

JUJUTSU KAISEN

0

BLINDING DARKNESS

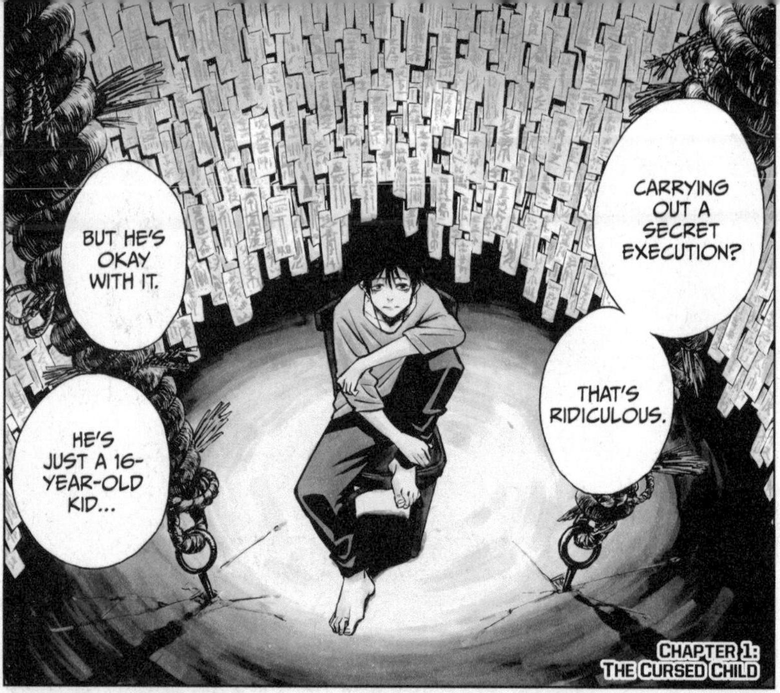
CARRYING OUT A SECRET EXECUTION?
THAT'S RIDICULOUS.
BUT HE'S OKAY WITH IT.
HE'S JUST A 16-YEAR-OLD KID...
CHAPTER 1: THE CURSED CHILD

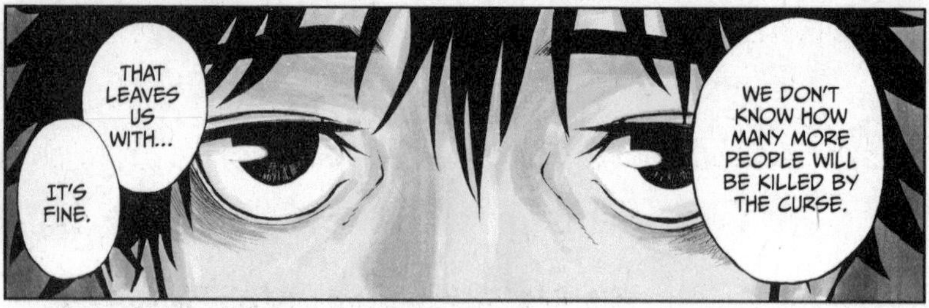
WE DON'T KNOW HOW MANY MORE PEOPLE WILL BE KILLED BY THE CURSE.
THAT LEAVES US WITH...
IT'S FINE.

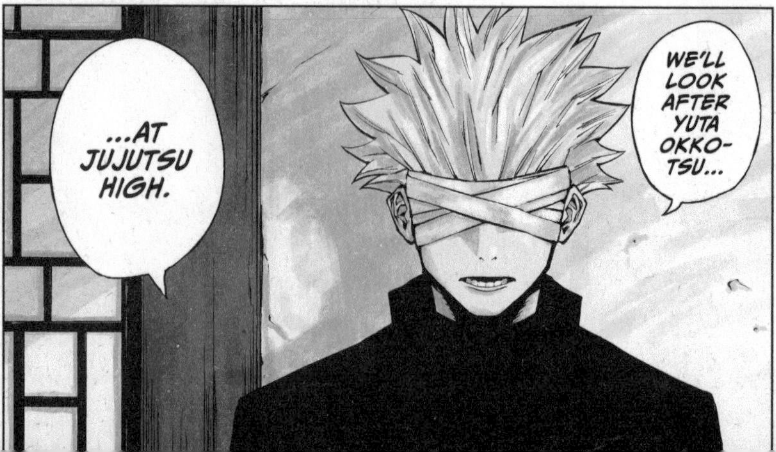
WE'LL LOOK AFTER YUTA OKKOTSU...
...AT JUJUTSU HIGH.

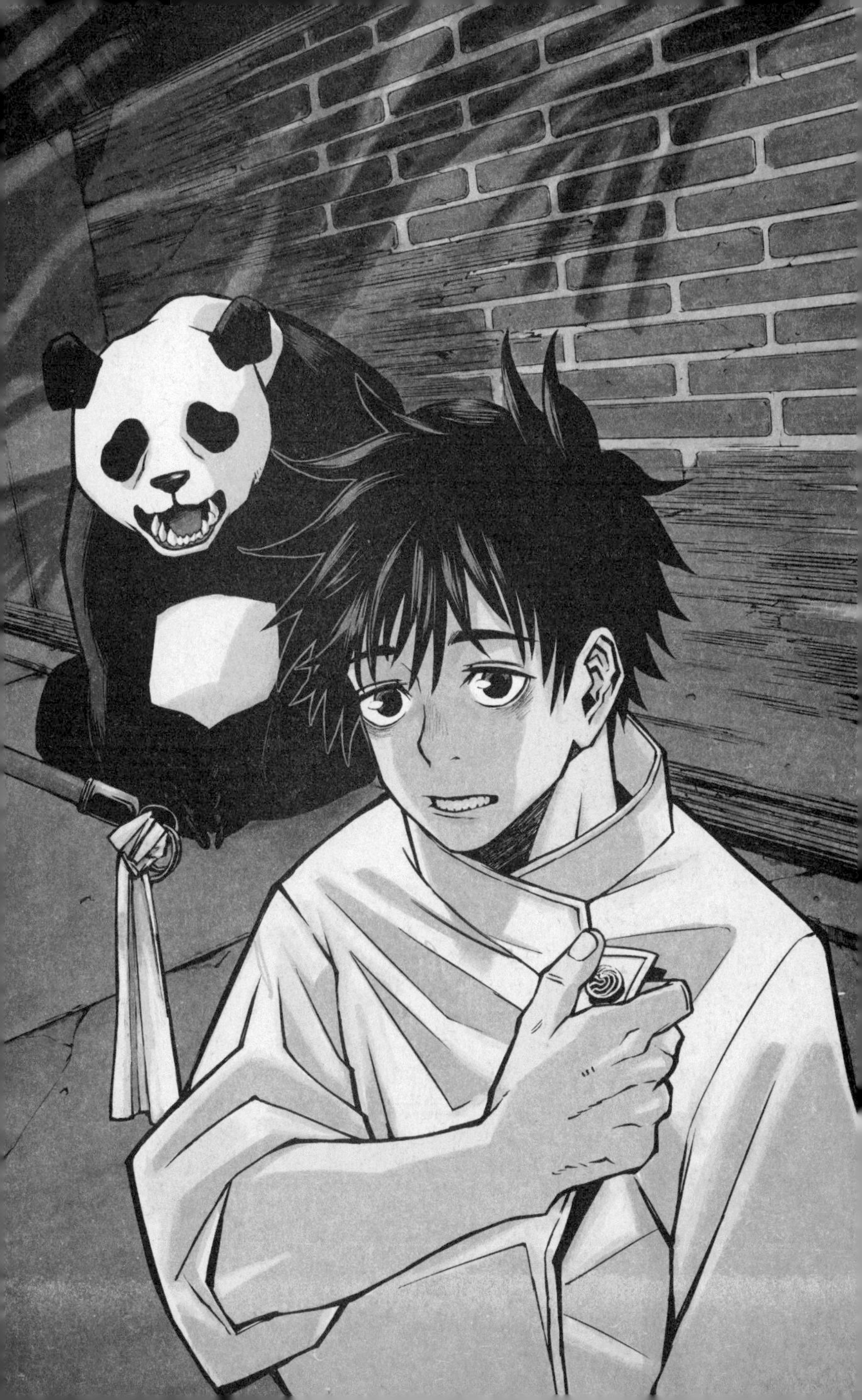

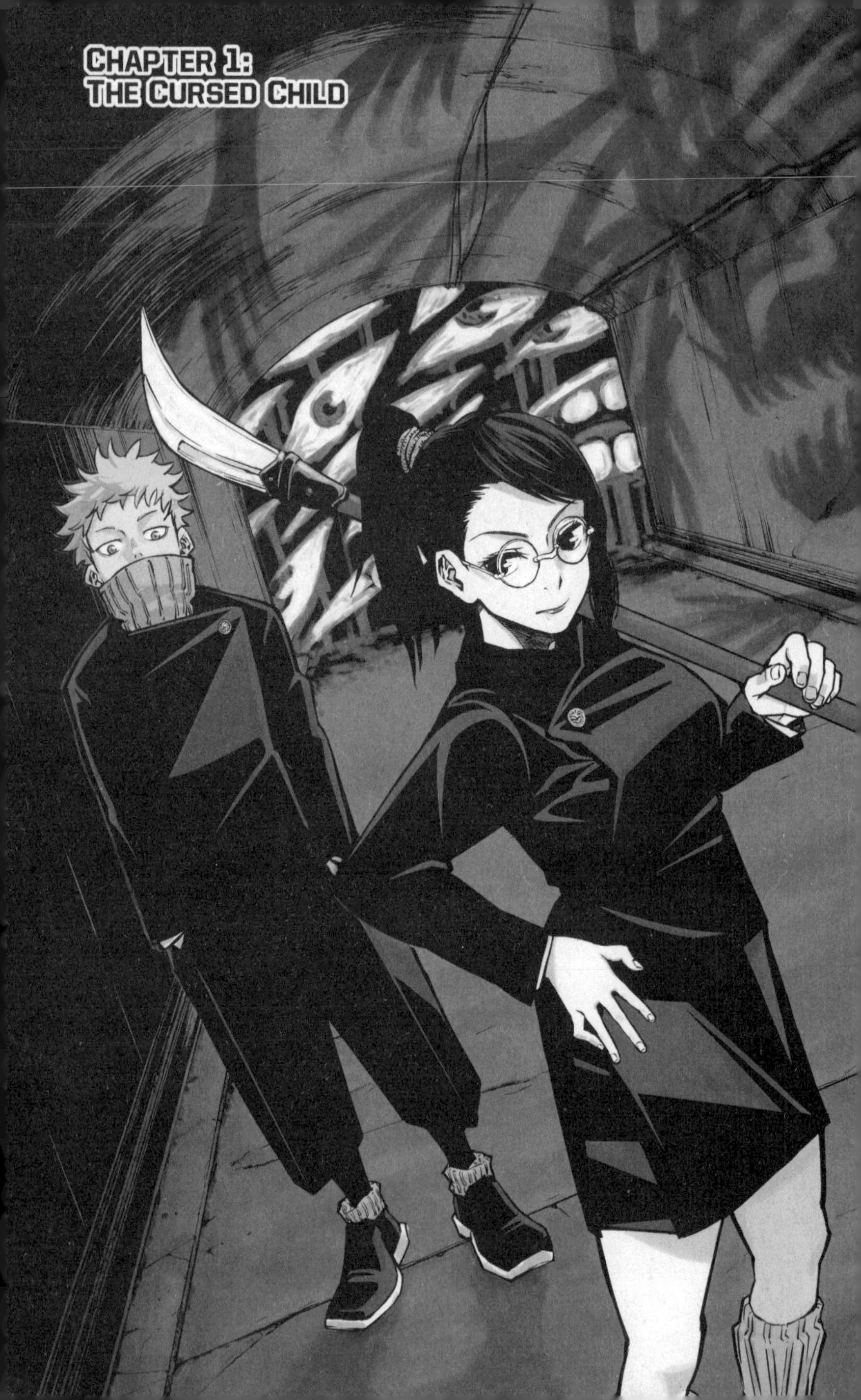
CHAPTER 1:
THE CURSED CHILD

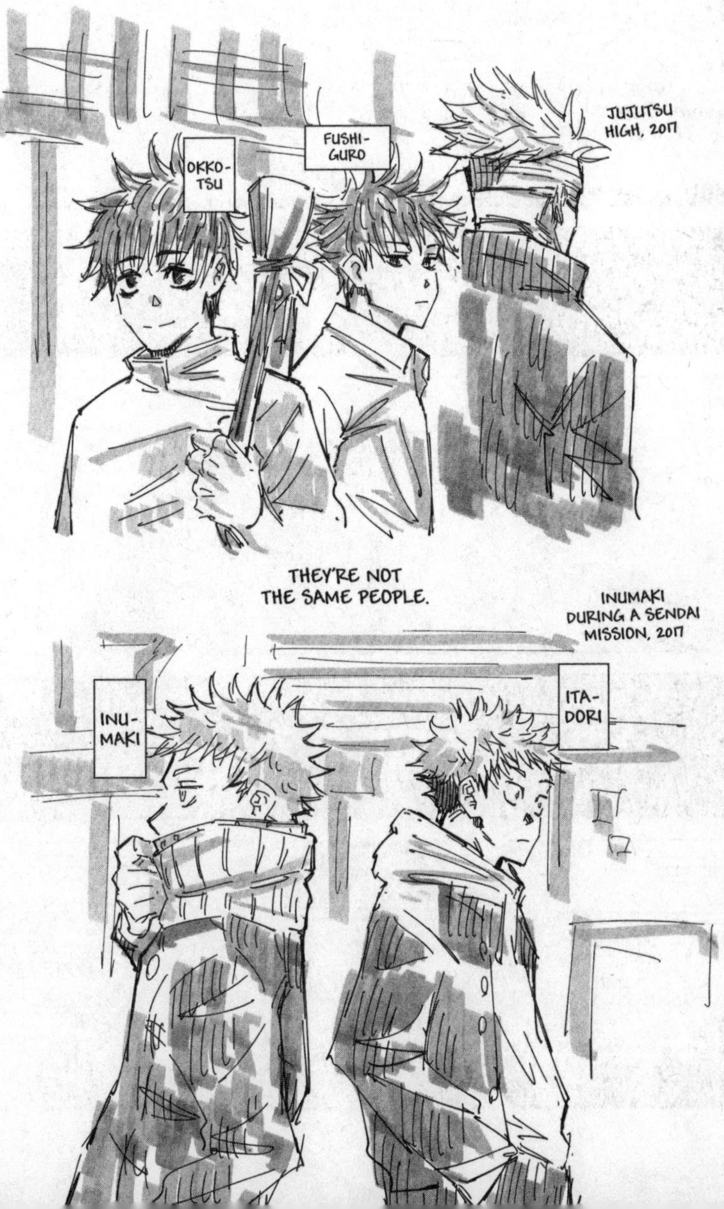
JUJUTSU HIGH, 2017
FUSHI-GURO
OKKO-TSU
THEY'RE NOT THE SAME PEOPLE.
INUMAKI DURING A SENDAI MISSION, 2017
ITA-DORI
INU-MAKI

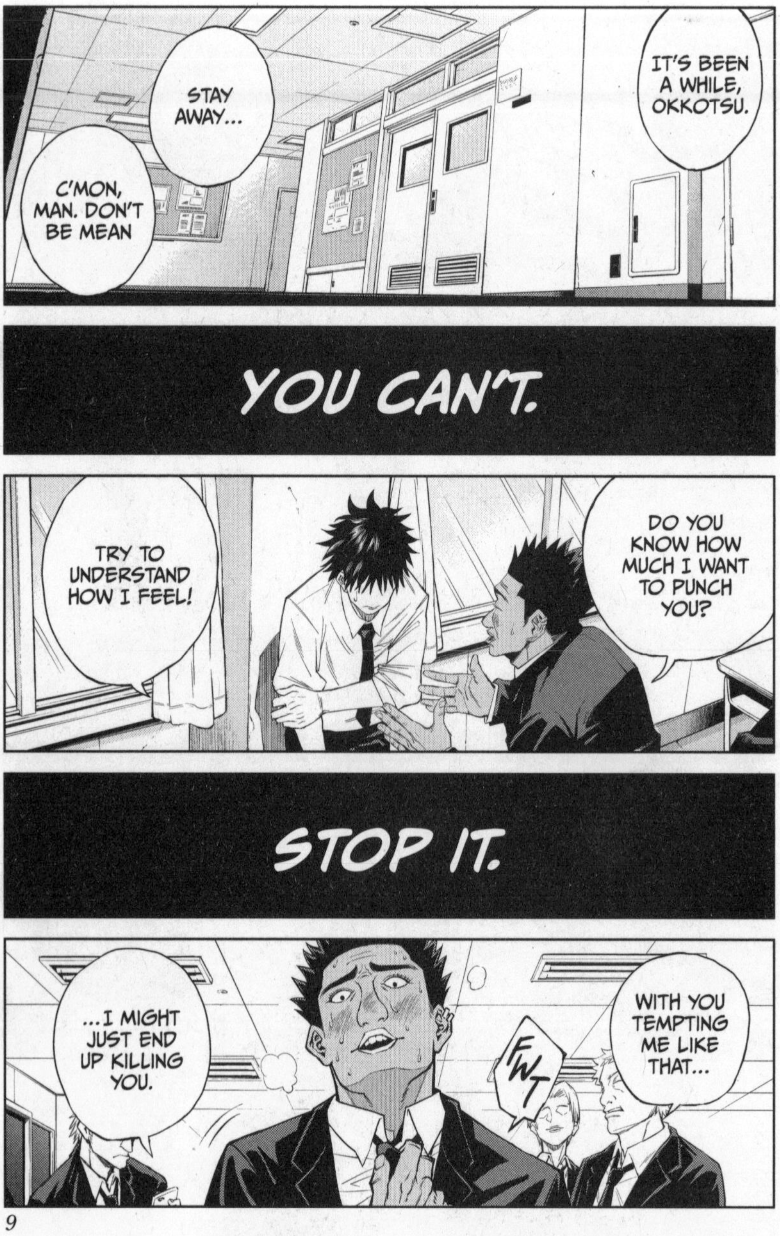
IT'S BEEN A WHILE, OKKOTSU.
STAY AWAY...
C'MON, MAN. DON'T BE MEAN
YOU CAN'T.
DO YOU KNOW HOW MUCH I WANT TO PUNCH YOU?
TRY TO UNDERSTAND HOW I FEEL!
STOP IT.
WITH YOU TEMPTING ME LIKE THAT...
FWT
...I MIGHT JUST END UP KILLING YOU.

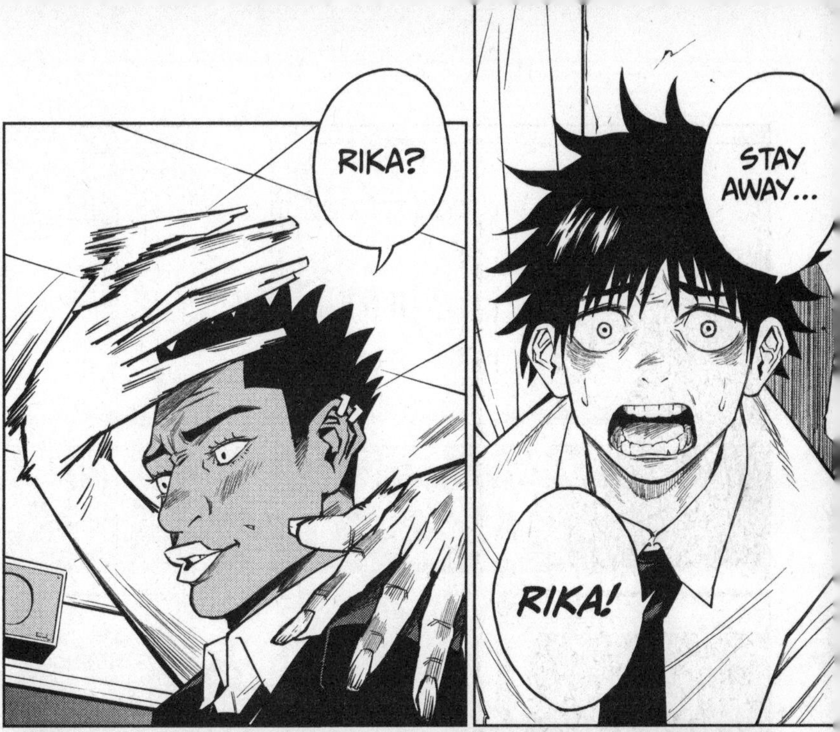
STAY AWAY...
RIKA!
RIKA?

REPORT—TOKYO, NOVEMBER 2016
FOUR STUDENTS, INCLUDING THE RINGLEADER, SUFFER SEVERE INJURIES IN RESPONSE TO THEIR PERSISTENT BULLYING BEHAVIOR.

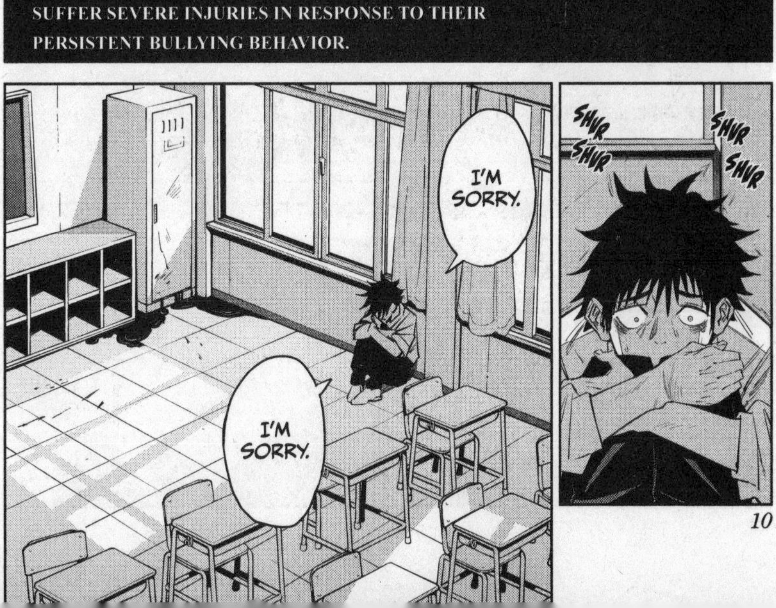
SHVR SHVR
SHVR SHVR
I'M SORRY.
I'M SORRY.

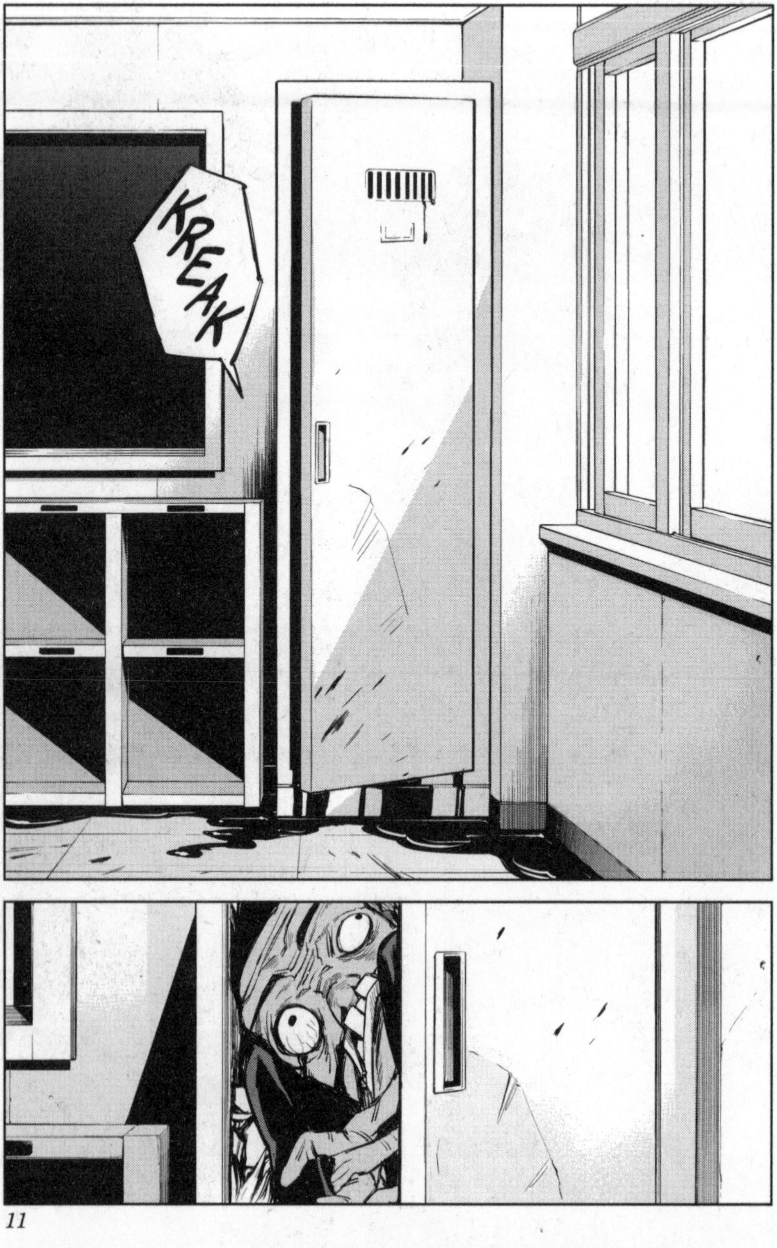
KREAK

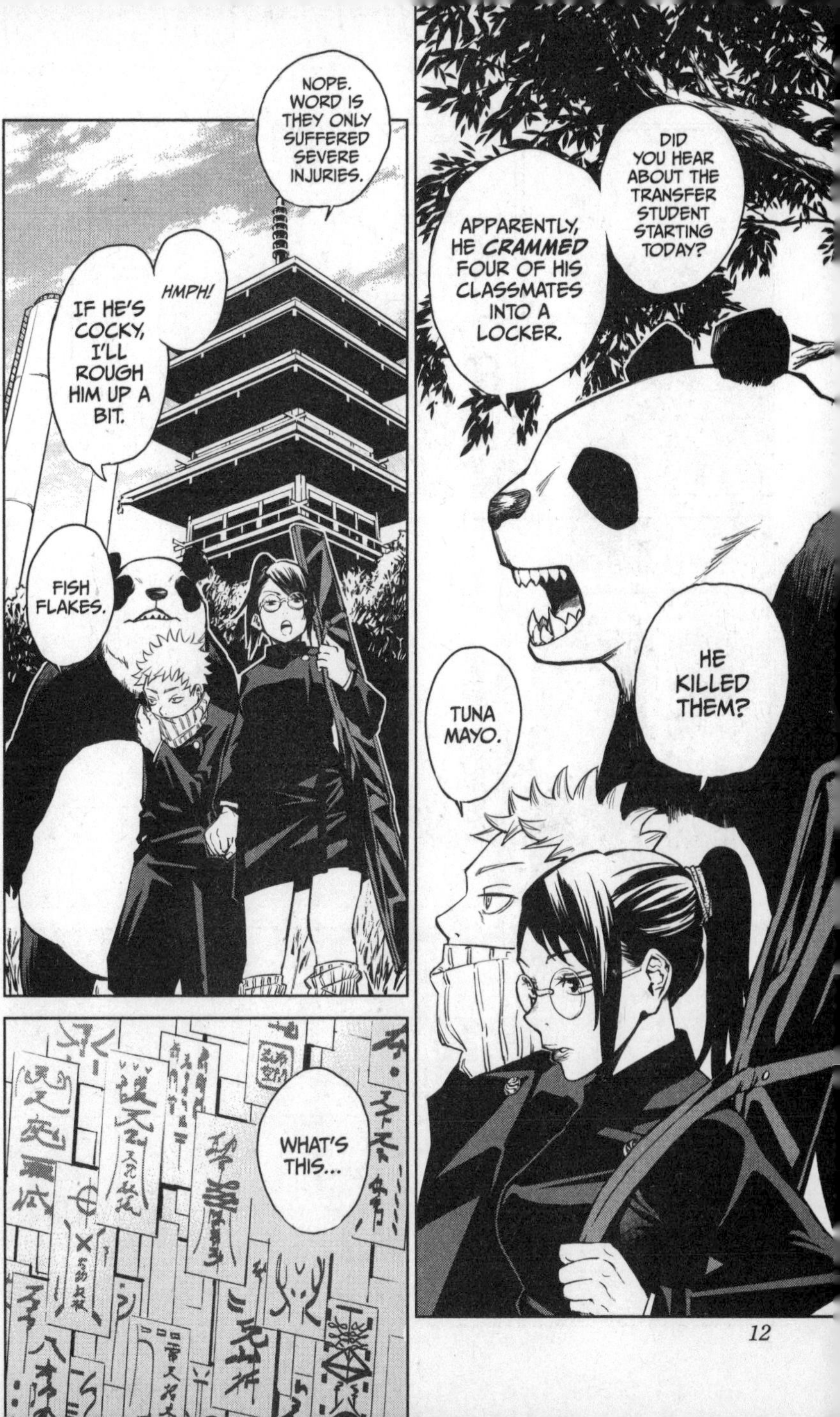
DID YOU HEAR ABOUT THE TRANSFER STUDENT STARTING TODAY?
APPARENTLY, HE *CRAMMED* FOUR OF HIS CLASSMATES INTO A LOCKER.
HE KILLED THEM?
TUNA MAYO.
NOPE. WORD IS THEY ONLY SUFFERED SEVERE INJURIES.
HMPH!
IF HE'S COCKY, I'LL ROUGH HIM UP A BIT.
FISH FLAKES.
WHAT'S THIS...

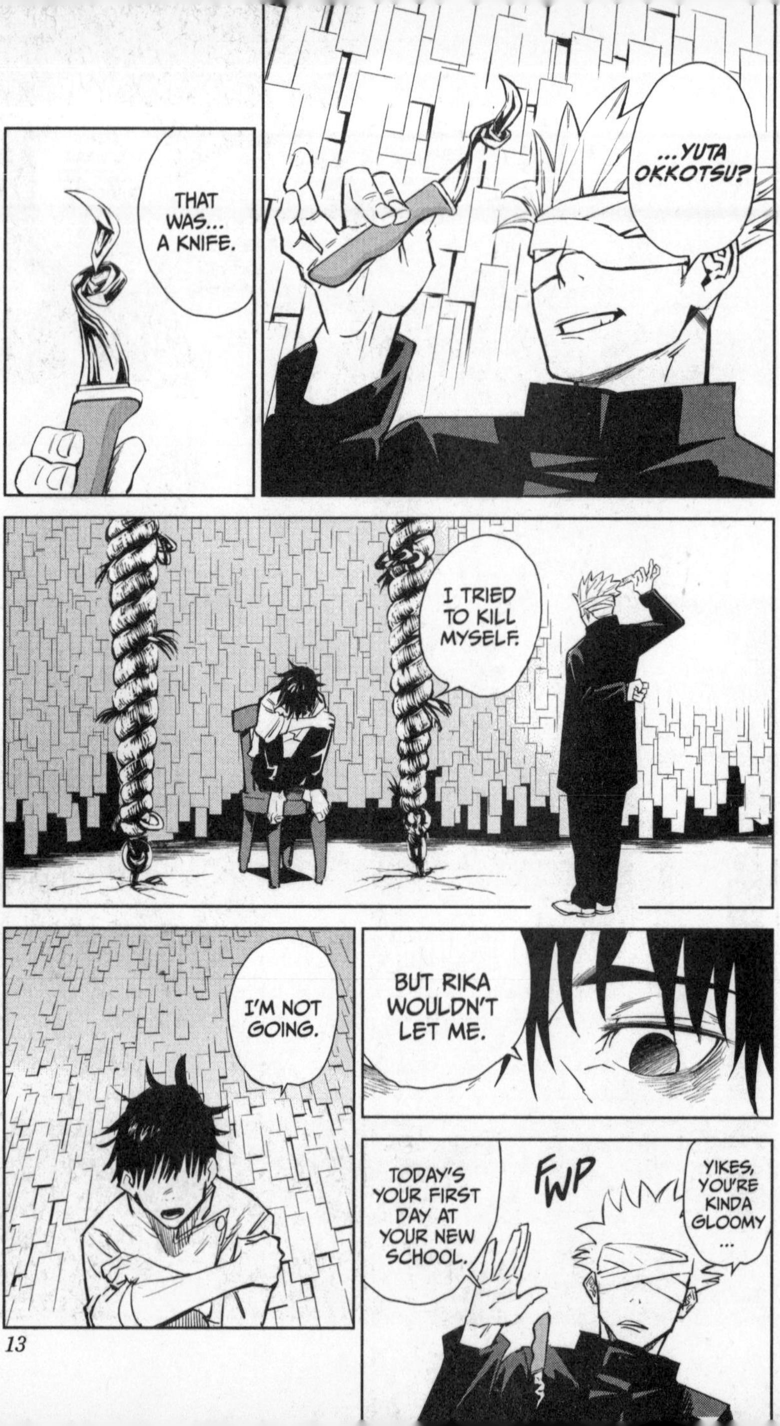
...YUTA OKKOTSU?
THAT WAS... A KNIFE.
I TRIED TO KILL MYSELF.
BUT RIKA WOULDN'T LET ME.
YIKES, YOU'RE KINDA GLOOMY ...
FWP
TODAY'S YOUR FIRST DAY AT YOUR NEW SCHOOL.
I'M NOT GOING.

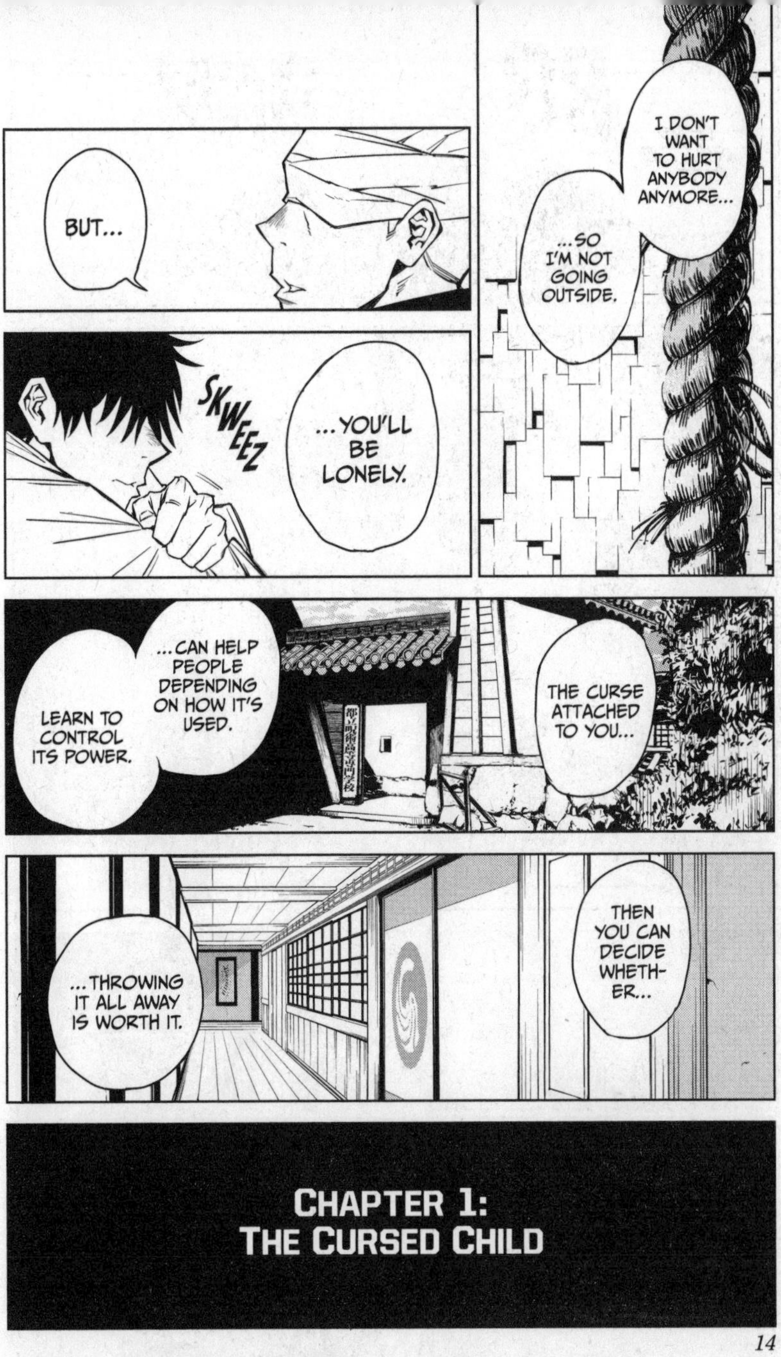
I DON'T WANT TO HURT ANYBODY ANYMORE...
...SO I'M NOT GOING OUTSIDE.
BUT...
...YOU'LL BE LONELY.
SKWEEZ
THE CURSE ATTACHED TO YOU...
...CAN HELP PEOPLE DEPENDING ON HOW IT'S USED.
LEARN TO CONTROL ITS POWER.
THEN YOU CAN DECIDE WHETH-ER...
...THROWING IT ALL AWAY IS WORTH IT.

Chapter 1: The Cursed Child

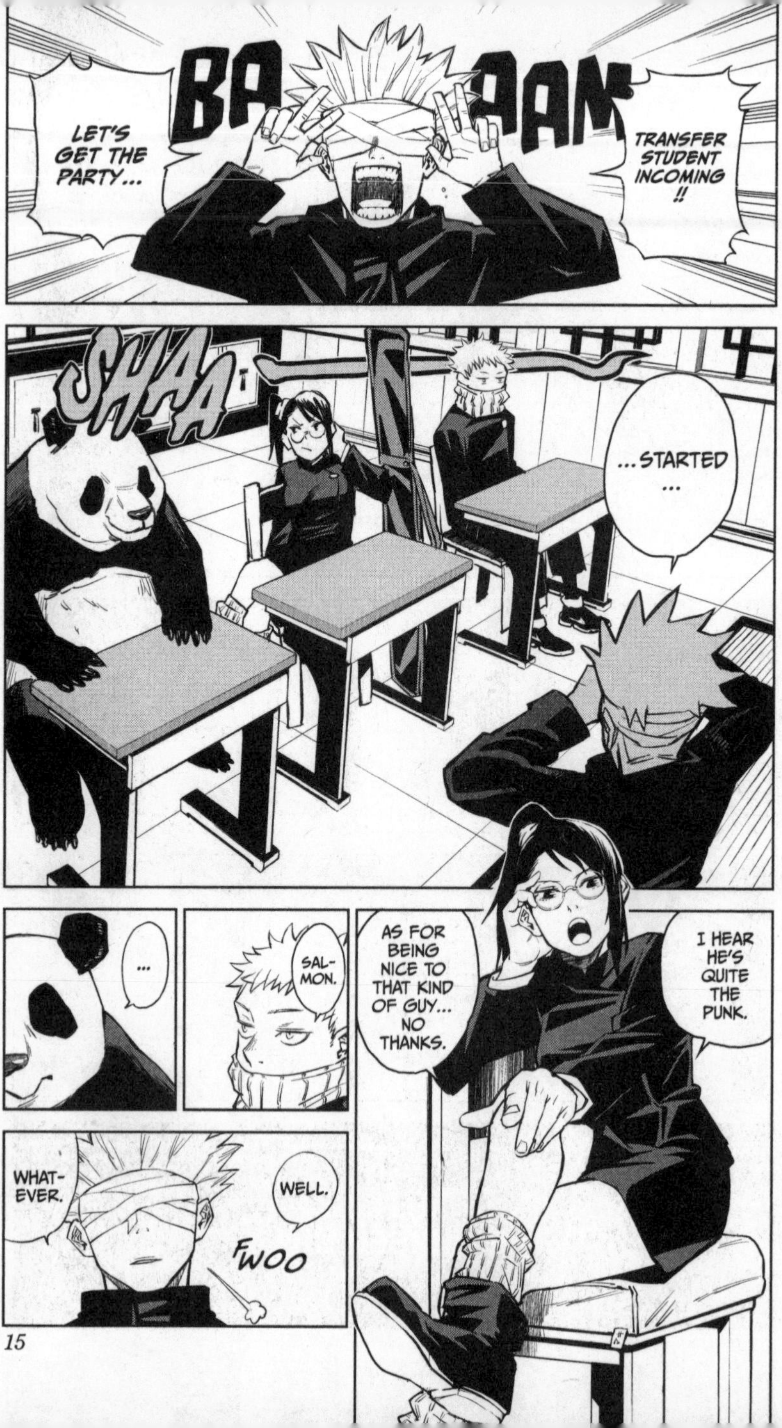
TRANSFER STUDENT INCOMING!!
BA AAM
LET'S GET THE PARTY...
...STARTED...
SHAA
I HEAR HE'S QUITE THE PUNK.
AS FOR BEING NICE TO THAT KIND OF GUY... NO THANKS.
SAL-MON.
...
WELL.
WHAT-EVER.
FWOO

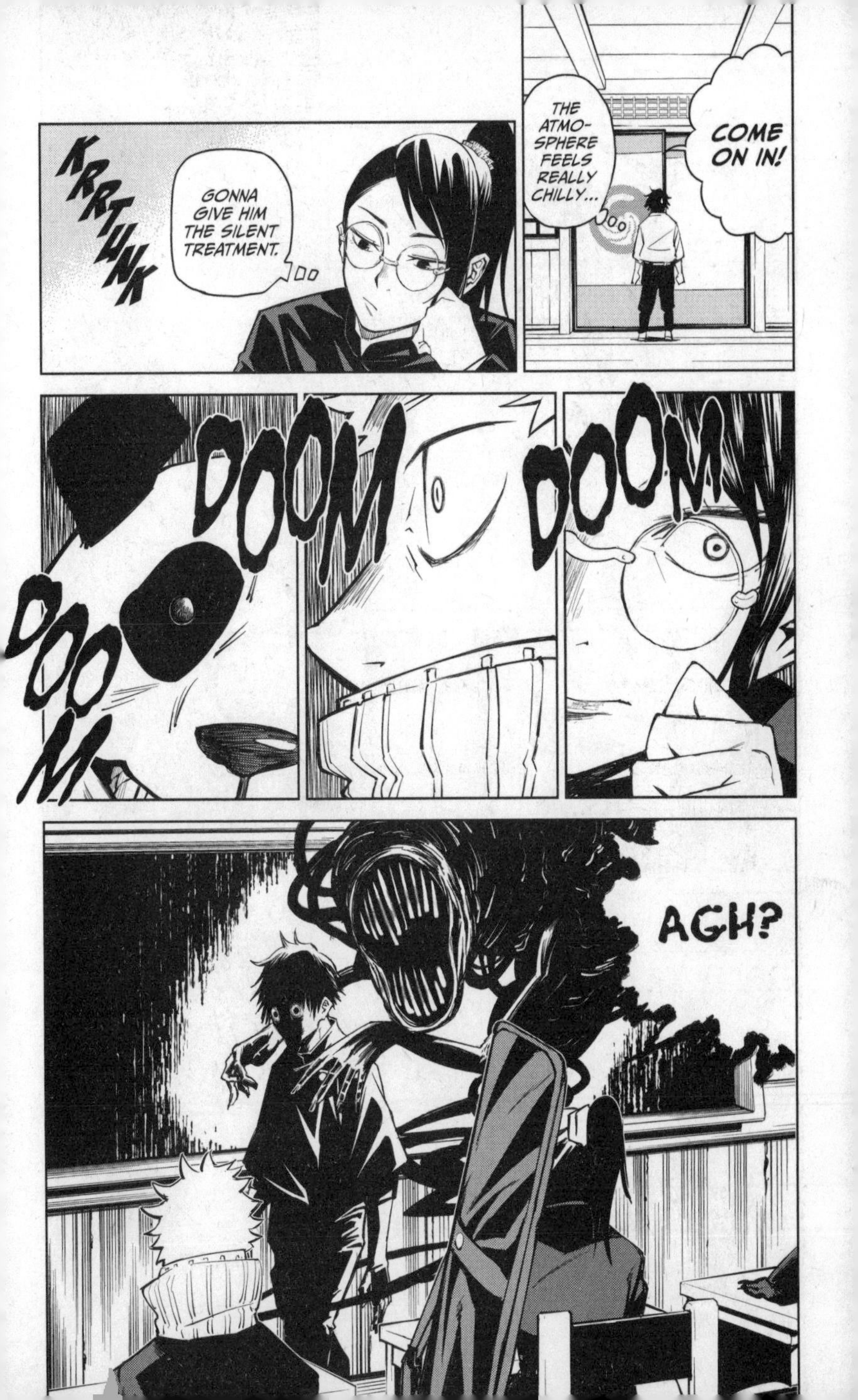
COME ON IN!
THE ATMOSPHERE FEELS REALLY CHILLY...
KRRTUNK
GONNA GIVE HIM THE SILENT TREATMENT.
DOOM
DOOM
DOOM
AGH?

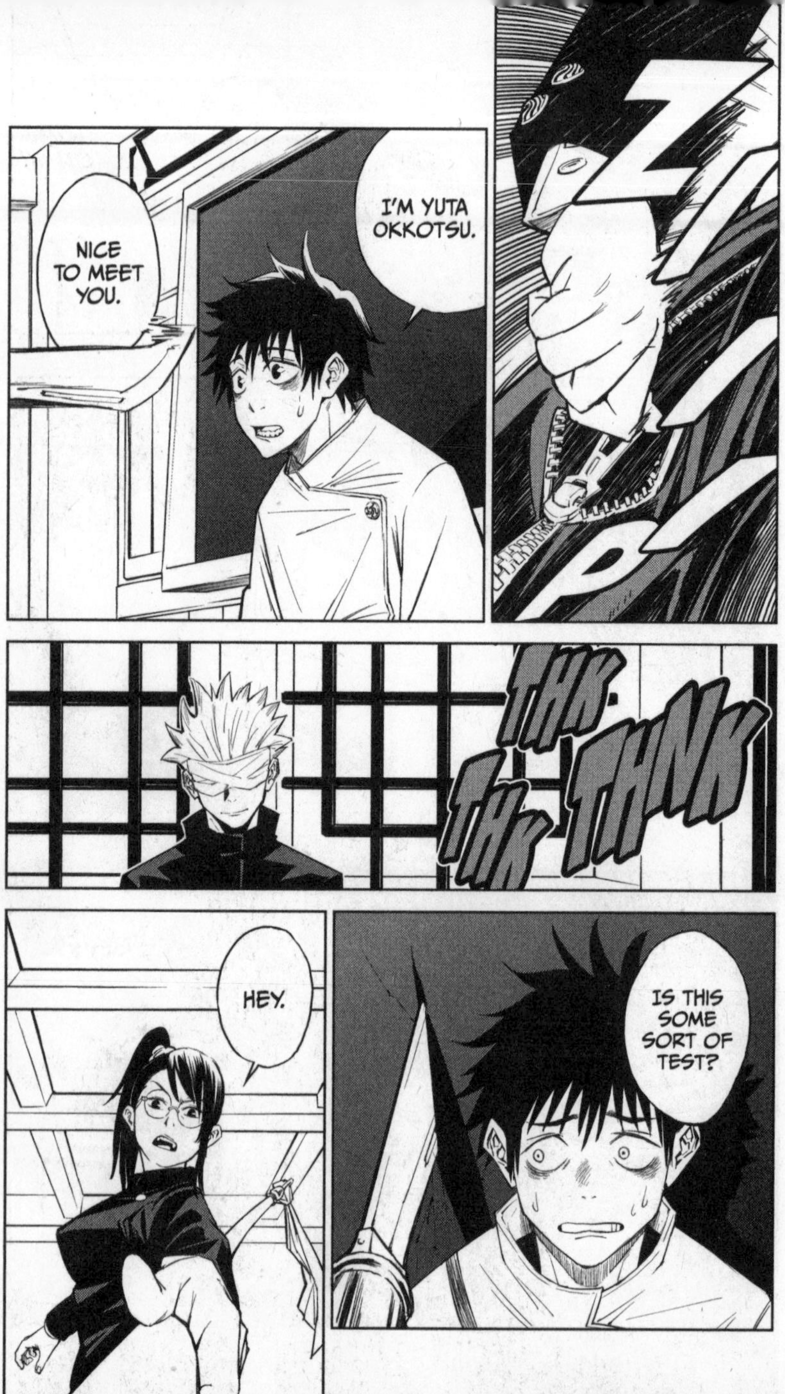
ZIP
I'M YUTA OKKOTSU.
NICE TO MEET YOU.
THK. THK THUNK
IS THIS SOME SORT OF TEST?
HEY.

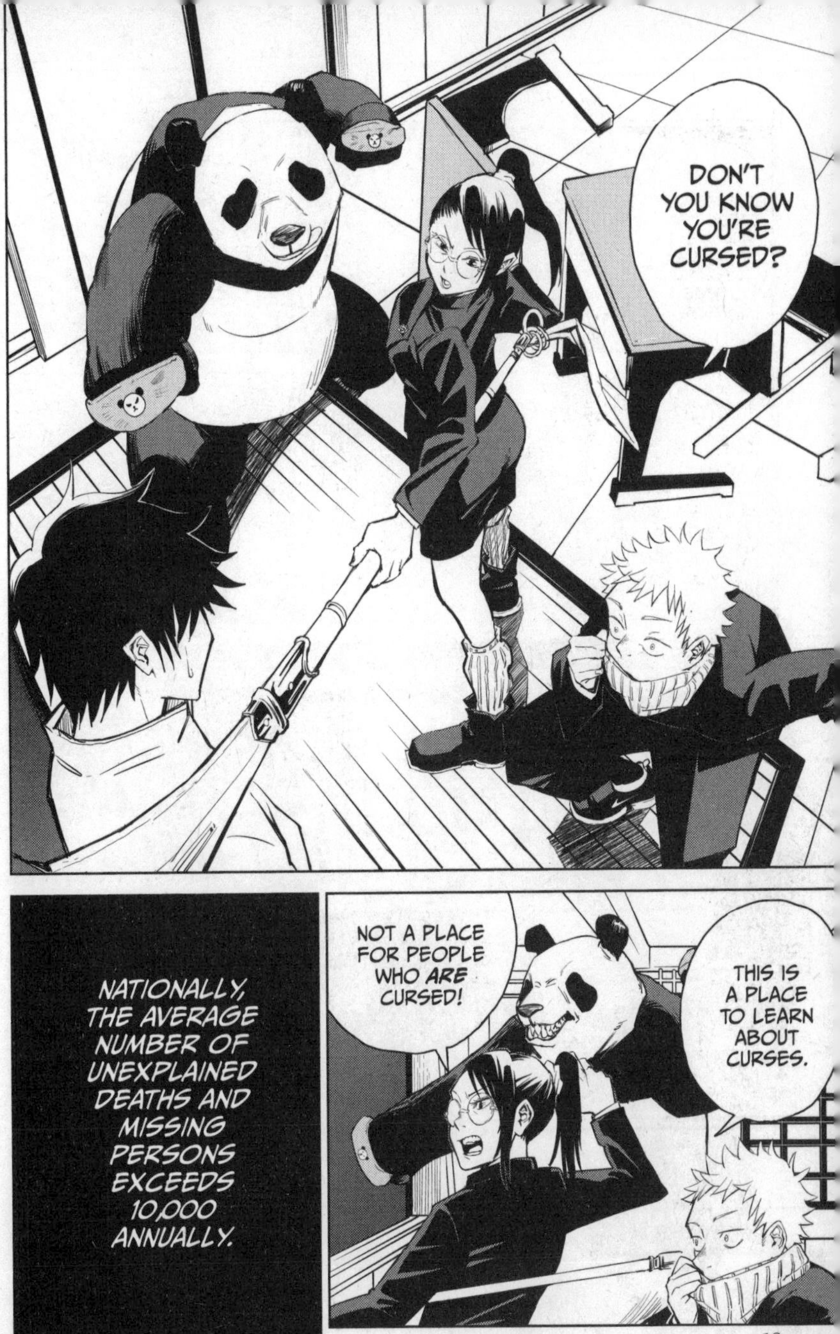
DON'T YOU KNOW YOU'RE CURSED?
THIS IS A PLACE TO LEARN ABOUT CURSES.
NOT A PLACE FOR PEOPLE WHO *ARE* CURSED!
NATIONALLY, THE AVERAGE NUMBER OF UNEXPLAINED DEATHS AND MISSING PERSONS EXCEEDS 10,000 ANNUALLY.

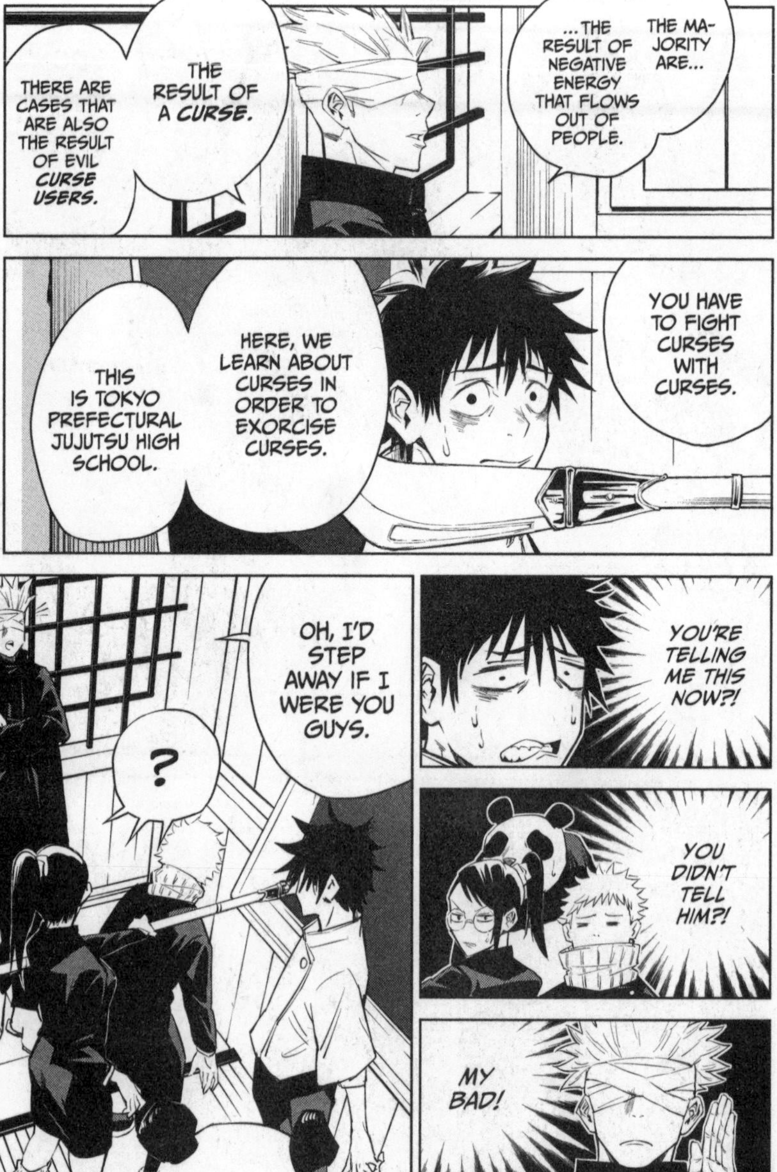
THE MAJORITY ARE...
...THE RESULT OF NEGATIVE ENERGY THAT FLOWS OUT OF PEOPLE.
THE RESULT OF A *CURSE.*
THERE ARE CASES THAT ARE ALSO THE RESULT OF EVIL *CURSE USERS.*
YOU HAVE TO FIGHT CURSES WITH CURSES.
HERE, WE LEARN ABOUT CURSES IN ORDER TO EXORCISE CURSES.
THIS IS TOKYO PREFECTURAL JUJUTSU HIGH SCHOOL.
YOU'RE TELLING ME THIS NOW?!
YOU DIDN'T TELL HIM?!
MY BAD!
OH, I'D STEP AWAY IF I WERE YOU GUYS.
?

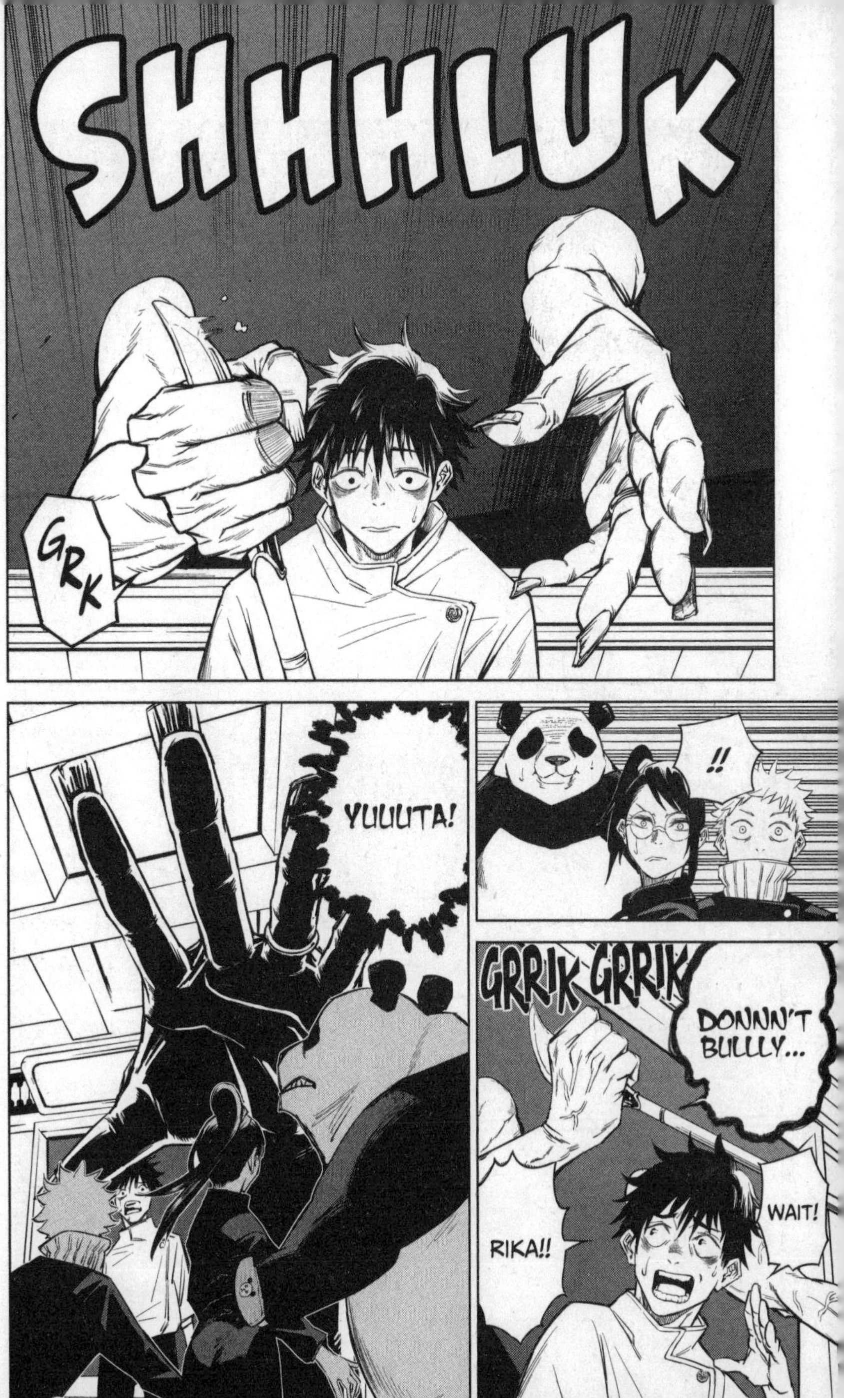
SHHHLUK
GRK
!!
DONNN'T BULLLY...
GRRIK GRRIK
WAIT!
RIKA!!
YUUUTA!

SPECIAL GRADE CURSED HUMAN: YUTA OKKOTSU

SPECIAL GRADE VENGEFUL CURSED SPIRIT: RIKA

RECORD—SIX YEARS AGO, SENDAI CITY, MIYAGI PREFECTURE

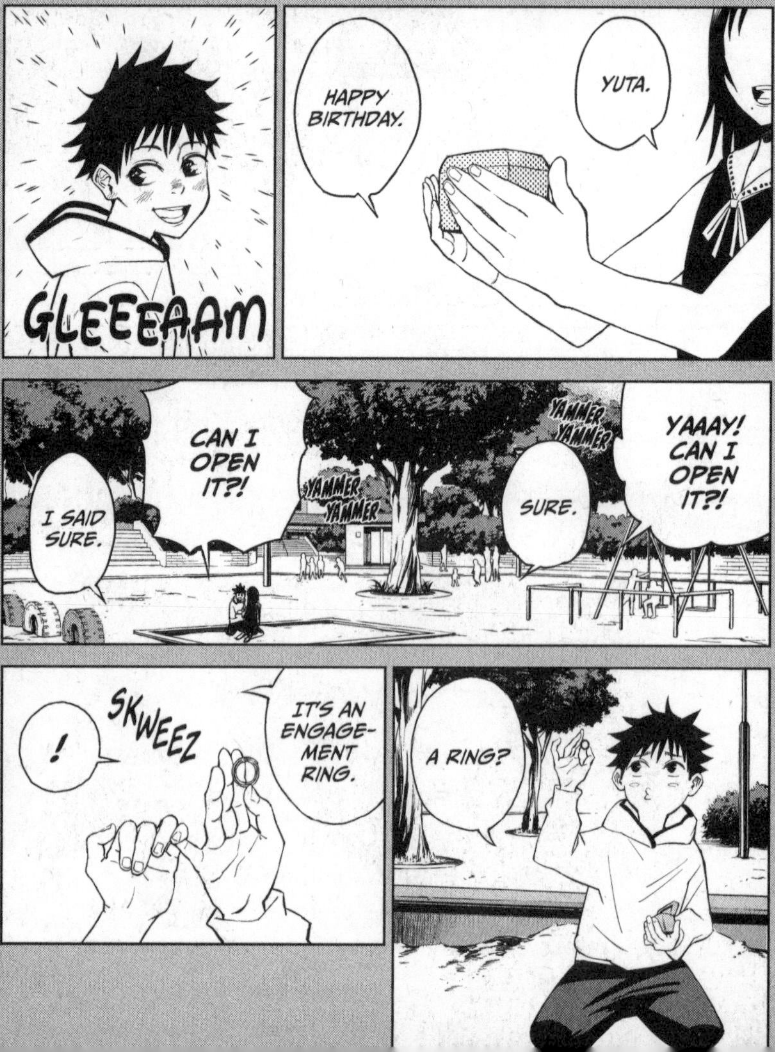
YUTA.
HAPPY BIRTHDAY.
GLEEEAAM
YAAAY! CAN I OPEN IT?!
YAMMER YAMMER
SURE.
YAMMER YAMMER
CAN I OPEN IT?!
I SAID SURE.
A RING?
IT'S AN ENGAGE-MENT RING.
SKWEEZ
!

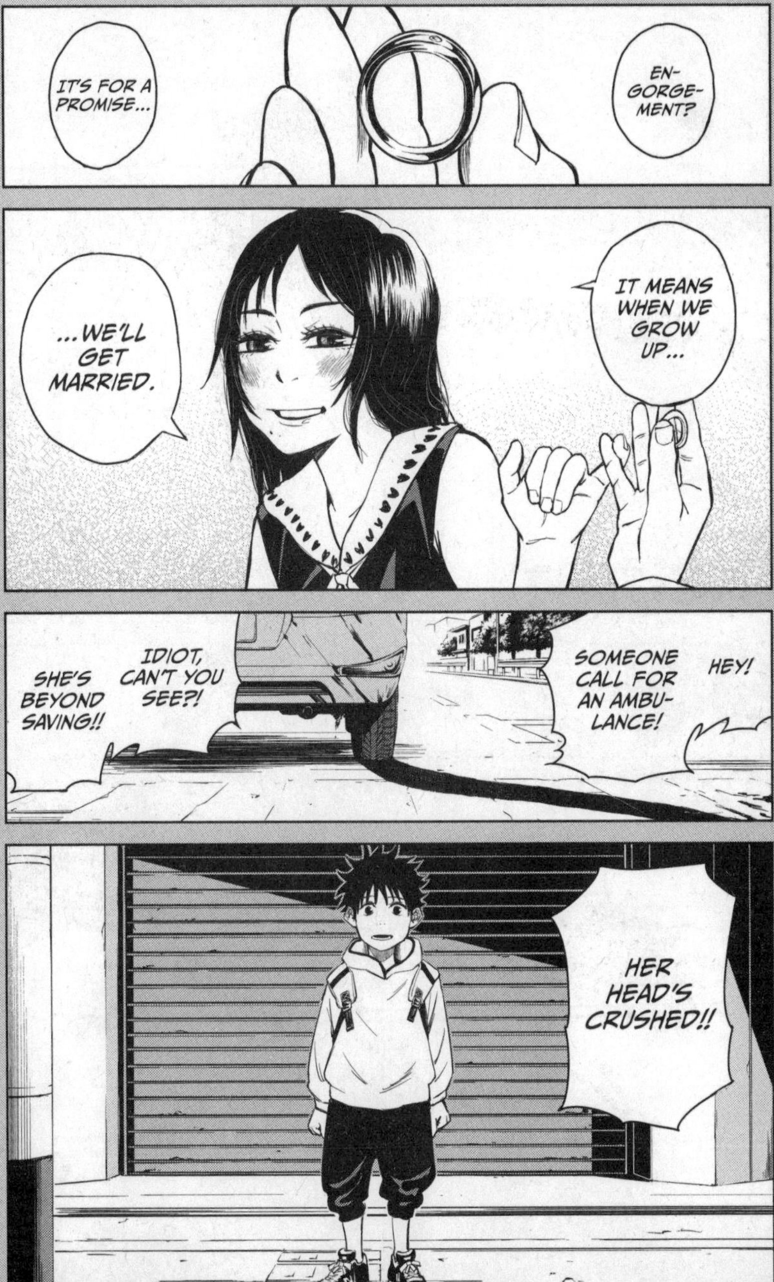
EN-GORGE-MENT?
IT'S FOR A PROMISE...
IT MEANS WHEN WE GROW UP...
...WE'LL GET MARRIED.
HEY!
SOMEONE CALL FOR AN AMBU-LANCE!
IDIOT, CAN'T YOU SEE?!
SHE'S BEYOND SAVING!!
HER HEAD'S CRUSHED!!

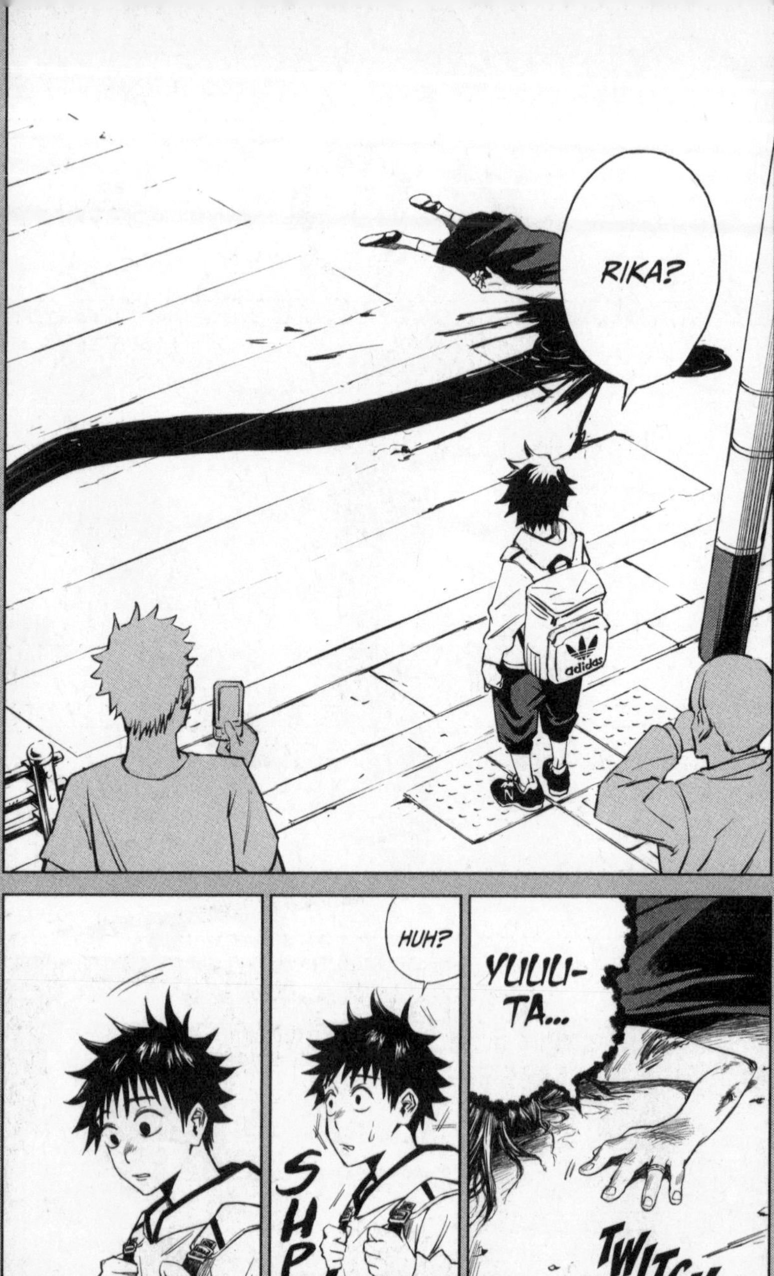
RIKA?
adidas
YUUU-TA...
TWITCH
HUH?
SHP

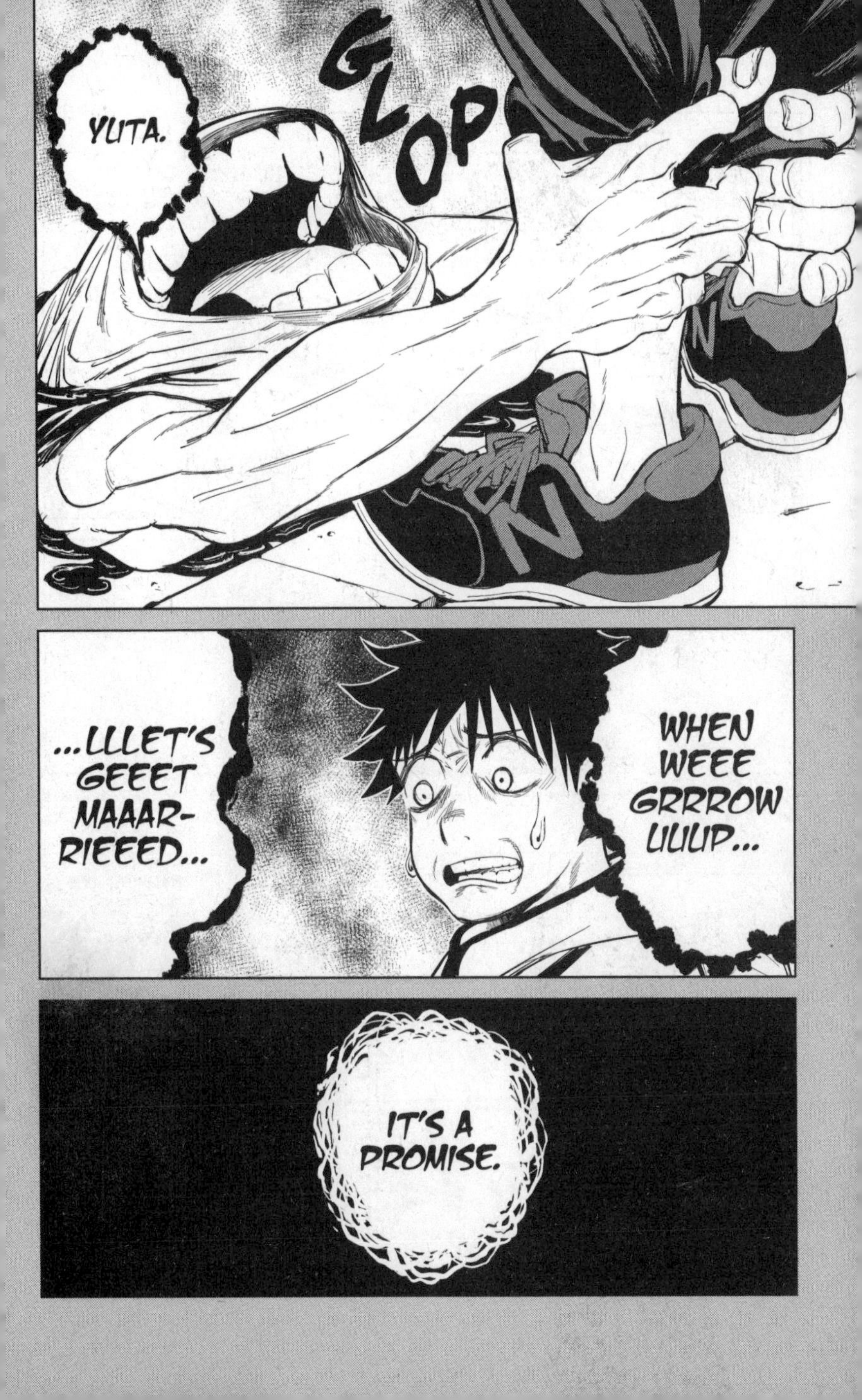
GLOP
YUTA.
WHEN WEEE GRRROW UUUP...
...LLLET'S GEEET MAAAR-RIEEED...
IT'S A PROMISE.

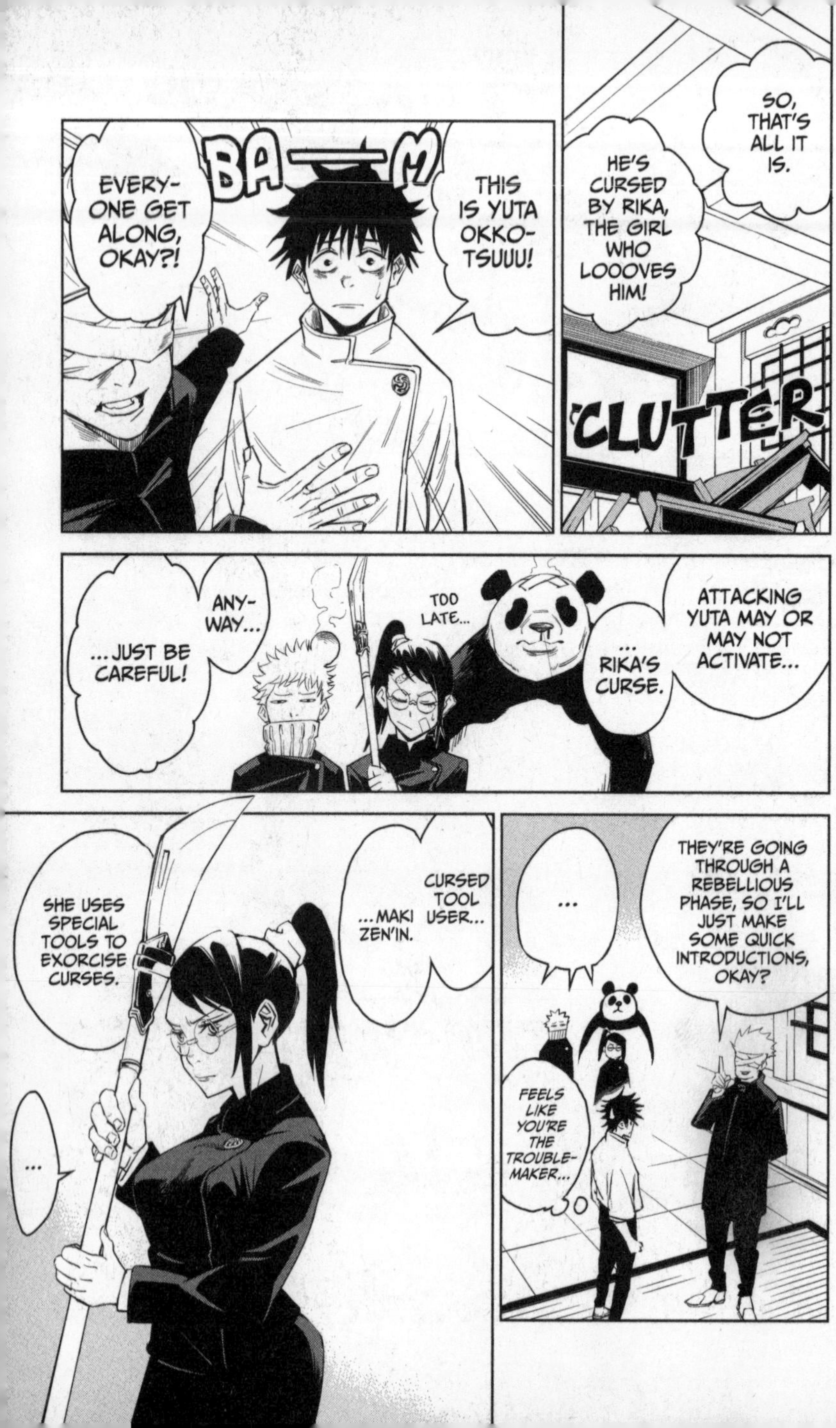
SO, THAT'S ALL IT IS.
HE'S CURSED BY RIKA, THE GIRL WHO LOOOVES HIM!
CLUTTER
BA—M
THIS IS YUTA OKKOTSUUU!
EVERYONE GET ALONG, OKAY?!
ATTACKING YUTA MAY OR MAY NOT ACTIVATE...
... RIKA'S CURSE.
TOO LATE...
ANYWAY...
...JUST BE CAREFUL!
THEY'RE GOING THROUGH A REBELLIOUS PHASE, SO I'LL JUST MAKE SOME QUICK INTRODUCTIONS, OKAY?
...
FEELS LIKE YOU'RE THE TROUBLEMAKER...
CURSED TOOL USER...
...MAKI ZEN'IN.
SHE USES SPECIAL TOOLS TO EXORCISE CURSES.
...

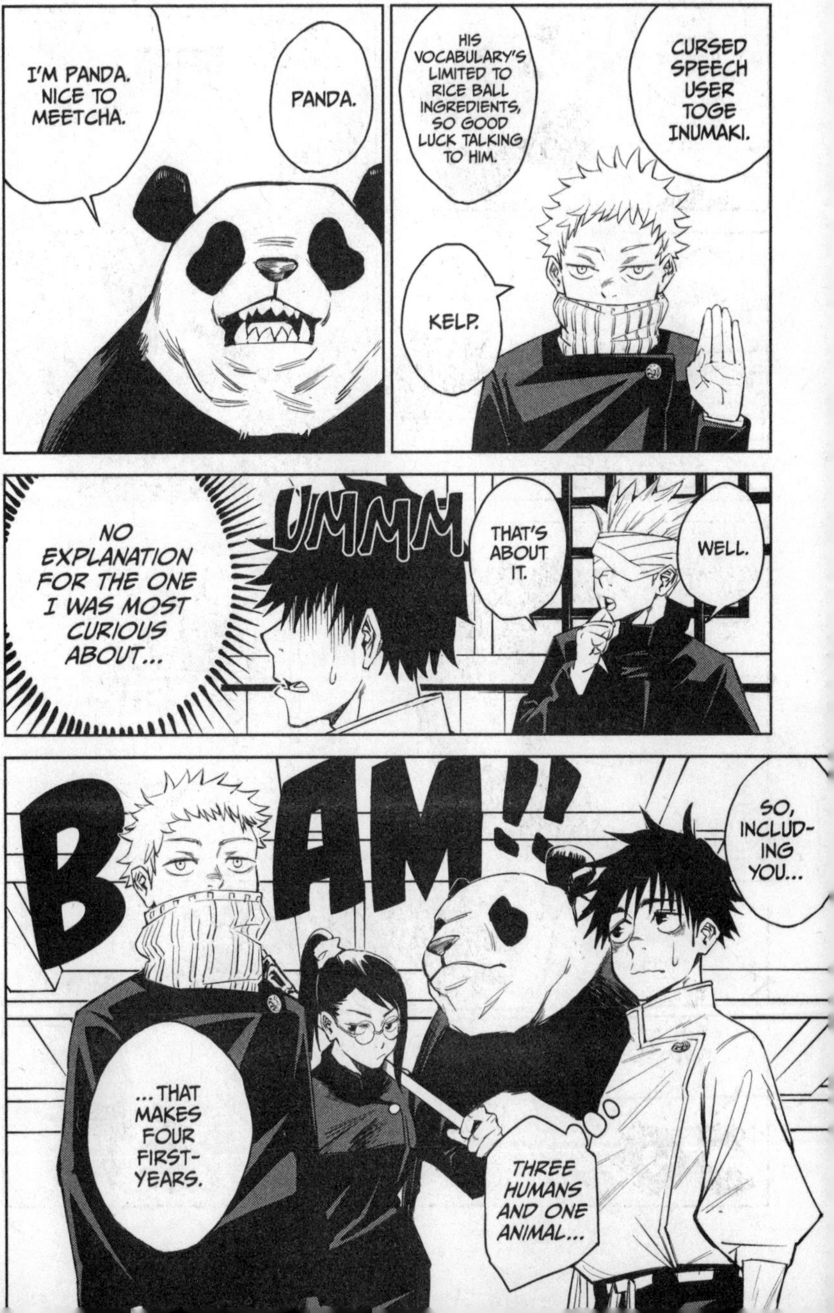
CURSED SPEECH USER TOGE INUMAKI.
HIS VOCABULARY'S LIMITED TO RICE BALL INGREDIENTS, SO GOOD LUCK TALKING TO HIM.
KELP.
PANDA.
I'M PANDA. NICE TO MEETCHA.
WELL.
THAT'S ABOUT IT.
UMMM
NO EXPLANATION FOR THE ONE I WAS MOST CURIOUS ABOUT...
SO, INCLUDING YOU...
BAM!!
...THAT MAKES FOUR FIRST-YEARS.
THREE HUMANS AND ONE ANIMAL...

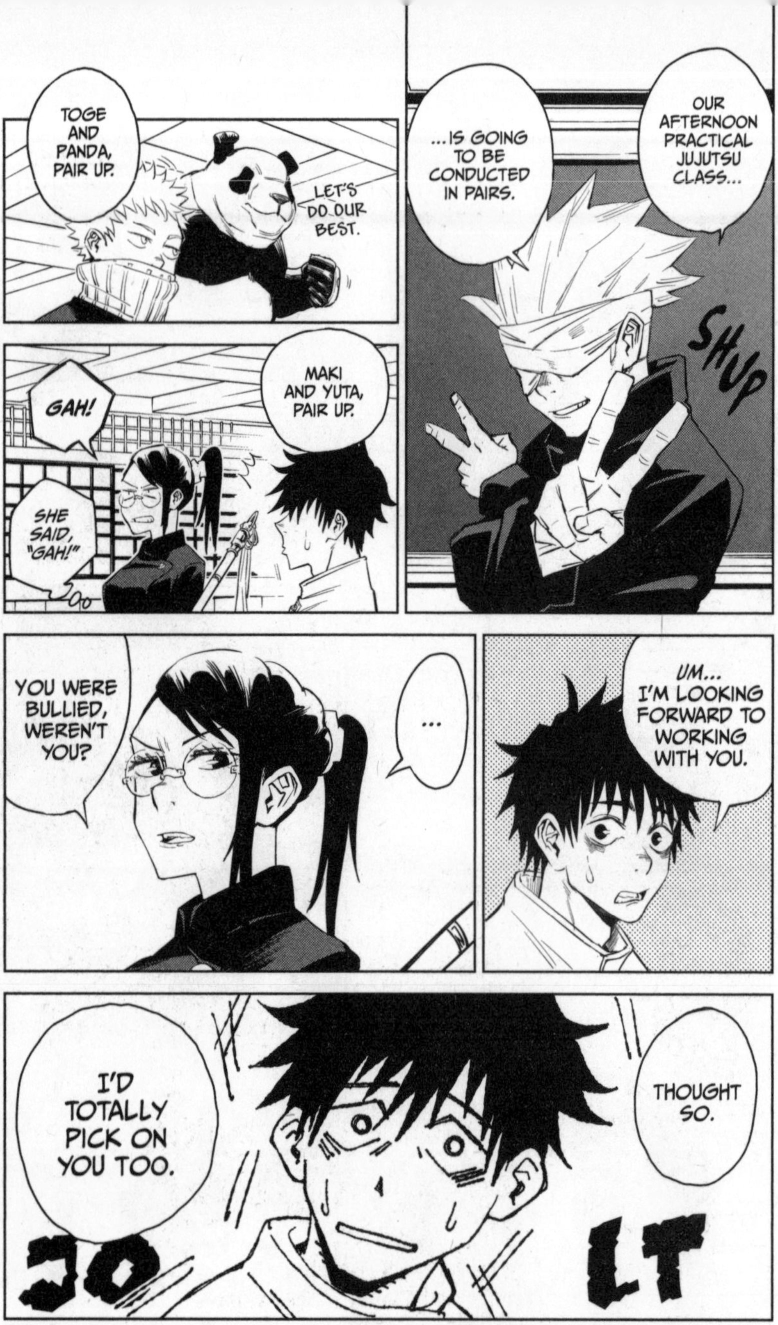
OUR AFTERNOON PRACTICAL JUJUTSU CLASS...
...IS GOING TO BE CONDUCTED IN PAIRS.
SHUP
TOGE AND PANDA, PAIR UP.
LET'S DO OUR BEST.
MAKI AND YUTA, PAIR UP.
GAH!
SHE SAID, "GAH!"
UM... I'M LOOKING FORWARD TO WORKING WITH YOU.
...
YOU WERE BULLIED, WEREN'T YOU?
THOUGHT SO.
I'D TOTALLY PICK ON YOU TOO.
JOLT

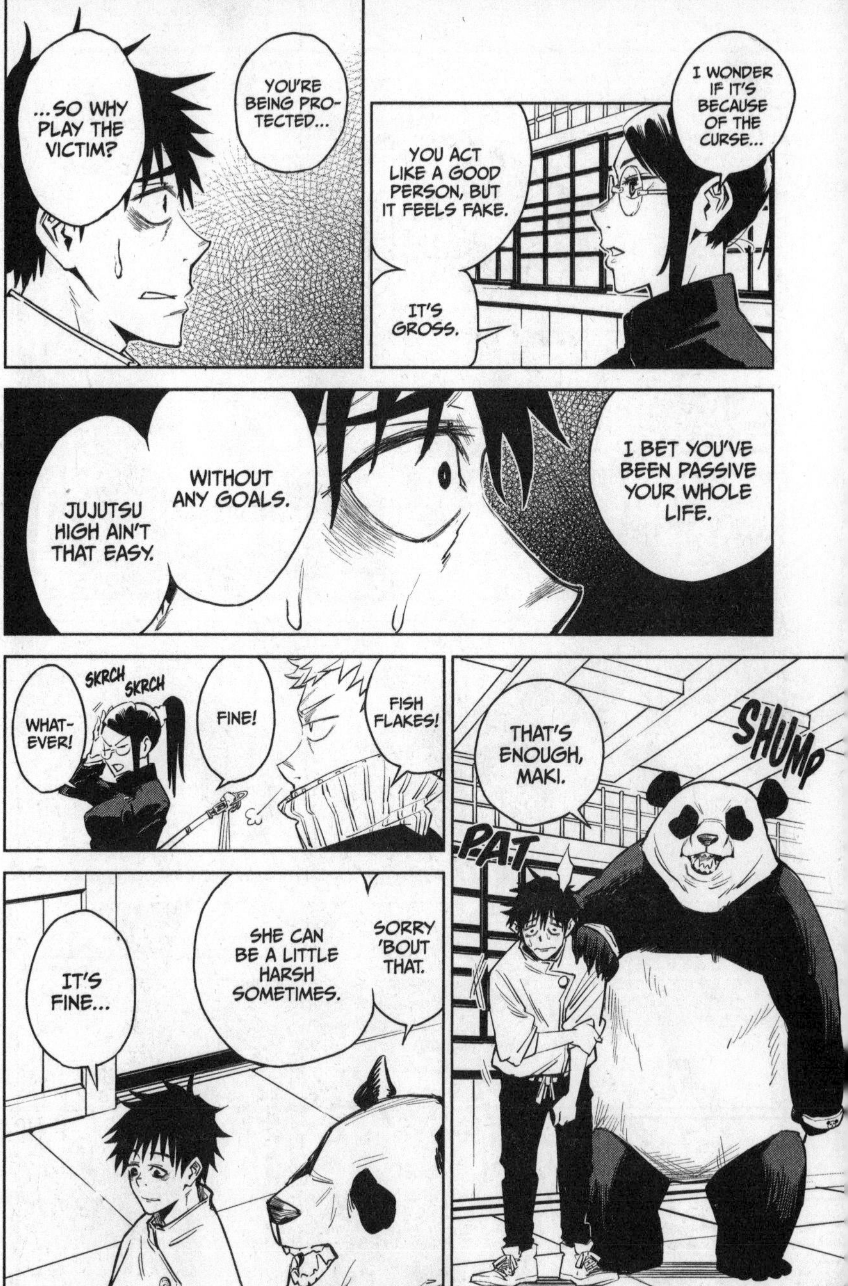
I WONDER IF IT'S BECAUSE OF THE CURSE...
YOU ACT LIKE A GOOD PERSON, BUT IT FEELS FAKE.
IT'S GROSS.
YOU'RE BEING PROTECTED...
...SO WHY PLAY THE VICTIM?
I BET YOU'VE BEEN PASSIVE YOUR WHOLE LIFE.
WITHOUT ANY GOALS.
JUJUTSU HIGH AIN'T THAT EASY.
SHUMP
THAT'S ENOUGH, MAKI.
PAT
FISH FLAKES!
FINE!
SKRCH SKRCH
WHAT-EVER!
SORRY 'BOUT THAT.
SHE CAN BE A LITTLE HARSH SOMETIMES.
IT'S FINE...

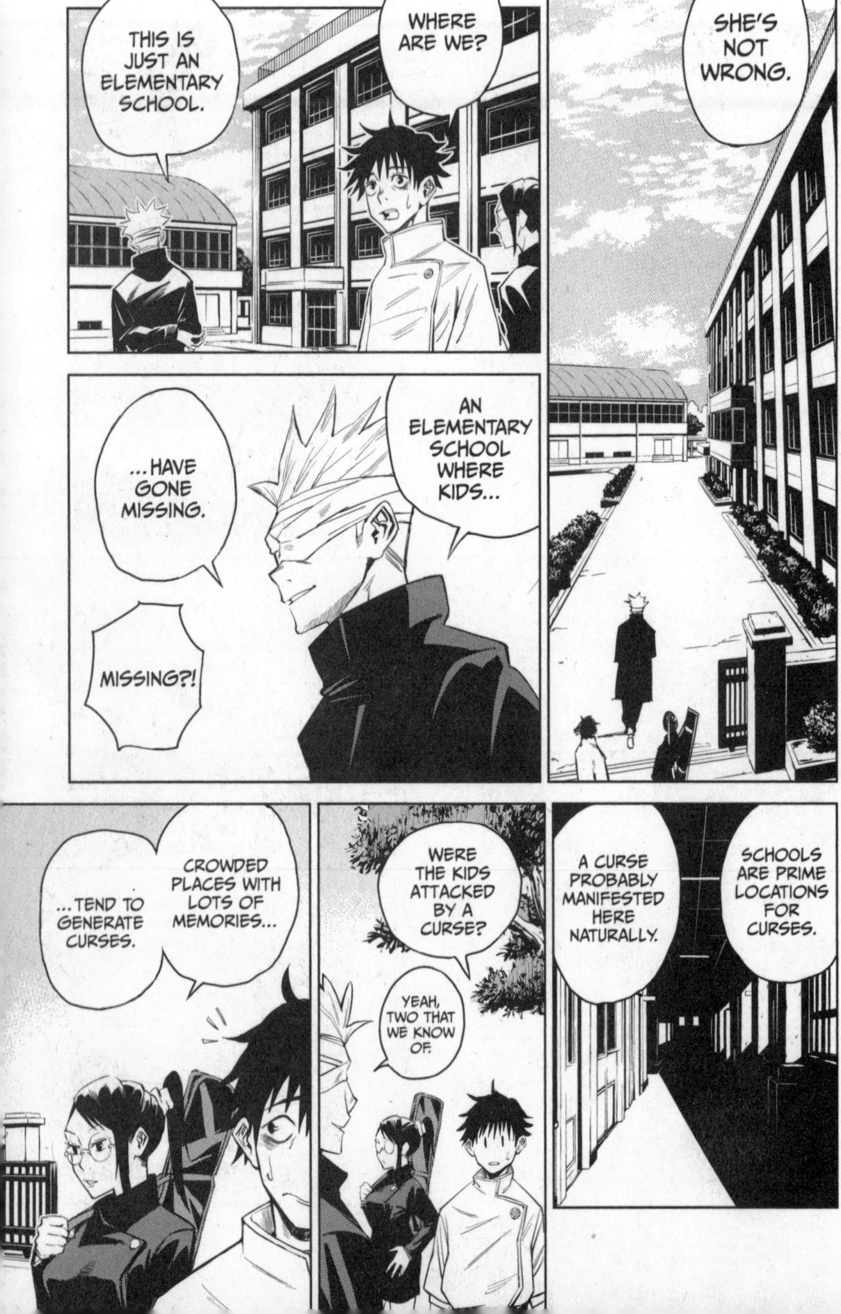
SHE'S NOT WRONG.
WHERE ARE WE?
THIS IS JUST AN ELEMENTARY SCHOOL.
AN ELEMENTARY SCHOOL WHERE KIDS...
...HAVE GONE MISSING.
MISSING?!
SCHOOLS ARE PRIME LOCATIONS FOR CURSES.
A CURSE PROBABLY MANIFESTED HERE NATURALLY.
WERE THE KIDS ATTACKED BY A CURSE?
YEAH, TWO THAT WE KNOW OF.
CROWDED PLACES WITH LOTS OF MEMORIES...
...TEND TO GENERATE CURSES.

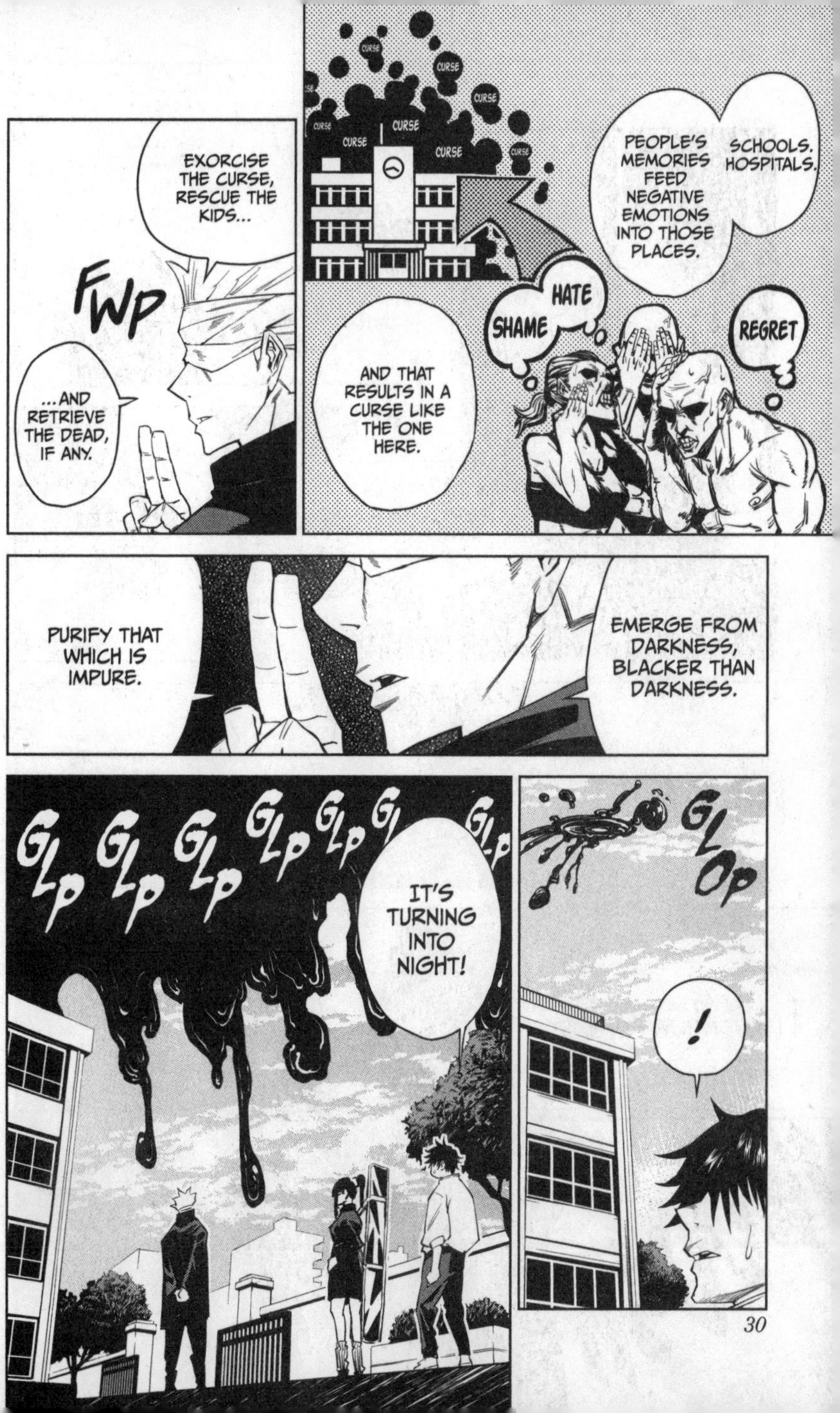
SCHOOLS. HOSPITALS.
PEOPLE'S MEMORIES FEED NEGATIVE EMOTIONS INTO THOSE PLACES.
CURSE
CURSE
CURSE
CURSE
CURSE
CURSE
CURSE
HATE
SHAME
REGRET
AND THAT RESULTS IN A CURSE LIKE THE ONE HERE.
EXORCISE THE CURSE, RESCUE THE KIDS...
FWP
...AND RETRIEVE THE DEAD, IF ANY.
EMERGE FROM DARKNESS, BLACKER THAN DARKNESS.
PURIFY THAT WHICH IS IMPURE.
GLOP
!
GLP
GLP
GLP
GLP
GLP
GLP
IT'S TURNING INTO NIGHT!

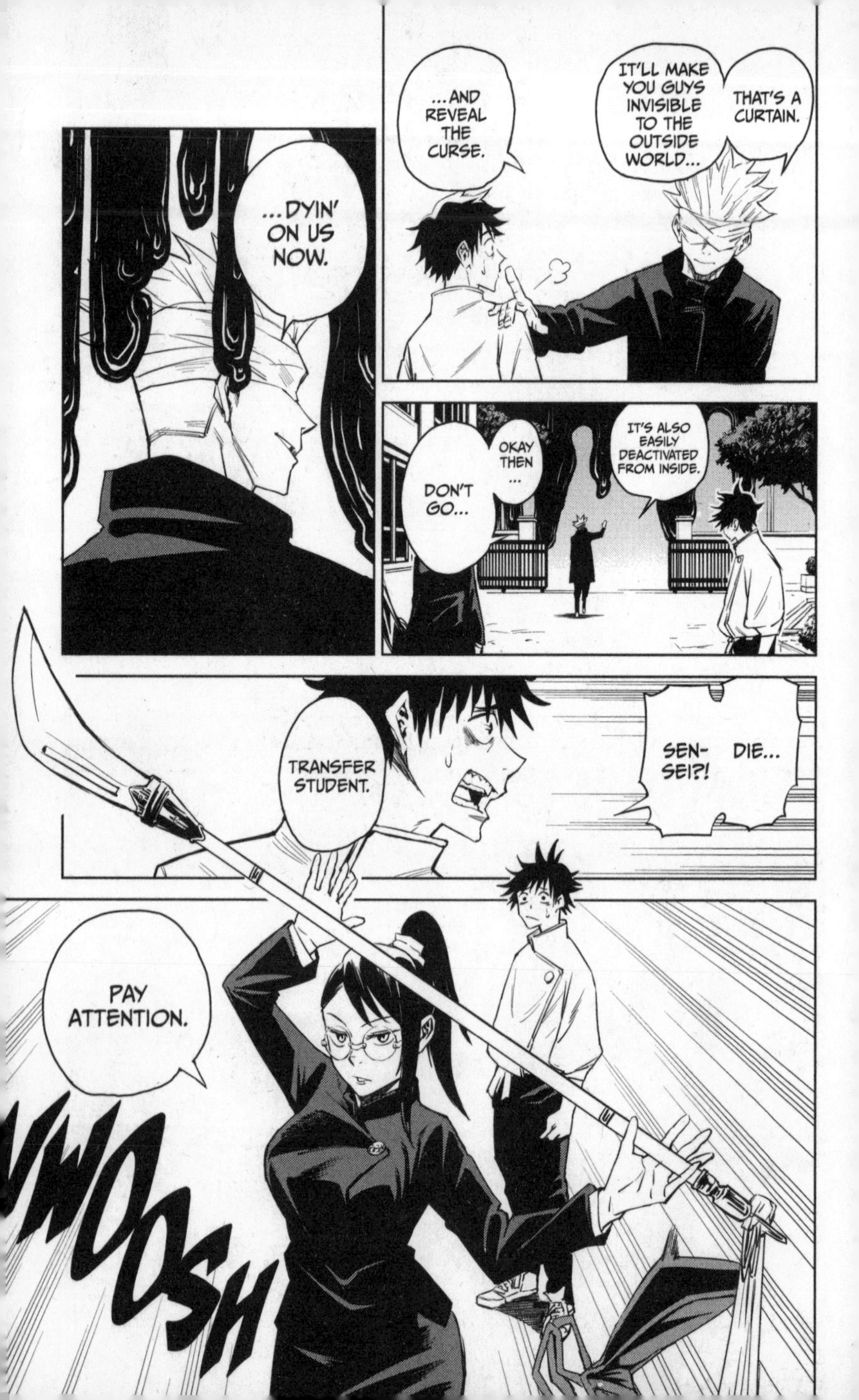
THAT'S A CURTAIN.
IT'LL MAKE YOU GUYS INVISIBLE TO THE OUTSIDE WORLD...
...AND REVEAL THE CURSE.
IT'S ALSO EASILY DEACTIVATED FROM INSIDE.
OKAY THEN ...
DON'T GO...
...DYIN' ON US NOW.
DIE...
SEN-SEI?!
TRANSFER STUDENT.
PAY ATTENTION.
WHOOSH

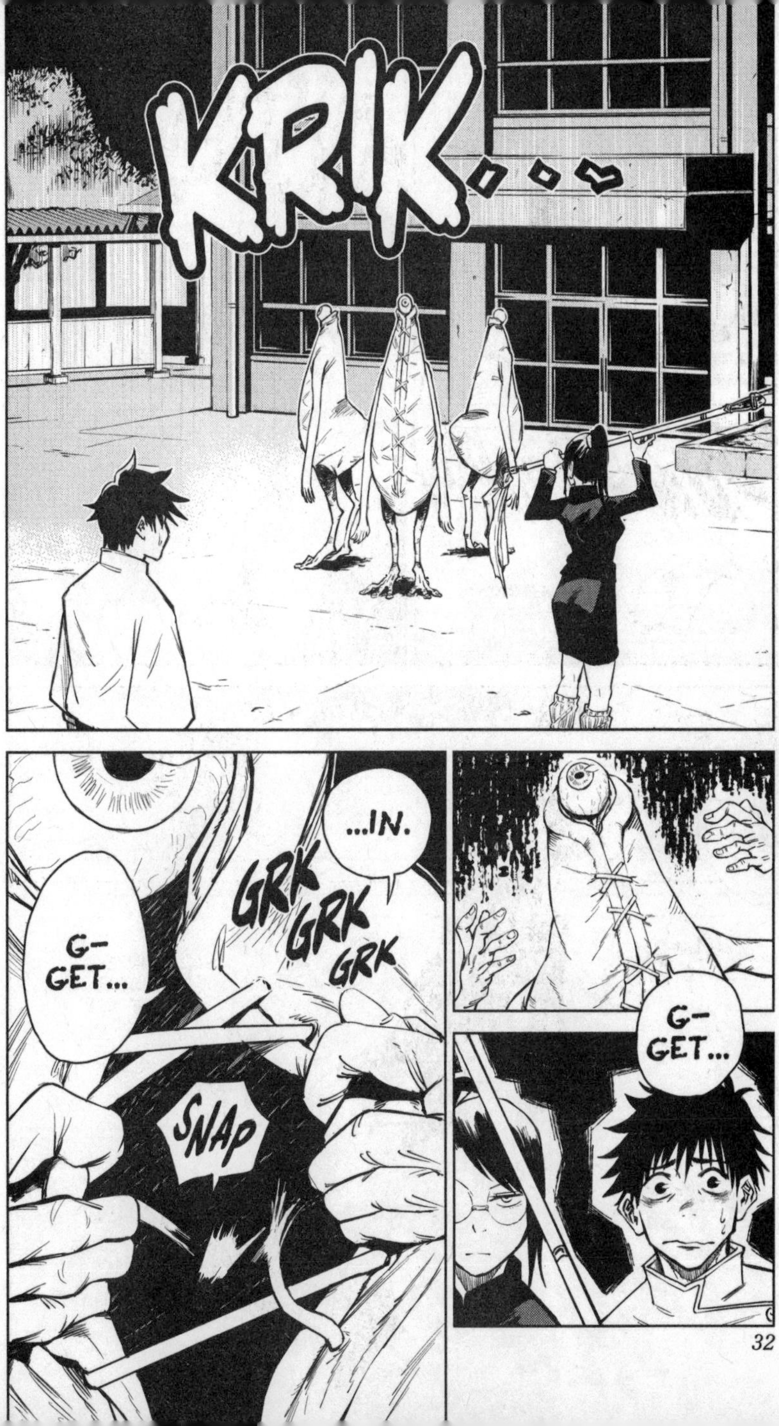
KRIK...
G- GET...
...IN.
GRK GRK GRK
G- GET...
SNAP

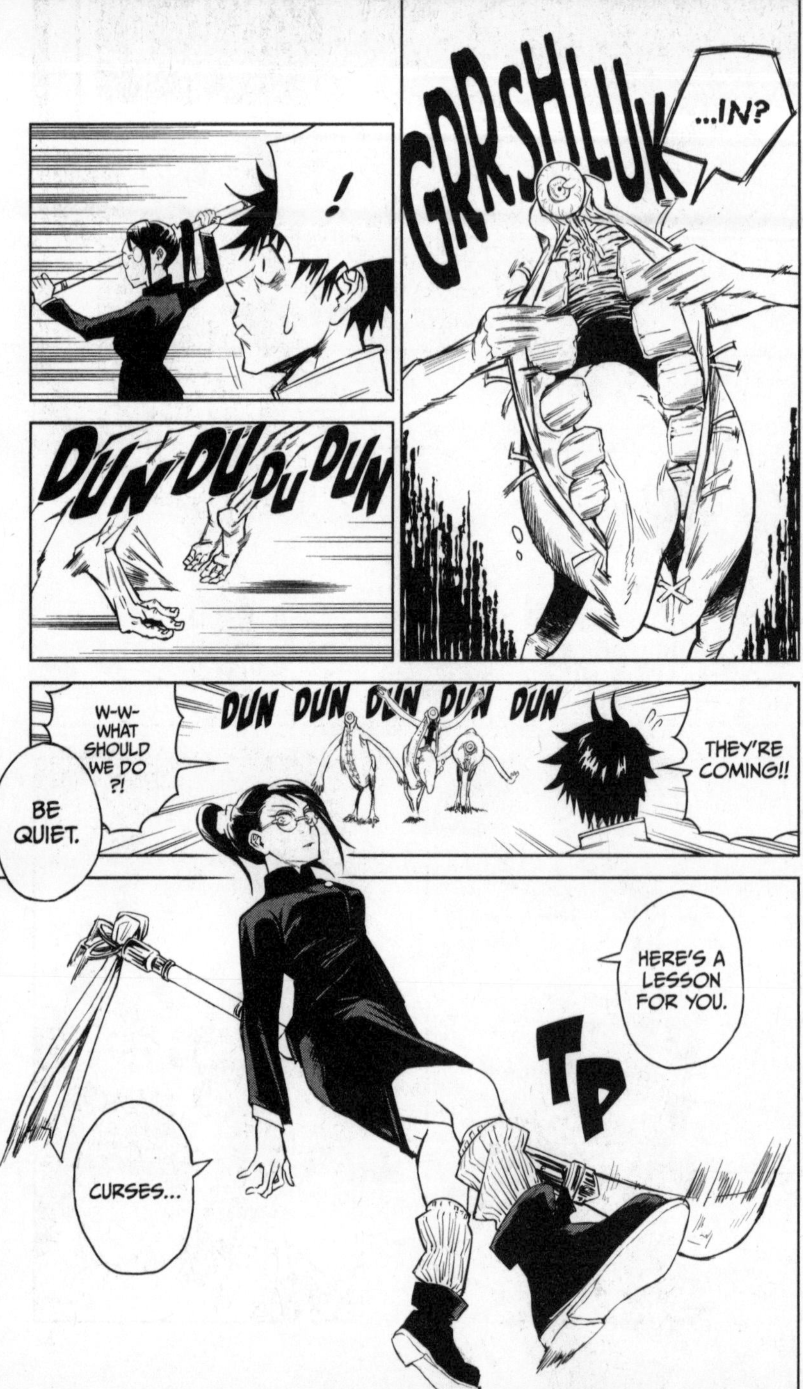
GRRSHLUK
...IN?
!
DUN DU DU DUN
THEY'RE COMING!!
DUN DUN DUN DUN DUN
W-W-WHAT SHOULD WE DO ?!
BE QUIET.
HERE'S A LESSON FOR YOU.
TP
CURSES...

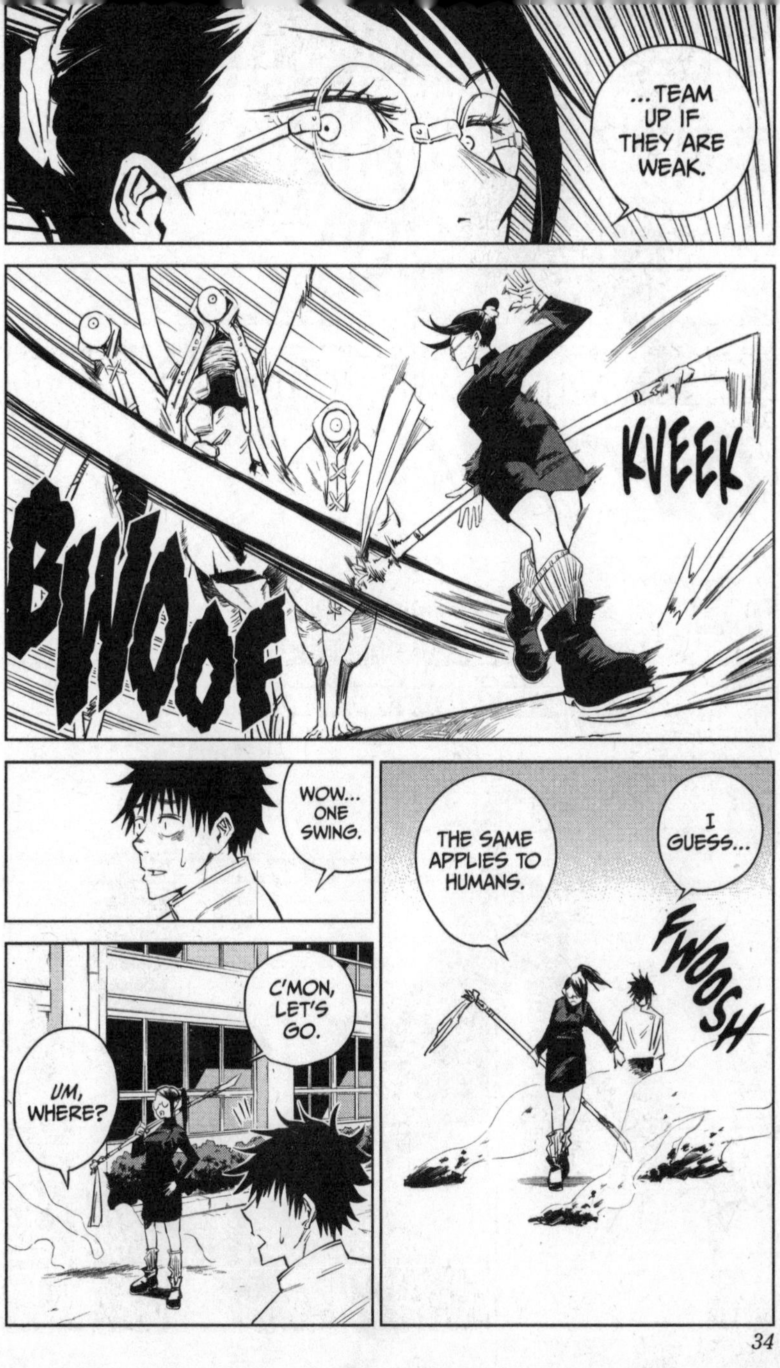
...TEAM UP IF THEY ARE WEAK.
KVEEK
BWOOF
I GUESS...
THE SAME APPLIES TO HUMANS.
FWOOSH
WOW... ONE SWING.
C'MON, LET'S GO.
UM, WHERE?

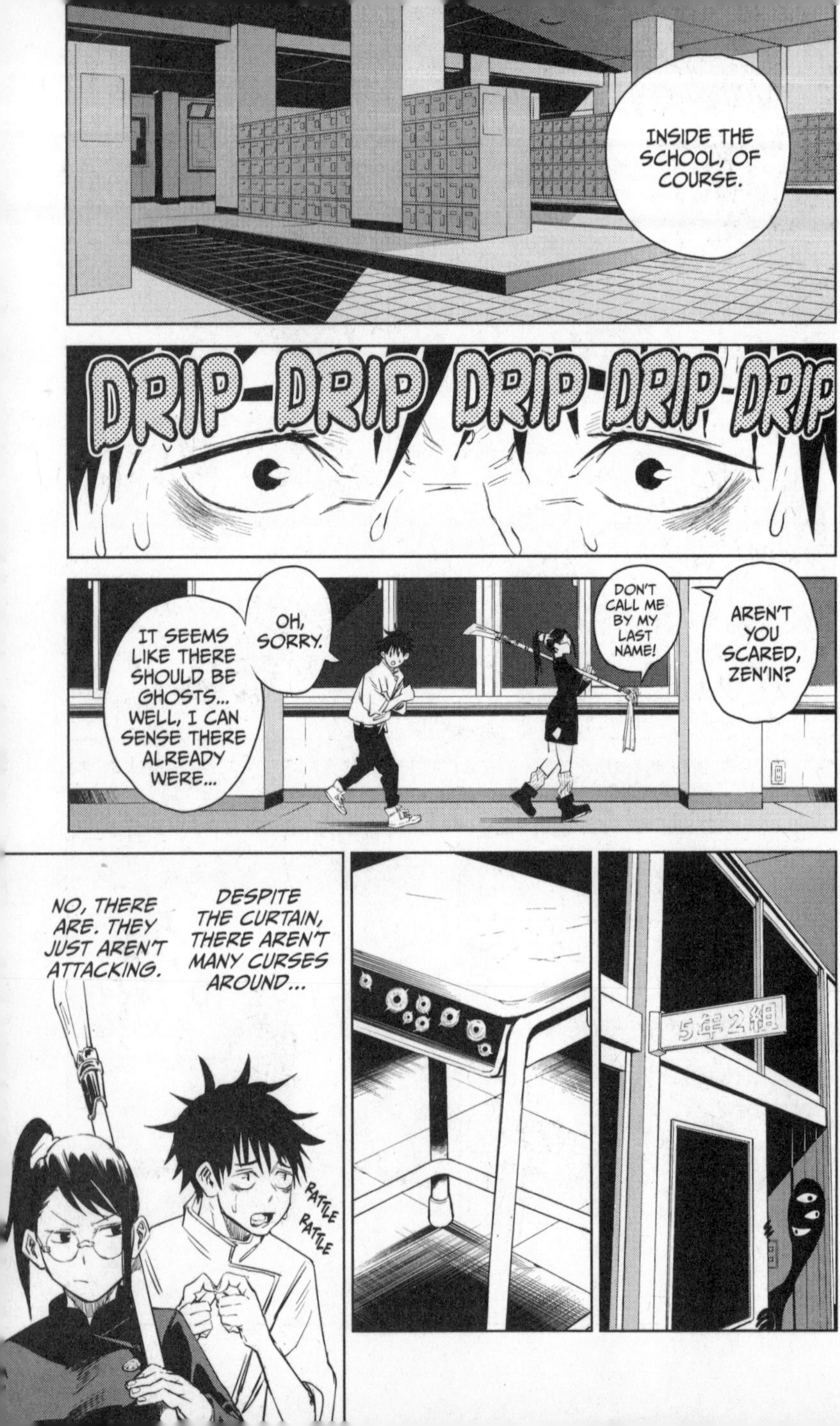

INSIDE THE SCHOOL, OF COURSE.
DRIP DRIP DRIP DRIP DRIP
AREN'T YOU SCARED, ZEN'IN?
DON'T CALL ME BY MY LAST NAME!
OH, SORRY.
IT SEEMS LIKE THERE SHOULD BE GHOSTS... WELL, I CAN SENSE THERE ALREADY WERE...
5年2組
DESPITE THE CURTAIN, THERE AREN'T MANY CURSES AROUND...
NO, THERE ARE. THEY JUST AREN'T ATTACKING.
RATTLE RATTLE

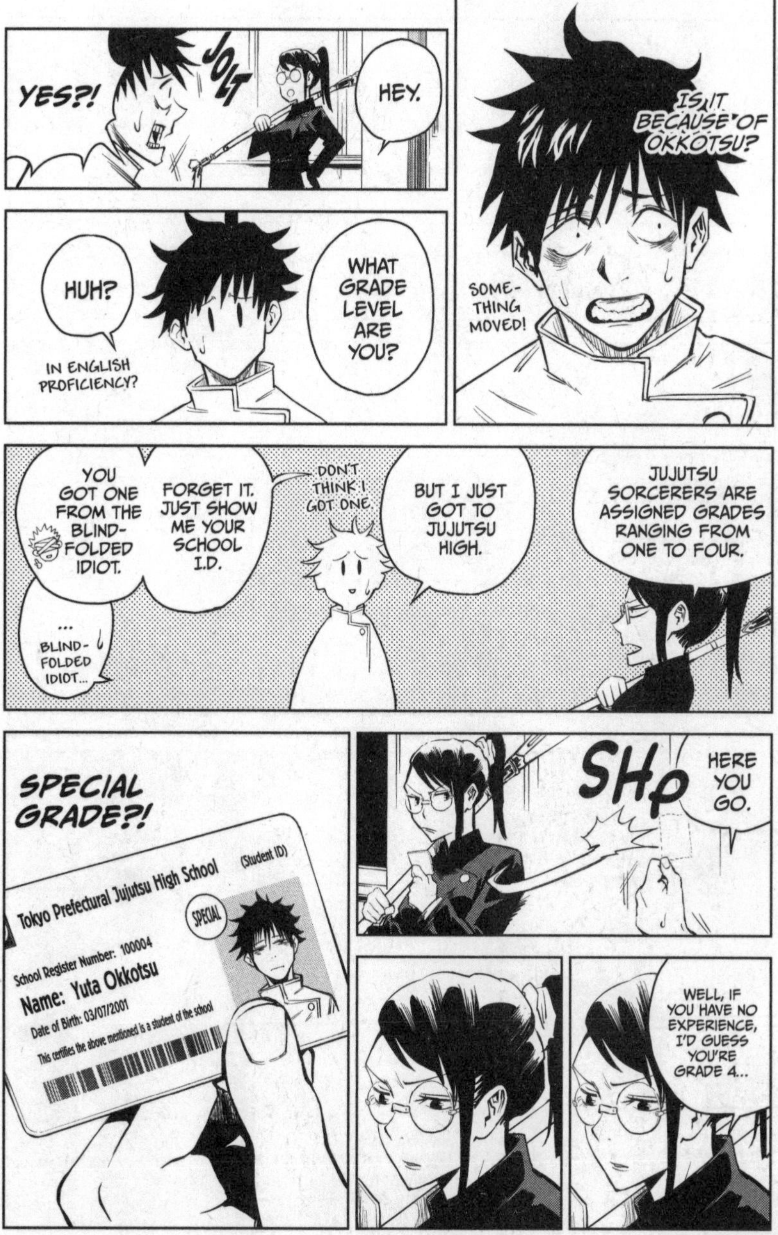
IS IT BECAUSE OF OKKOTSU?
SOME-THING MOVED!
HEY.
JOLT
YES?!
WHAT GRADE LEVEL ARE YOU?
HUH?
IN ENGLISH PROFICIENCY?
JUJUTSU SORCERERS ARE ASSIGNED GRADES RANGING FROM ONE TO FOUR.
BUT I JUST GOT TO JUJUTSU HIGH.
DON'T THINK I GOT ONE.
FORGET IT. JUST SHOW ME YOUR SCHOOL I.D.
YOU GOT ONE FROM THE BLIND-FOLDED IDIOT.
... BLIND-FOLDED IDIOT...
HERE YOU GO.
SHP
WELL, IF YOU HAVE NO EXPERIENCE, I'D GUESS YOU'RE GRADE 4...
SPECIAL GRADE?!
(Student ID)
Tokyo Prefectural Jujutsu High School
SPECIAL
School Register Number: 100004
Name: Yuta Okkotsu
Date of Birth: 03/07/2001
This certifies the above mentioned is a student of the school

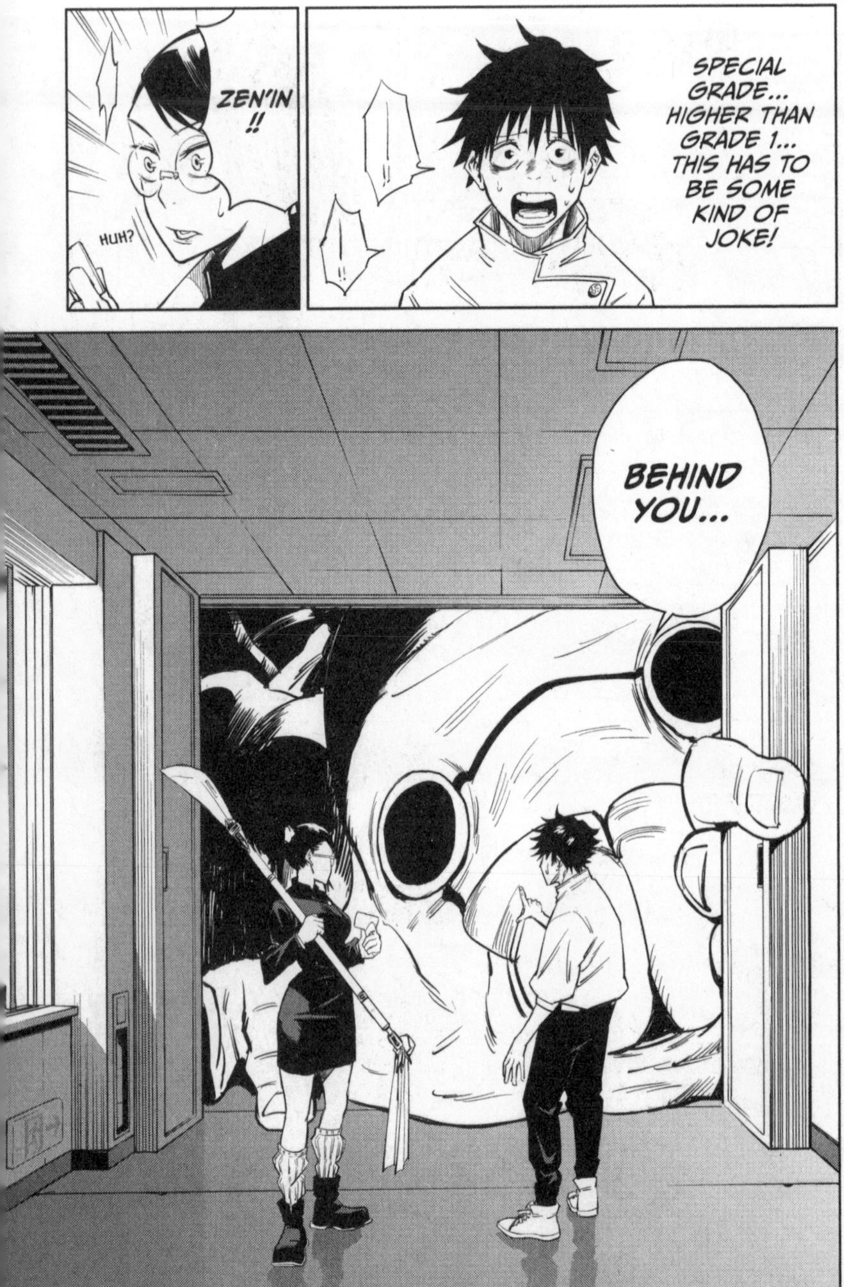
SPECIAL GRADE... HIGHER THAN GRADE 1... THIS HAS TO BE SOME KIND OF JOKE!
ZEN'IN !!
HUH?
BEHIND YOU...

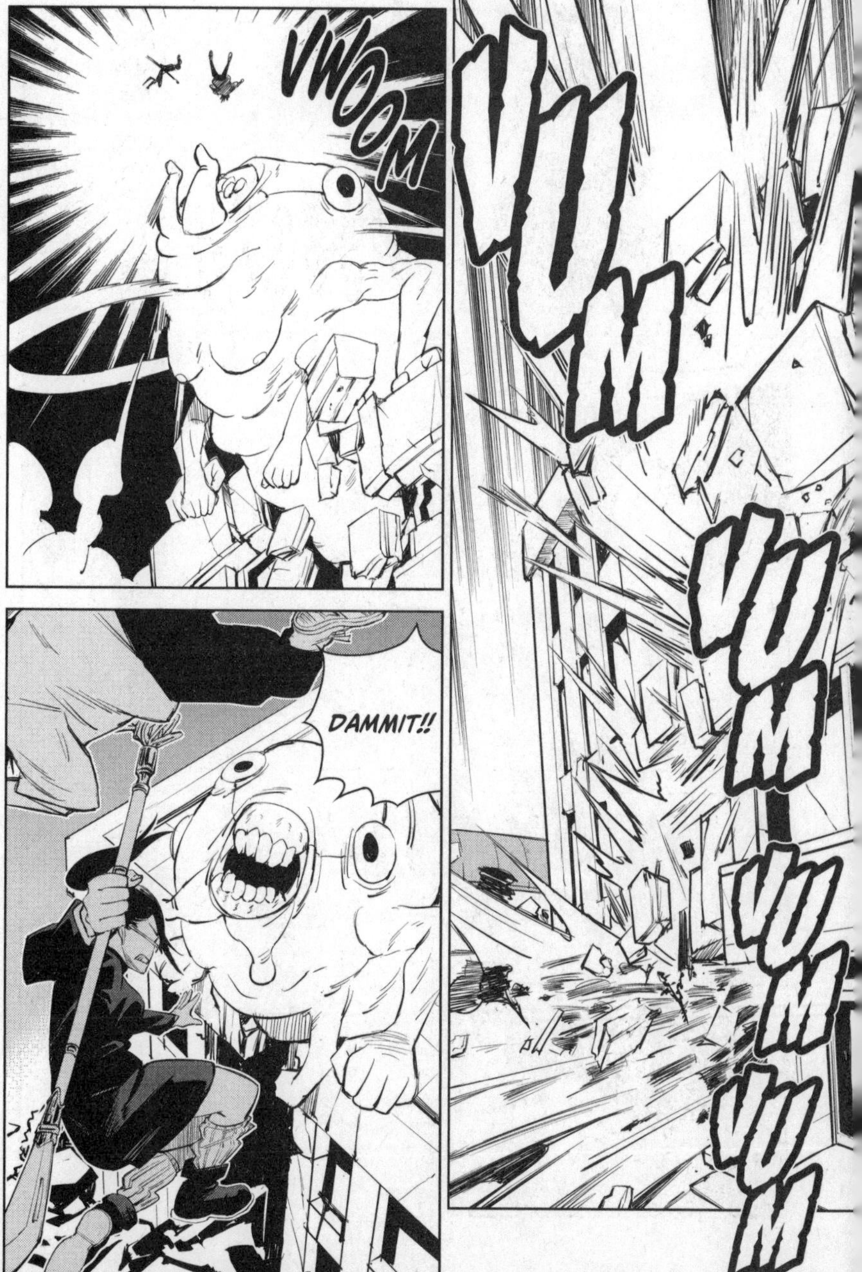
VUM
VUM VUM VUM VUM
VWOOM
DAMMIT!!

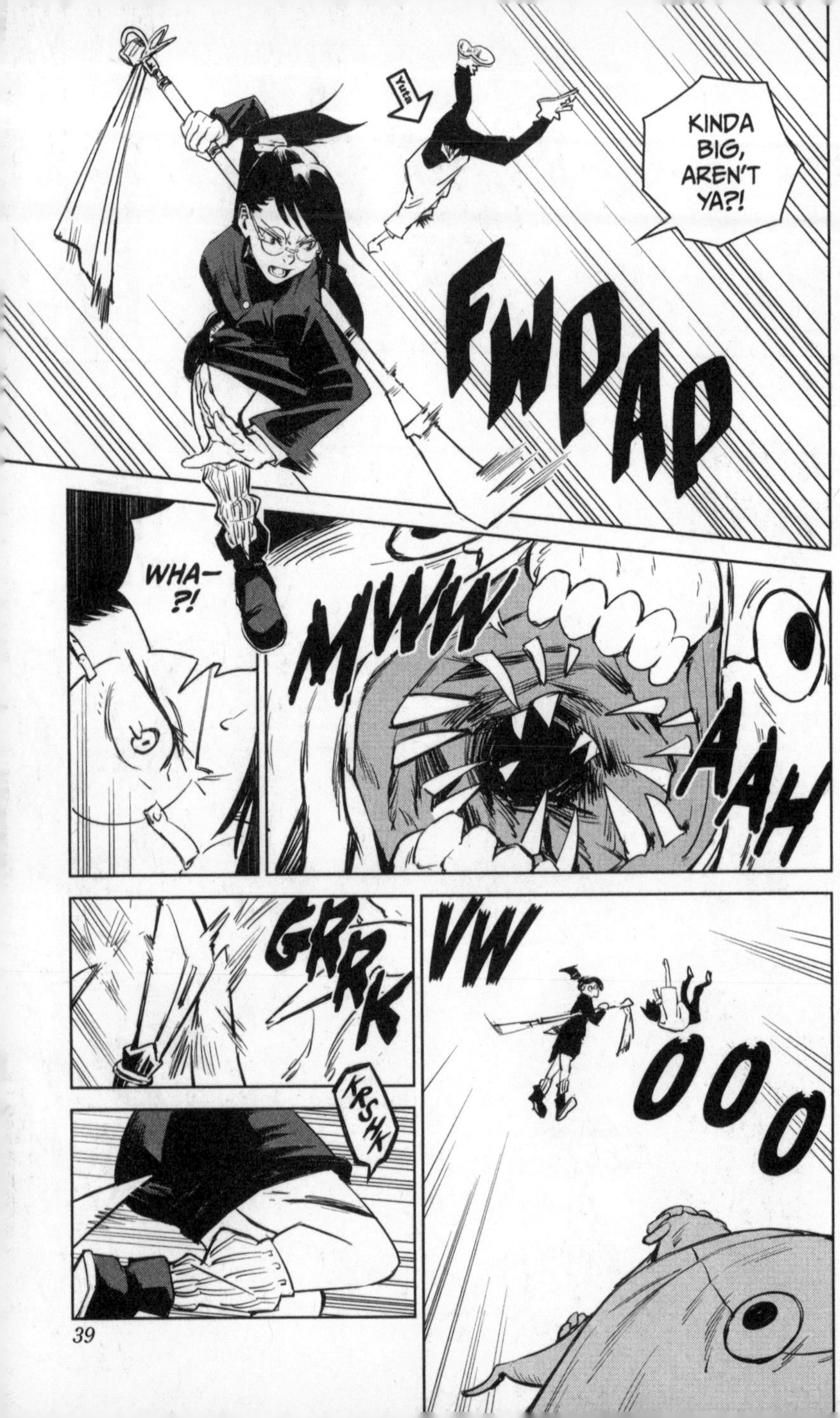
KINDA BIG, AREN'T YA?!
Yuta
FWPAP
MWW
AAH
WHA— ?!
VW
OOOO
GRRK
KRSHK

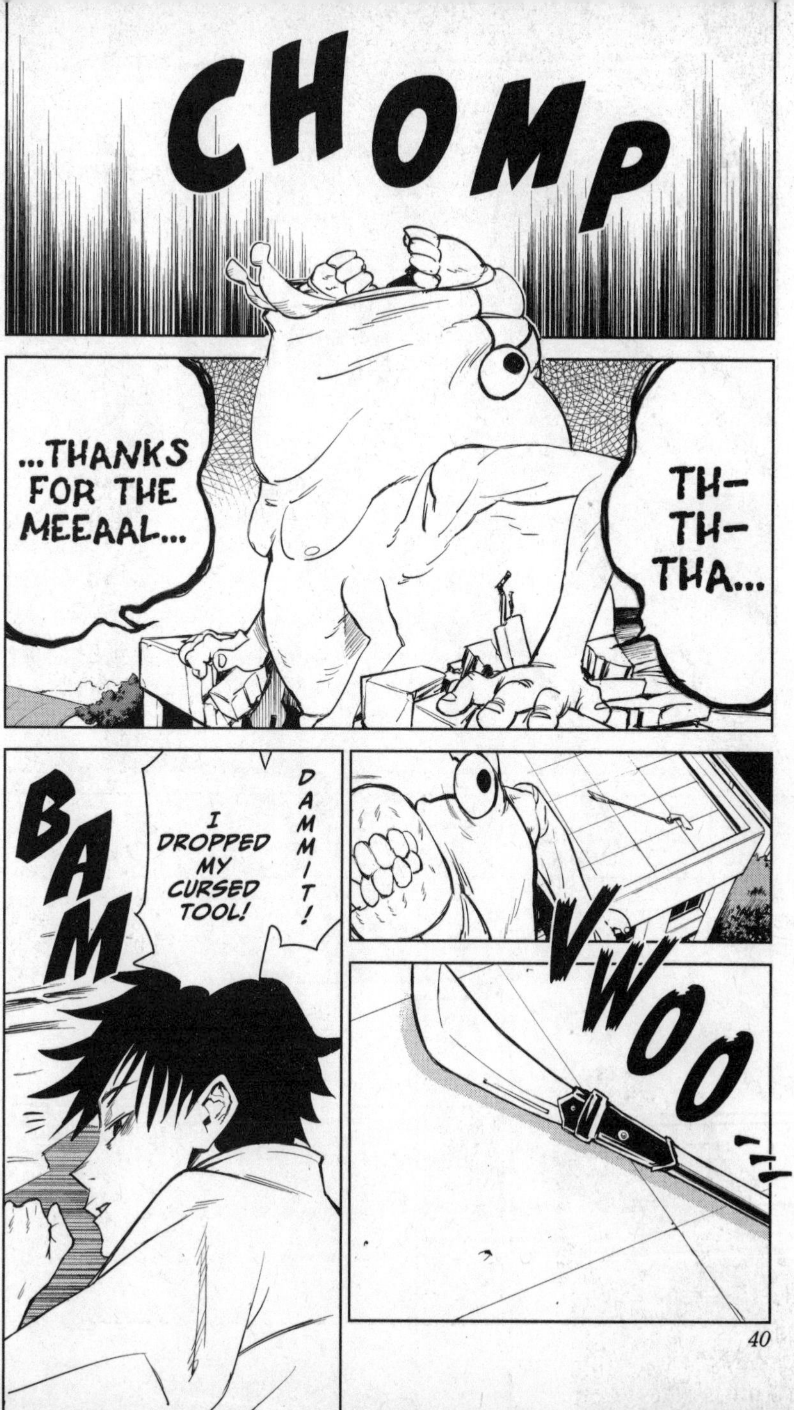
CHOMP
TH-TH-THA...
...THANKS FOR THE MEEAAL...
VWOO
DAMMIT!
I DROPPED MY CURSED TOOL!
BAM

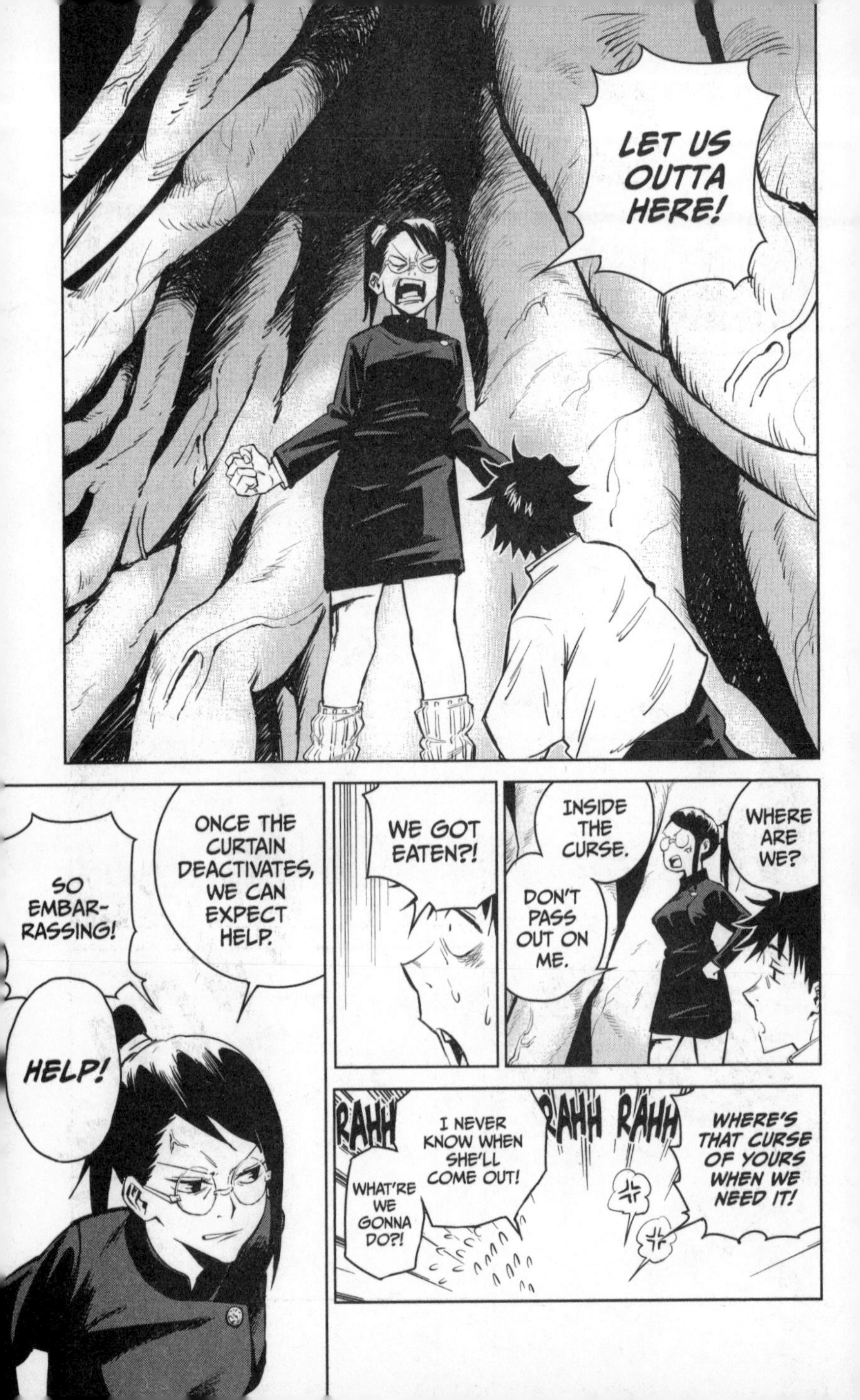
LET US OUTTA HERE!
WHERE ARE WE?
INSIDE THE CURSE.
DON'T PASS OUT ON ME.
WE GOT EATEN?!
WHERE'S THAT CURSE OF YOURS WHEN WE NEED IT!
RAHH RAHH
I NEVER KNOW WHEN SHE'LL COME OUT!
RAHH
WHAT'RE WE GONNA DO?!
ONCE THE CURTAIN DEACTIVATES, WE CAN EXPECT HELP.
SO EMBAR-RASSING!
HELP!

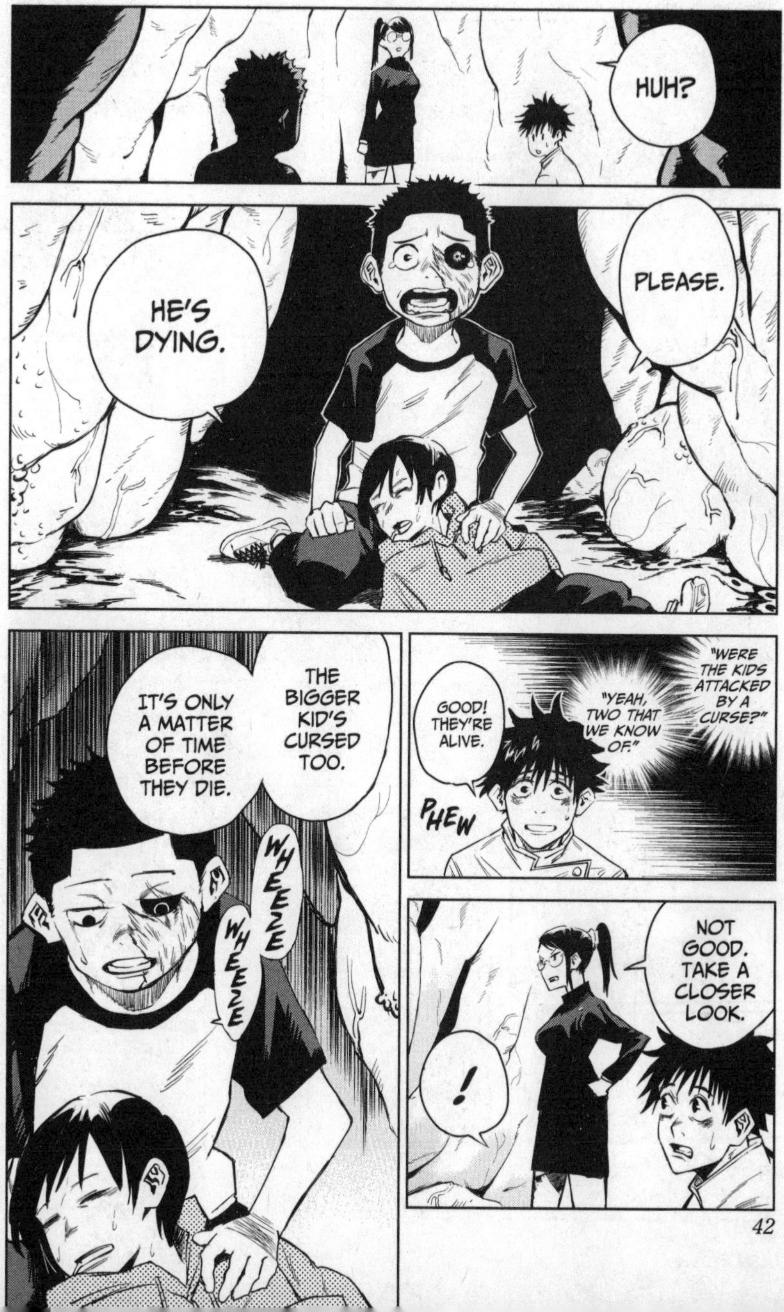
HUH?
PLEASE.
HE'S DYING.
"WERE THE KIDS ATTACKED BY A CURSE?"
"YEAH, TWO THAT WE KNOW OF."
GOOD! THEY'RE ALIVE.
PHEW
NOT GOOD. TAKE A CLOSER LOOK.
!
THE BIGGER KID'S CURSED TOO.
IT'S ONLY A MATTER OF TIME BEFORE THEY DIE.
WHEEZE
WHEEZE

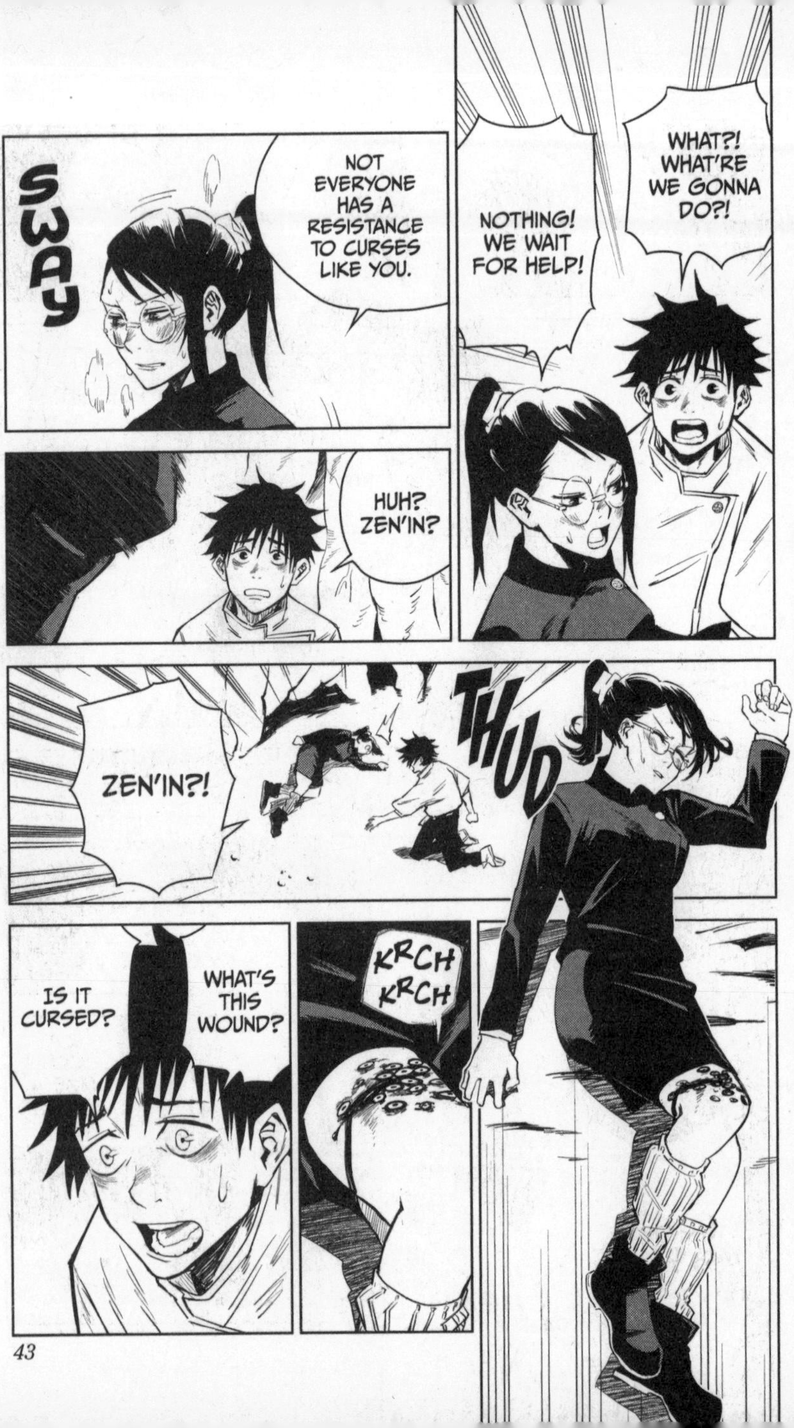
WHAT?! WHAT'RE WE GONNA DO?!
NOTHING! WE WAIT FOR HELP!
NOT EVERYONE HAS A RESISTANCE TO CURSES LIKE YOU.
SWAY
HUH? ZEN'IN?
THUD
ZEN'IN?!
KRCH KRCH
WHAT'S THIS WOUND?
IS IT CURSED?

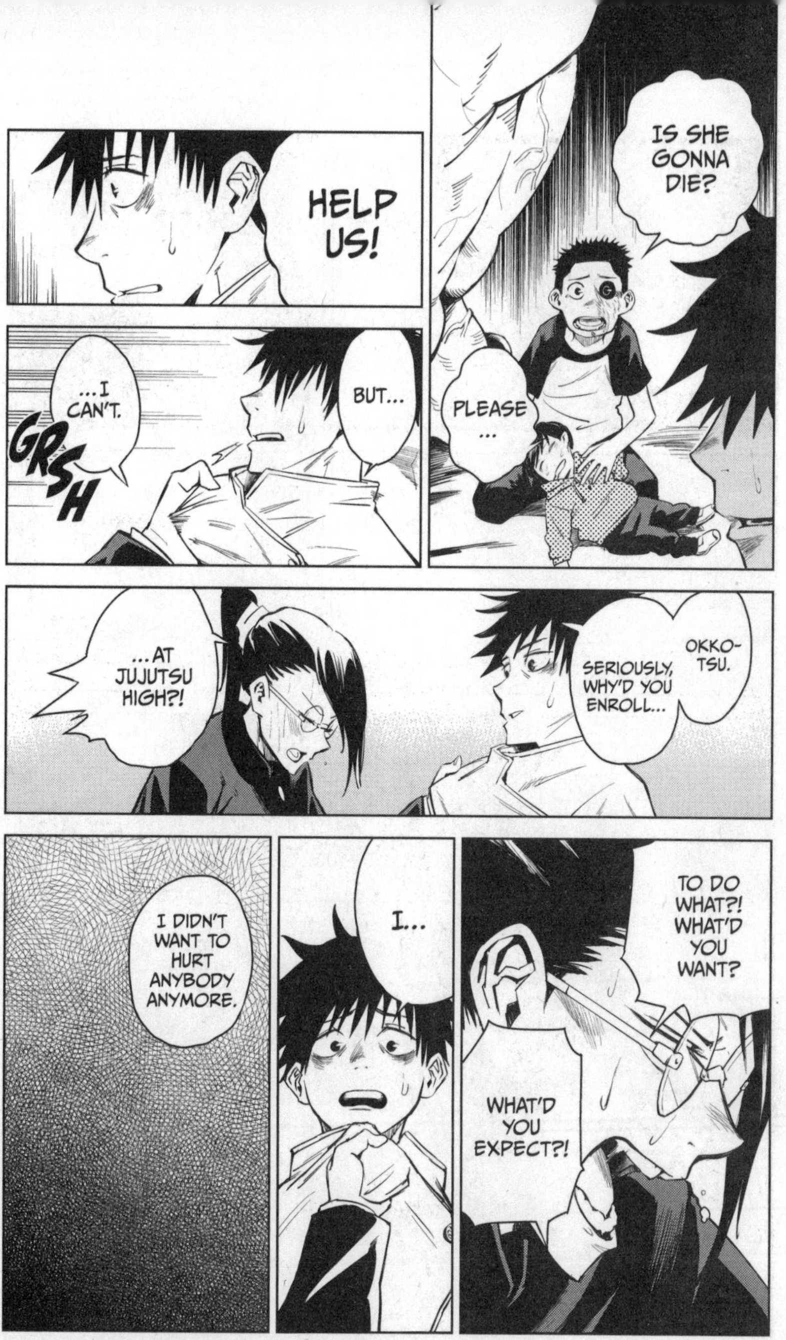
IS SHE GONNA DIE?
PLEASE ...
HELP US!
BUT...
...I CAN'T.
GRSH
OKKO-TSU.
SERIOUSLY, WHY'D YOU ENROLL...
...AT JUJUTSU HIGH?!
TO DO WHAT?! WHAT'D YOU WANT?
WHAT'D YOU EXPECT?!
I...
I DIDN'T WANT TO HURT ANYBODY ANYMORE.

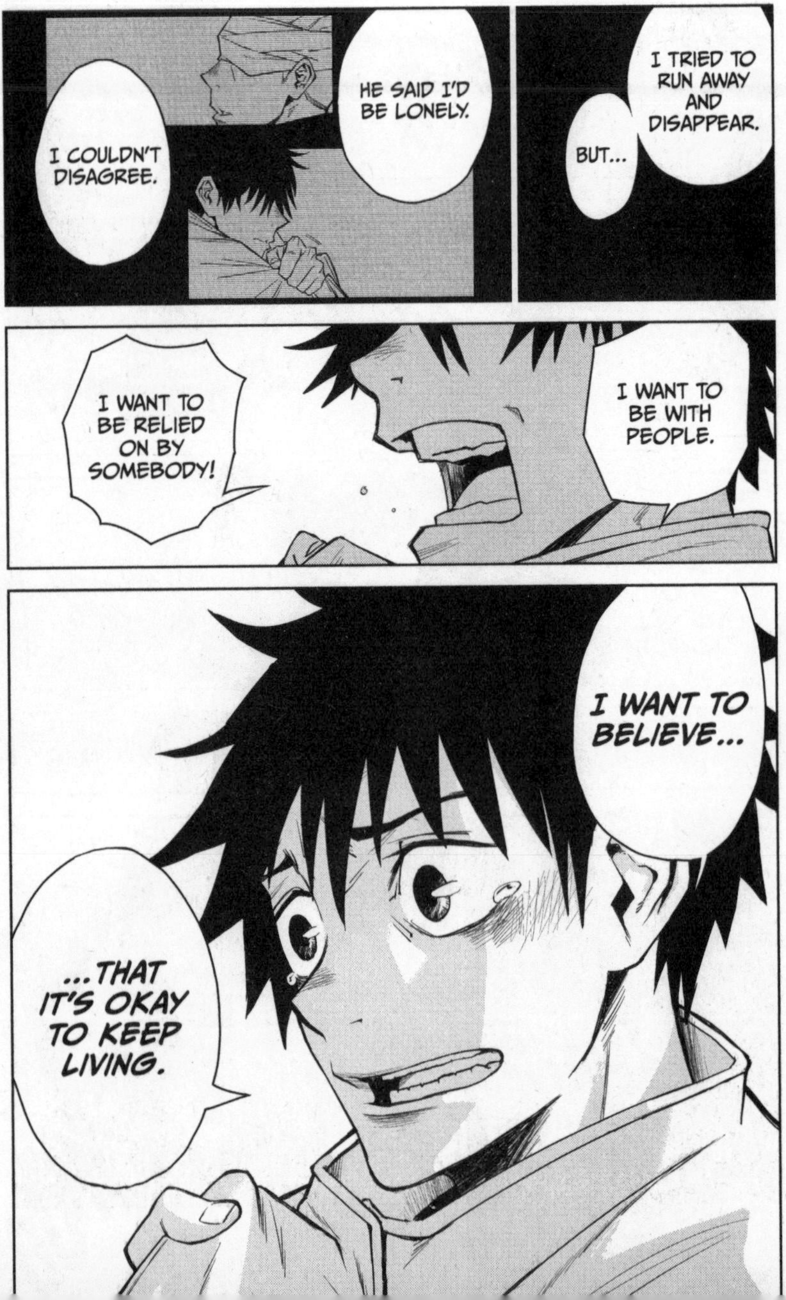
I TRIED TO RUN AWAY AND DISAPPEAR.
BUT...
HE SAID I'D BE LONELY.
I COULDN'T DISAGREE.
I WANT TO BE WITH PEOPLE.
I WANT TO BE RELIED ON BY SOMEBODY!
I WANT TO BELIEVE...
...THAT IT'S OKAY TO KEEP LIVING.

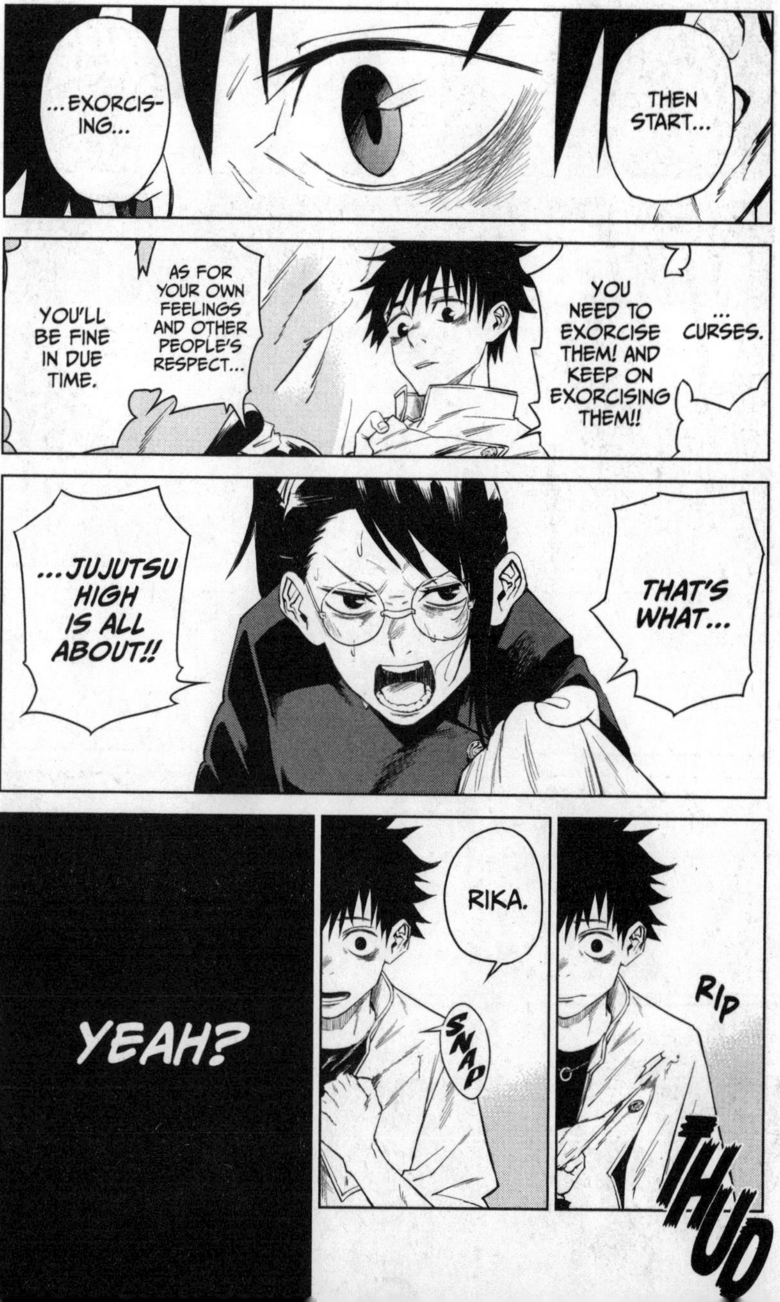
THEN START...
...EXORCIS-ING...
... CURSES.
YOU NEED TO EXORCISE THEM! AND KEEP ON EXORCISING THEM!!
AS FOR YOUR OWN FEELINGS AND OTHER PEOPLE'S RESPECT...
YOU'LL BE FINE IN DUE TIME.
THAT'S WHAT...
...JUJUTSU HIGH IS ALL ABOUT!!
RIP
THUD
RIKA.
SNAP
YEAH?

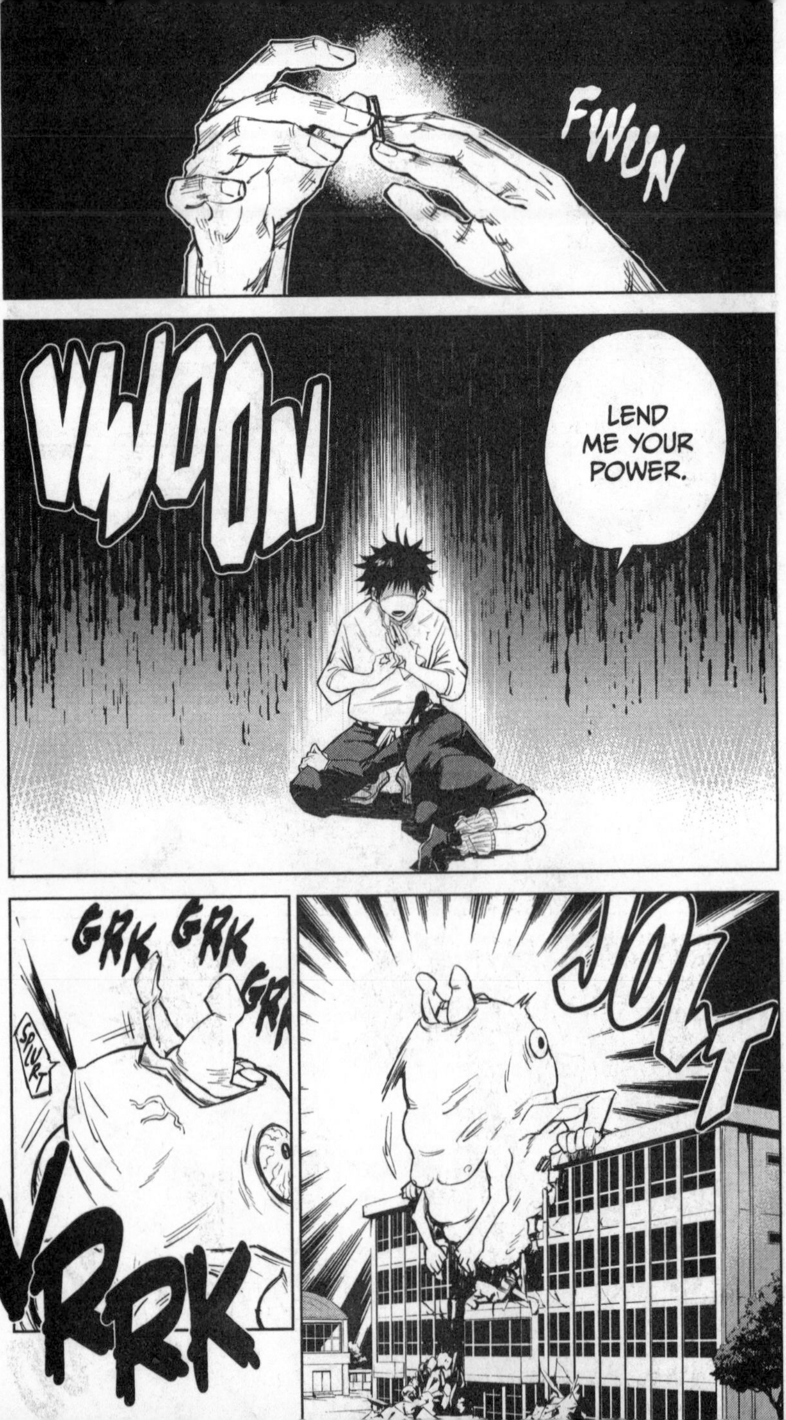
FWUN
LEND ME YOUR POWER.
VWOON
JOLT
GRK GRK
SPLURT
VRRK

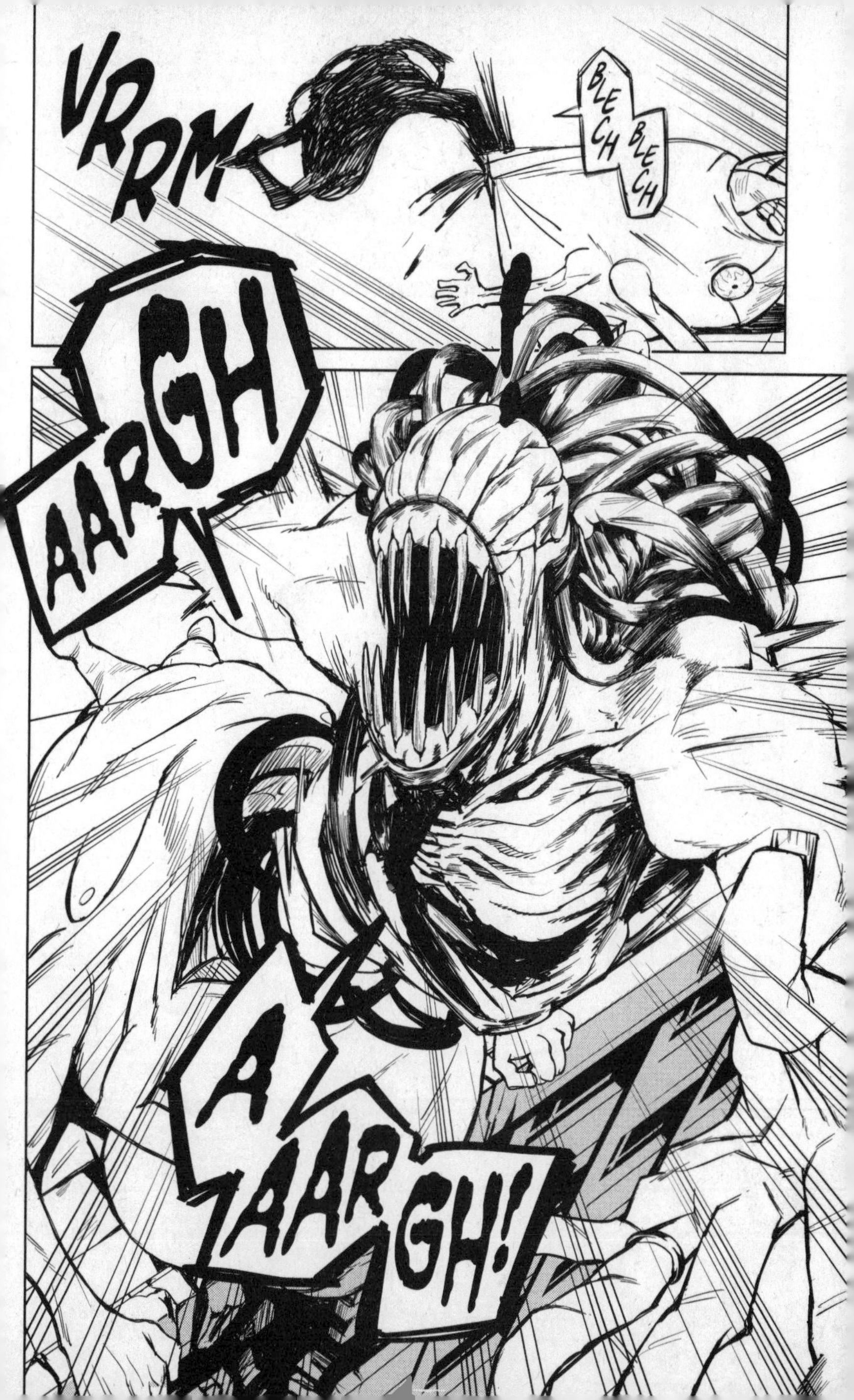
BLECH
BLECH
VRRM
AARGH
AAAARGH!

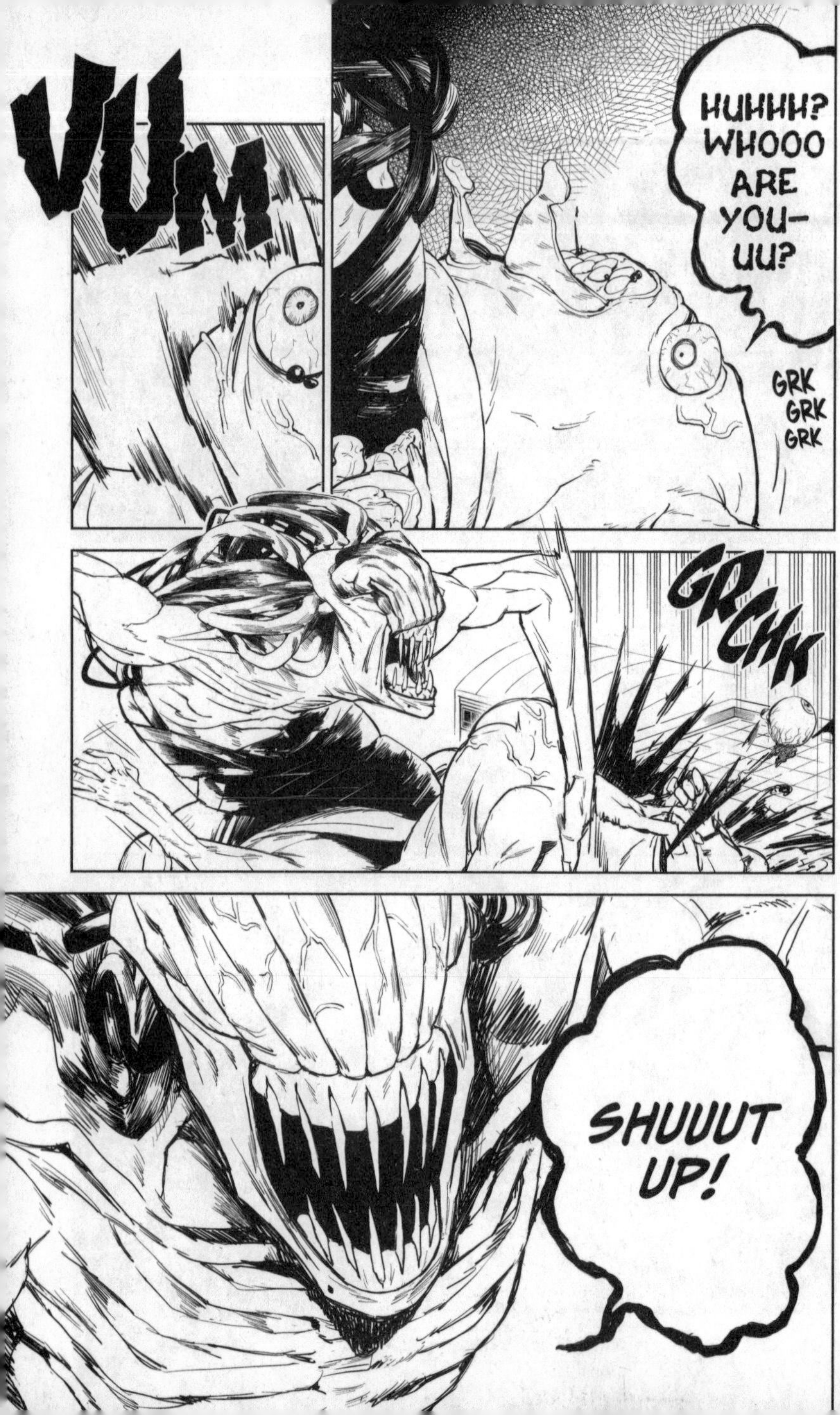
HUHHH? WHOOO ARE YOU-UU?
GRK GRK GRK
VUM
GRCHK
SHUUUT UP!

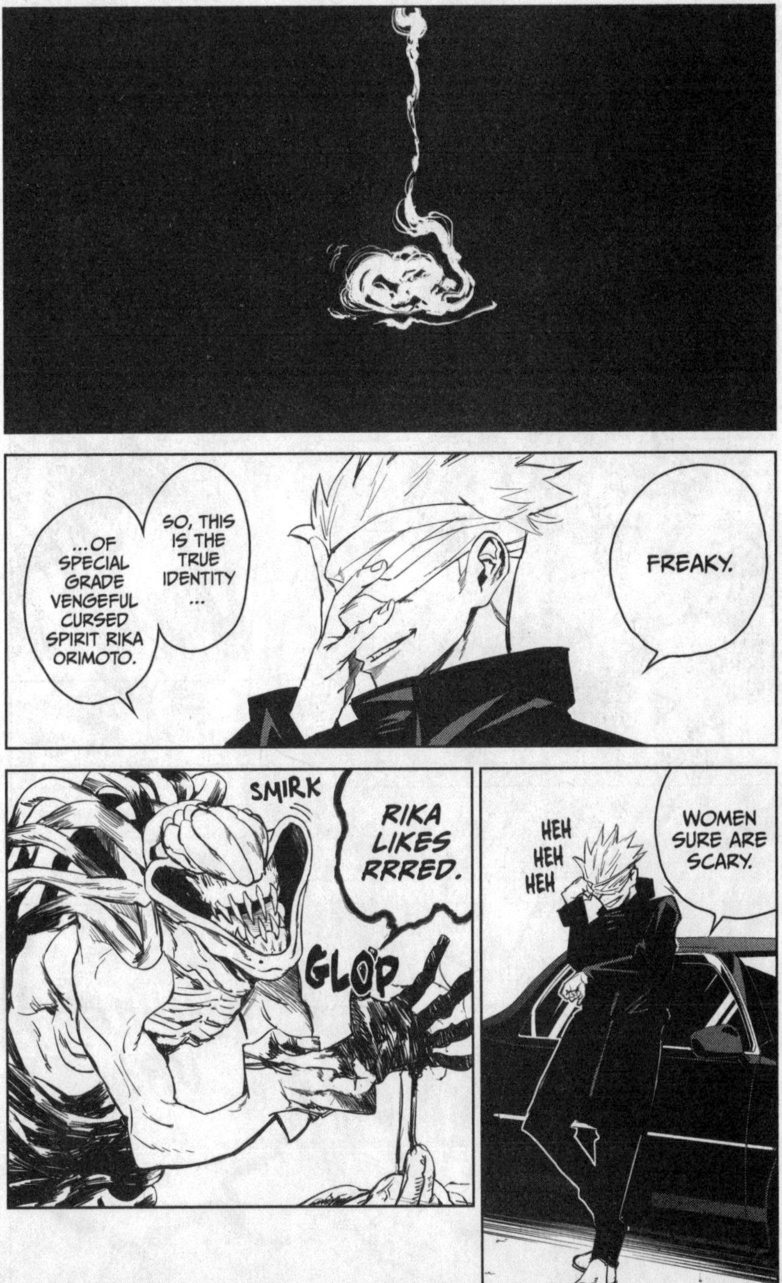
FREAKY.
SO, THIS IS THE TRUE IDENTITY...
...OF SPECIAL GRADE VENGEFUL CURSED SPIRIT RIKA ORIMOTO.
WOMEN SURE ARE SCARY.
HEH HEH HEH
RIKA LIKES RRRED.
SMIRK
GLOP

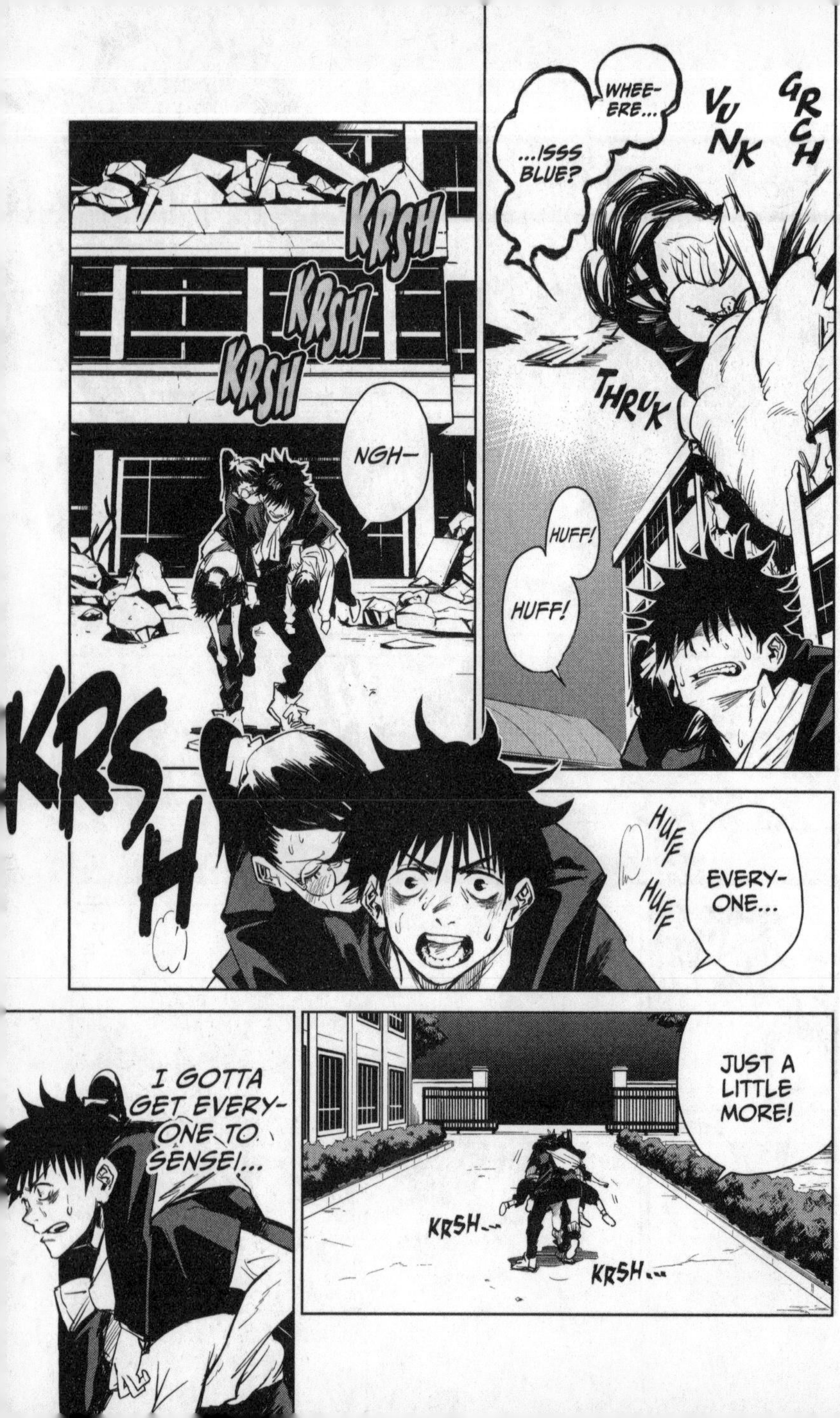
WHEE-ERE...
...ISSS BLUE?
GRCH
VUNK
THRUK
HUFF!
HUFF!
KRSH
KRSH
KRSH
NGH—
KRSH
HUFF
HUFF
EVERY-ONE...
JUST A LITTLE MORE!
KRSH...
KRSH...
I GOTTA GET EVERY-ONE TO SENSEI...

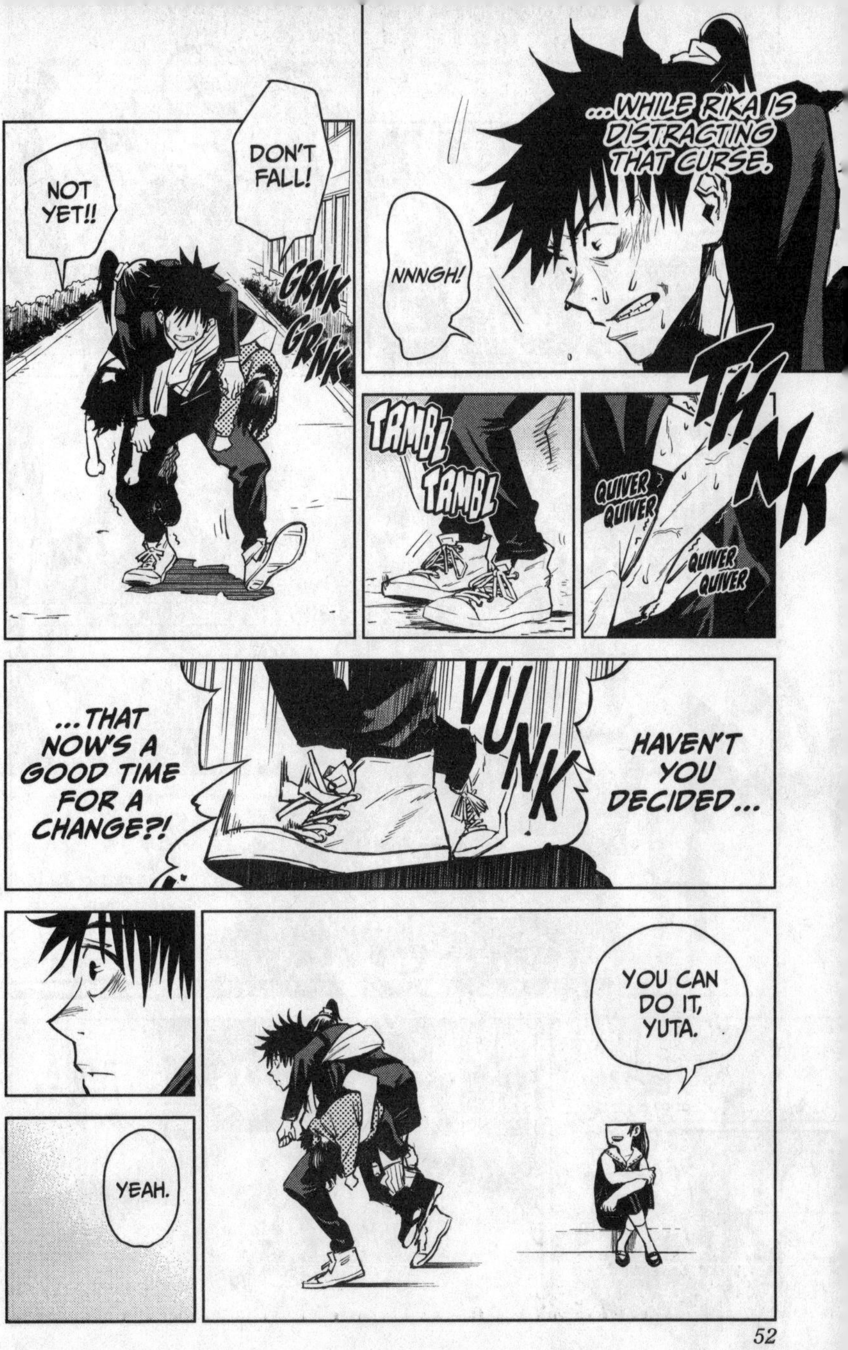
...WHILE RIKA IS DISTRACTING THAT CURSE.
NNNGH!
THNK
QUIVER QUIVER
QUIVER QUIVER
TRMBL TRMBL
DON'T FALL!
NOT YET!!
GRNK GRNK
HAVEN'T YOU DECIDED...
VUNK
...THAT NOW'S A GOOD TIME FOR A CHANGE?!
YOU CAN DO IT, YUTA.
YEAH.

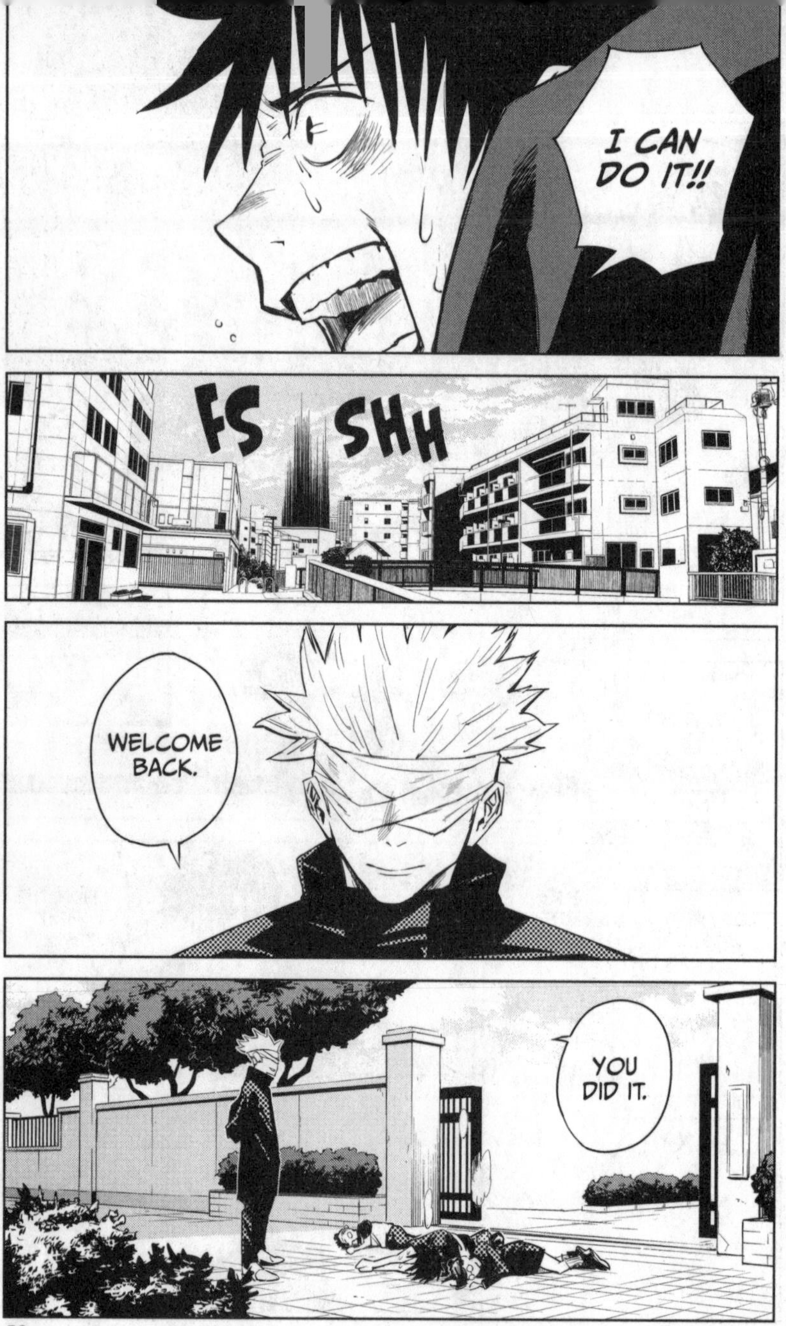
I CAN DO IT!!
FS SHH
WELCOME BACK.
YOU DID IT.

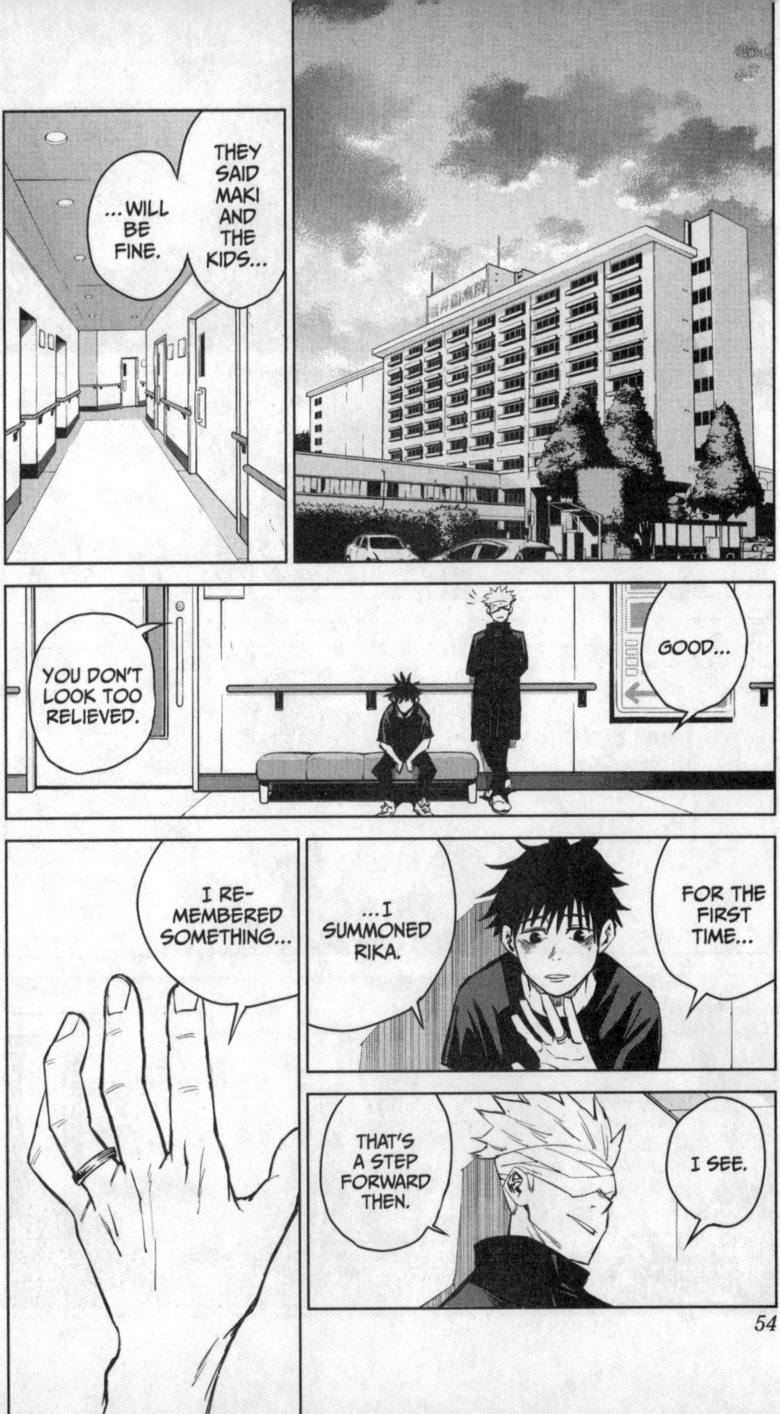
THEY SAID MAKI AND THE KIDS...
...WILL BE FINE.
GOOD...
YOU DON'T LOOK TOO RELIEVED.
FOR THE FIRST TIME...
...I SUMMONED RIKA.
I SEE.
THAT'S A STEP FORWARD THEN.
I RE-MEMBERED SOMETHING...

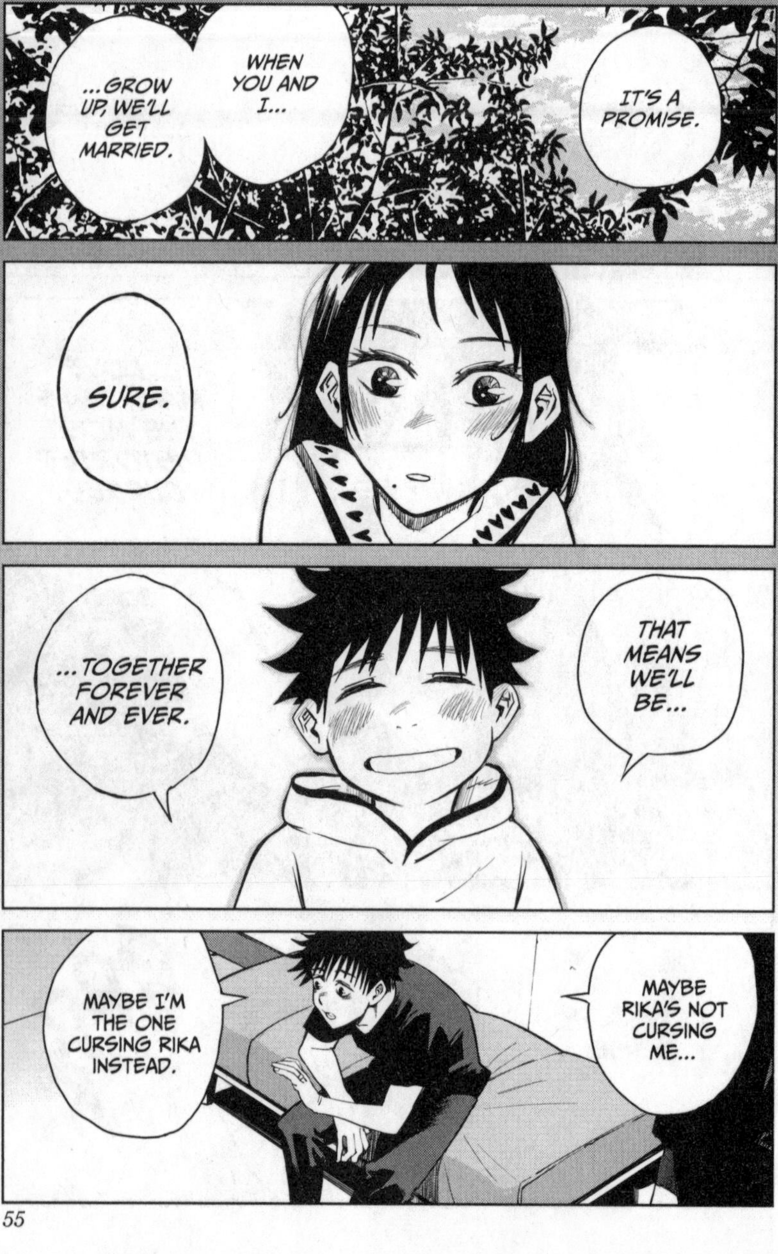
IT'S A PROMISE.
WHEN YOU AND I...
...GROW UP, WE'LL GET MARRIED.
SURE.
THAT MEANS WE'LL BE...
...TOGETHER FOREVER AND EVER.
MAYBE RIKA'S NOT CURSING ME...
MAYBE I'M THE ONE CURSING RIKA INSTEAD.

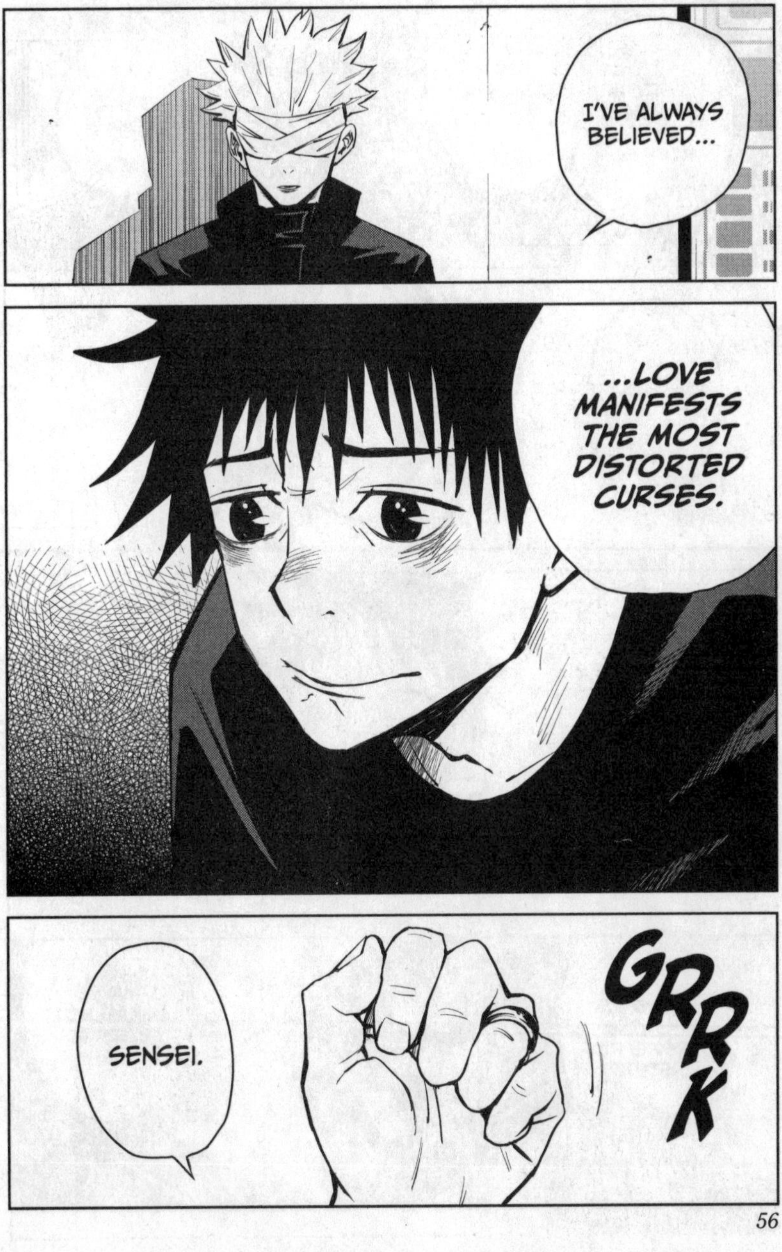
I'VE ALWAYS BELIEVED...
...LOVE MANIFESTS THE MOST DISTORTED CURSES.
GRRK
SENSEI.

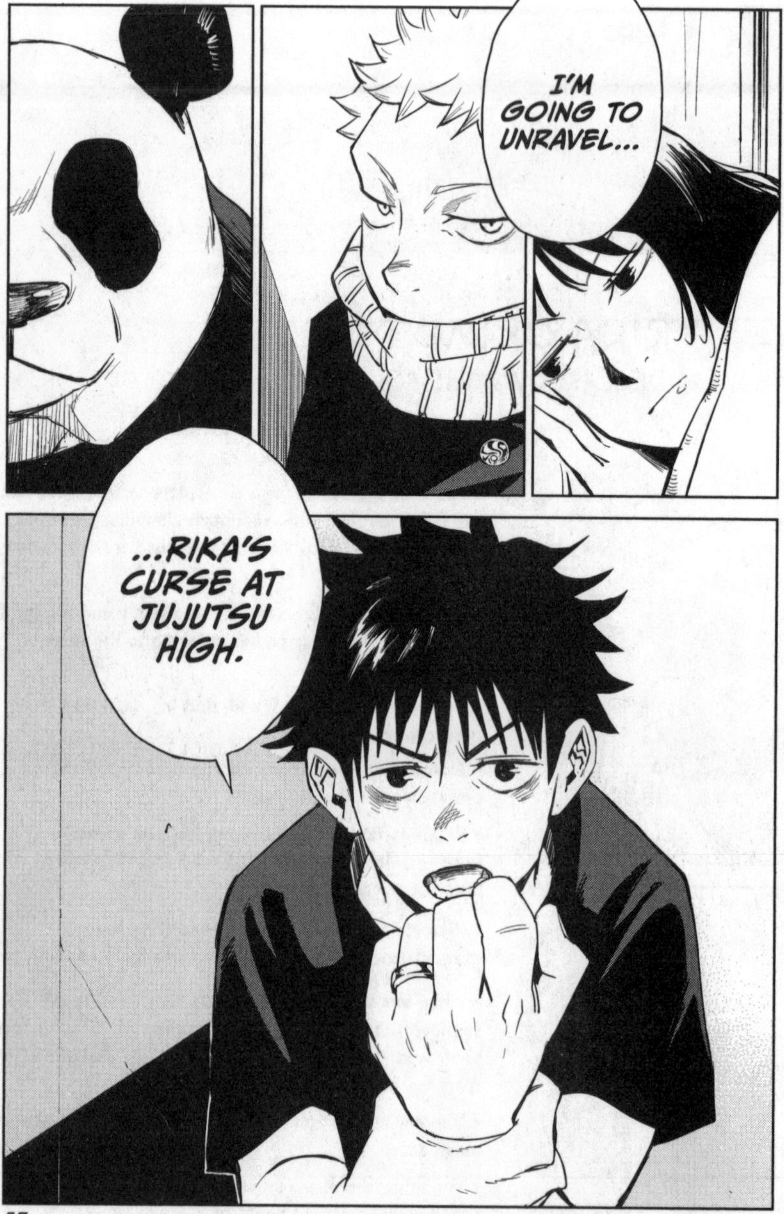
I'M GOING TO UNRAVEL...
...RIKA'S CURSE AT JUJUTSU HIGH.

RIKA ORIMOTO
(DECEASED AT THE AGE OF 11)

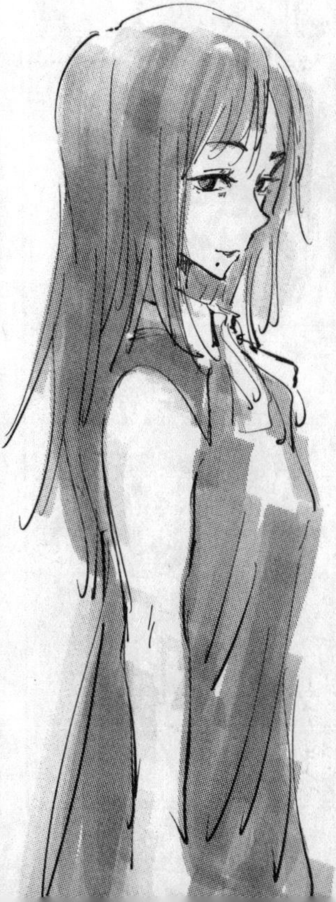

- Rika's mother died suddenly from unknown causes when Rika was five.
- Two days before entering elementary school, Rika and her father got lost while mountain climbing. One week later, Rika was found alone and rescued from a shelter near the summit.
- At the hospital, she met Yuta, who was being treated for pneumonia. They later ended up going to the same elementary school.
- Her father was never found, and his death has never been confirmed.
- Aware of how her appearance is perceived, Rika sometimes manipulates adults.
- Rika was taken in by her grandmother on her father's side, who strongly believes that Rika killed both her parents.
- Rika stole the ring she gave Yuta from her grandmother's dresser. It was her mother's wedding ring.
- When she was human, Rika was very friendly with Yuta's younger sister. However, after becoming a vengeful curse, she became aggressive, which is why Yuta distanced himself from his family.
- She dislikes everyone besides Yuta—especially girls and older guys.
- The thing she dislikes the most in the world is her grandmother's stewed eggplant.
- She loves Yuta.

Chapter 2:
Blacker and Blacker

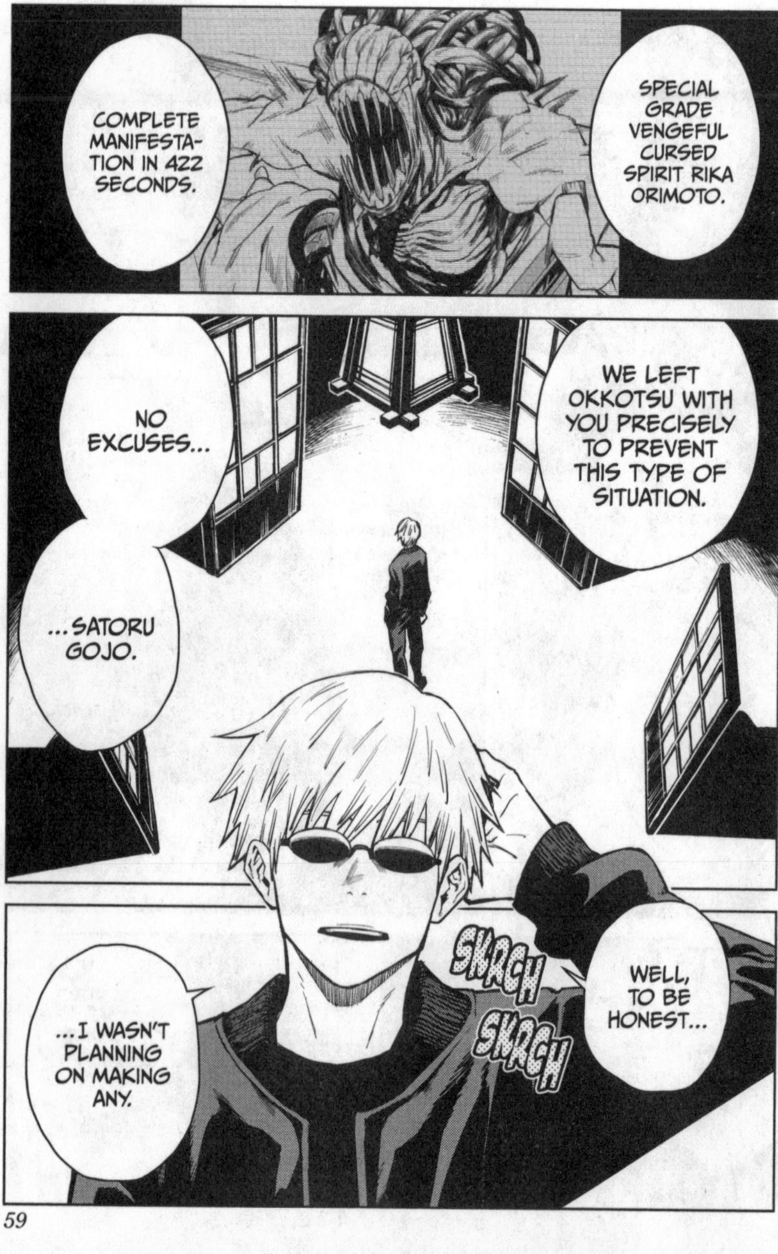
SPECIAL GRADE VENGEFUL CURSED SPIRIT RIKA ORIMOTO.
COMPLETE MANIFESTATION IN 422 SECONDS.
WE LEFT OKKOTSU WITH YOU PRECISELY TO PREVENT THIS TYPE OF SITUATION.
NO EXCUSES...
...SATORU GOJO.
WELL, TO BE HONEST...
SKRCH
SKRCH
...I WASN'T PLANNING ON MAKING ANY.

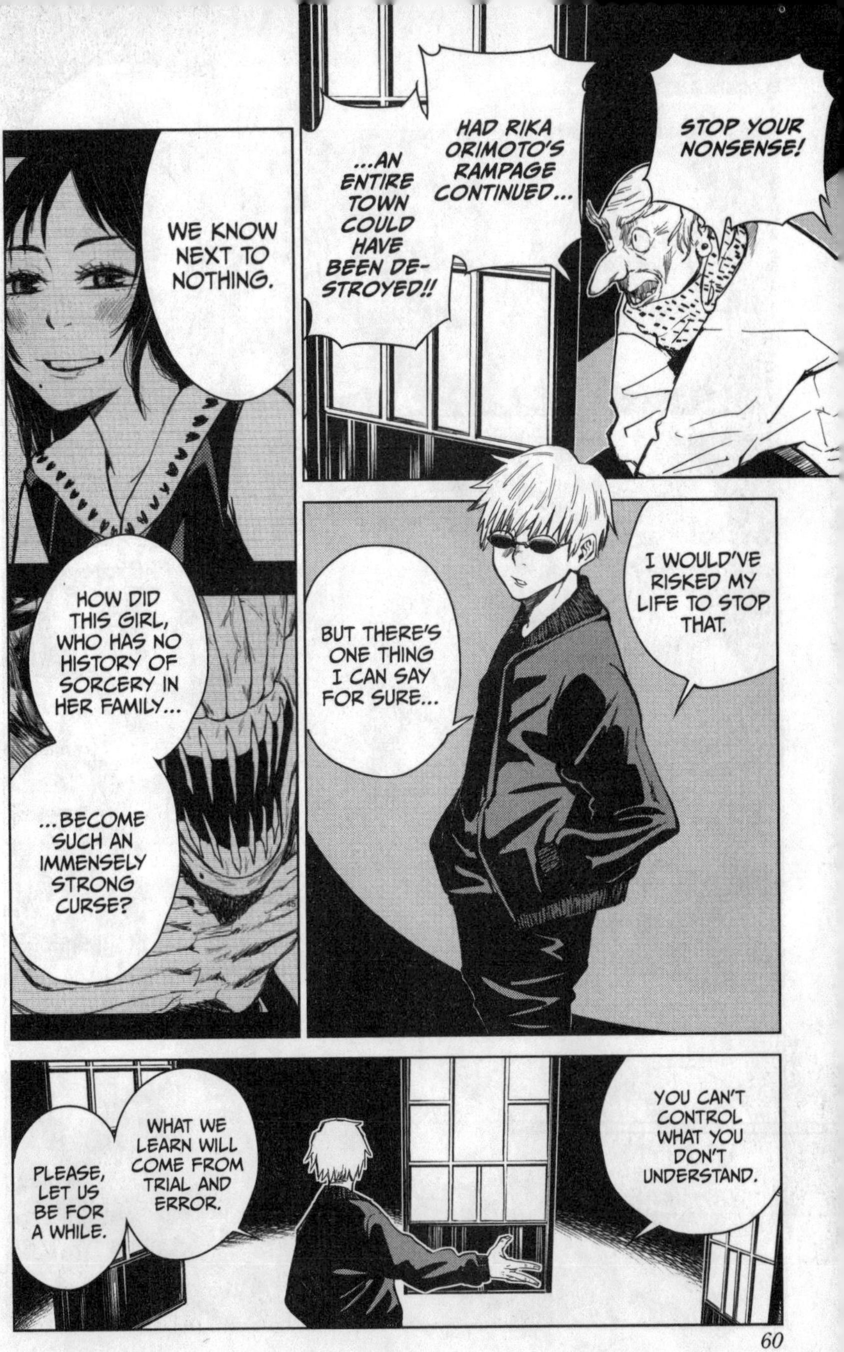
STOP YOUR NONSENSE!
HAD RIKA ORIMOTO'S RAMPAGE CONTINUED...
...AN ENTIRE TOWN COULD HAVE BEEN DE-STROYED!!
I WOULD'VE RISKED MY LIFE TO STOP THAT.
BUT THERE'S ONE THING I CAN SAY FOR SURE...
WE KNOW NEXT TO NOTHING.
HOW DID THIS GIRL, WHO HAS NO HISTORY OF SORCERY IN HER FAMILY...
...BECOME SUCH AN IMMENSELY STRONG CURSE?
YOU CAN'T CONTROL WHAT YOU DON'T UNDERSTAND.
WHAT WE LEARN WILL COME FROM TRIAL AND ERROR.
PLEASE, LET US BE FOR A WHILE.

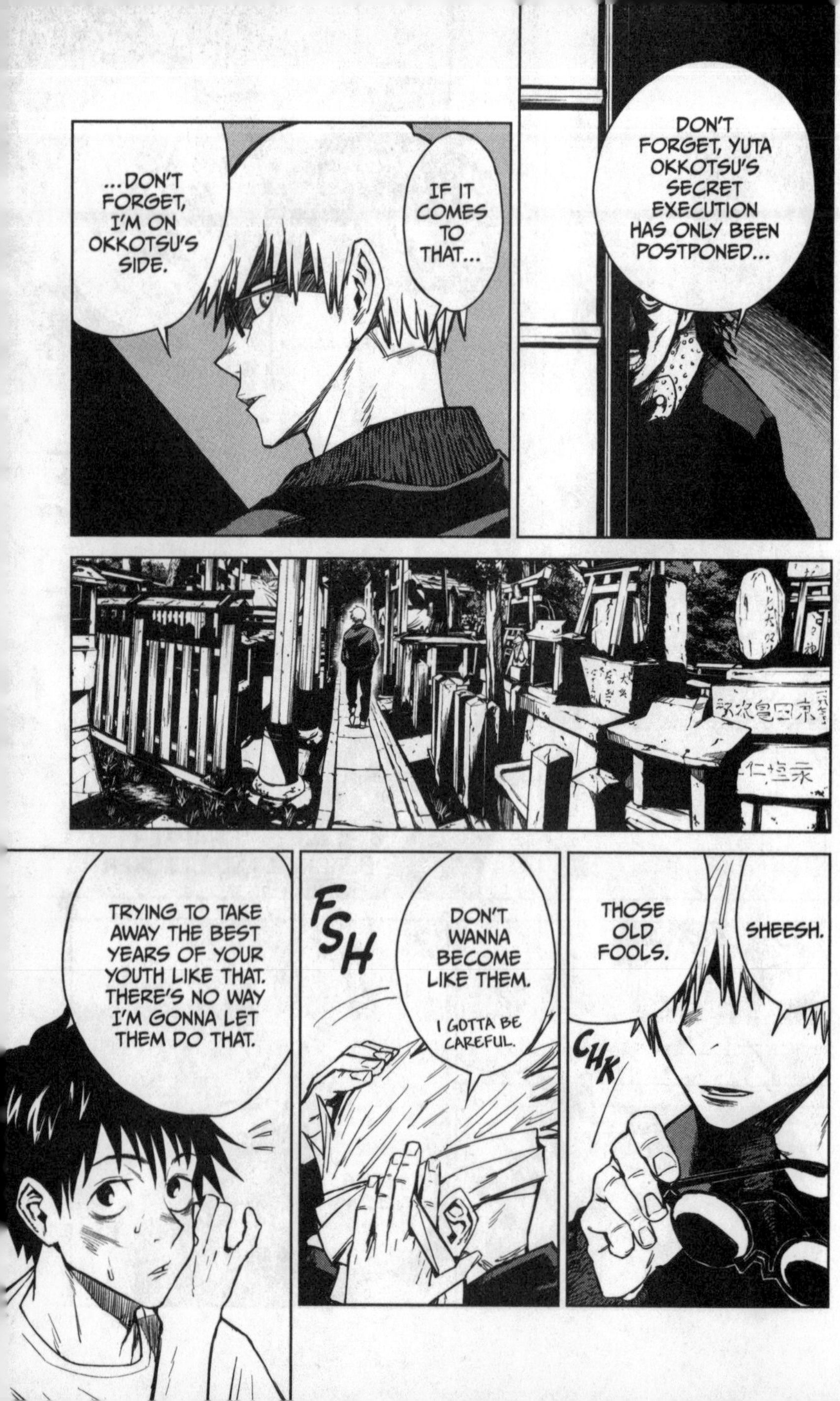
DON'T FORGET, YUTA OKKOTSU'S SECRET EXECUTION HAS ONLY BEEN POSTPONED...
IF IT COMES TO THAT...
...DON'T FORGET, I'M ON OKKOTSU'S SIDE.
SHEESH.
THOSE OLD FOOLS.
CHK
DON'T WANNA BECOME LIKE THEM.
I GOTTA BE CAREFUL.
FSH
TRYING TO TAKE AWAY THE BEST YEARS OF YOUR YOUTH LIKE THAT. THERE'S NO WAY I'M GONNA LET THEM DO THAT.

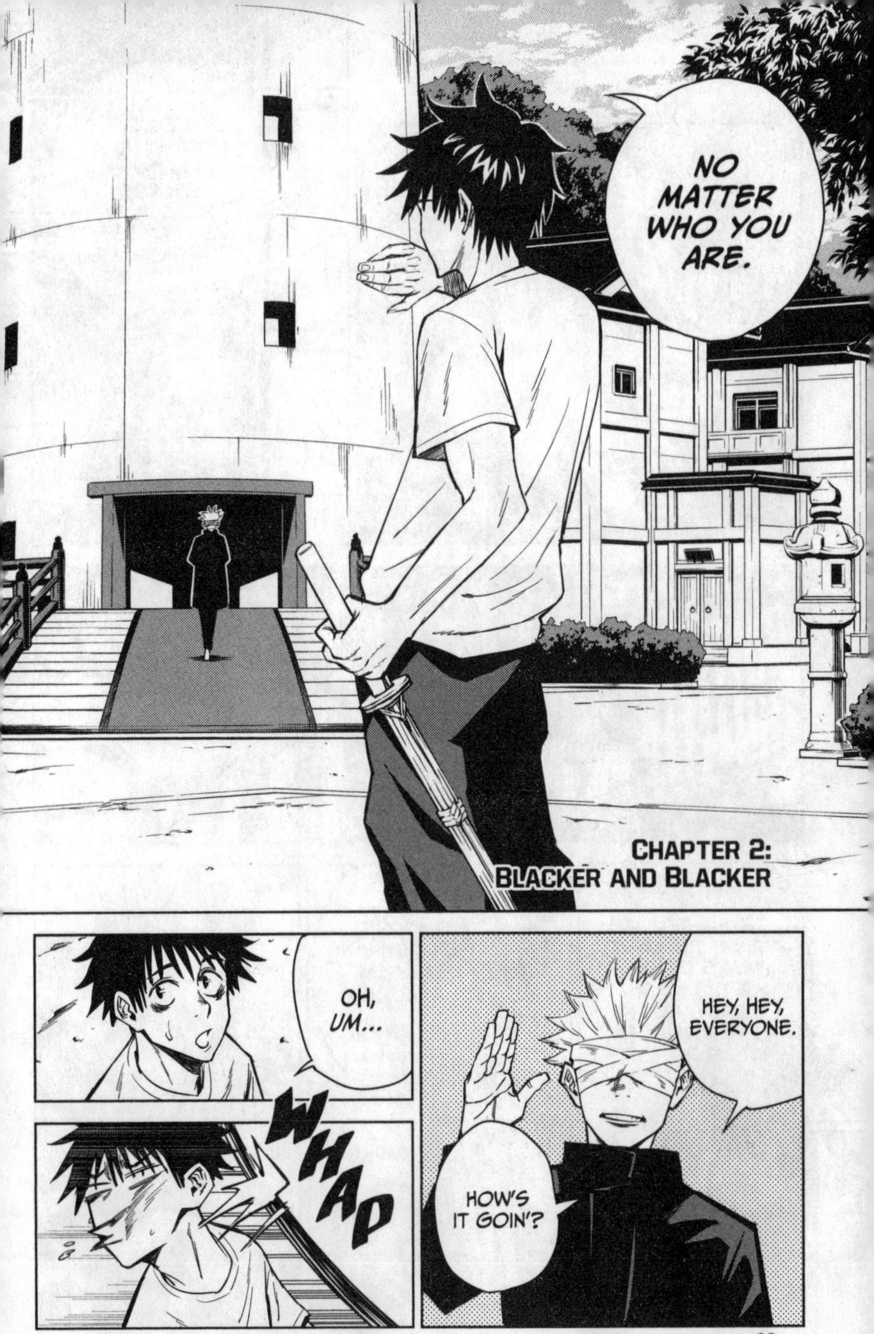
NO MATTER WHO YOU ARE.
CHAPTER 2: BLACKER AND BLACKER
HEY, HEY, EVERYONE.
HOW'S IT GOIN'?
OH, UM...
WHAP

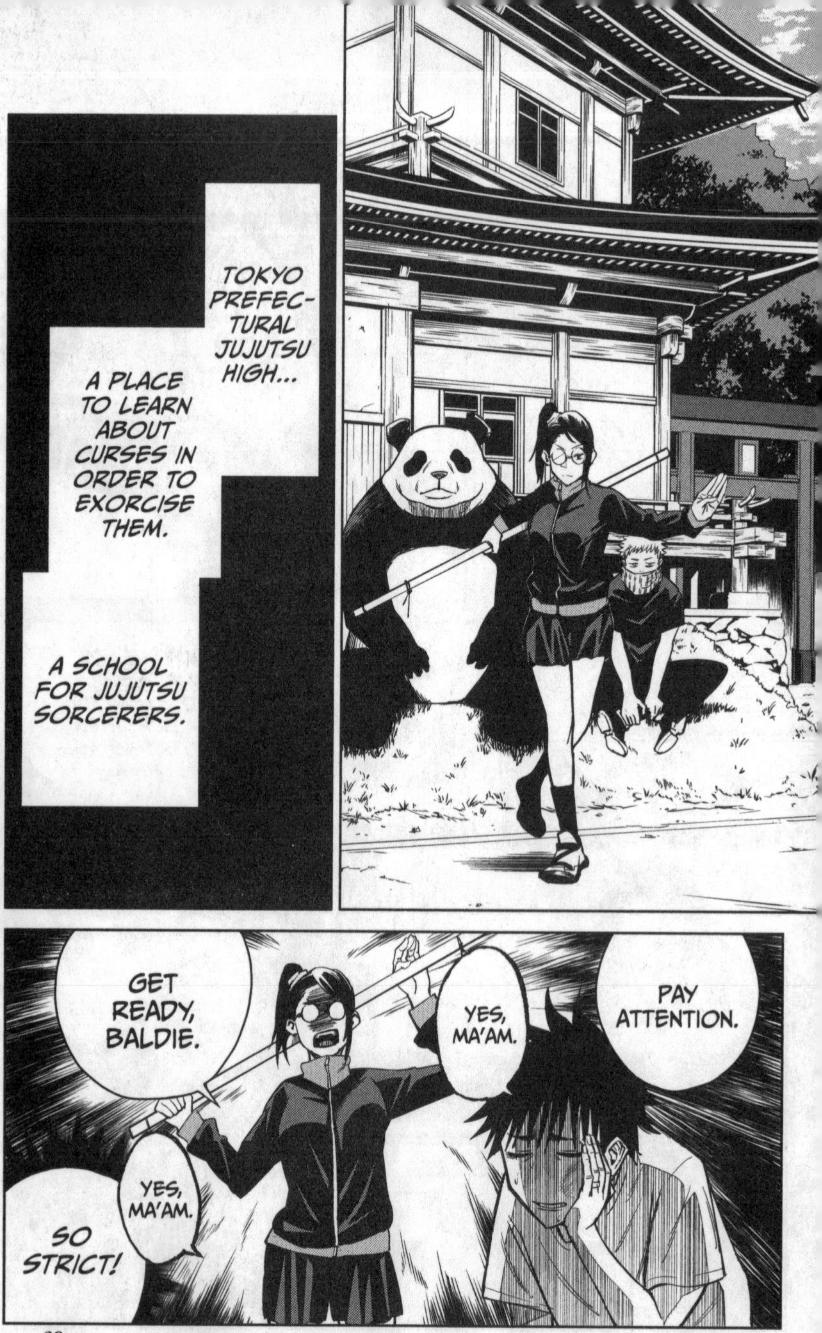
TOKYO PREFECTURAL JUJUTSU HIGH...
A PLACE TO LEARN ABOUT CURSES IN ORDER TO EXORCISE THEM.
A SCHOOL FOR JUJUTSU SORCERERS.
PAY ATTENTION.
YES, MA'AM.
GET READY, BALDIE.
YES, MA'AM.
SO STRICT!

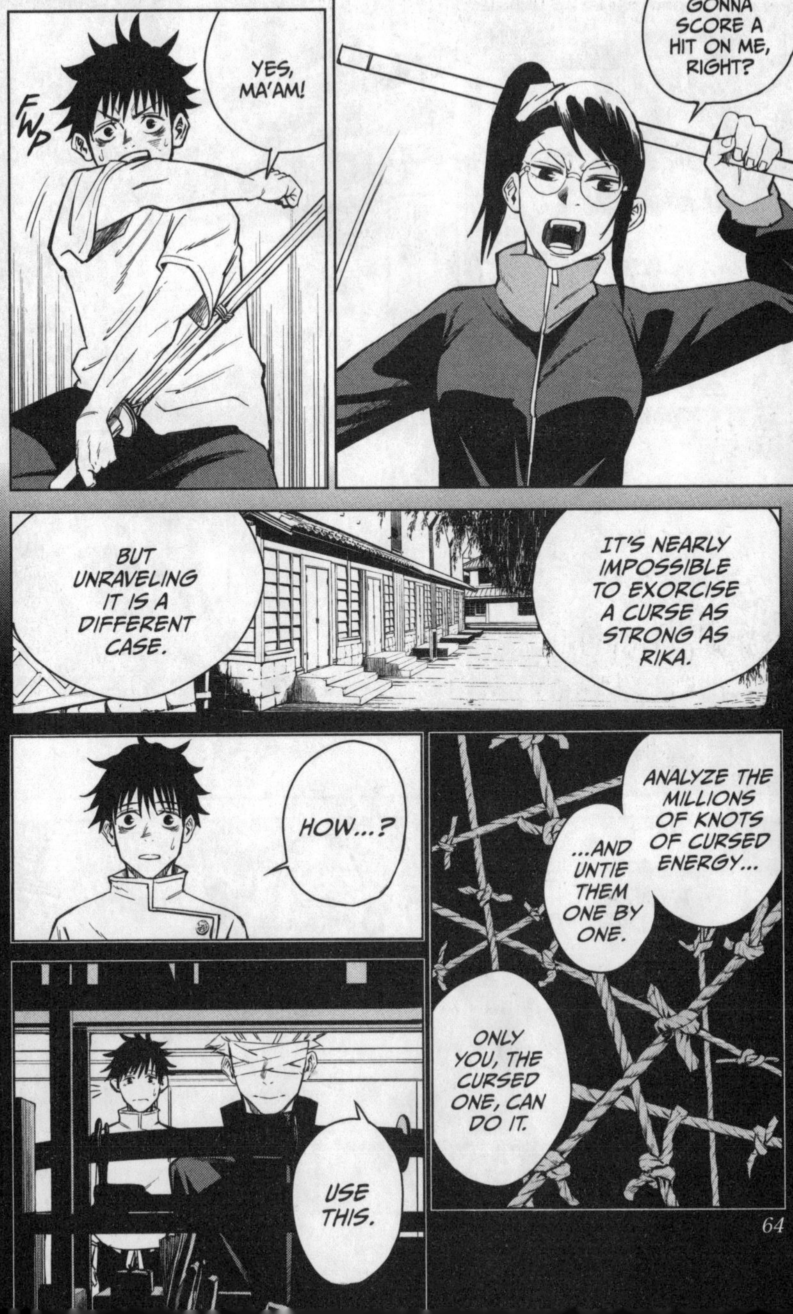
YOU'RE GONNA SCORE A HIT ON ME, RIGHT?
FWP
YES, MA'AM!
IT'S NEARLY IMPOSSIBLE TO EXORCISE A CURSE AS STRONG AS RIKA.
BUT UNRAVELING IT IS A DIFFERENT CASE.
ANALYZE THE MILLIONS OF KNOTS OF CURSED ENERGY...
...AND UNTIE THEM ONE BY ONE.
ONLY YOU, THE CURSED ONE, CAN DO IT.
HOW...?
USE THIS.

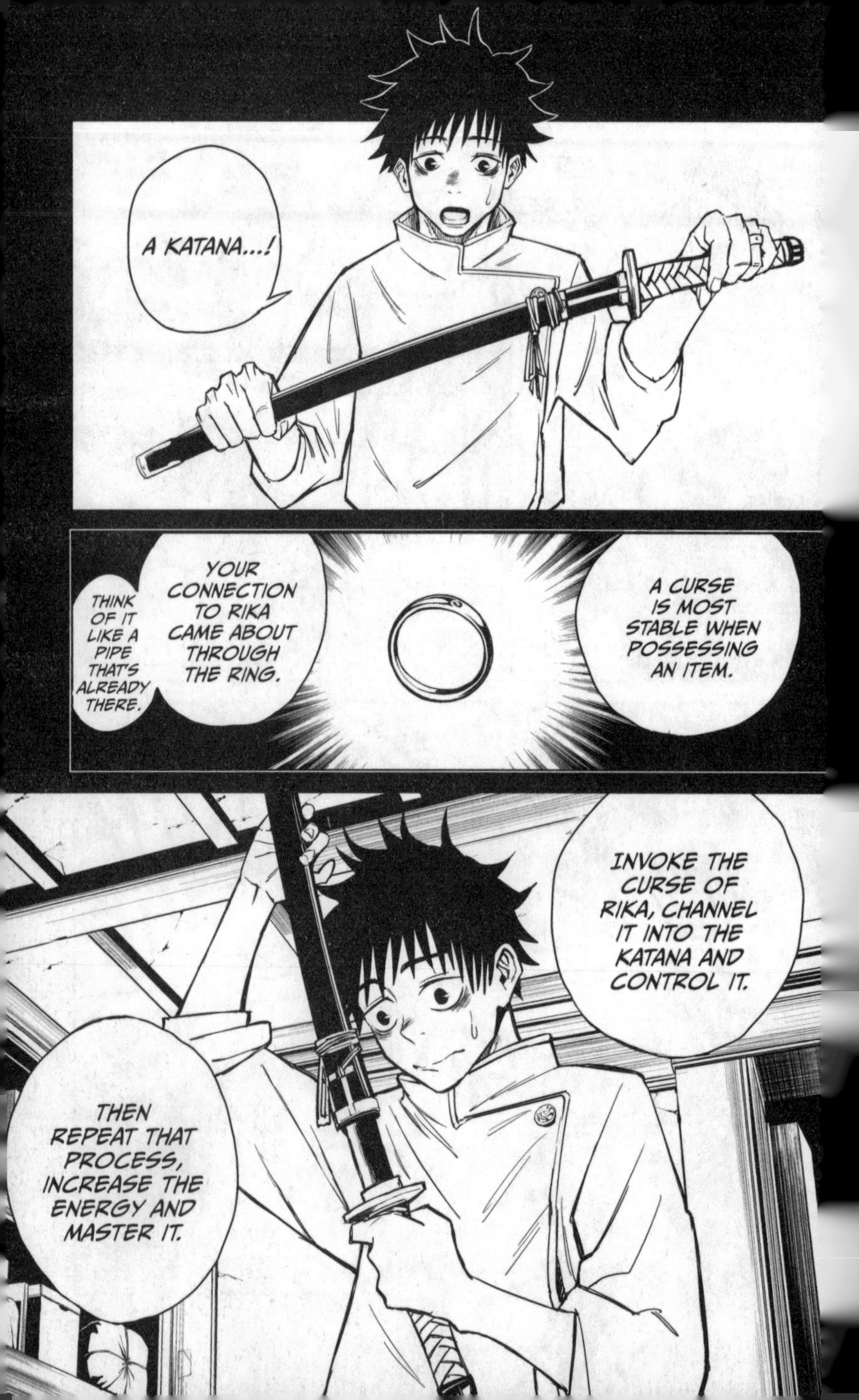
A KATANA...!
A CURSE IS MOST STABLE WHEN POSSESSING AN ITEM.
YOUR CONNECTION TO RIKA CAME ABOUT THROUGH THE RING.
THINK OF IT LIKE A PIPE THAT'S ALREADY THERE.
INVOKE THE CURSE OF RIKA, CHANNEL IT INTO THE KATANA AND CONTROL IT.
THEN REPEAT THAT PROCESS, INCREASE THE ENERGY AND MASTER IT.

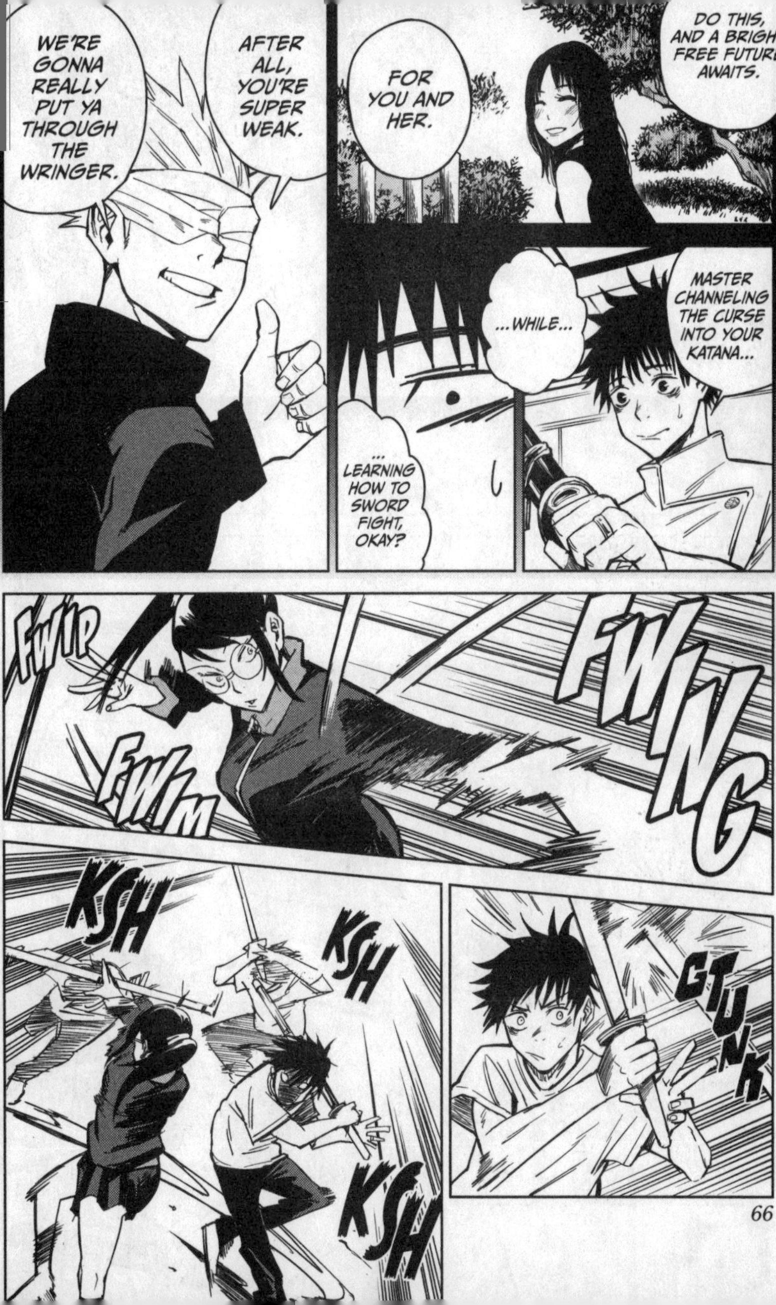
DO THIS, AND A BRIGHT, FREE FUTURE AWAITS.
FOR YOU AND HER.
MASTER CHANNELING THE CURSE INTO YOUR KATANA...
...WHILE...
...LEARNING HOW TO SWORD FIGHT, OKAY?
AFTER ALL, YOU'RE SUPER WEAK.
WE'RE GONNA REALLY PUT YA THROUGH THE WRINGER.
FWING
FWIP
FWIM
GTUNK
KSH
KSH
KSH

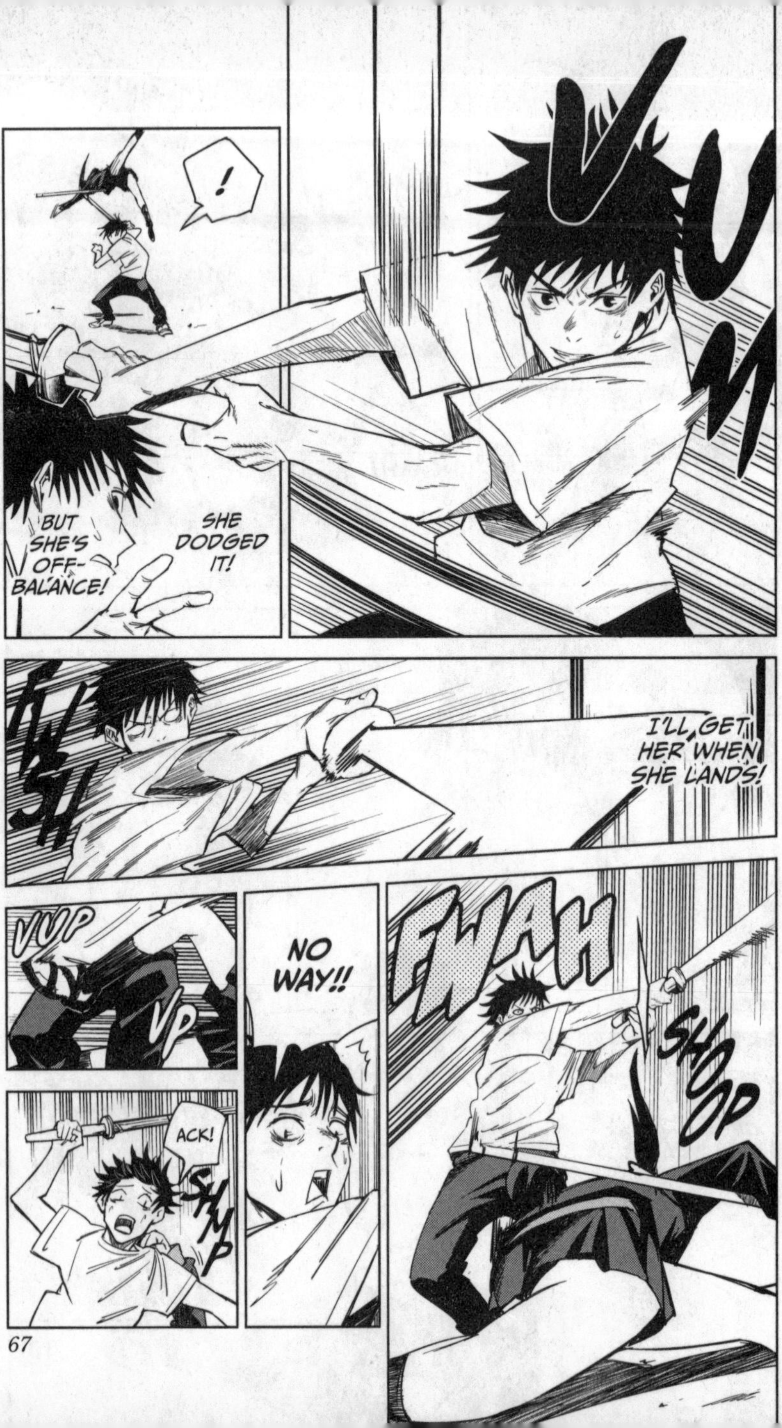

!
SHE DODGED IT!
BUT SHE'S OFF-BALANCE!
I'LL GET HER WHEN SHE LANDS!
FWASH
FWAH
SHOOOP
NO WAY!!
VUP
VP
ACK!
SHMP

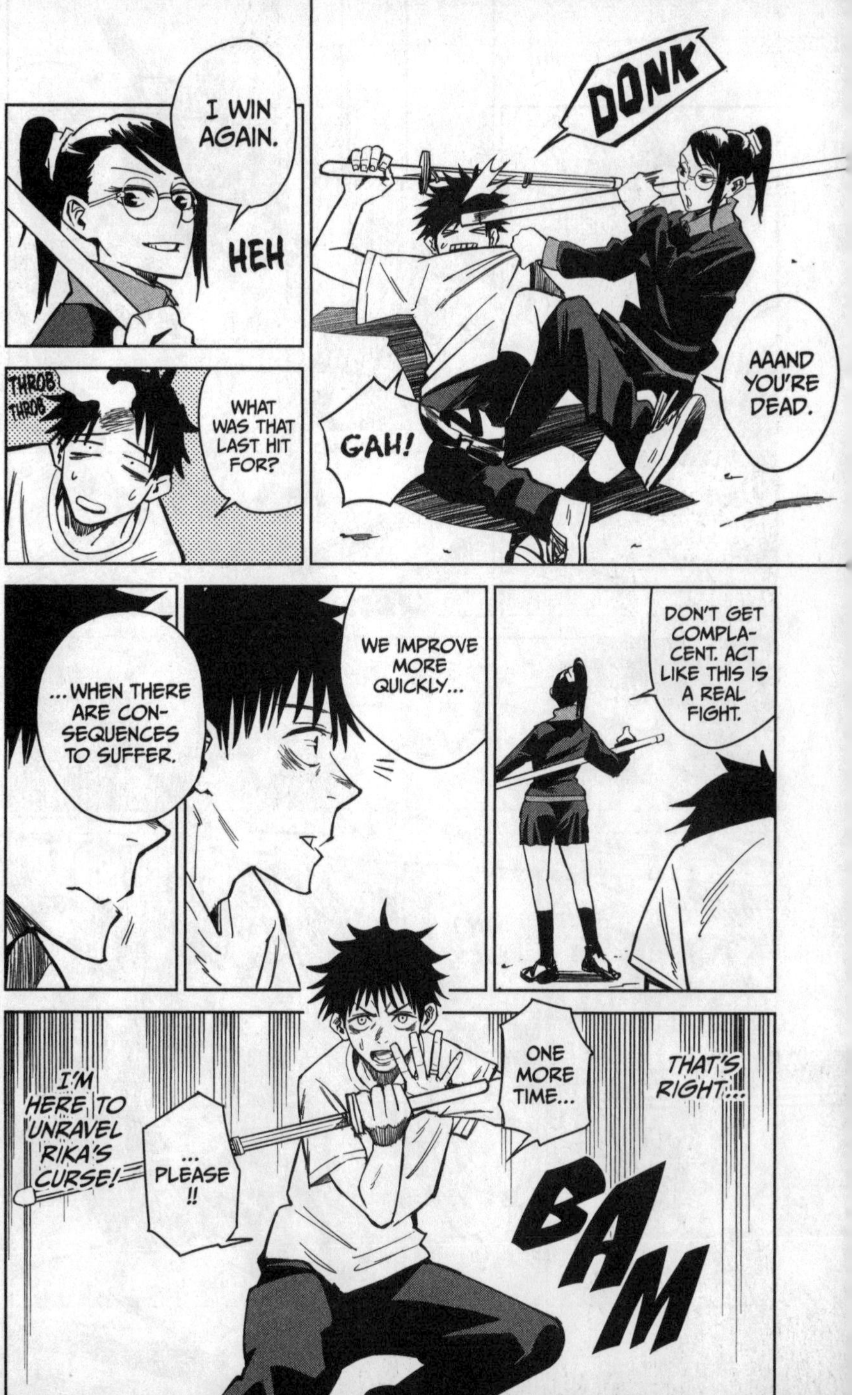
DONK
AAAND YOU'RE DEAD.
GAH!
I WIN AGAIN.
HEH
THROB THROB
WHAT WAS THAT LAST HIT FOR?
DON'T GET COMPLA-CENT. ACT LIKE THIS IS A REAL FIGHT.
WE IMPROVE MORE QUICKLY...
...WHEN THERE ARE CON-SEQUENCES TO SUFFER.
THAT'S RIGHT...
ONE MORE TIME...
I'M HERE TO UNRAVEL RIKA'S CURSE!
... PLEASE !!
BAM

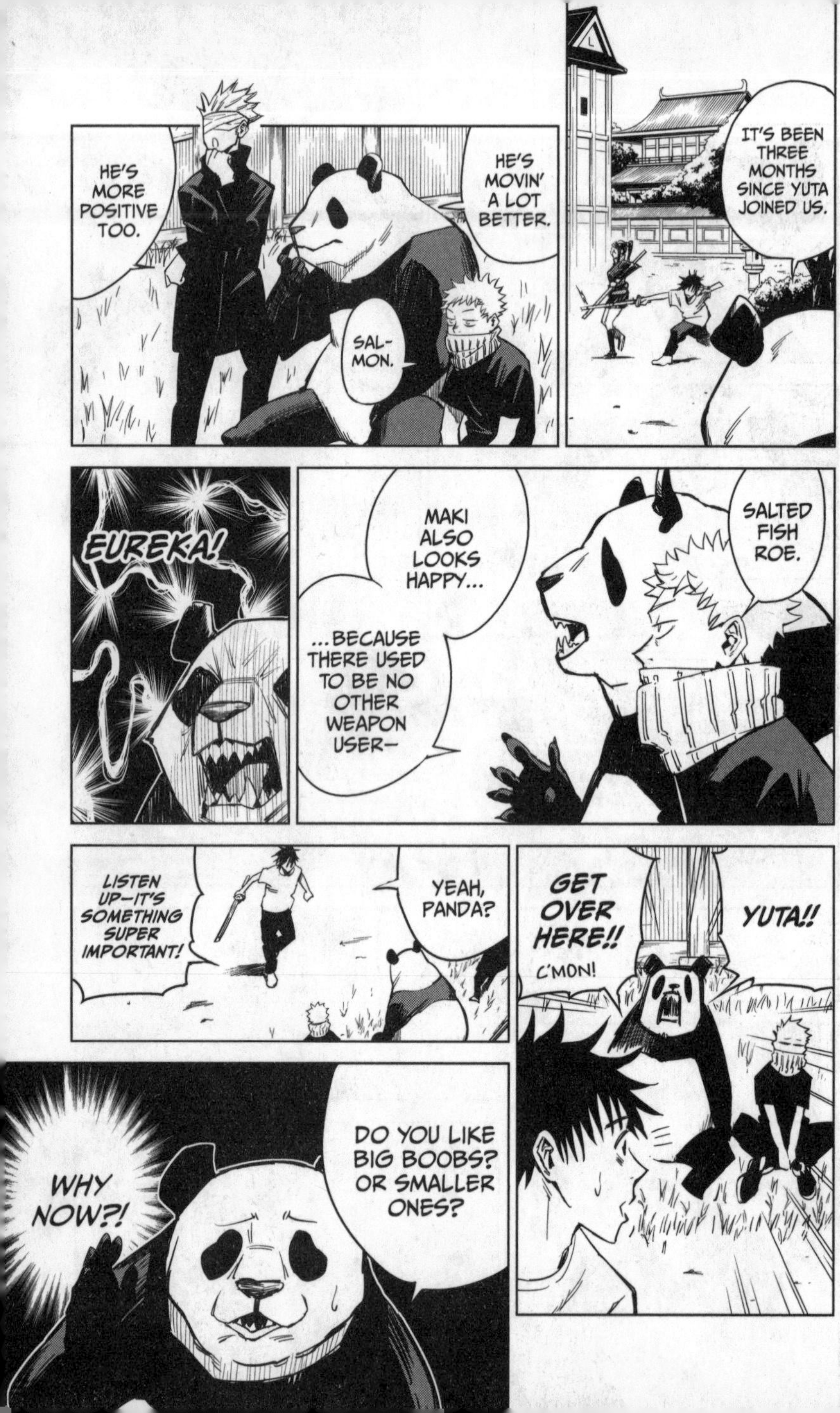
IT'S BEEN THREE MONTHS SINCE YUTA JOINED US.
HE'S MOVIN' A LOT BETTER.
HE'S MORE POSITIVE TOO.
SAL-MON.
SALTED FISH ROE.
MAKI ALSO LOOKS HAPPY...
...BECAUSE THERE USED TO BE NO OTHER WEAPON USER—
EUREKA!
YUTA!!
GET OVER HERE!!
C'MON!
YEAH, PANDA?
LISTEN UP—IT'S SOMETHING SUPER IMPORTANT!
DO YOU LIKE BIG BOOBS? OR SMALLER ONES?
WHY NOW?!

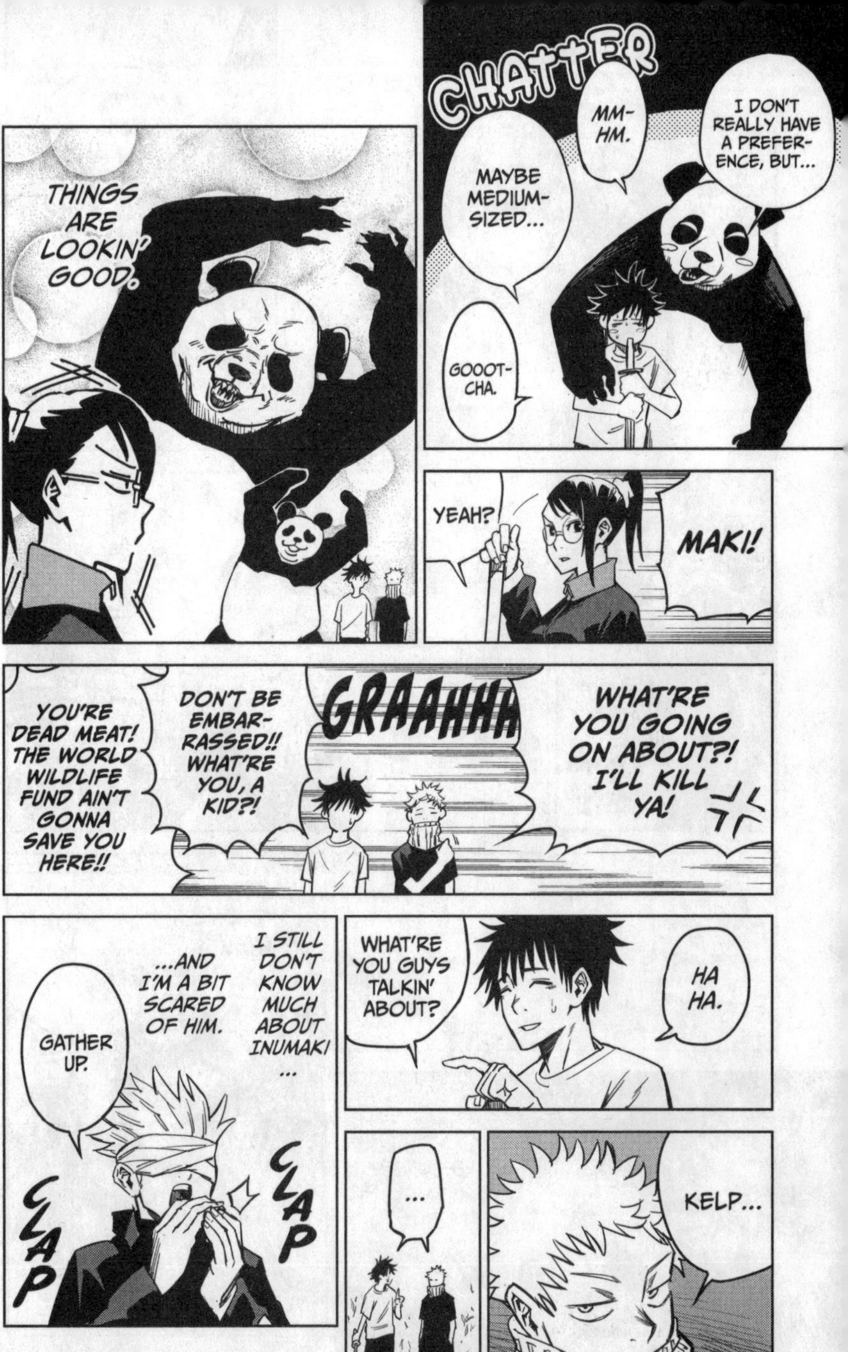
CHATTER
I DON'T REALLY HAVE A PREFERENCE, BUT...
MM-HM.
MAYBE MEDIUM-SIZED...
GOOOT-CHA.
MAKI!
YEAH?
THINGS ARE LOOKIN' GOOD.
WHAT'RE YOU GOING ON ABOUT?! I'LL KILL YA!
GRAAHHH
DON'T BE EMBARRASSED!! WHAT'RE YOU, A KID?!
YOU'RE DEAD MEAT! THE WORLD WILDLIFE FUND AIN'T GONNA SAVE YOU HERE!!
HA HA.
WHAT'RE YOU GUYS TALKIN' ABOUT?
KELP...
...
I STILL DON'T KNOW MUCH ABOUT INUMAKI...
...AND I'M A BIT SCARED OF HIM.
GATHER UP.
CLAP
CLAP

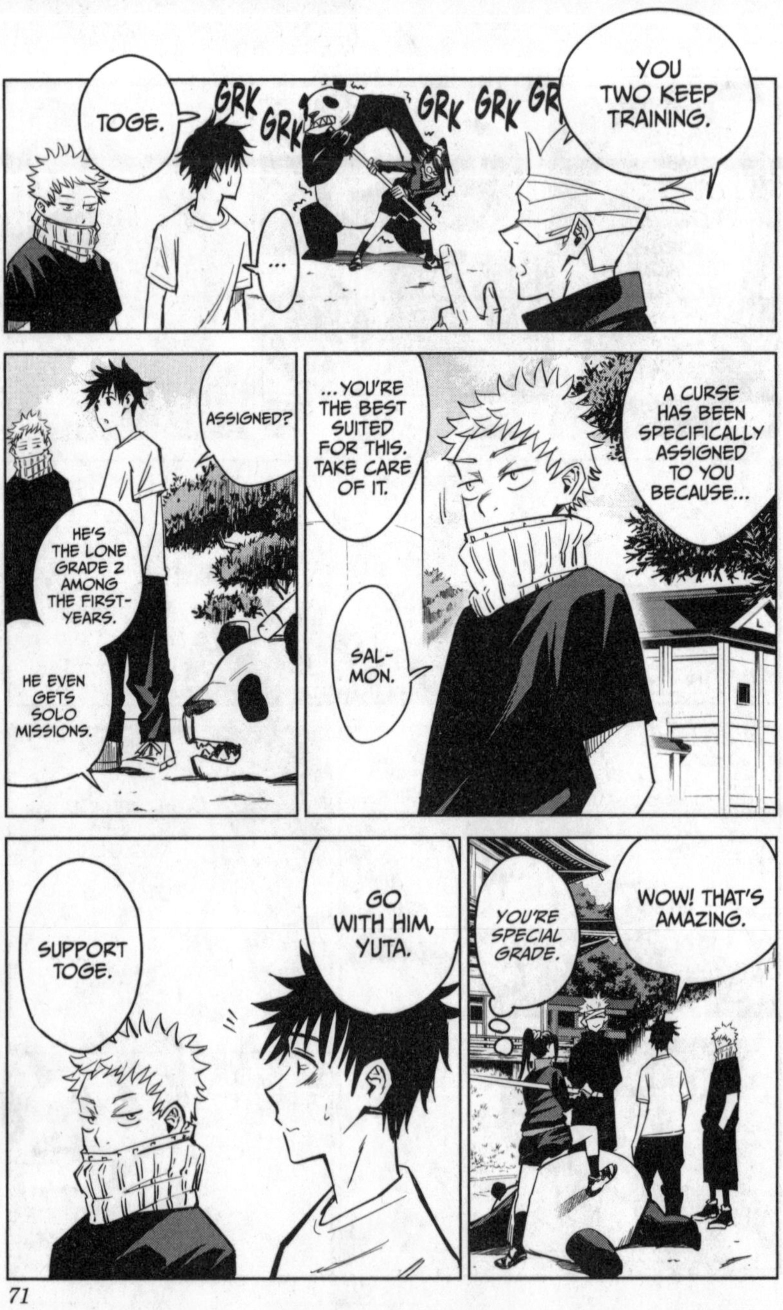
YOU TWO KEEP TRAINING.
GRK GRK
GRK
GRK
GRK
TOGE.
...
A CURSE HAS BEEN SPECIFICALLY ASSIGNED TO YOU BECAUSE...
...YOU'RE THE BEST SUITED FOR THIS. TAKE CARE OF IT.
SAL-MON.
ASSIGNED?
HE'S THE LONE GRADE 2 AMONG THE FIRST-YEARS.
HE EVEN GETS SOLO MISSIONS.
WOW! THAT'S AMAZING.
YOU'RE SPECIAL GRADE.
GO WITH HIM, YUTA.
SUPPORT TOGE.

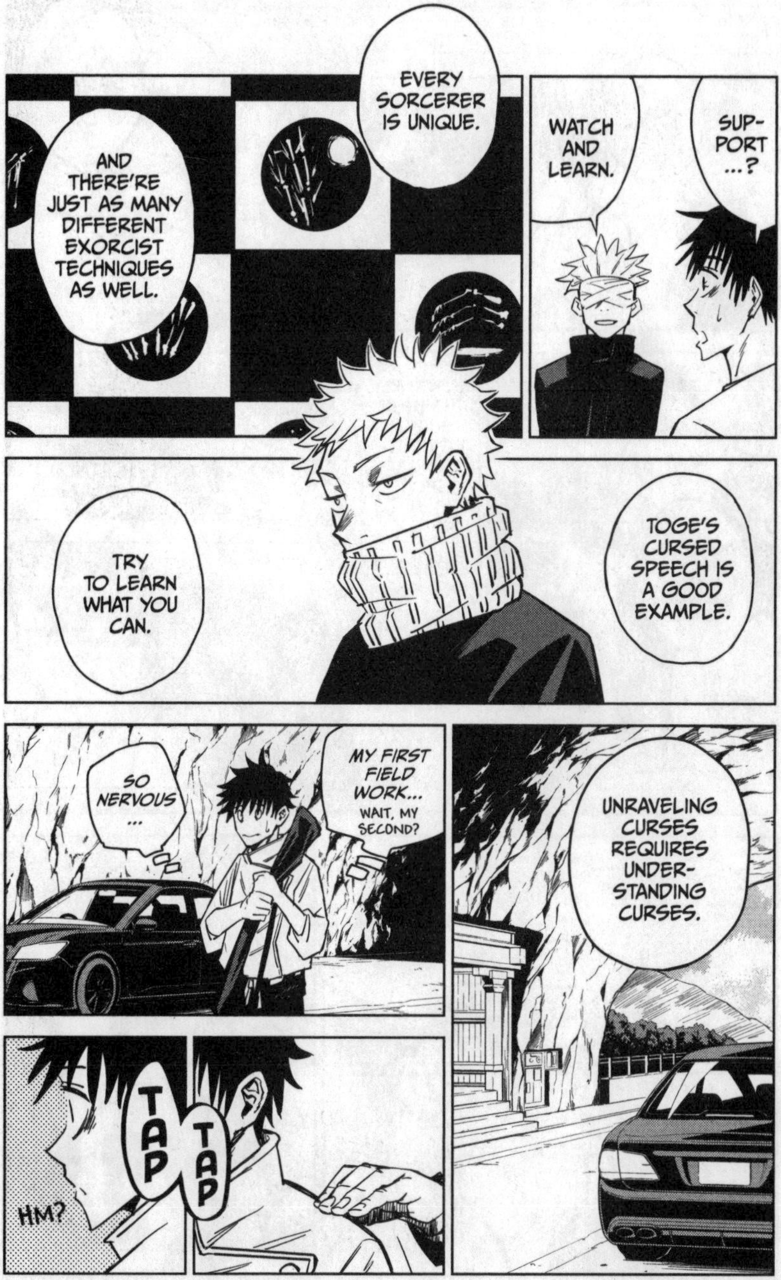
SUP-PORT ...?
WATCH AND LEARN.
EVERY SORCERER IS UNIQUE.
AND THERE'RE JUST AS MANY DIFFERENT EXORCIST TECHNIQUES AS WELL.
TOGE'S CURSED SPEECH IS A GOOD EXAMPLE.
TRY TO LEARN WHAT YOU CAN.
UNRAVELING CURSES REQUIRES UNDER-STANDING CURSES.
MY FIRST FIELD WORK... WAIT, MY SECOND?
SO NERVOUS ...
TAP TAP
HM?

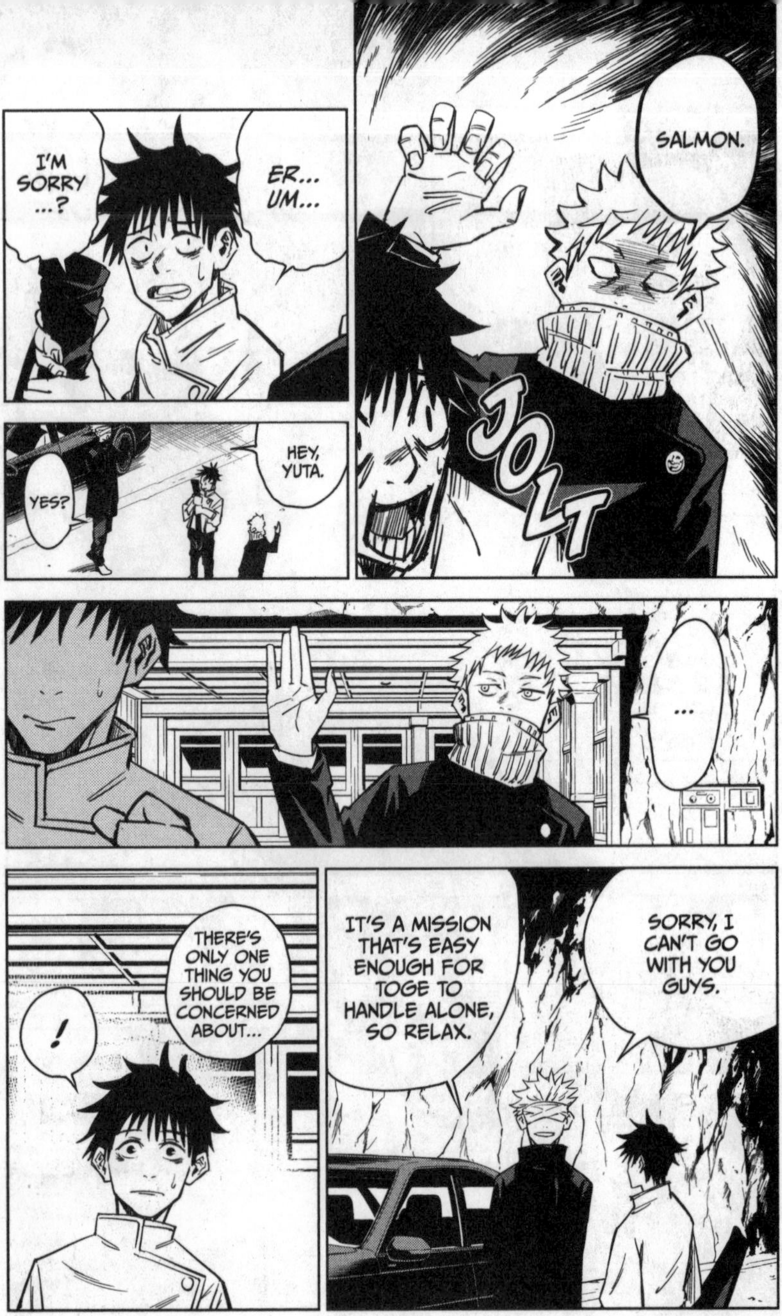
SALMON.
JOLT
ER... UM...
I'M SORRY ...?
HEY, YUTA.
YES?
...
SORRY, I CAN'T GO WITH YOU GUYS.
IT'S A MISSION THAT'S EASY ENOUGH FOR TOGE TO HANDLE ALONE, SO RELAX.
THERE'S ONLY ONE THING YOU SHOULD BE CONCERNED ABOUT...
!

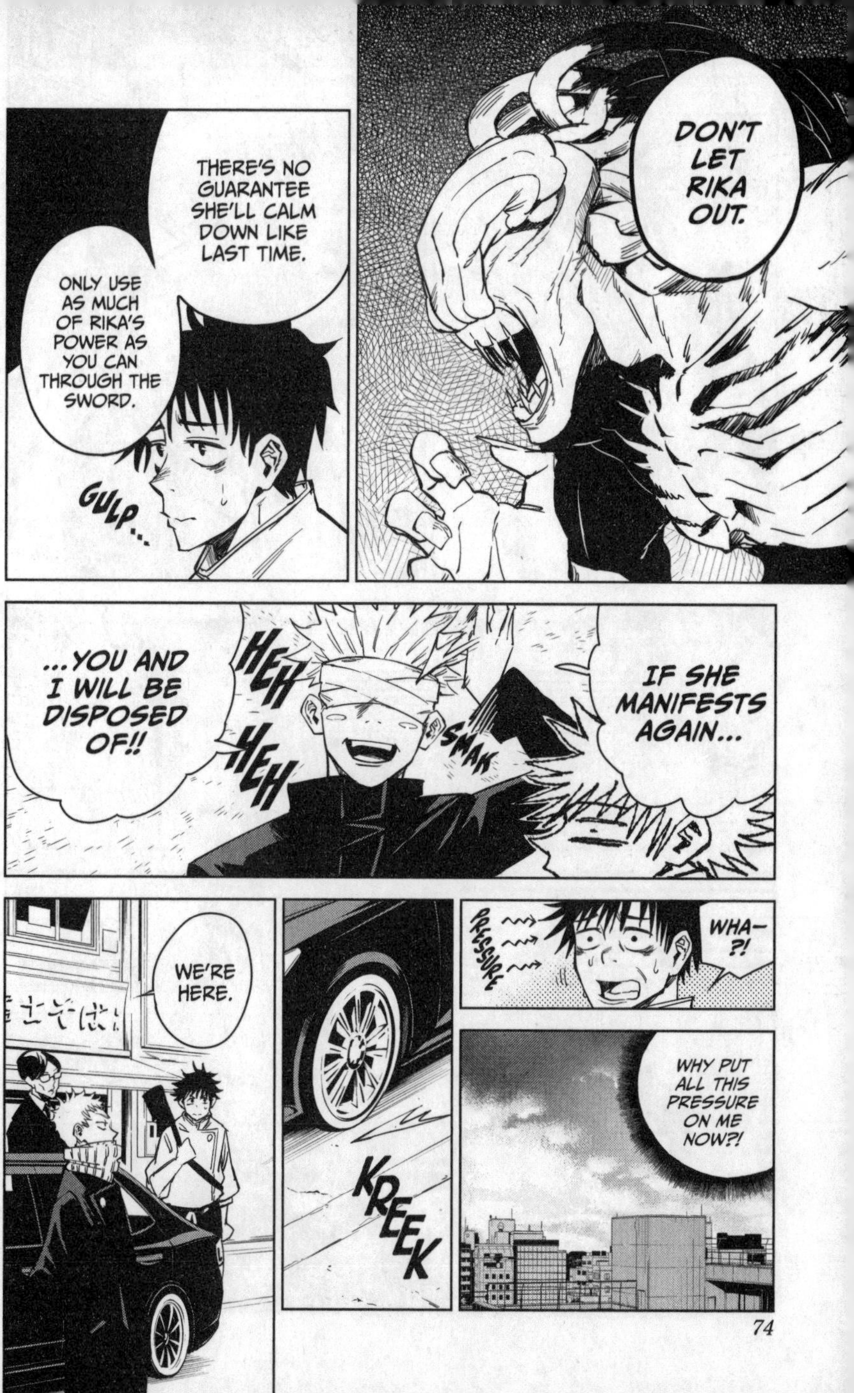
DON'T LET RIKA OUT.
THERE'S NO GUARANTEE SHE'LL CALM DOWN LIKE LAST TIME.
ONLY USE AS MUCH OF RIKA'S POWER AS YOU CAN THROUGH THE SWORD.
GULP...
IF SHE MANIFESTS AGAIN...
SMAK
HEH HEH
...YOU AND I WILL BE DISPOSED OF!!
WHA-?!
PRESSURE
WHY PUT ALL THIS PRESSURE ON ME NOW?!
KREEK
WE'RE HERE.

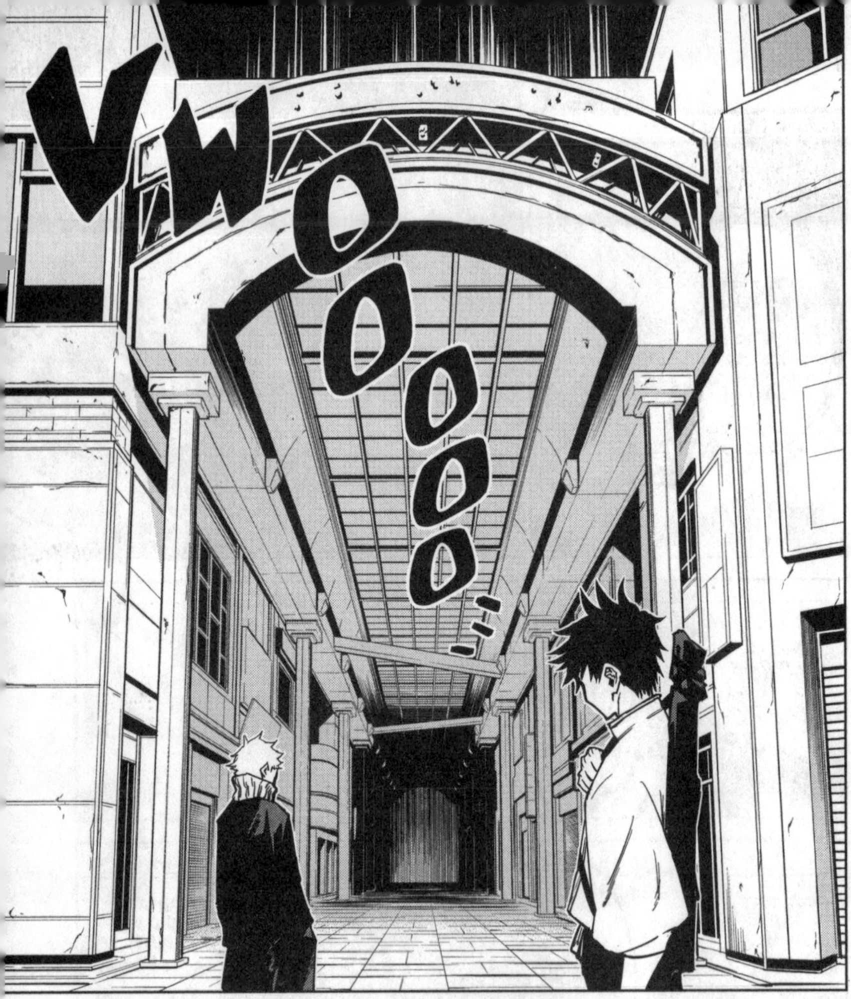
VWOOOOOO

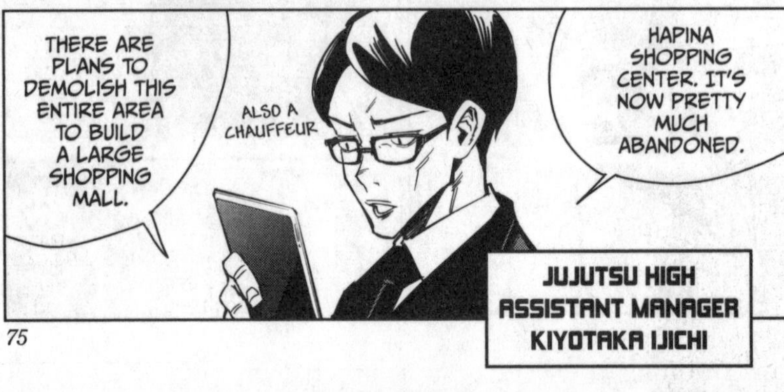
HAPINA SHOPPING CENTER. IT'S NOW PRETTY MUCH ABANDONED.
THERE ARE PLANS TO DEMOLISH THIS ENTIRE AREA TO BUILD A LARGE SHOPPING MALL.
ALSO A CHAUFFEUR
JUJUTSU HIGH ASSISTANT MANAGER KIYOTAKA IJICHI

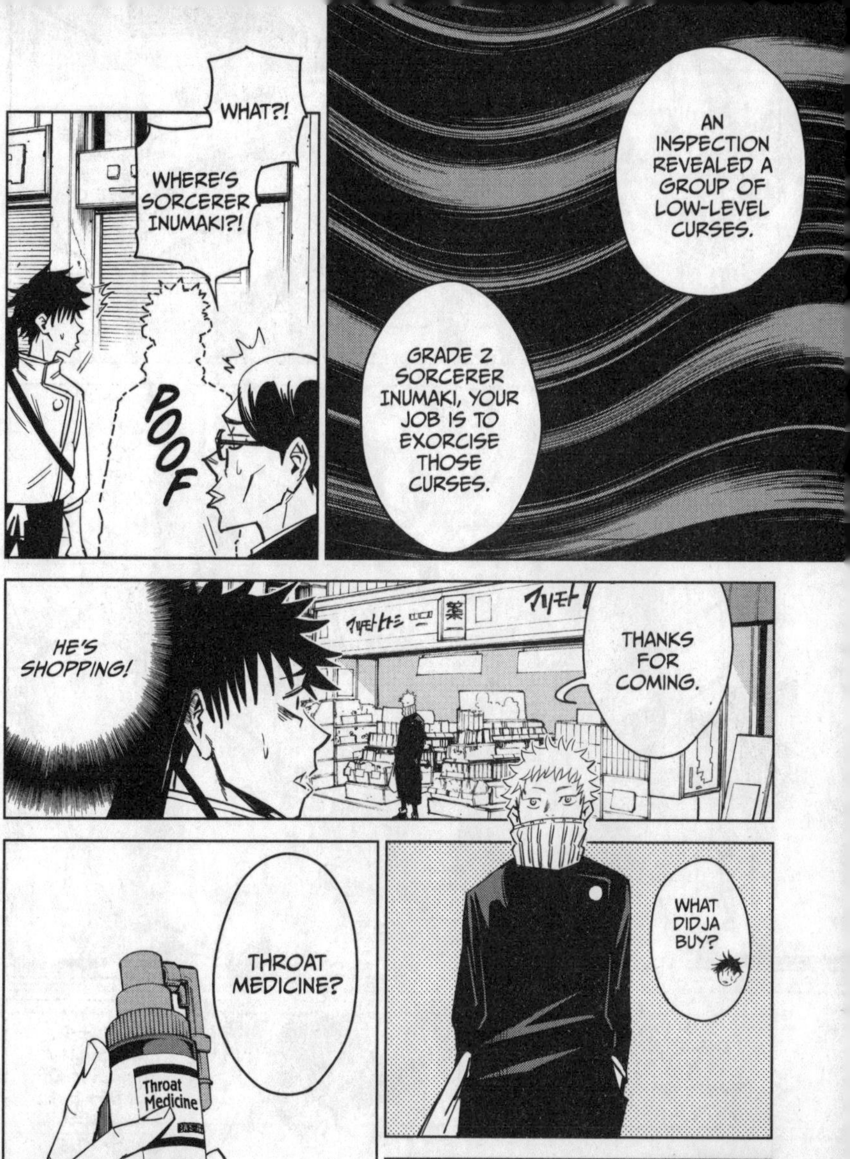
AN INSPECTION REVEALED A GROUP OF LOW-LEVEL CURSES.
GRADE 2 SORCERER INUMAKI, YOUR JOB IS TO EXORCISE THOSE CURSES.
WHAT?!
WHERE'S SORCERER INUMAKI?!
POOF
THANKS FOR COMING.
HE'S SHOPPING!
WHAT DIDJA BUY?
!
RSTL
RSTL
THROAT MEDICINE?
Throat Medicine

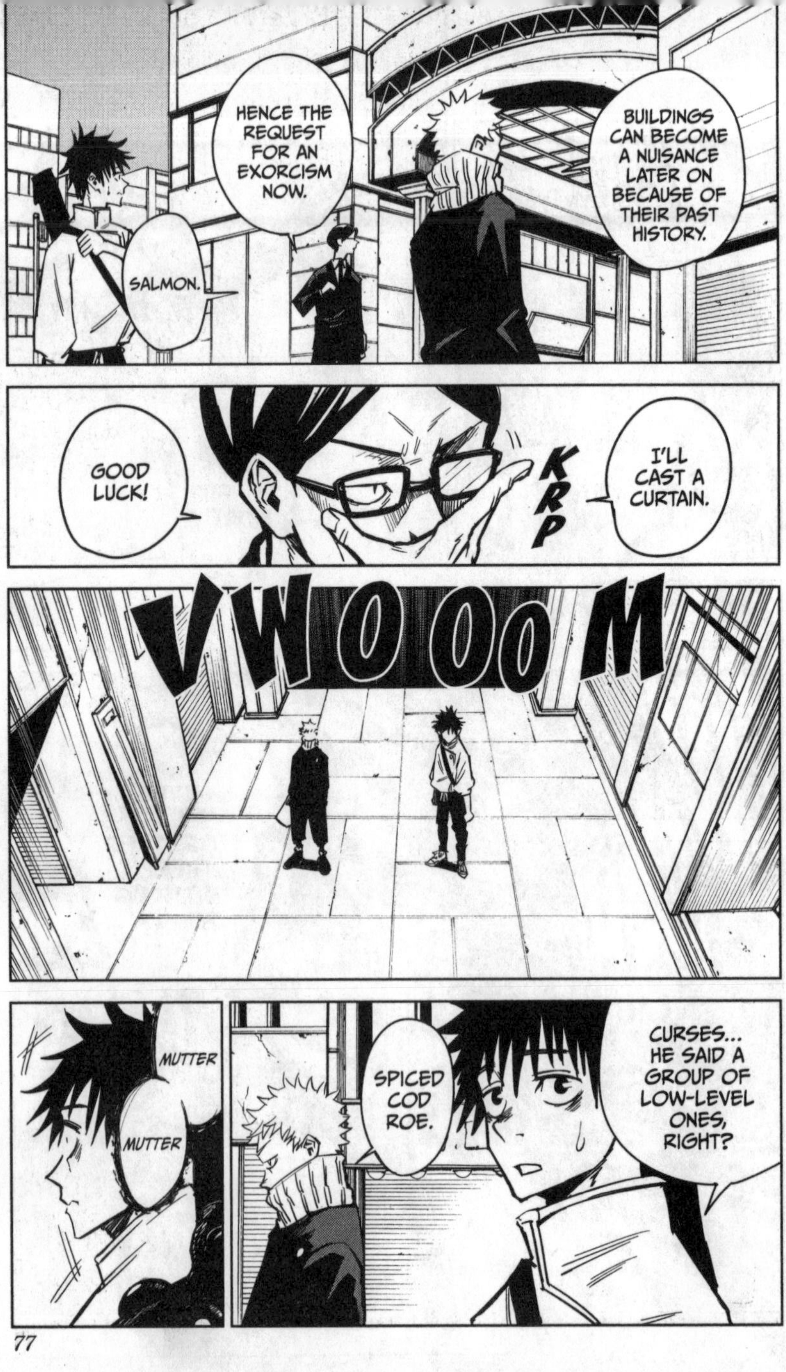
BUILDINGS CAN BECOME A NUISANCE LATER ON BECAUSE OF THEIR PAST HISTORY.
HENCE THE REQUEST FOR AN EXORCISM NOW.
SALMON.
I'LL CAST A CURTAIN.
KRP
GOOD LUCK!
VWOOOM
CURSES... HE SAID A GROUP OF LOW-LEVEL ONES, RIGHT?
SPICED COD ROE.
MUTTER
MUTTER

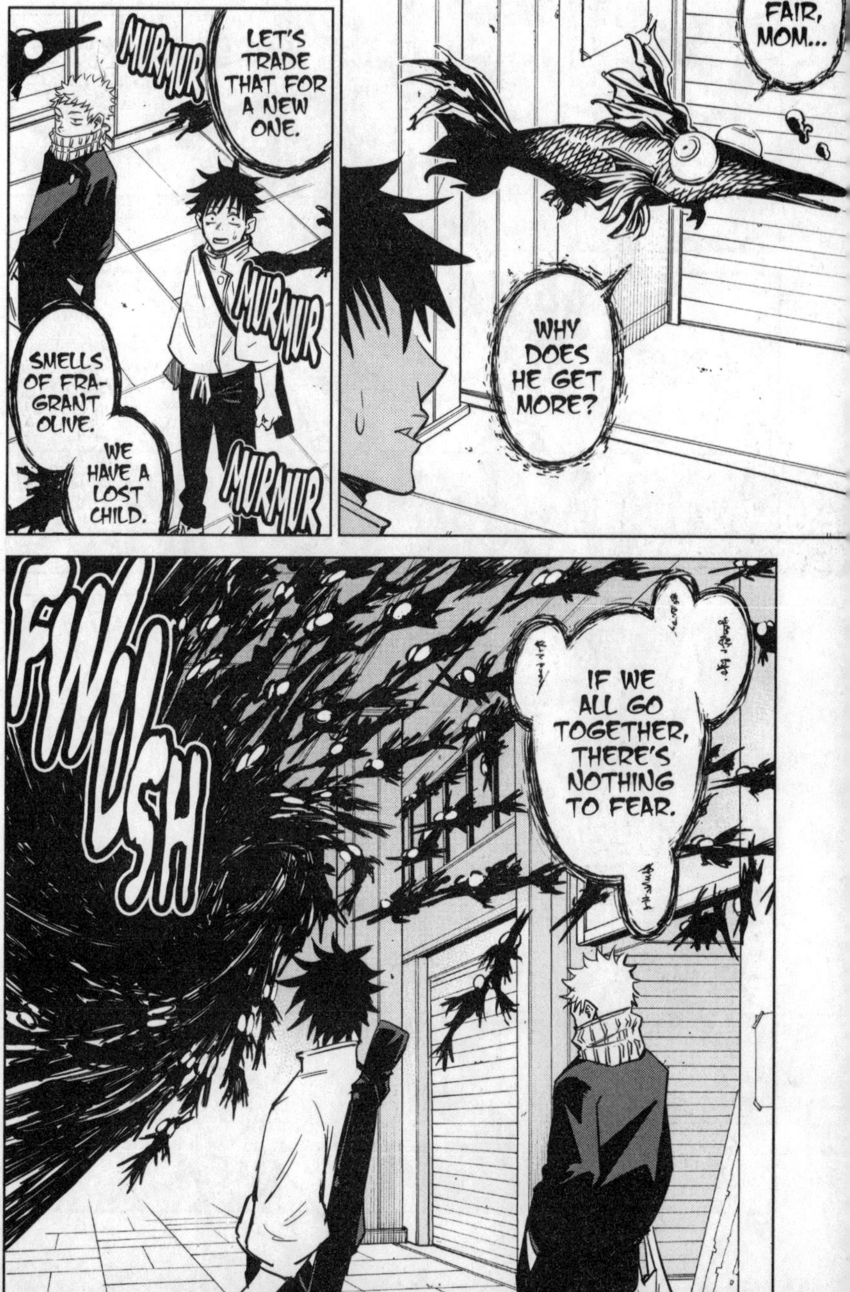
NO FAIR, MOM...
WHY DOES HE GET MORE?
LET'S TRADE THAT FOR A NEW ONE.
MURMUR
MURMUR
SMELLS OF FRA-GRANT OLIVE.
WE HAVE A LOST CHILD.
MURMUR
IF WE ALL GO TOGETHER, THERE'S NOTHING TO FEAR.
FWOOSH

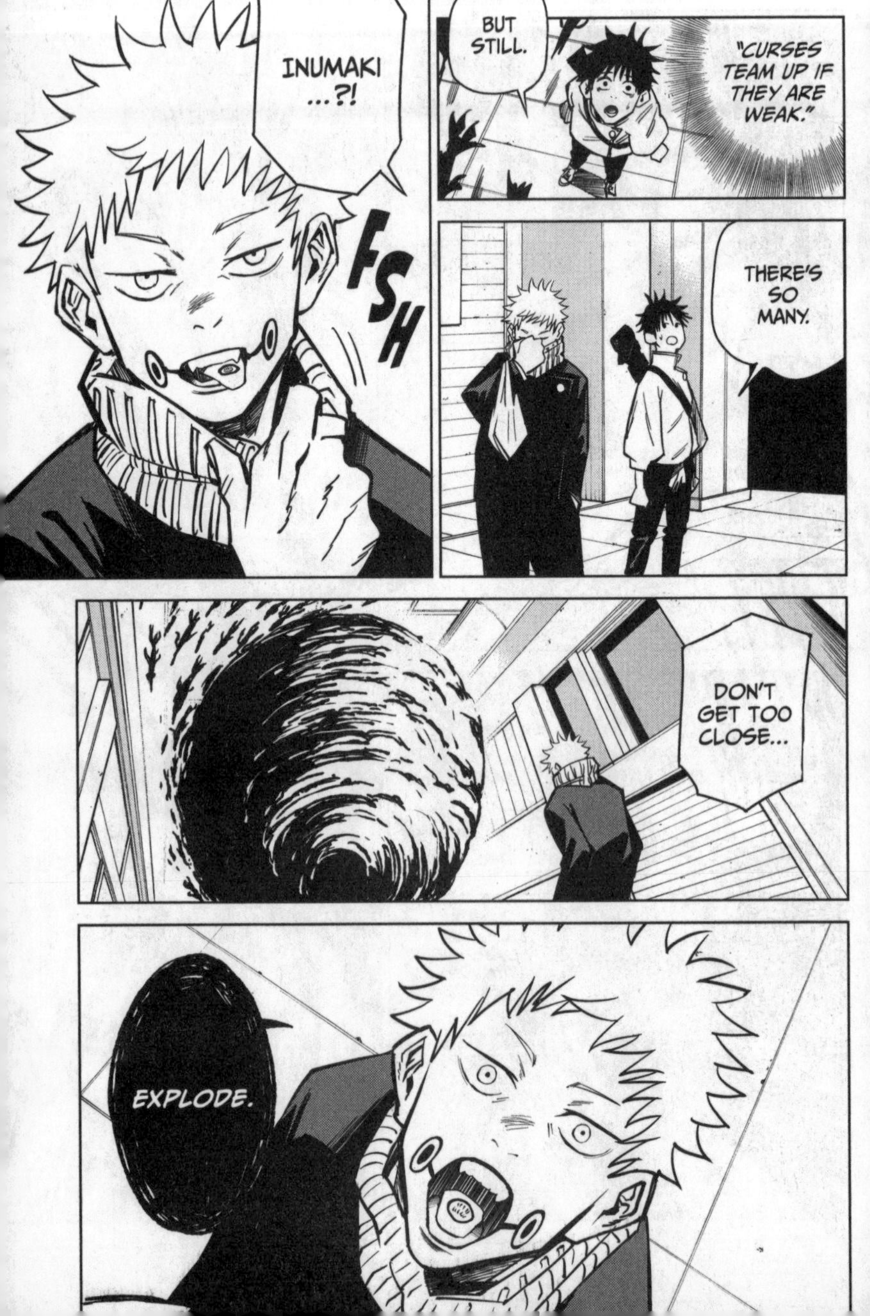
"CURSES TEAM UP IF THEY ARE WEAK."
BUT STILL.
THERE'S SO MANY.
INUMAKI ...?!
FSH
DON'T GET TOO CLOSE...
EXPLODE.

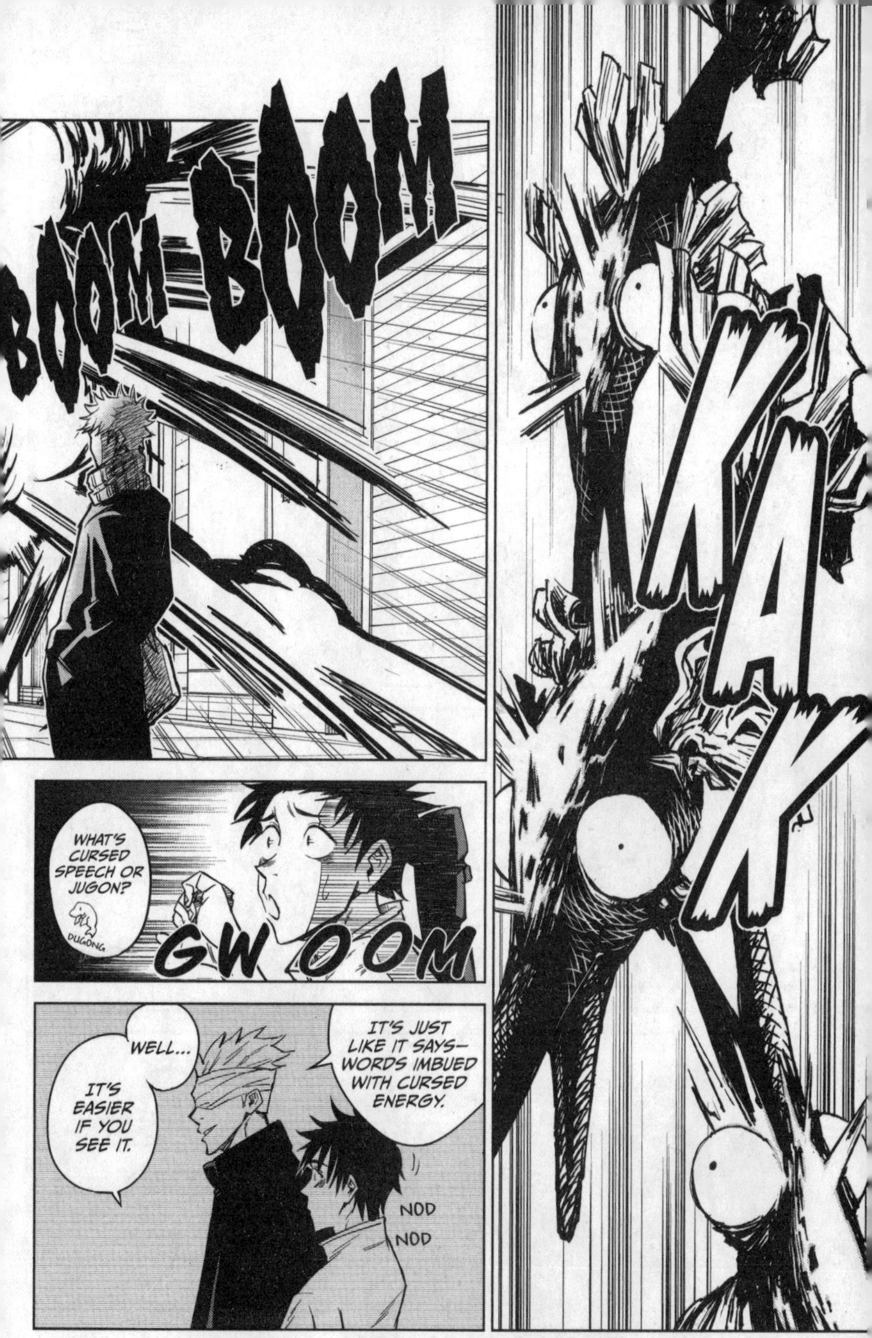
WAK
BOOM BOOM
GWOOM
WHAT'S CURSED SPEECH OR JUGON?
DUGONG
IT'S JUST LIKE IT SAYS—WORDS IMBUED WITH CURSED ENERGY.
WELL...
IT'S EASIER IF YOU SEE IT.
NOD
NOD

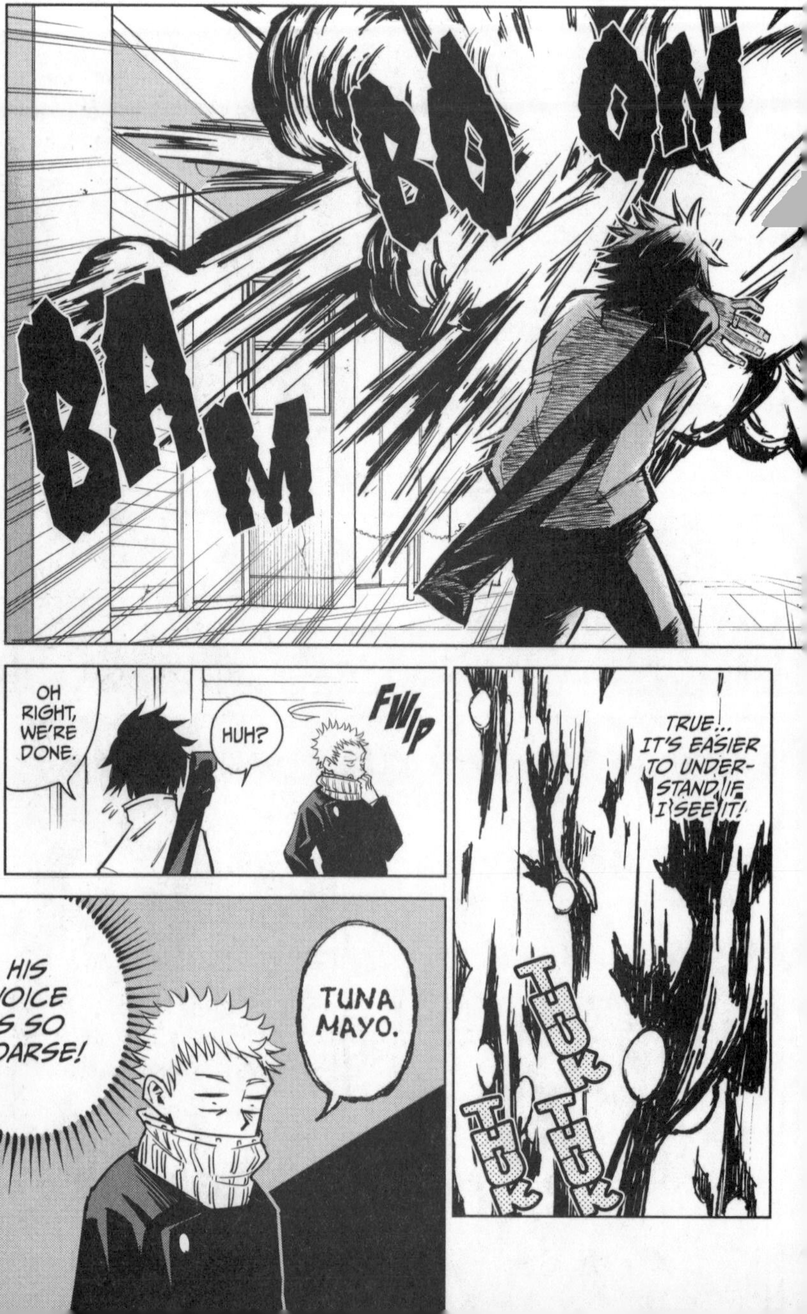
BOOM
BAM
TRUE... IT'S EASIER TO UNDER-STAND IF I SEE IT!
THUK THUK
THUK THUK
FWIP
HUH?
OH RIGHT, WE'RE DONE.
TUNA MAYO.
HIS VOICE IS SO HOARSE!

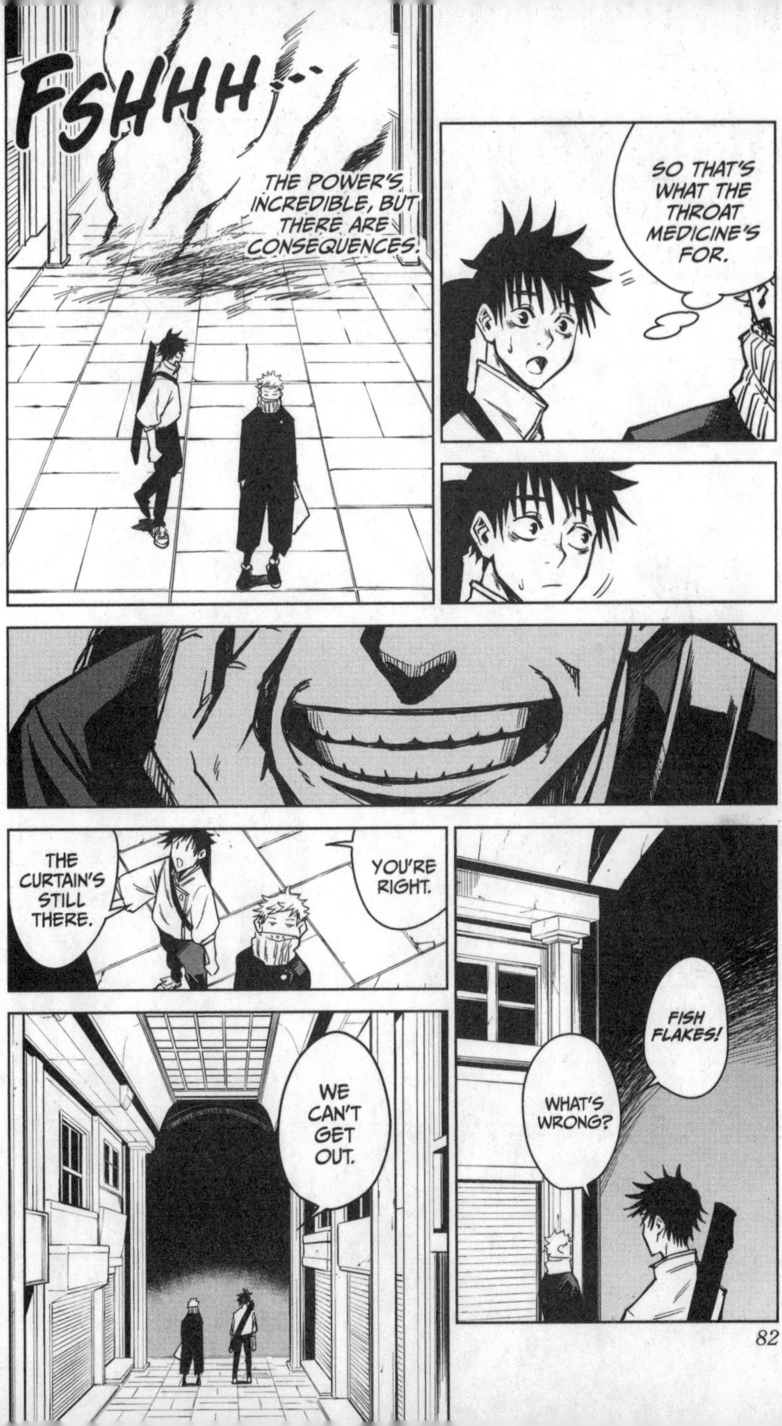
SO THAT'S WHAT THE THROAT MEDICINE'S FOR.
FSHHH
THE POWER'S INCREDIBLE, BUT THERE ARE CONSEQUENCES.
FISH FLAKES!
WHAT'S WRONG?
YOU'RE RIGHT.
THE CURTAIN'S STILL THERE.
WE CAN'T GET OUT.

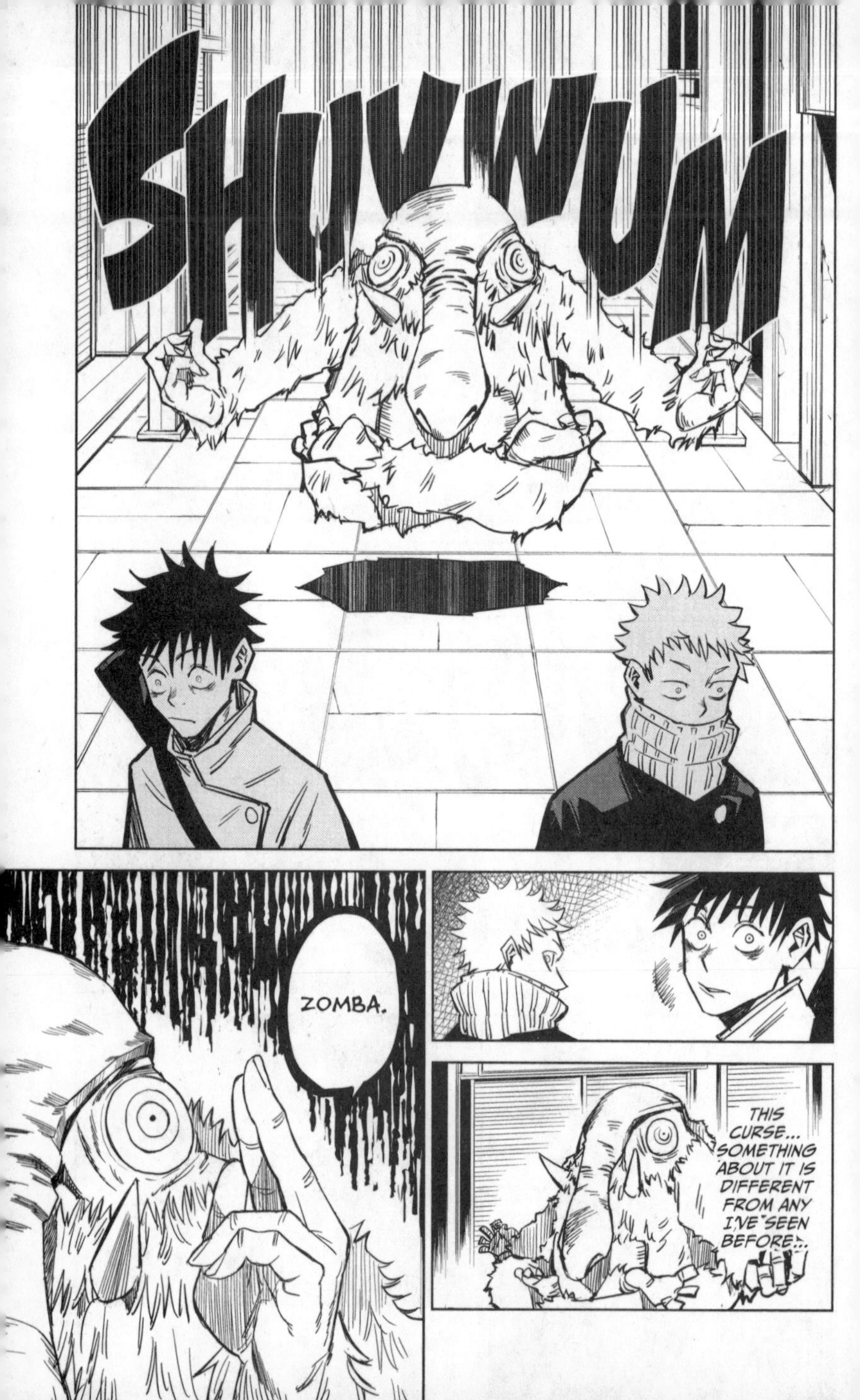
SHUWUM
THIS CURSE... SOMETHING ABOUT IT IS DIFFERENT FROM ANY I'VE SEEN BEFORE...
ZOMBA.

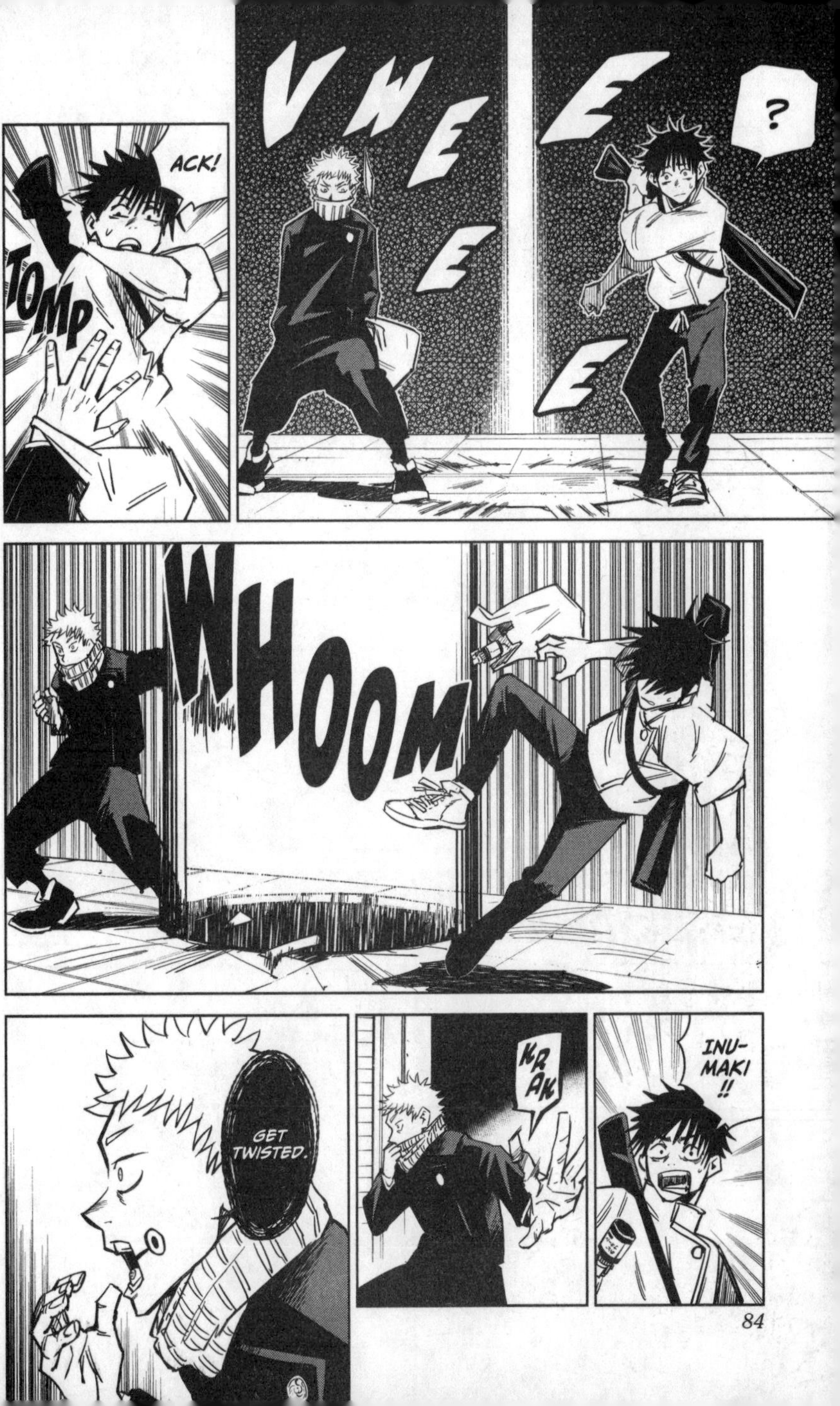
?
VWEEEE
ACK!
TOMP
WHOOM
INU-
MAKI
!!
KRAK
GET
TWISTED.

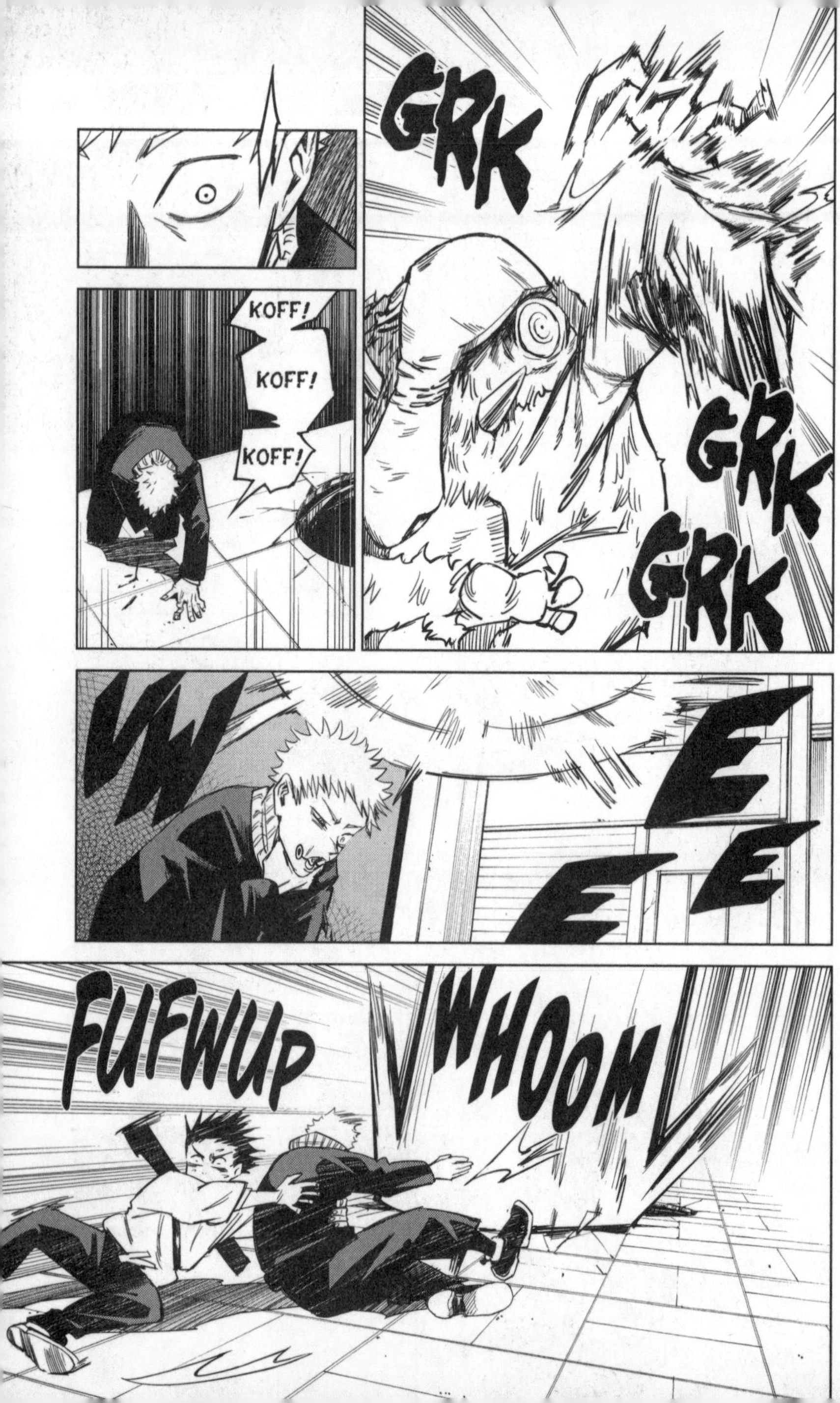
GRK
GRK
GRK
KOFF!
KOFF!
KOFF!
WEEEEE
WHOOM
FUFWUP

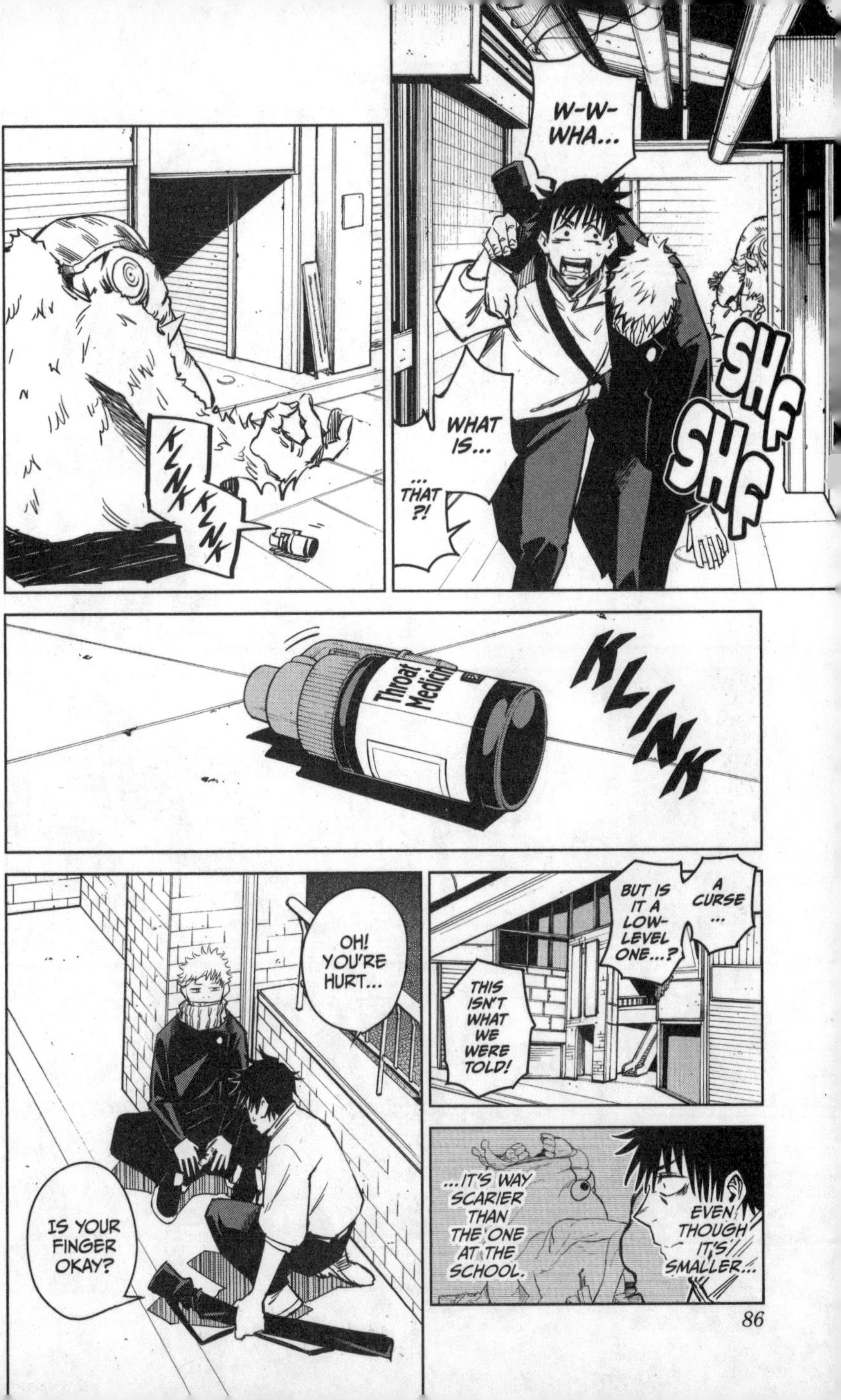
W-W-WHA...
WHAT IS...
...THAT?!
SHF SHF
KLINK KLINK KLINK
KLINK
Throat Medicine
A CURSE...
BUT IS IT A LOW-LEVEL ONE...?
THIS ISN'T WHAT WE WERE TOLD!
EVEN THOUGH IT'S SMALLER...
...IT'S WAY SCARIER THAN THE ONE AT THE SCHOOL.
OH! YOU'RE HURT...
IS YOUR FINGER OKAY?

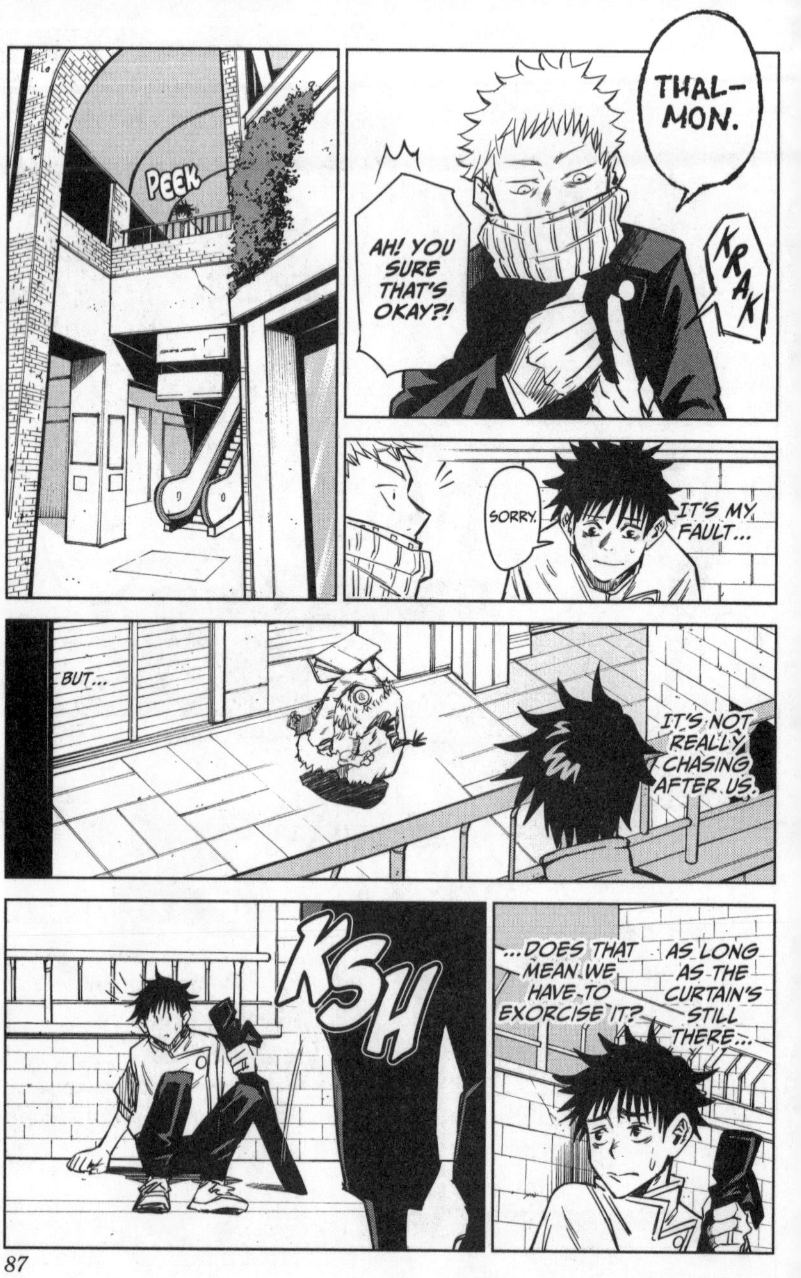
THAL-MON.
KRAK
AH! YOU SURE THAT'S OKAY?!
IT'S MY FAULT...
SORRY.
PEEK
IT'S NOT REALLY CHASING AFTER US.
BUT...
AS LONG AS THE CURTAIN'S STILL THERE...
...DOES THAT MEAN WE HAVE TO EXORCISE IT?
KSH

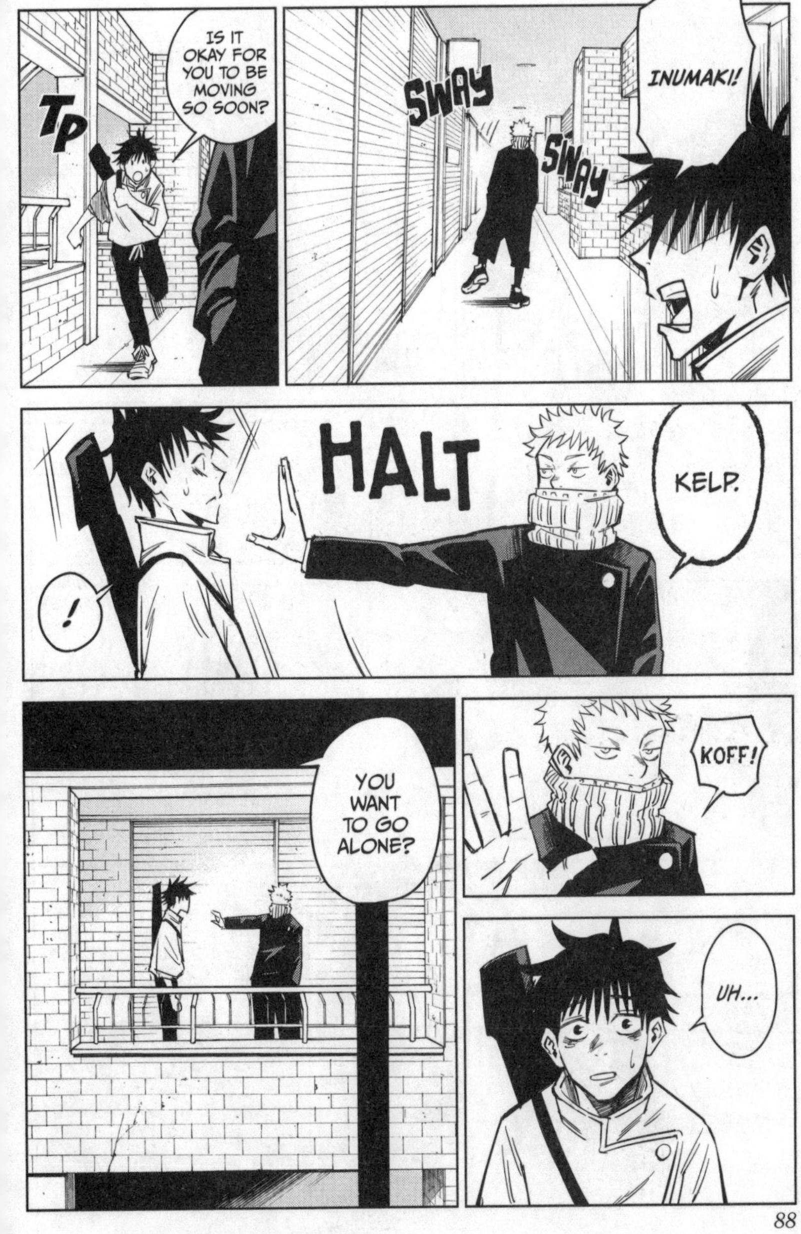
INUMAKI!
SWAY
SWAY
TP
IS IT OKAY FOR YOU TO BE MOVING SO SOON?
KELP.
HALT
!
KOFF!
UH...
YOU WANT TO GO ALONE?

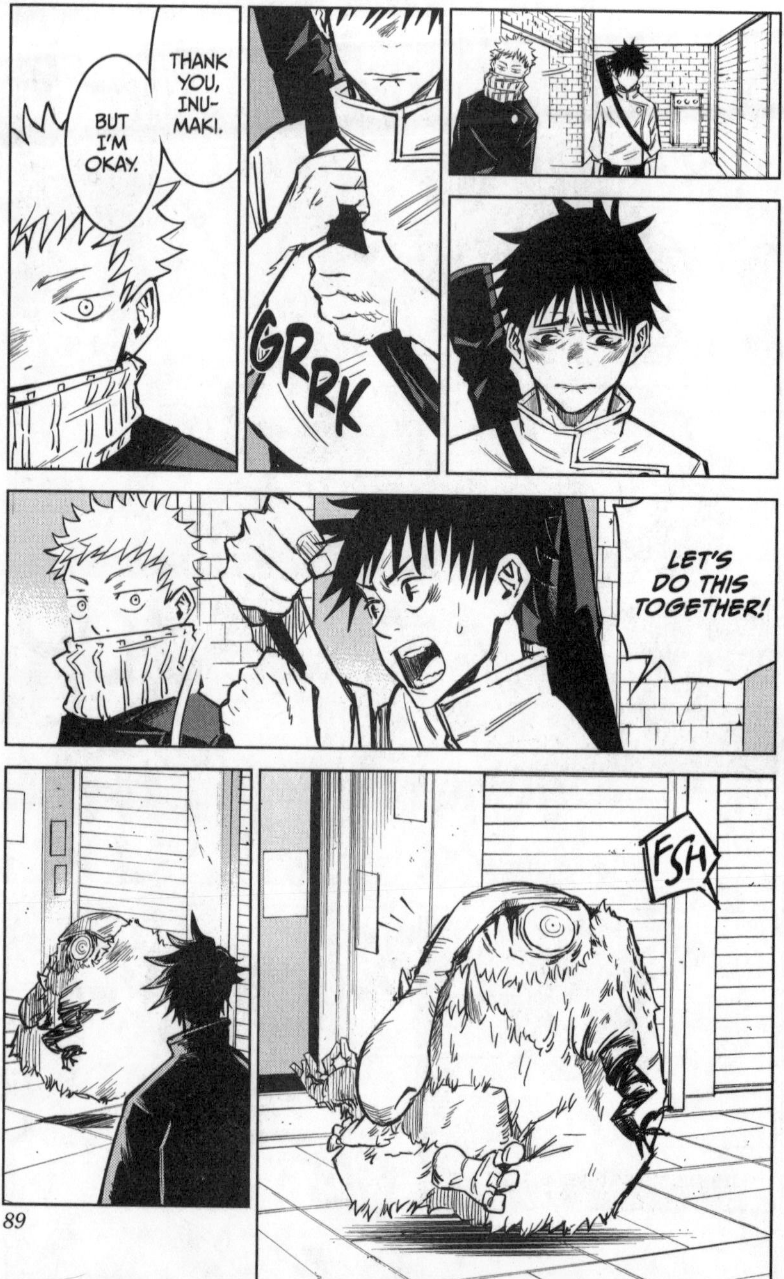
GRRK
THANK YOU, INU-MAKI.
BUT I'M OKAY.
LET'S DO THIS TOGETHER!
FSH

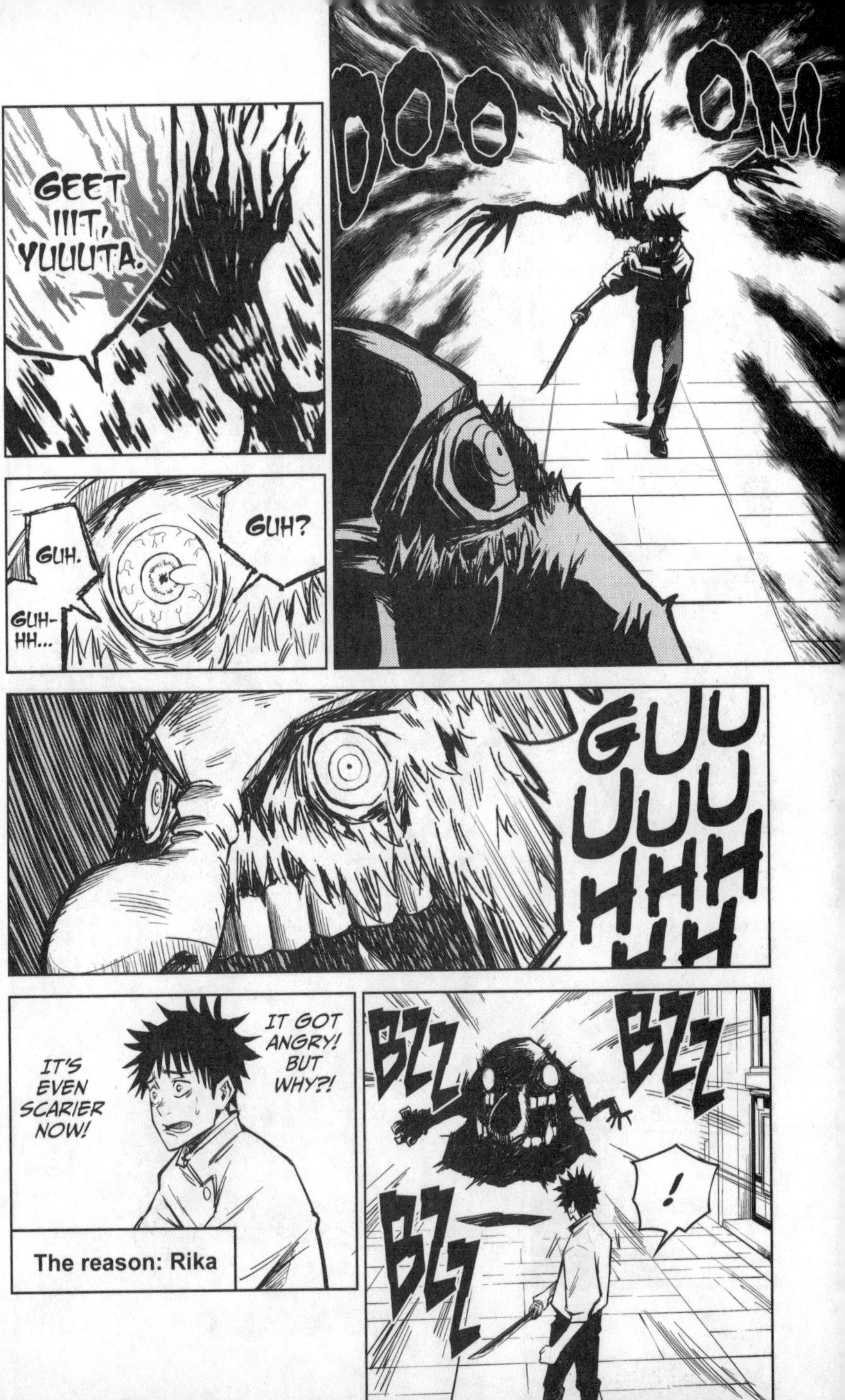
DOOOOM
GEET IIIT, YUUUTA.
GUH?
GUH.
GUH-HH...
GUUUUUHHHHHH
BZZ BZZ BZZ
!
IT GOT ANGRY! BUT WHY?!
IT'S EVEN SCARIER NOW!
The reason: Rika

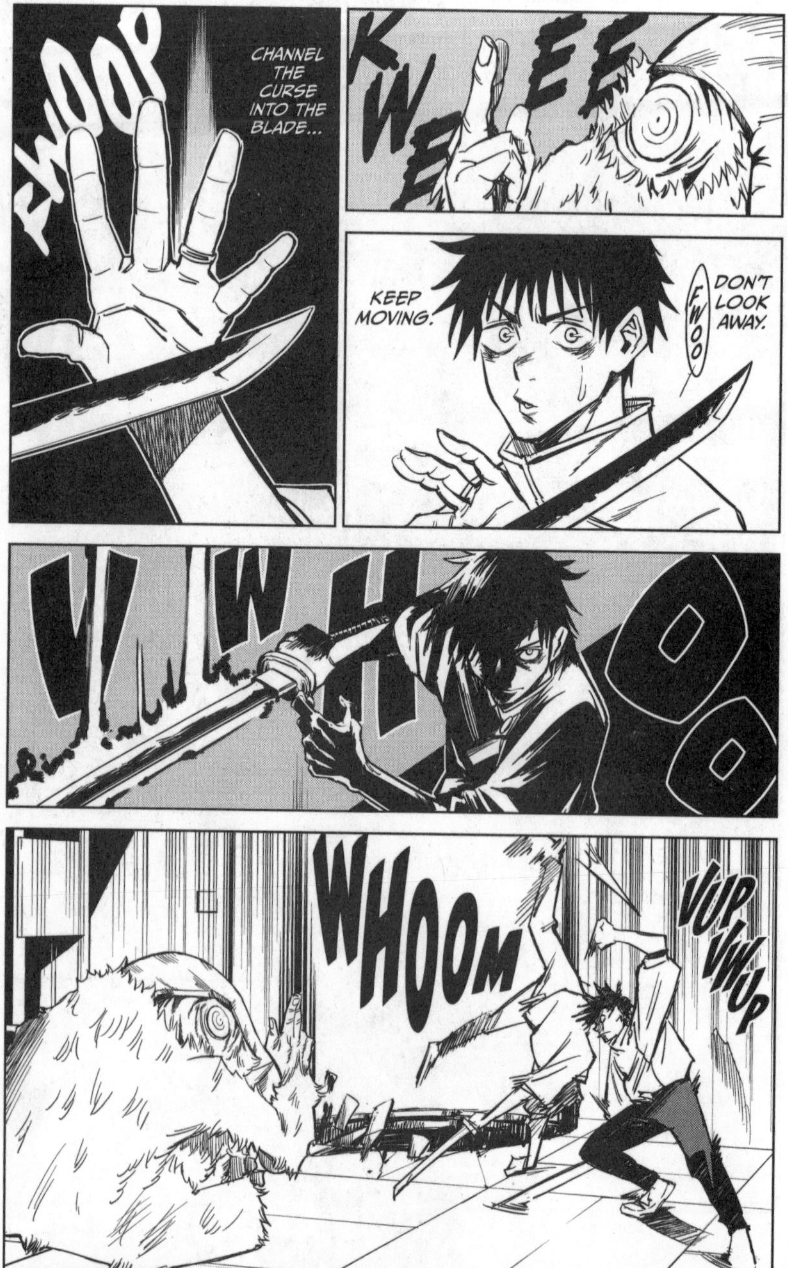
KWEEE
DON'T LOOK AWAY.
FWOO
KEEP MOVING.
CHANNEL THE CURSE INTO THE BLADE...
FWOOP
VWHOOO
VUP VWUP
WHOOM

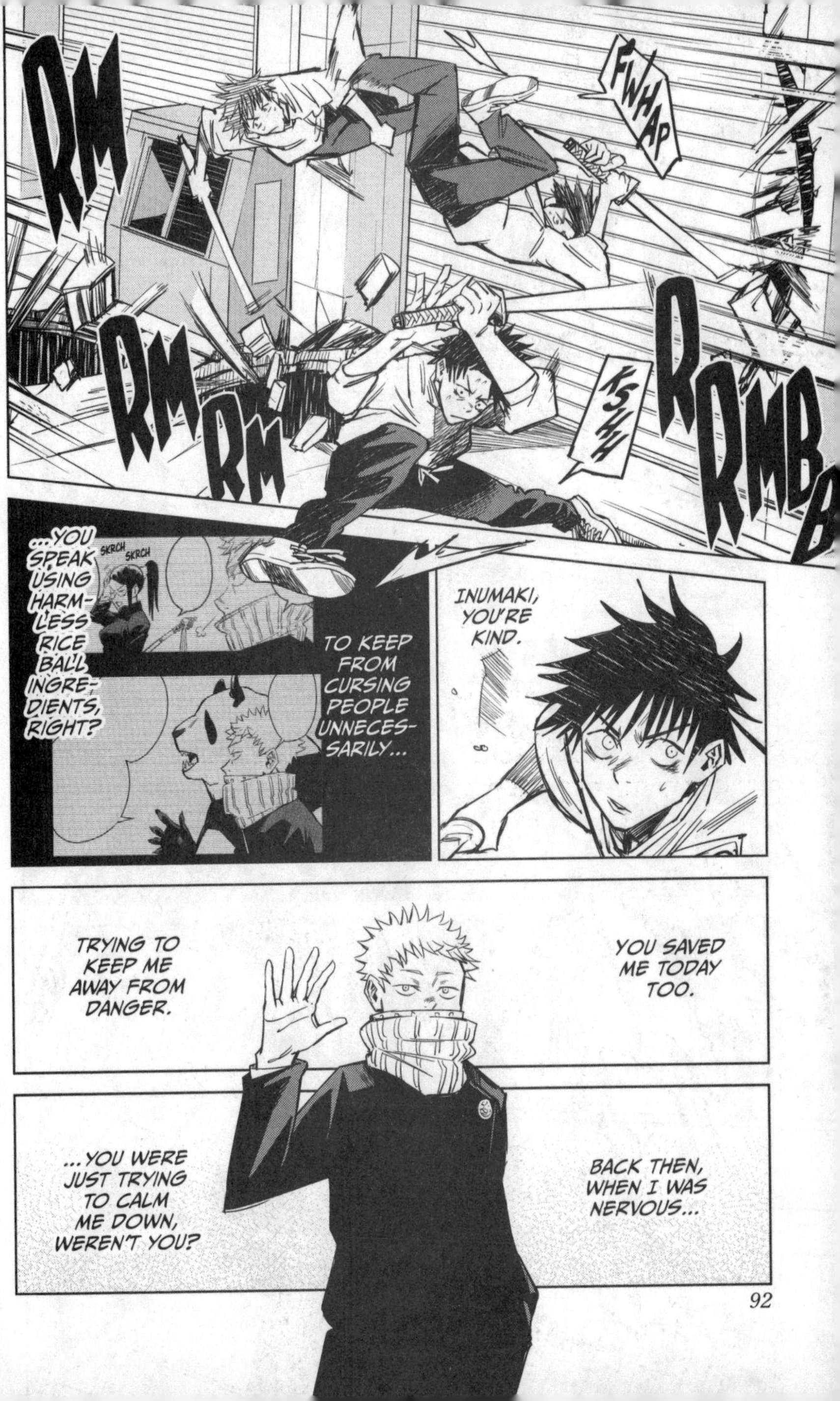
FWHAP
RRMBB
KSHH
RM
RM
RM
INUMAKI, YOU'RE KIND.
...YOU SPEAK USING HARMLESS RICE BALL INGREDIENTS, RIGHT?
SKRCH SKRCH
TO KEEP FROM CURSING PEOPLE UNNECESSARILY...
YOU SAVED ME TODAY TOO.
TRYING TO KEEP ME AWAY FROM DANGER.
BACK THEN, WHEN I WAS NERVOUS...
...YOU WERE JUST TRYING TO CALM ME DOWN, WEREN'T YOU?

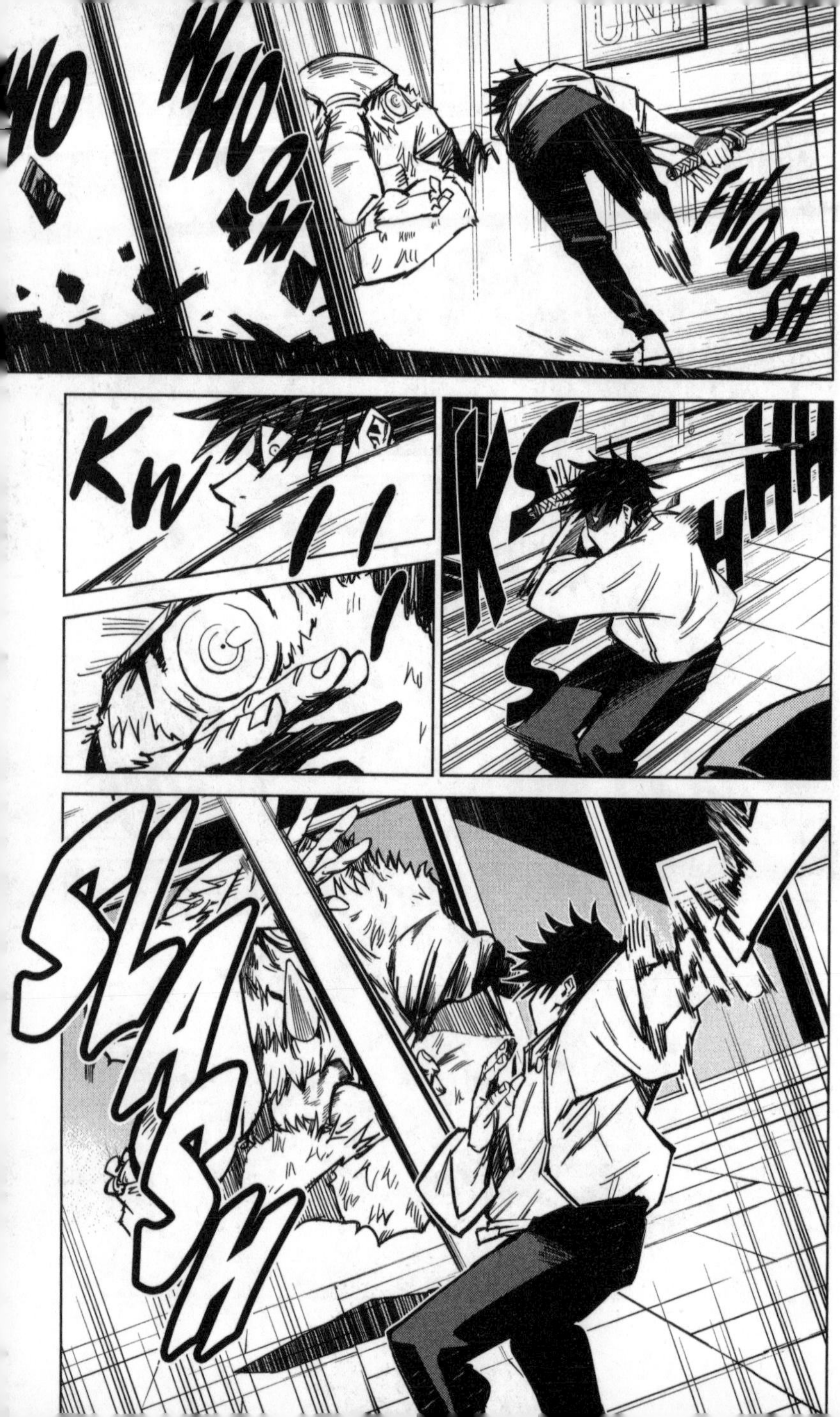
FWOOSH
WHOOM
WHO
KSHHHH
KW!!
SLASH

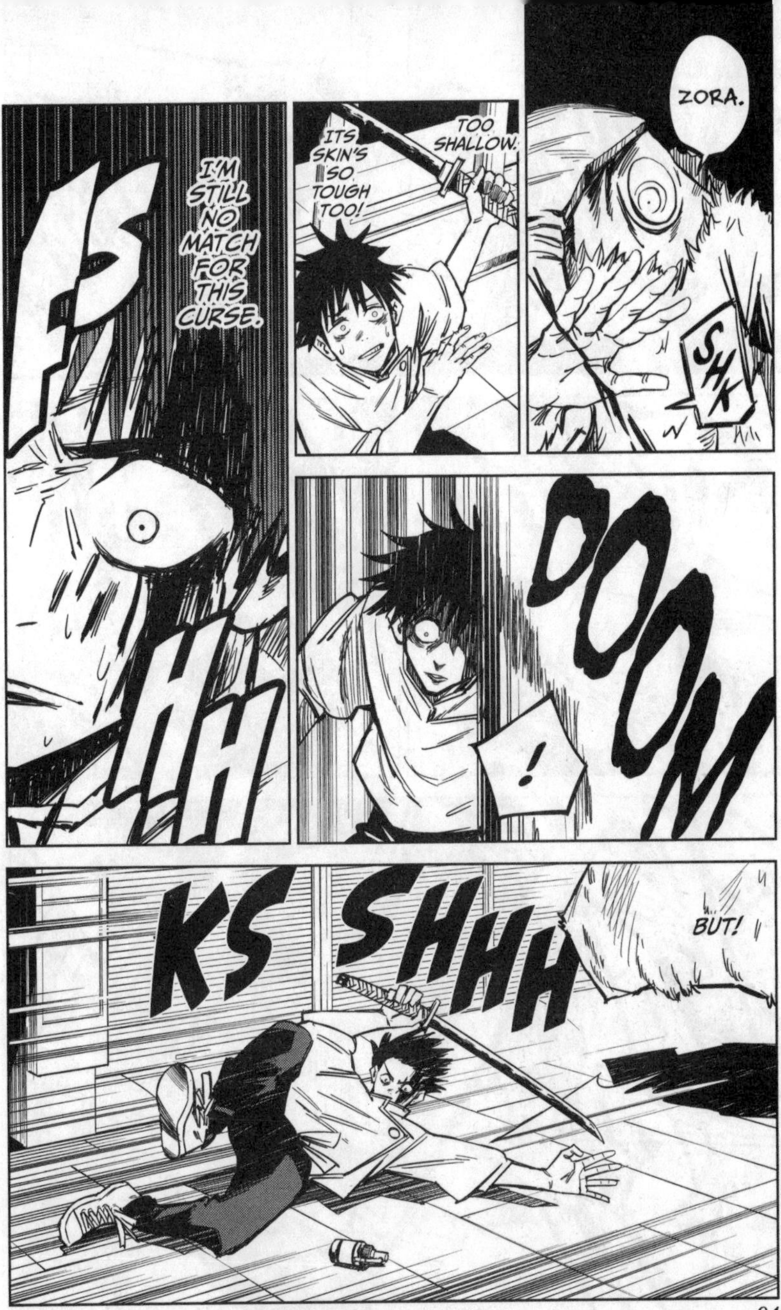
ZORA.
SHK
TOO SHALLOW.
ITS SKIN'S SO TOUGH TOO!
DOOOM
!
I'M STILL NO MATCH FOR THIS CURSE.
BUT!
KS SHHH

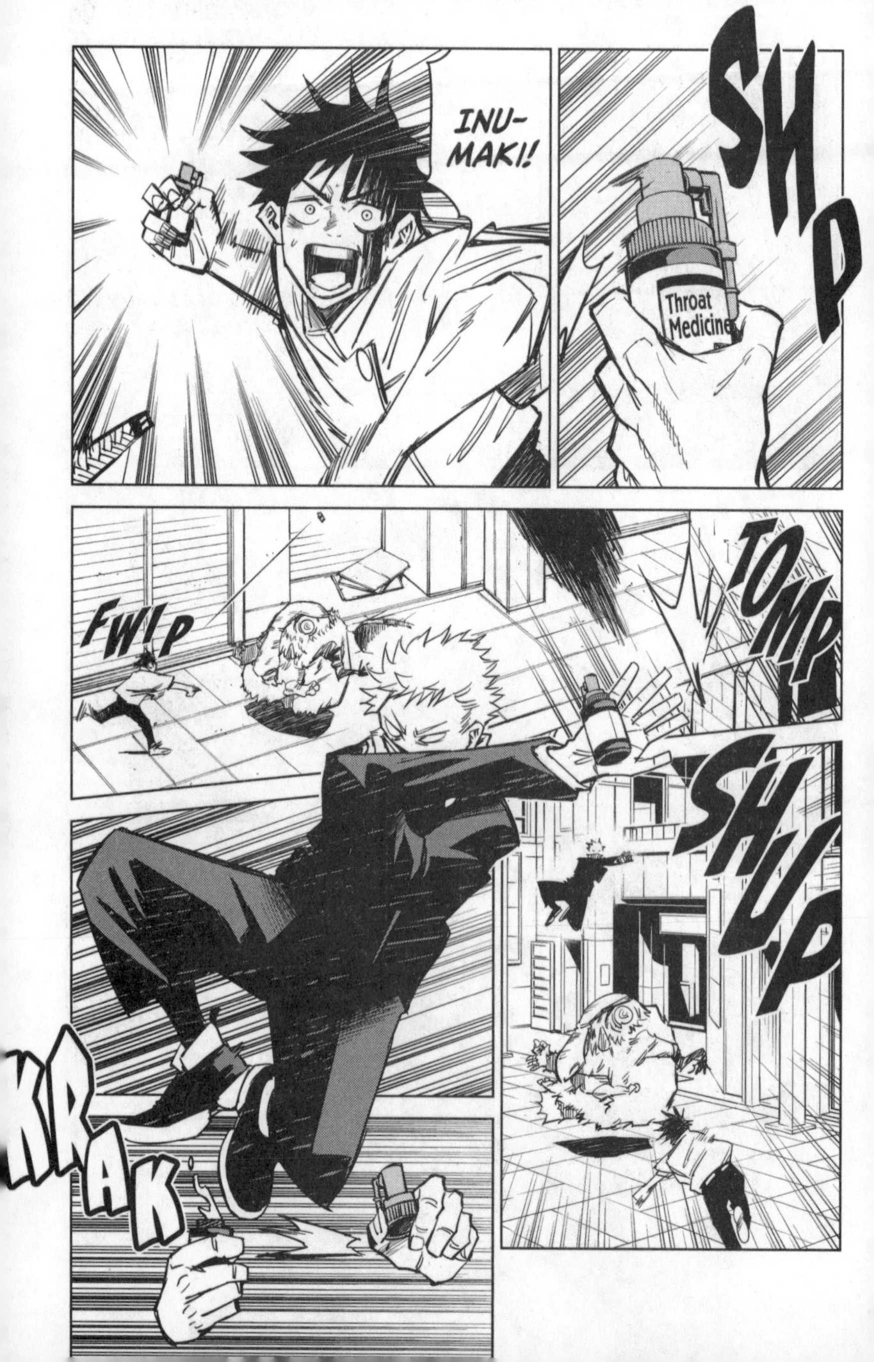
SHP
Throat Medicine
INU-MAKI!
TOMP
FWIP
SHUP
KRAK

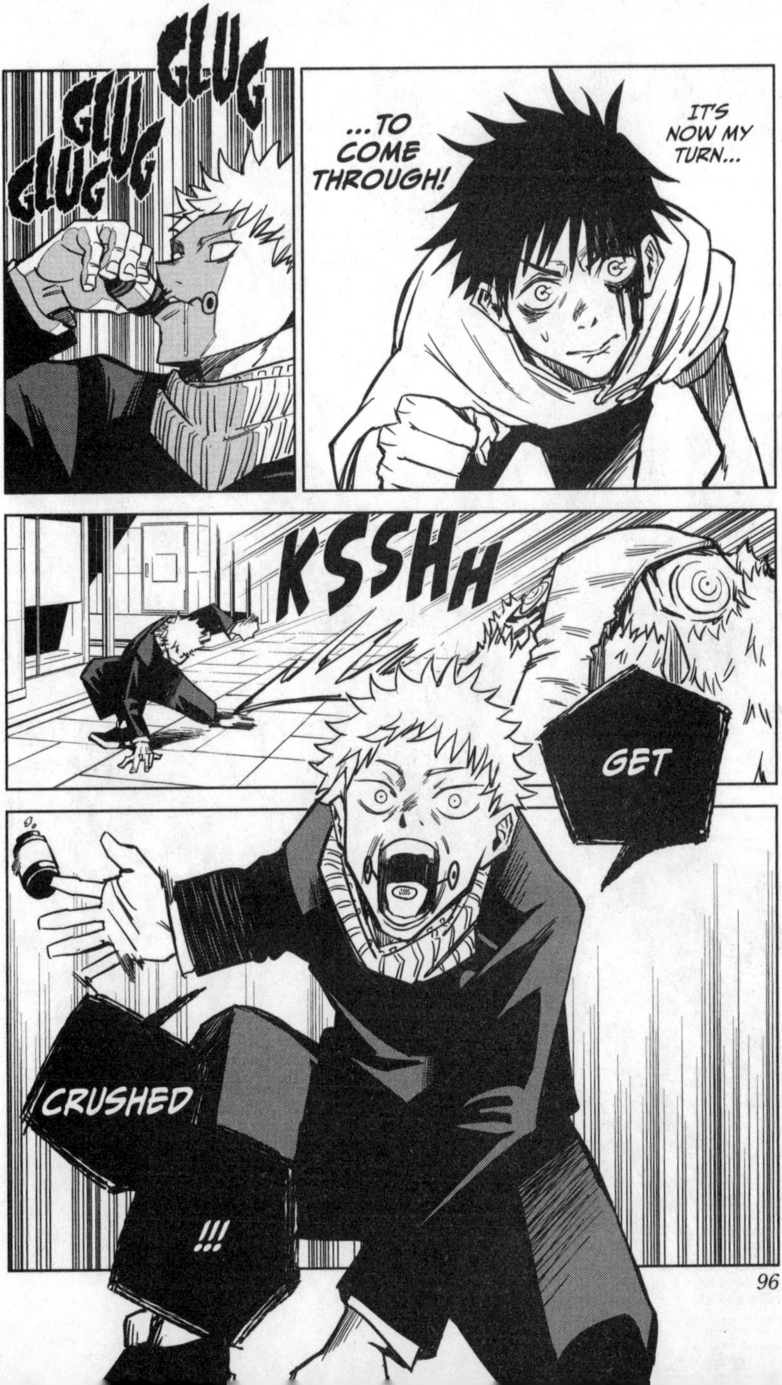
IT'S NOW MY TURN...
...TO COME THROUGH!
GLUG GLUG GLUG
KSSHH
GET
CRUSHED
!!!

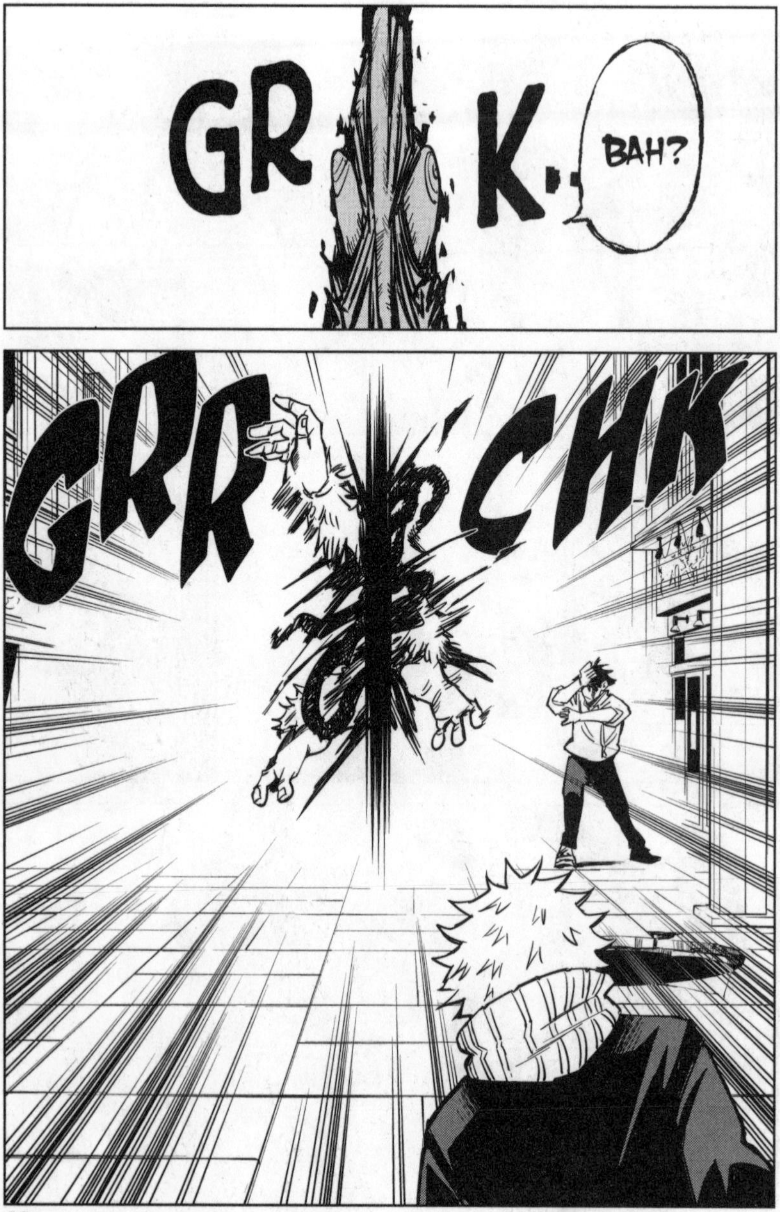
GR
K..
BAH?
GRR
CHK

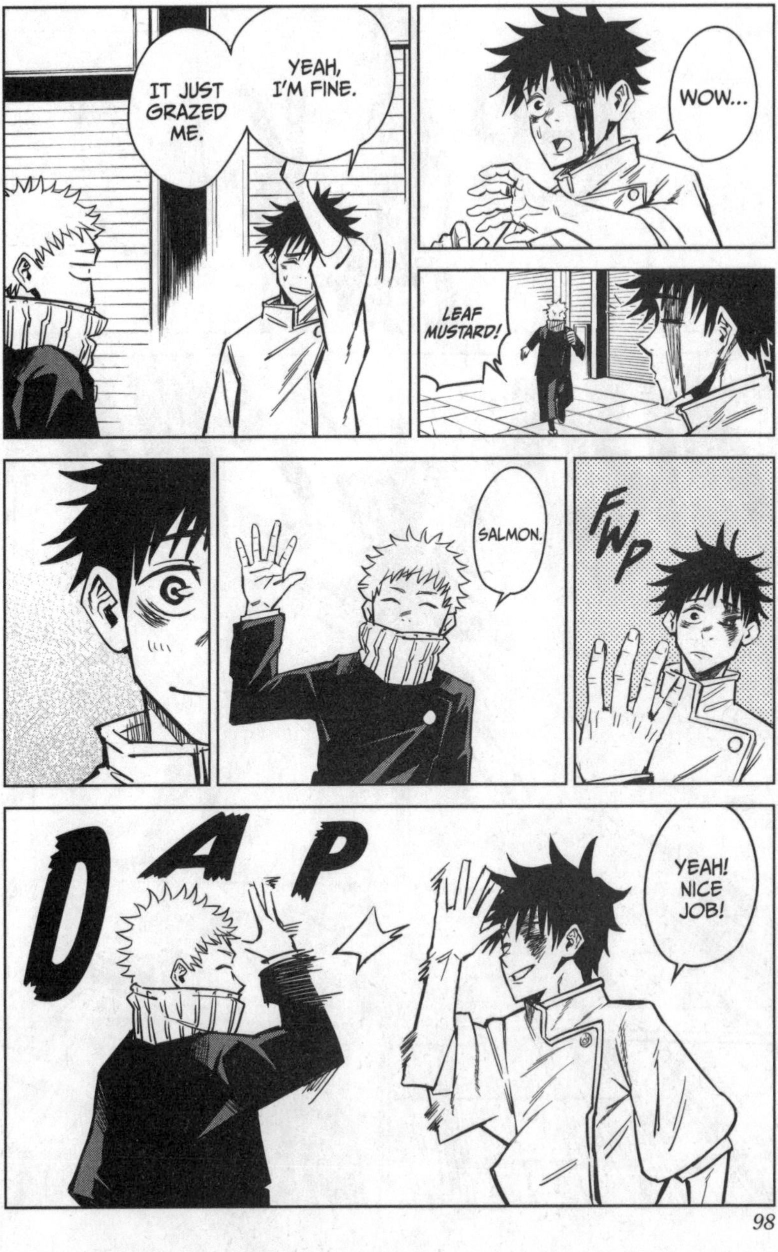
WOW...
LEAF MUSTARD!
YEAH, I'M FINE.
IT JUST GRAZED ME.
FWP
SALMON.
YEAH! NICE JOB!
DAP

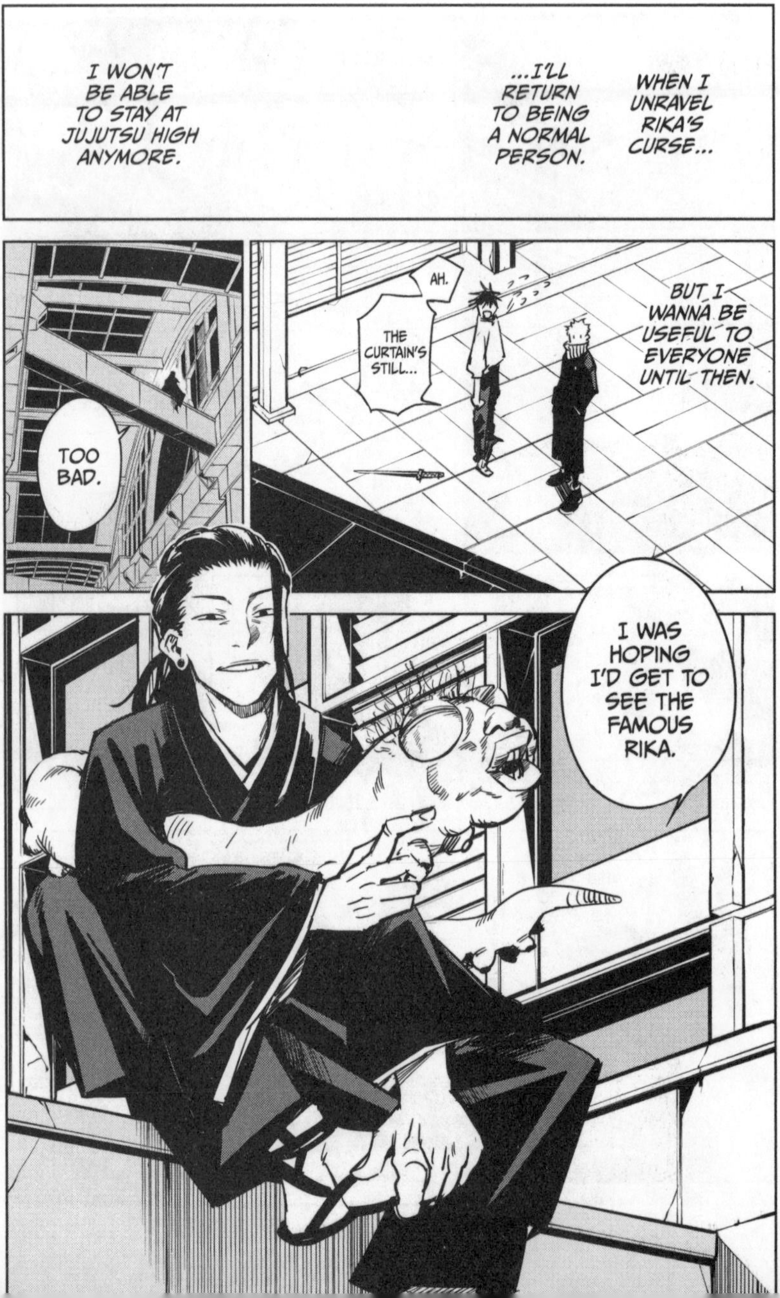
WHEN I UNRAVEL RIKA'S CURSE...
...I'LL RETURN TO BEING A NORMAL PERSON.
I WON'T BE ABLE TO STAY AT JUJUTSU HIGH ANYMORE.
BUT I WANNA BE USEFUL TO EVERYONE UNTIL THEN.
AH.
THE CURTAIN'S STILL...
TOO BAD.
I WAS HOPING I'D GET TO SEE THE FAMOUS RIKA.

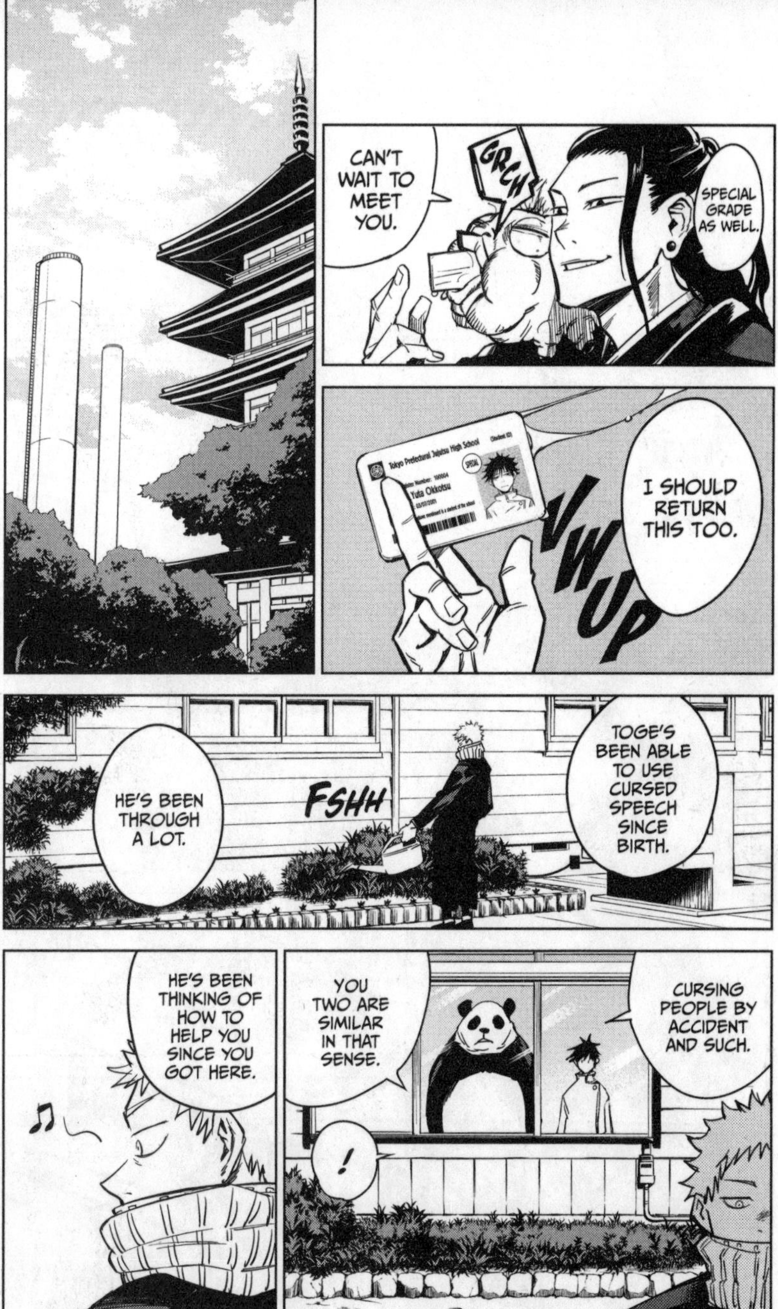
SPECIAL GRADE AS WELL.
GRCH
CAN'T WAIT TO MEET YOU.
I SHOULD RETURN THIS TOO.
Tokyo Prefectural Jujutsu High School
SPECIAL
Yuta Okkotsu
VWUP
TOGE'S BEEN ABLE TO USE CURSED SPEECH SINCE BIRTH.
FSHH
HE'S BEEN THROUGH A LOT.
CURSING PEOPLE BY ACCIDENT AND SUCH.
YOU TWO ARE SIMILAR IN THAT SENSE.
!
HE'S BEEN THINKING OF HOW TO HELP YOU SINCE YOU GOT HERE.

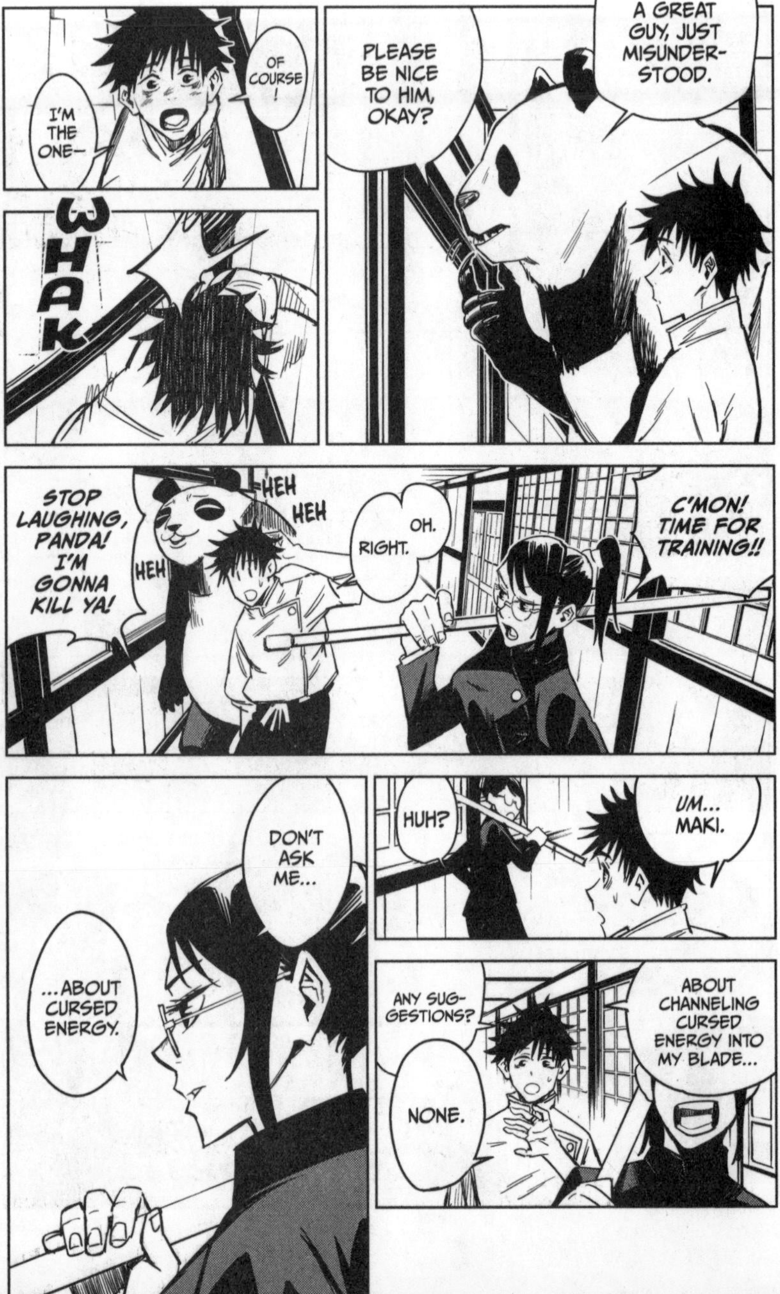
HE'S A GREAT GUY, JUST MISUNDERSTOOD.
PLEASE BE NICE TO HIM, OKAY?
OF COURSE!
I'M THE ONE—
WHAK
C'MON! TIME FOR TRAINING!!
OH. RIGHT.
HEH HEH HEH
STOP LAUGHING, PANDA! I'M GONNA KILL YA!
UM... MAKI.
HUH?
ABOUT CHANNELING CURSED ENERGY INTO MY BLADE...
ANY SUG-GESTIONS?
NONE.
DON'T ASK ME...
...ABOUT CURSED ENERGY.

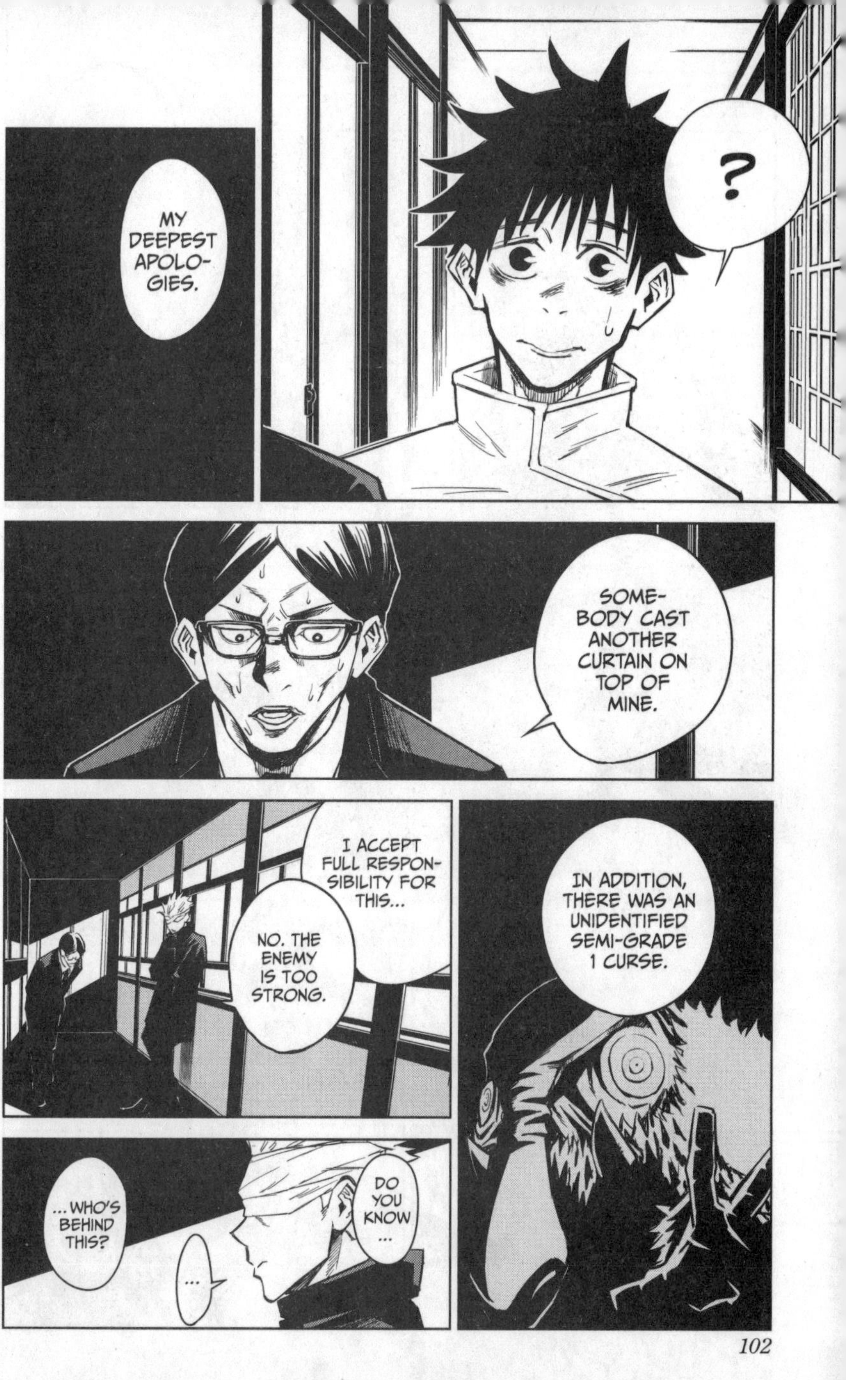
?
MY DEEPEST APOLO-GIES.
SOME-BODY CAST ANOTHER CURTAIN ON TOP OF MINE.
IN ADDITION, THERE WAS AN UNIDENTIFIED SEMI-GRADE 1 CURSE.
I ACCEPT FULL RESPON-SIBILITY FOR THIS...
NO. THE ENEMY IS TOO STRONG.
DO YOU KNOW ...
...WHO'S BEHIND THIS?
...

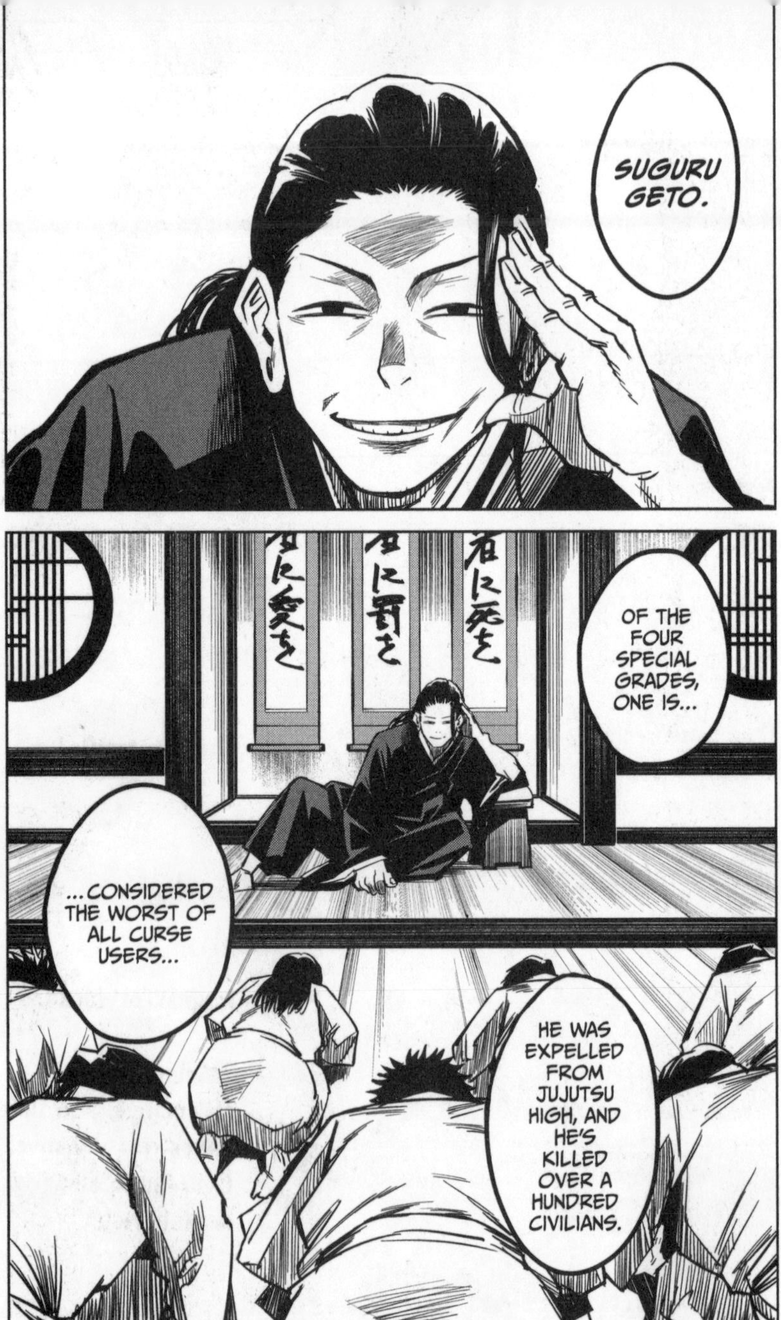
SUGURU GETO.
君に死を
君に罰を
君に愛を
OF THE FOUR SPECIAL GRADES, ONE IS...
...CONSIDERED THE WORST OF ALL CURSE USERS...
HE WAS EXPELLED FROM JUJUTSU HIGH, AND HE'S KILLED OVER A HUNDRED CIVILIANS.

Inumaki's Words

Salmon is an affirmative, and fish flakes is a negative. Everything else is gibberish.

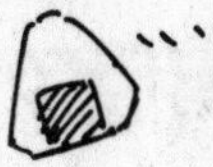

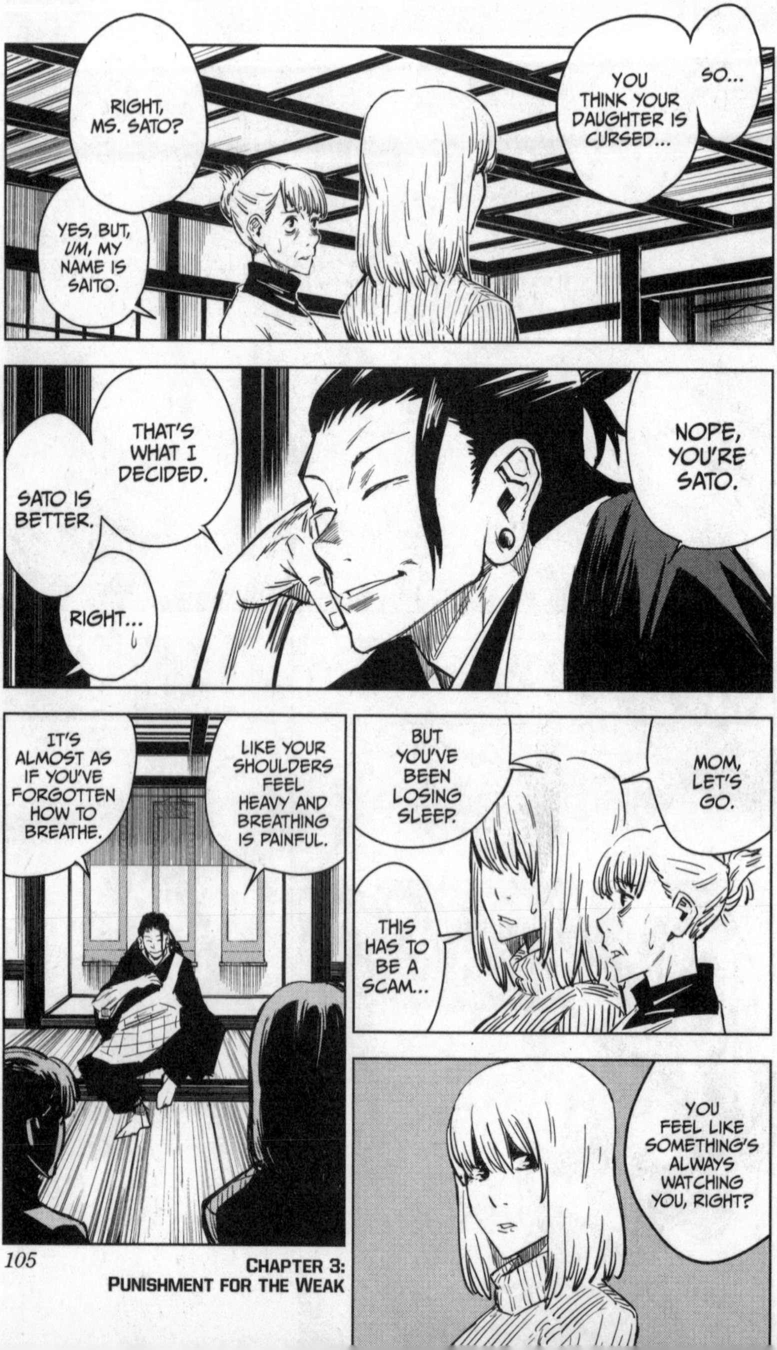
SO...
YOU THINK YOUR DAUGHTER IS CURSED...
RIGHT, MS. SATO?
YES, BUT, *UM*, MY NAME IS SAITO.
NOPE, YOU'RE SATO.
THAT'S WHAT I DECIDED.
SATO IS BETTER.
RIGHT...
MOM, LET'S GO.
BUT YOU'VE BEEN LOSING SLEEP.
THIS HAS TO BE A SCAM...
YOU FEEL LIKE SOMETHING'S ALWAYS WATCHING YOU, RIGHT?
LIKE YOUR SHOULDERS FEEL HEAVY AND BREATHING IS PAINFUL.
IT'S ALMOST AS IF YOU'VE FORGOTTEN HOW TO BREATHE.

CHAPTER 3: PUNISHMENT FOR THE WEAK

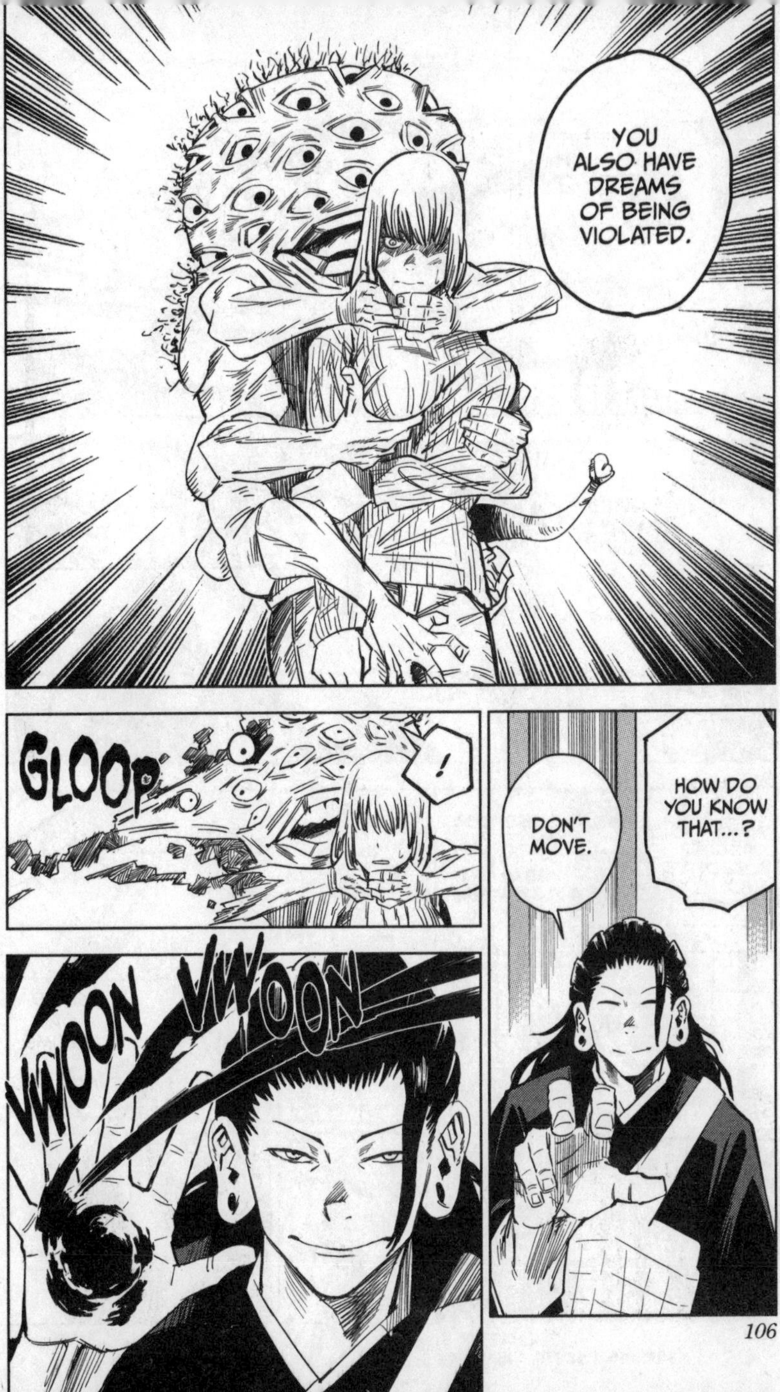
YOU ALSO HAVE DREAMS OF BEING VIOLATED.
HOW DO YOU KNOW THAT...?
DON'T MOVE.
GLOOP
!
VWOON VWOON

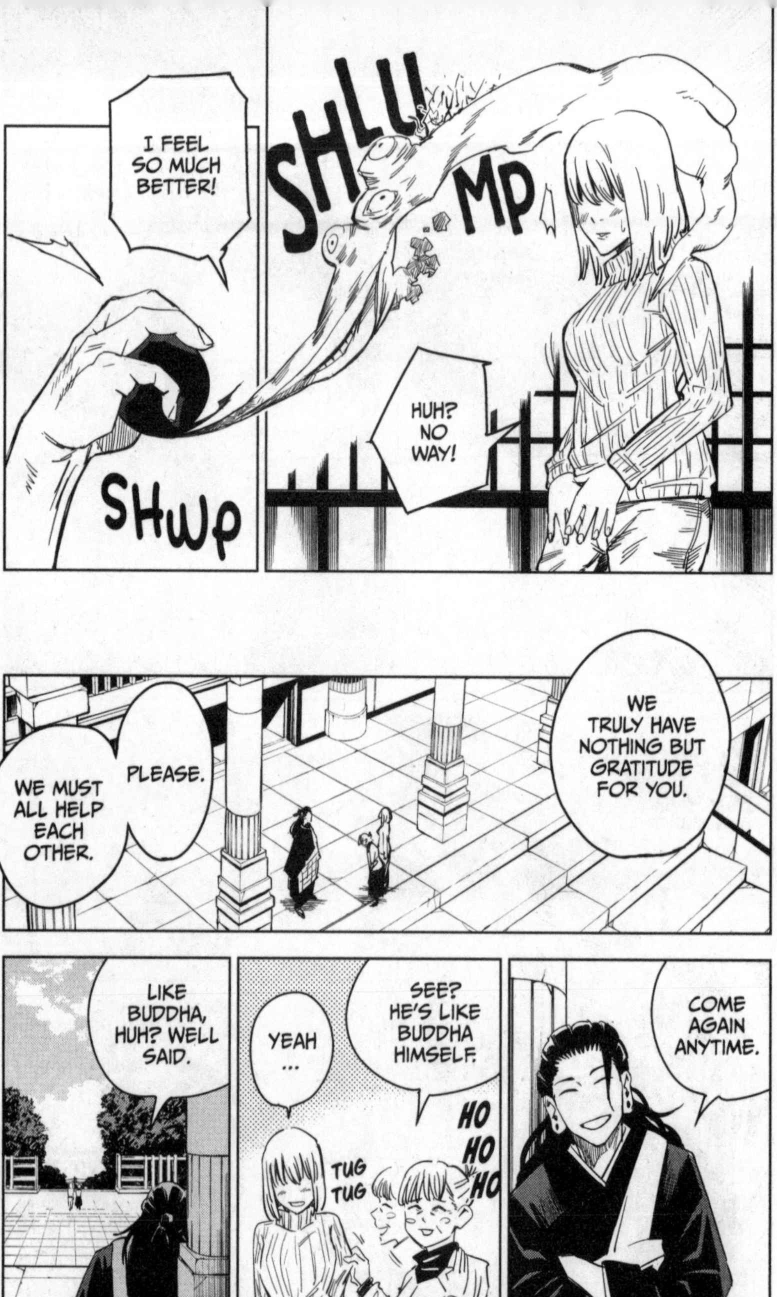
SHLUMP
HUH? NO WAY!
I FEEL SO MUCH BETTER!
SHWP
WE TRULY HAVE NOTHING BUT GRATITUDE FOR YOU.
PLEASE.
WE MUST ALL HELP EACH OTHER.
COME AGAIN ANYTIME.
SEE? HE'S LIKE BUDDHA HIMSELF.
HO HO HO
YEAH ...
TUG TUG
LIKE BUDDHA, HUH? WELL SAID.

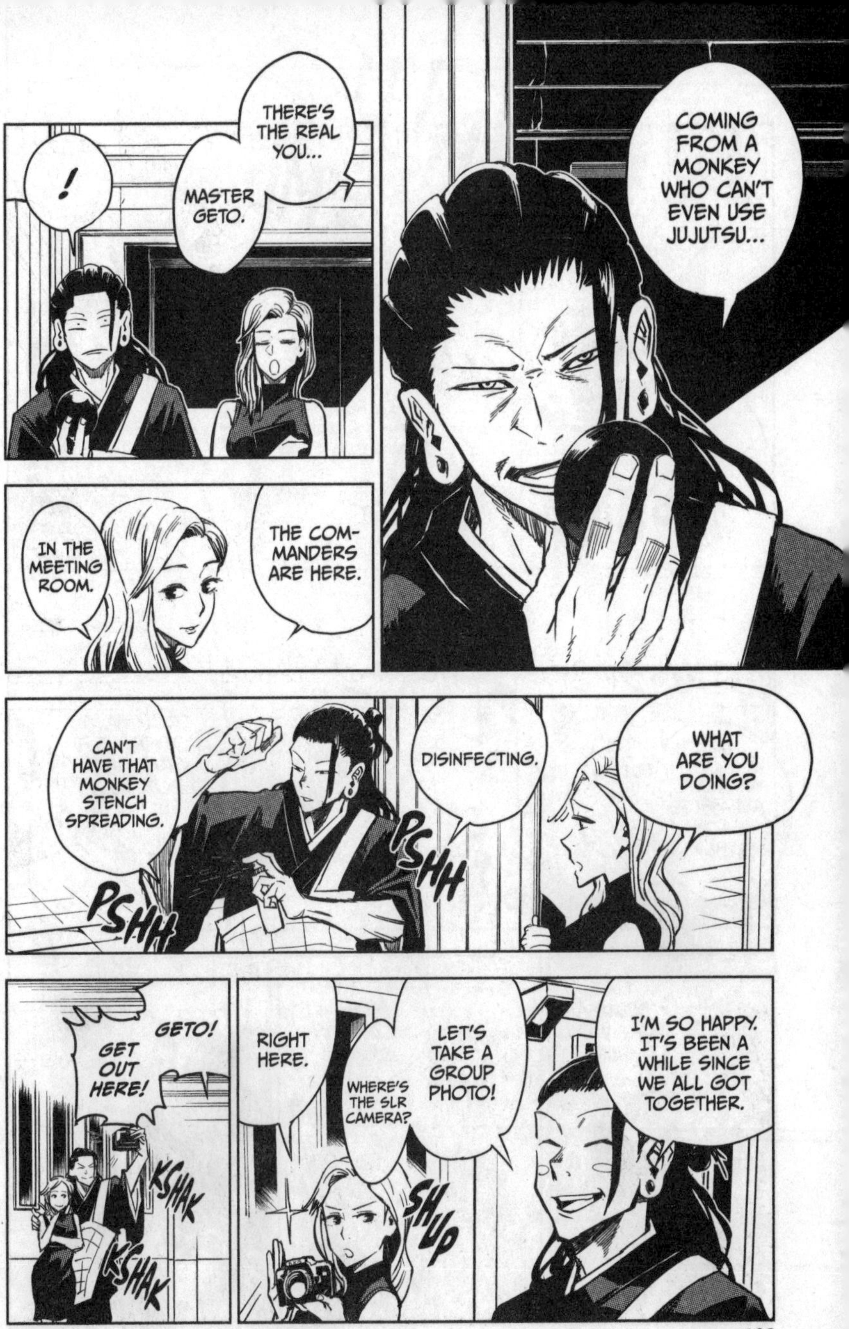
COMING FROM A MONKEY WHO CAN'T EVEN USE JUJUTSU...
THERE'S THE REAL YOU...
MASTER GETO.
!
THE COM-MANDERS ARE HERE.
IN THE MEETING ROOM.
WHAT ARE YOU DOING?
DISINFECTING.
PSHH
CAN'T HAVE THAT MONKEY STENCH SPREADING.
PSHH
I'M SO HAPPY. IT'S BEEN A WHILE SINCE WE ALL GOT TOGETHER.
LET'S TAKE A GROUP PHOTO!
SHUP
WHERE'S THE SLR CAMERA?
RIGHT HERE.
GETO!
GET OUT HERE!
KSHAK
KSHAK

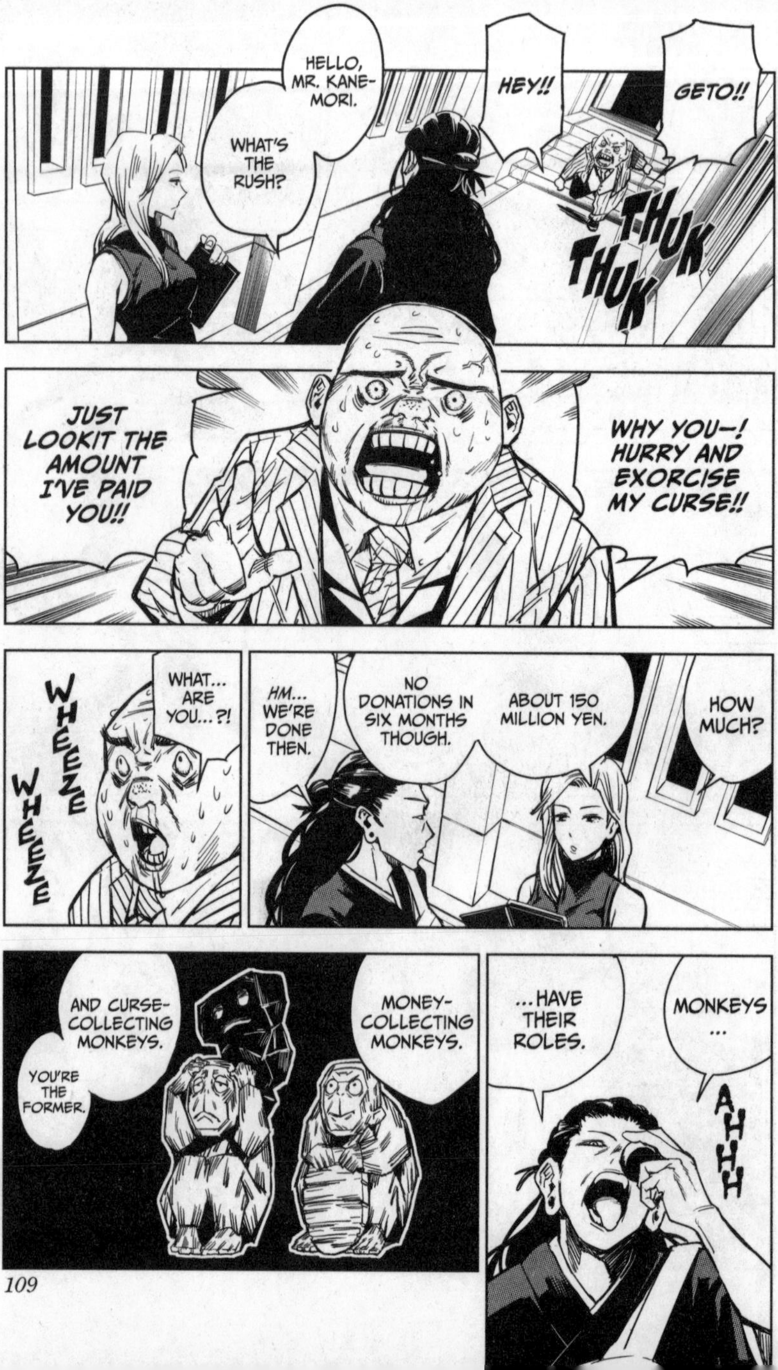
GETO!!
HEY!!
HELLO, MR. KANE-MORI.
WHAT'S THE RUSH?
THUK THUK
WHY YOU—! HURRY AND EXORCISE MY CURSE!!
JUST LOOKIT THE AMOUNT I'VE PAID YOU!!
HOW MUCH?
ABOUT 150 MILLION YEN.
NO DONATIONS IN SIX MONTHS THOUGH.
HM... WE'RE DONE THEN.
WHAT... ARE YOU...?!
WHEEZE WHEEZE
MONKEYS ...
AHHH
...HAVE THEIR ROLES.
MONEY-COLLECTING MONKEYS.
AND CURSE-COLLECTING MONKEYS.
YOU'RE THE FORMER.

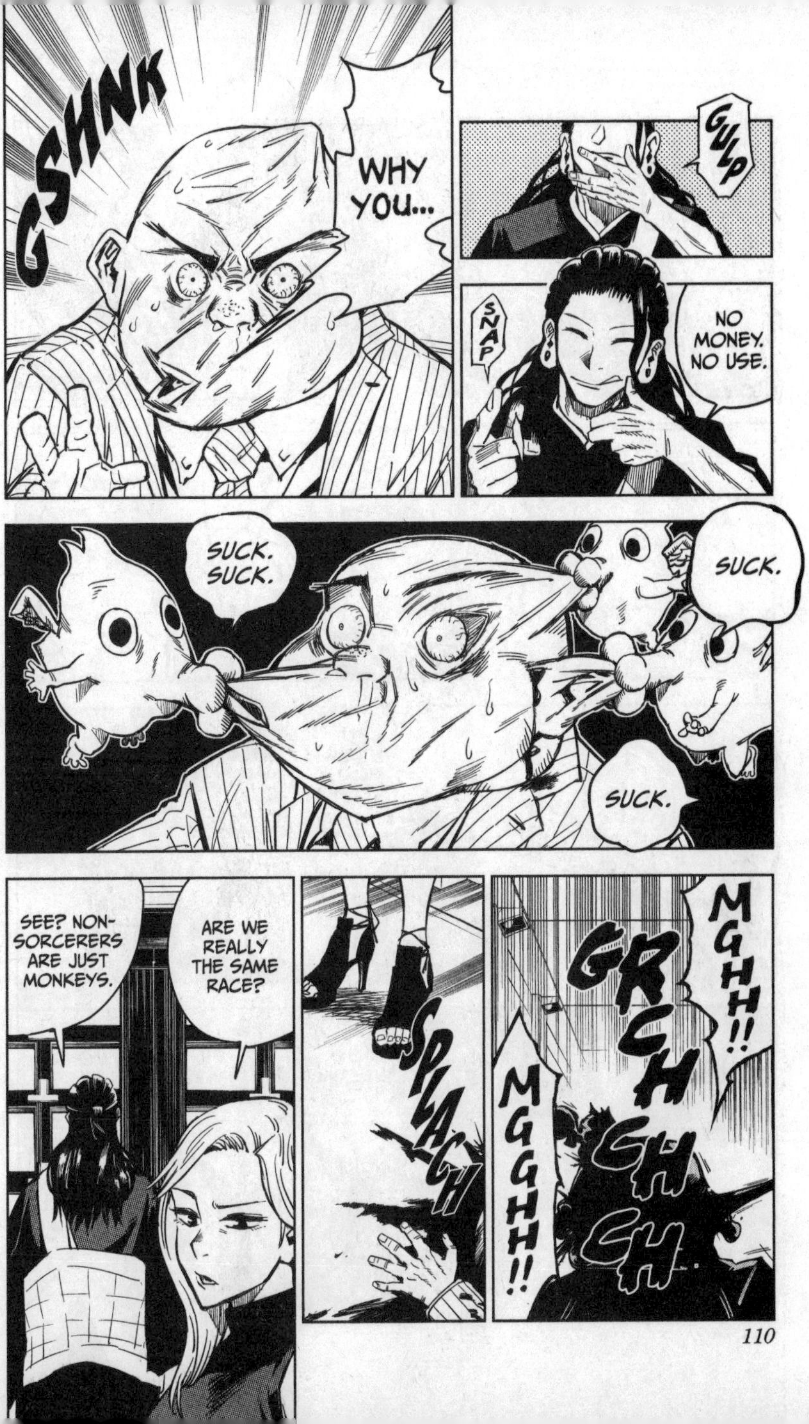
GULP
SNAP
NO MONEY. NO USE.
GSHNK
WHY YOU...
SUCK.
SUCK. SUCK.
SUCK.
MGHH!!
GRCH CH CH CH
MGGHH!!
SPLACH
ARE WE REALLY THE SAME RACE?
SEE? NON-SORCERERS ARE JUST MONKEYS.

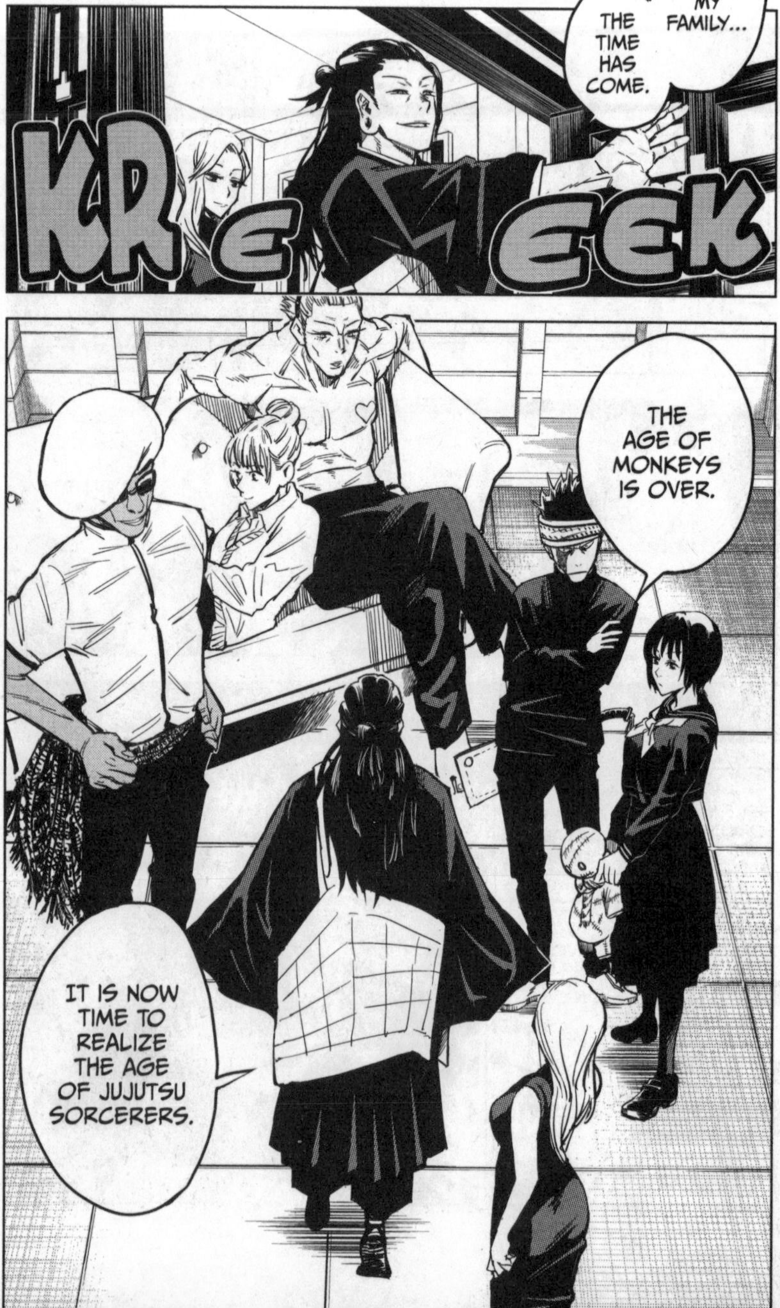
MY FAMILY...
THE TIME HAS COME.
KRRREECK
THE AGE OF MONKEYS IS OVER.
IT IS NOW TIME TO REALIZE THE AGE OF JUJUTSU SORCERERS.

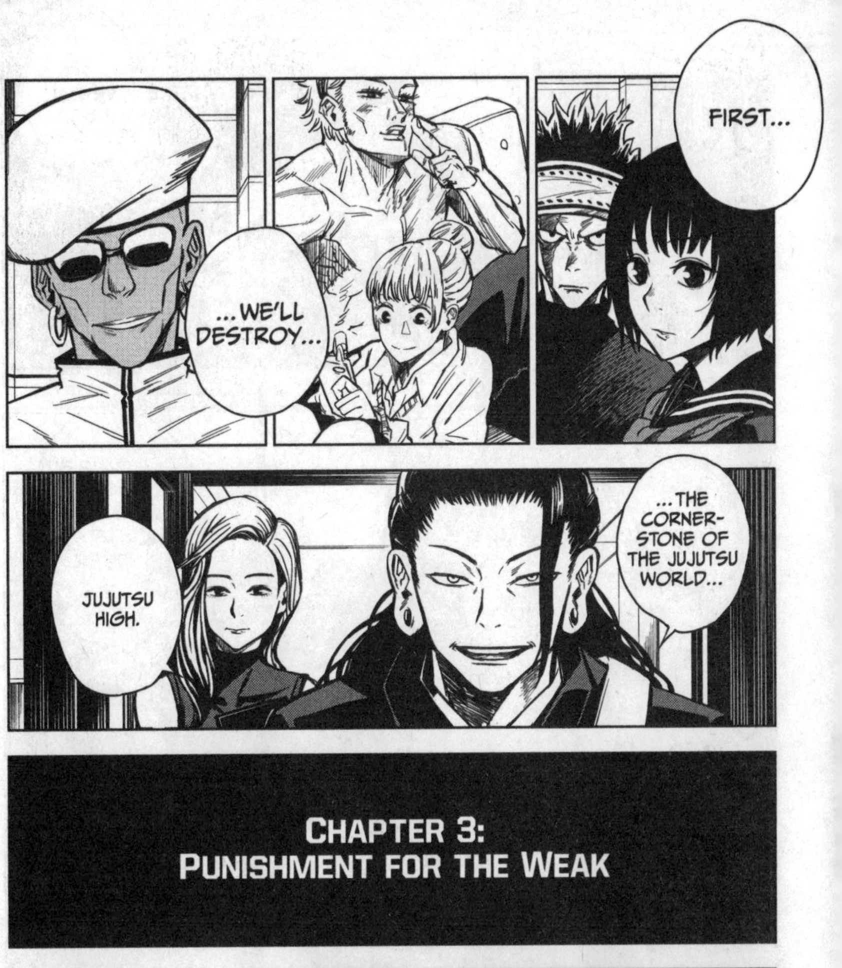
FIRST...
...WE'LL DESTROY...
...THE CORNER-STONE OF THE JUJUTSU WORLD...
JUJUTSU HIGH.

Chapter 3: Punishment for the Weak

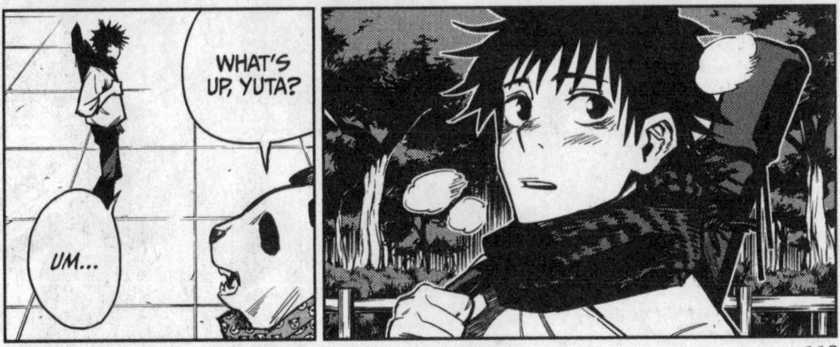
WHAT'S UP, YUTA?
UM...

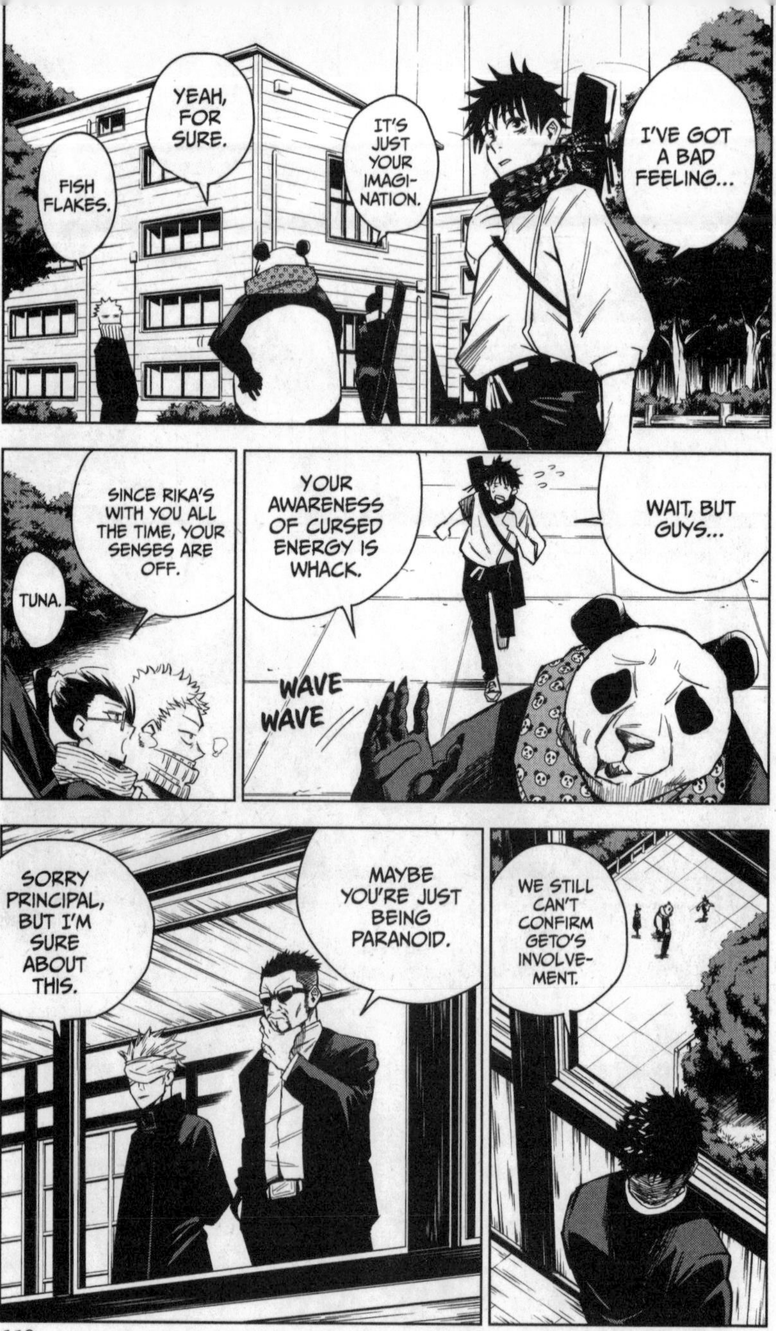
I'VE GOT A BAD FEELING...
IT'S JUST YOUR IMAGINATION.
YEAH, FOR SURE.
FISH FLAKES.
WAIT, BUT GUYS...
YOUR AWARENESS OF CURSED ENERGY IS WHACK.
WAVE WAVE
SINCE RIKA'S WITH YOU ALL THE TIME, YOUR SENSES ARE OFF.
TUNA.
WE STILL CAN'T CONFIRM GETO'S INVOLVEMENT.
MAYBE YOU'RE JUST BEING PARANOID.
SORRY PRINCIPAL, BUT I'M SURE ABOUT THIS.

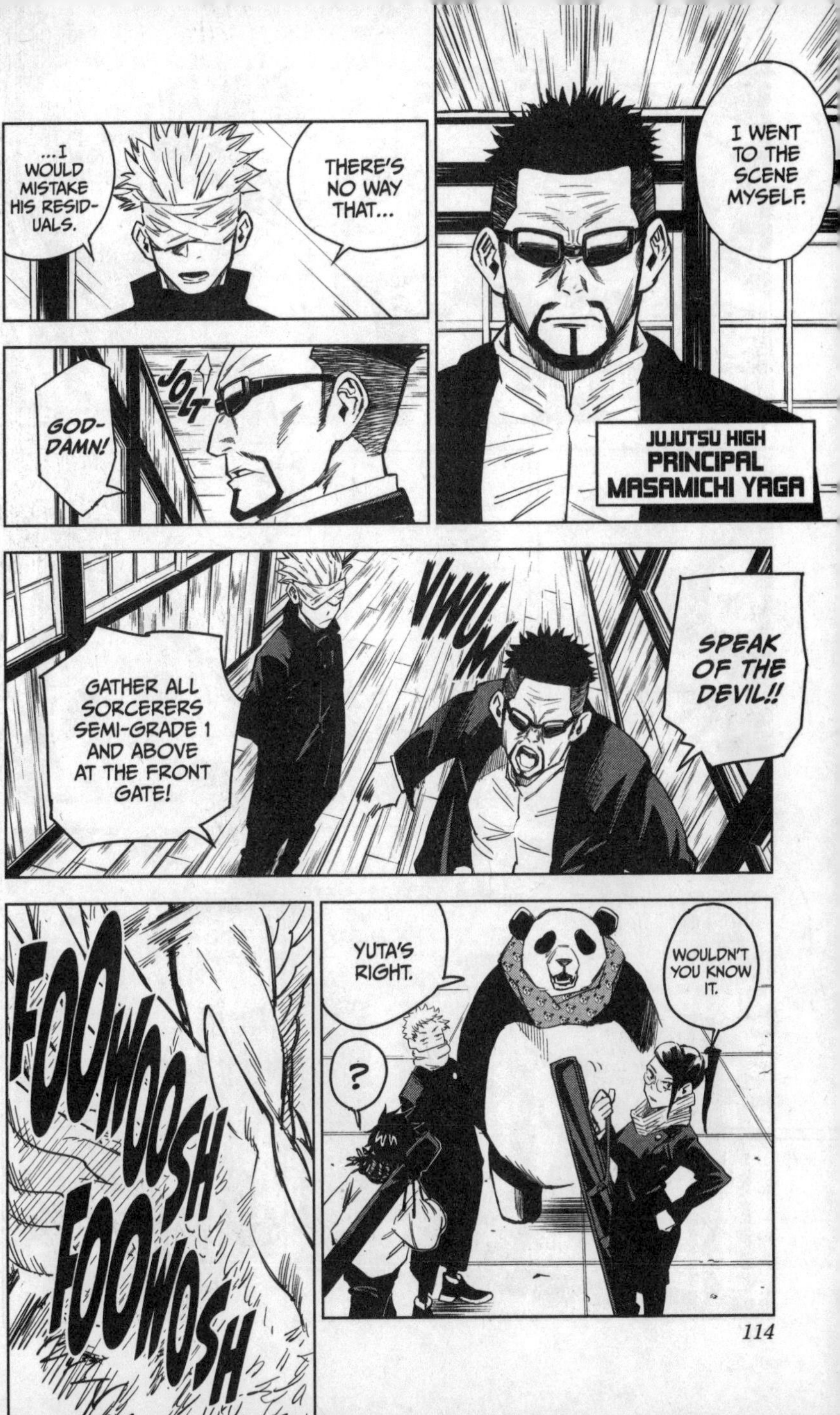
I WENT TO THE SCENE MYSELF.
JUJUTSU HIGH PRINCIPAL MASAMICHI YAGA
THERE'S NO WAY THAT...
...I WOULD MISTAKE HIS RESIDUALS.
JOLT
GOD-DAMN!
VWUM
SPEAK OF THE DEVIL!!
GATHER ALL SORCERERS SEMI-GRADE 1 AND ABOVE AT THE FRONT GATE!
WOULDN'T YOU KNOW IT.
YUTA'S RIGHT.
?
FOOWOOSH
FOOWOSH

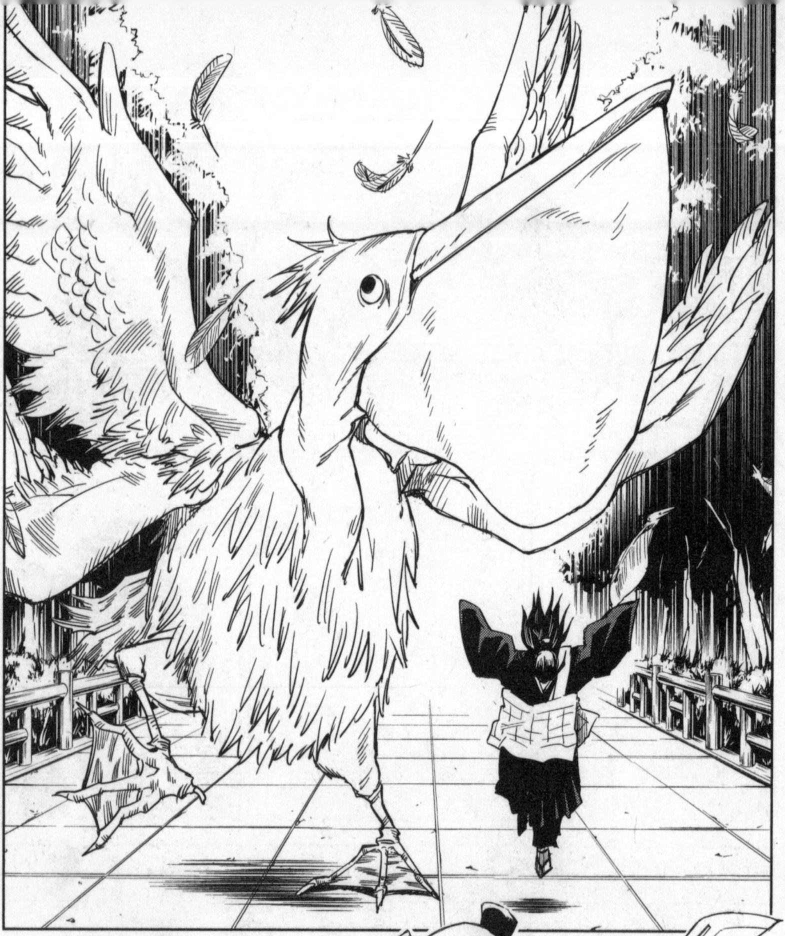

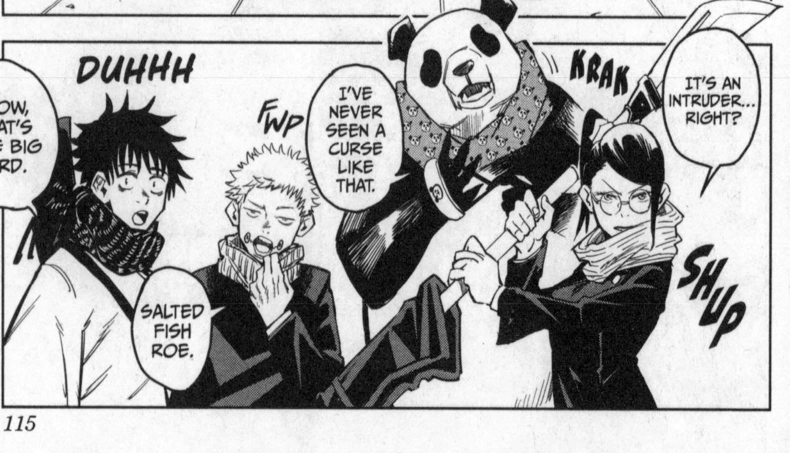
IT'S AN INTRUDER... RIGHT?
SHUP
KRAK
I'VE NEVER SEEN A CURSE LIKE THAT.
FWP
SALTED FISH ROE.
DUHHH
WOW, THAT'S ONE BIG BIRD.

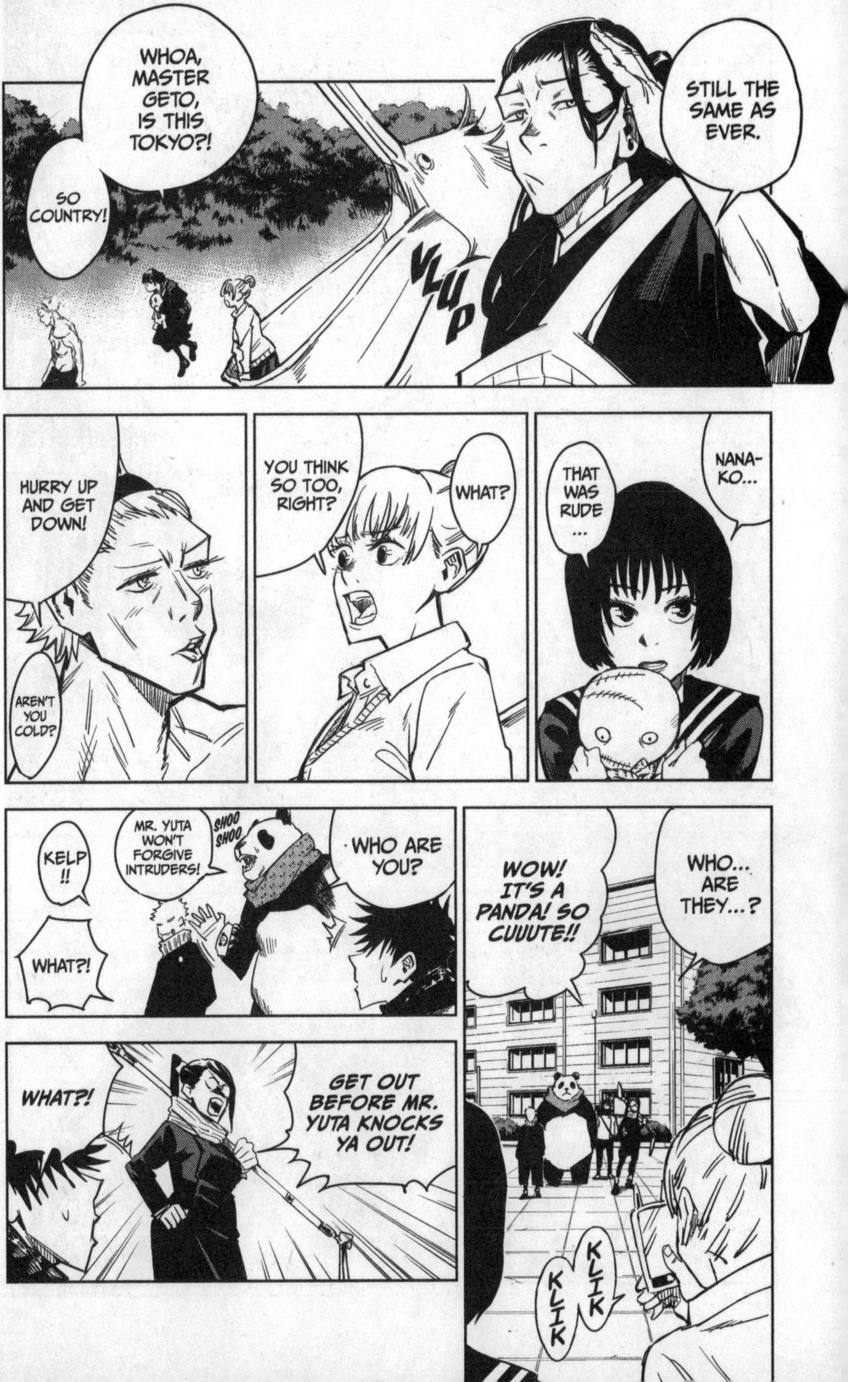
STILL THE SAME AS EVER.
WHOA, MASTER GETO, IS THIS TOKYO?!
SO COUNTRY!
VLUP
NANA-KO...
THAT WAS RUDE...
WHAT?
YOU THINK SO TOO, RIGHT?
HURRY UP AND GET DOWN!
AREN'T YOU COLD?
WHO... ARE THEY...?
WOW! IT'S A PANDA! SO CUUUTE!!
KLIK KLIK
KLIK KLIK
WHO ARE YOU?
SHOO SHOO
MR. YUTA WON'T FORGIVE INTRUDERS!
KELP!!
WHAT?!
GET OUT BEFORE MR. YUTA KNOCKS YA OUT!
WHAT?!

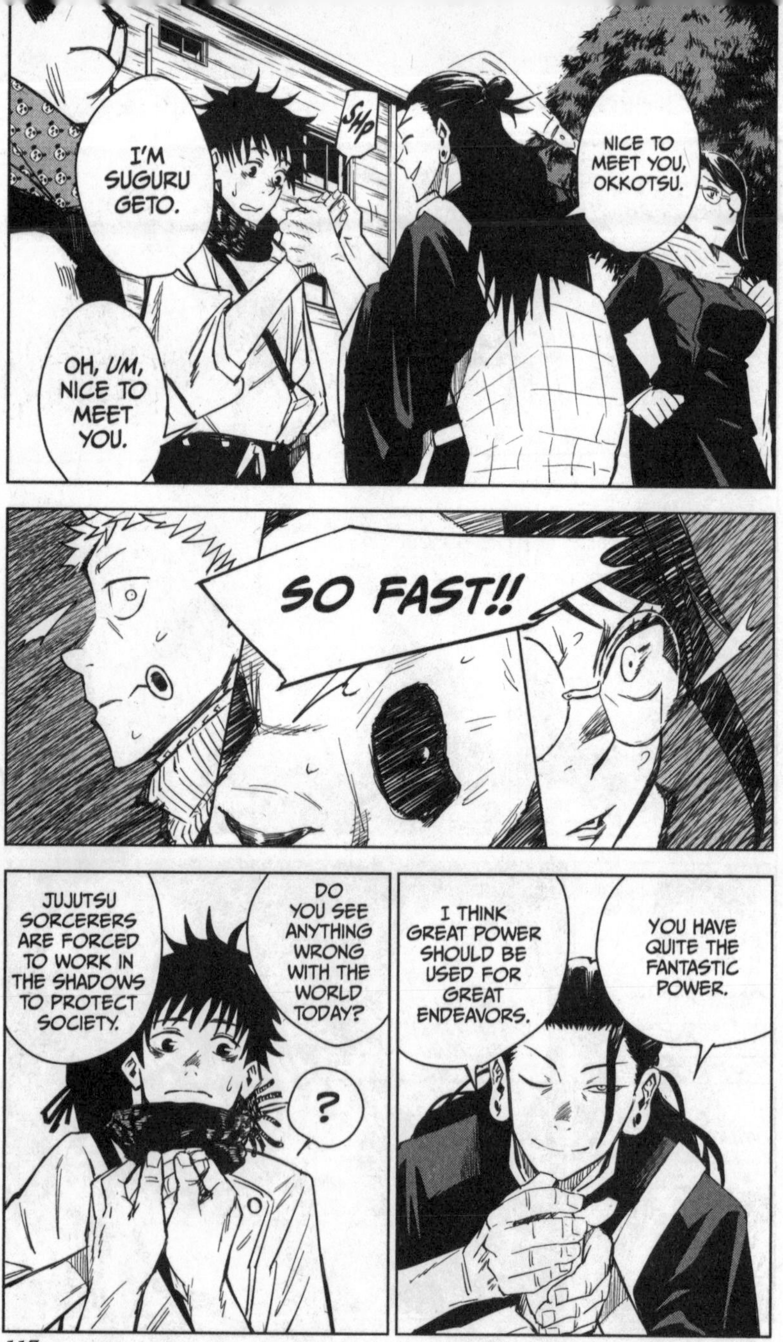
NICE TO MEET YOU, OKKOTSU.
SHP
I'M SUGURU GETO.
OH, UM, NICE TO MEET YOU.
SO FAST!!
YOU HAVE QUITE THE FANTASTIC POWER.
I THINK GREAT POWER SHOULD BE USED FOR GREAT ENDEAVORS.
DO YOU SEE ANYTHING WRONG WITH THE WORLD TODAY?
JUJUTSU SORCERERS ARE FORCED TO WORK IN THE SHADOWS TO PROTECT SOCIETY.
?

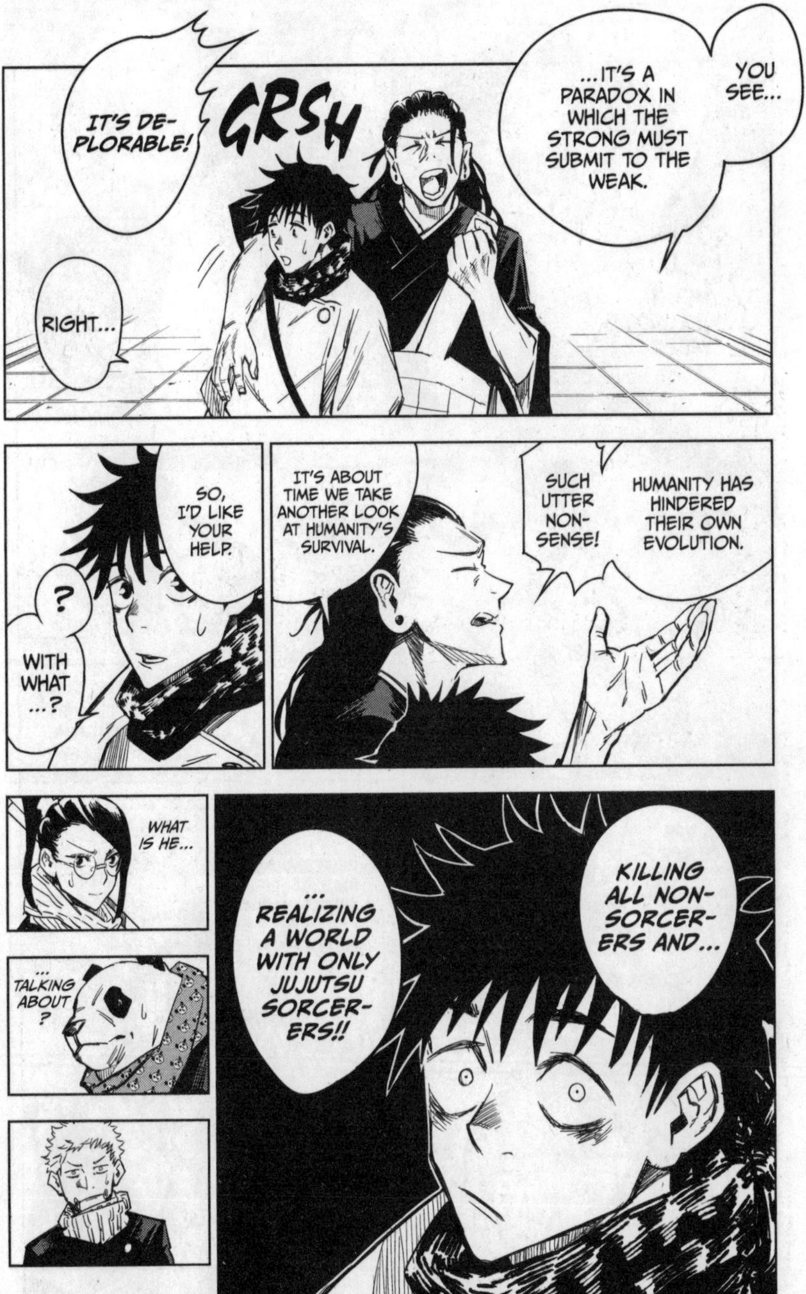
YOU SEE...
...IT'S A PARADOX IN WHICH THE STRONG MUST SUBMIT TO THE WEAK.
GRSH
IT'S DE-PLORABLE!
RIGHT...
HUMANITY HAS HINDERED THEIR OWN EVOLUTION.
SUCH UTTER NON-SENSE!
IT'S ABOUT TIME WE TAKE ANOTHER LOOK AT HUMANITY'S SURVIVAL.
SO, I'D LIKE YOUR HELP.
?
WITH WHAT ...?
KILLING ALL NON-SORCER-ERS AND...
...REALIZING A WORLD WITH ONLY JUJUTSU SORCER-ERS!!
WHAT IS HE...
...TALKING ABOUT?

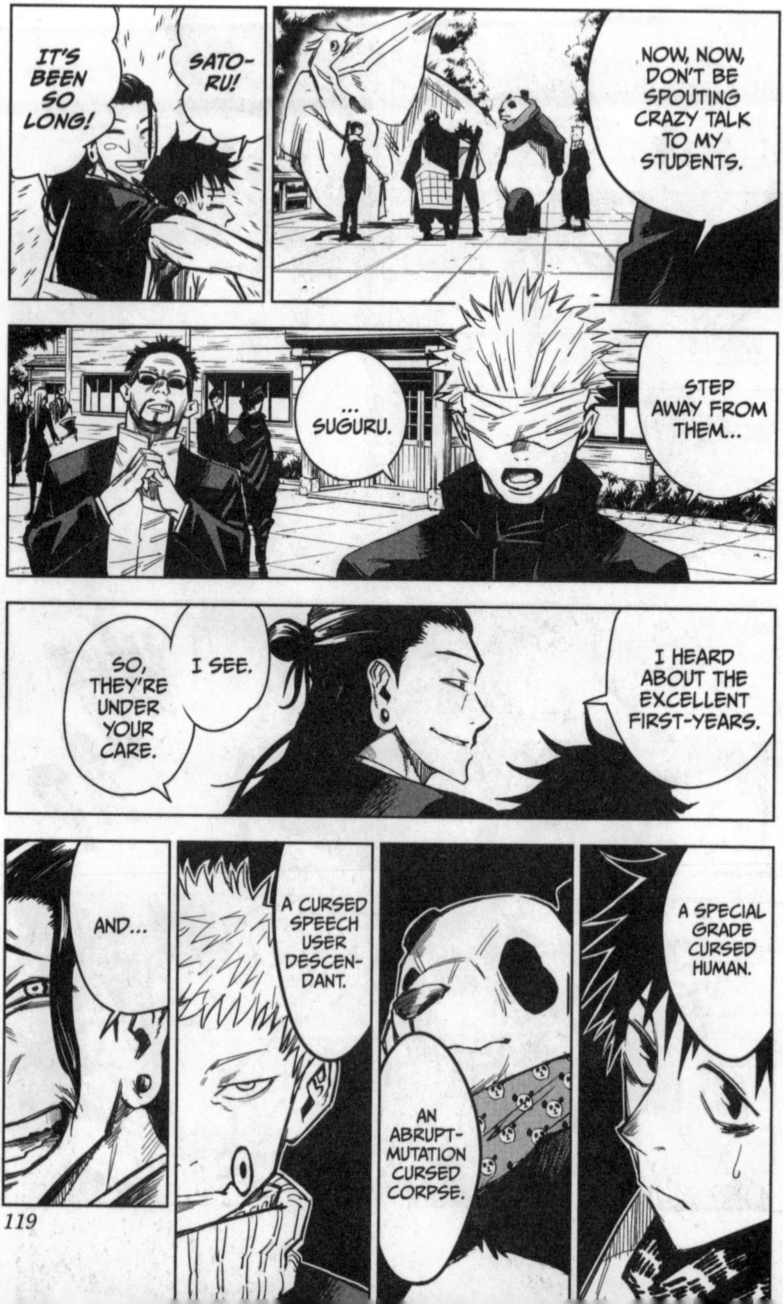
NOW, NOW, DON'T BE SPOUTING CRAZY TALK TO MY STUDENTS.
SATO-RU!
IT'S BEEN SO LONG!
STEP AWAY FROM THEM...
... SUGURU.
I HEARD ABOUT THE EXCELLENT FIRST-YEARS.
I SEE.
SO, THEY'RE UNDER YOUR CARE.
A SPECIAL GRADE CURSED HUMAN.
AN ABRUPT-MUTATION CURSED CORPSE.
A CURSED SPEECH USER DESCENDANT.
AND...

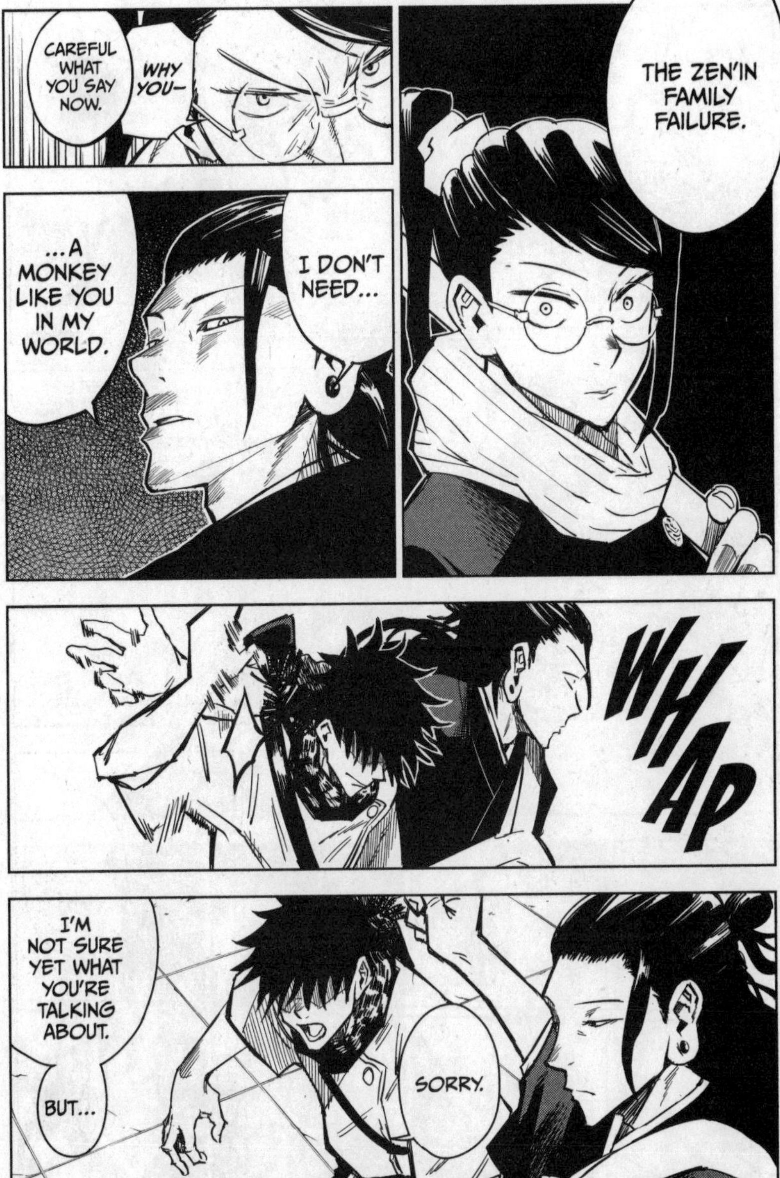
THE ZEN'IN FAMILY FAILURE.
WHY YOU—
CAREFUL WHAT YOU SAY NOW.
I DON'T NEED...
...A MONKEY LIKE YOU IN MY WORLD.
WHAP
SORRY.
I'M NOT SURE YET WHAT YOU'RE TALKING ABOUT.
BUT...

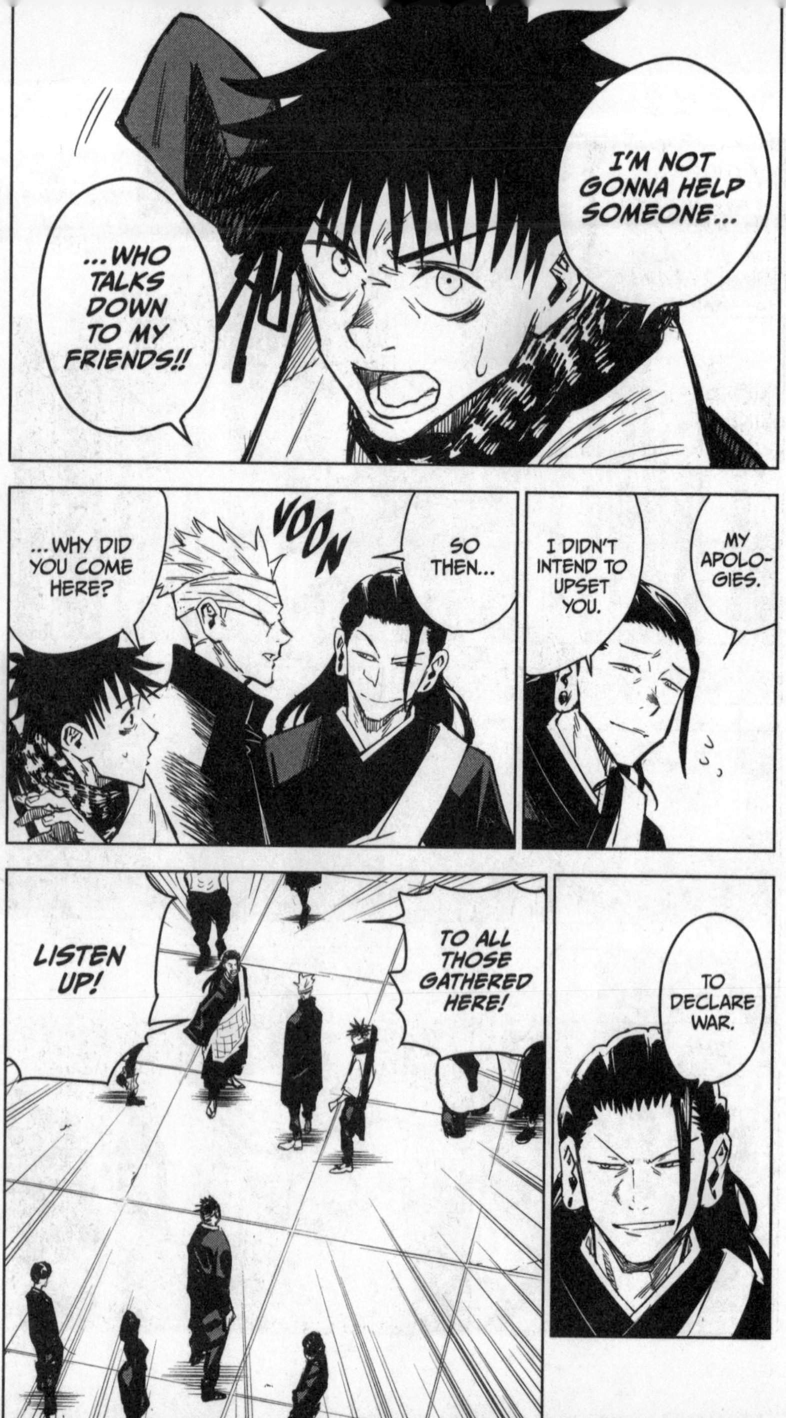
I'M NOT GONNA HELP SOMEONE...
...WHO TALKS DOWN TO MY FRIENDS!!
MY APOLO-GIES.
I DIDN'T INTEND TO UPSET YOU.
SO THEN...
VOON
...WHY DID YOU COME HERE?
TO DECLARE WAR.
TO ALL THOSE GATHERED HERE!
LISTEN UP!

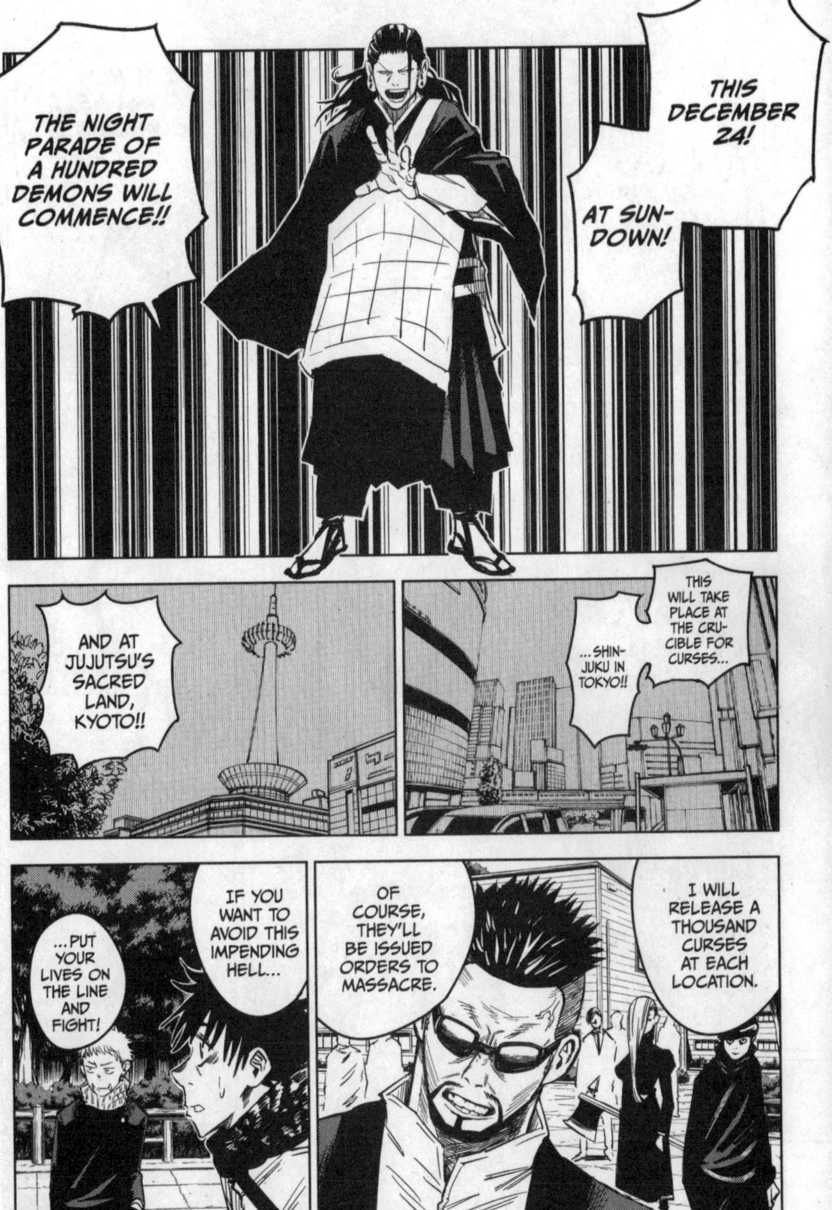
THIS DECEMBER 24!
AT SUN-DOWN!
THE NIGHT PARADE OF A HUNDRED DEMONS WILL COMMENCE!!
THIS WILL TAKE PLACE AT THE CRU-CIBLE FOR CURSES...
...SHIN-JUKU IN TOKYO!!
AND AT JUJUTSU'S SACRED LAND, KYOTO!!
I WILL RELEASE A THOUSAND CURSES AT EACH LOCATION.
OF COURSE, THEY'LL BE ISSUED ORDERS TO MASSACRE.
IF YOU WANT TO AVOID THIS IMPENDING HELL...
...PUT YOUR LIVES ON THE LINE AND FIGHT!

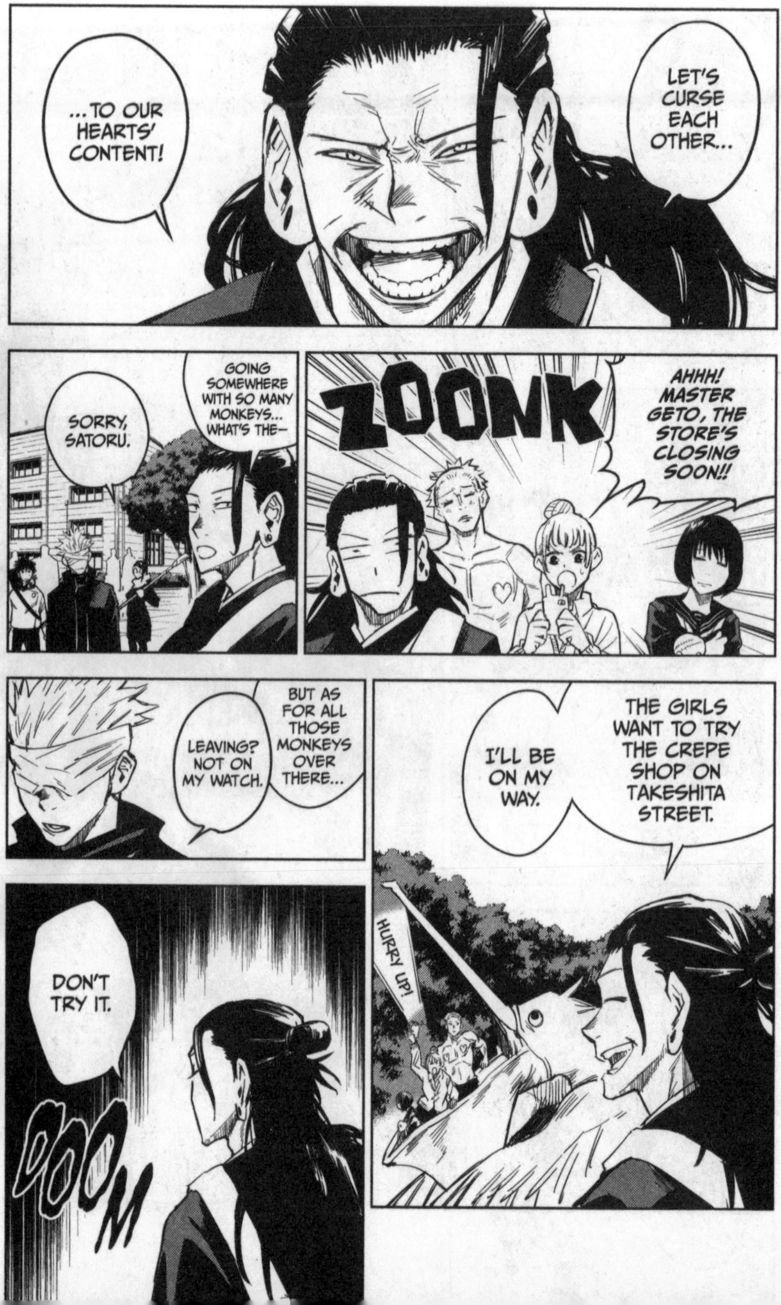
LET'S CURSE EACH OTHER...
...TO OUR HEARTS' CONTENT!
ZOONK
AHHH! MASTER GETO, THE STORE'S CLOSING SOON!!
GOING SOMEWHERE WITH SO MANY MONKEYS... WHAT'S THE—
SORRY, SATORU.
THE GIRLS WANT TO TRY THE CREPE SHOP ON TAKESHITA STREET.
I'LL BE ON MY WAY.
HURRY UP!
BUT AS FOR ALL THOSE MONKEYS OVER THERE...
LEAVING? NOT ON MY WATCH.
DON'T TRY IT.
DOOM

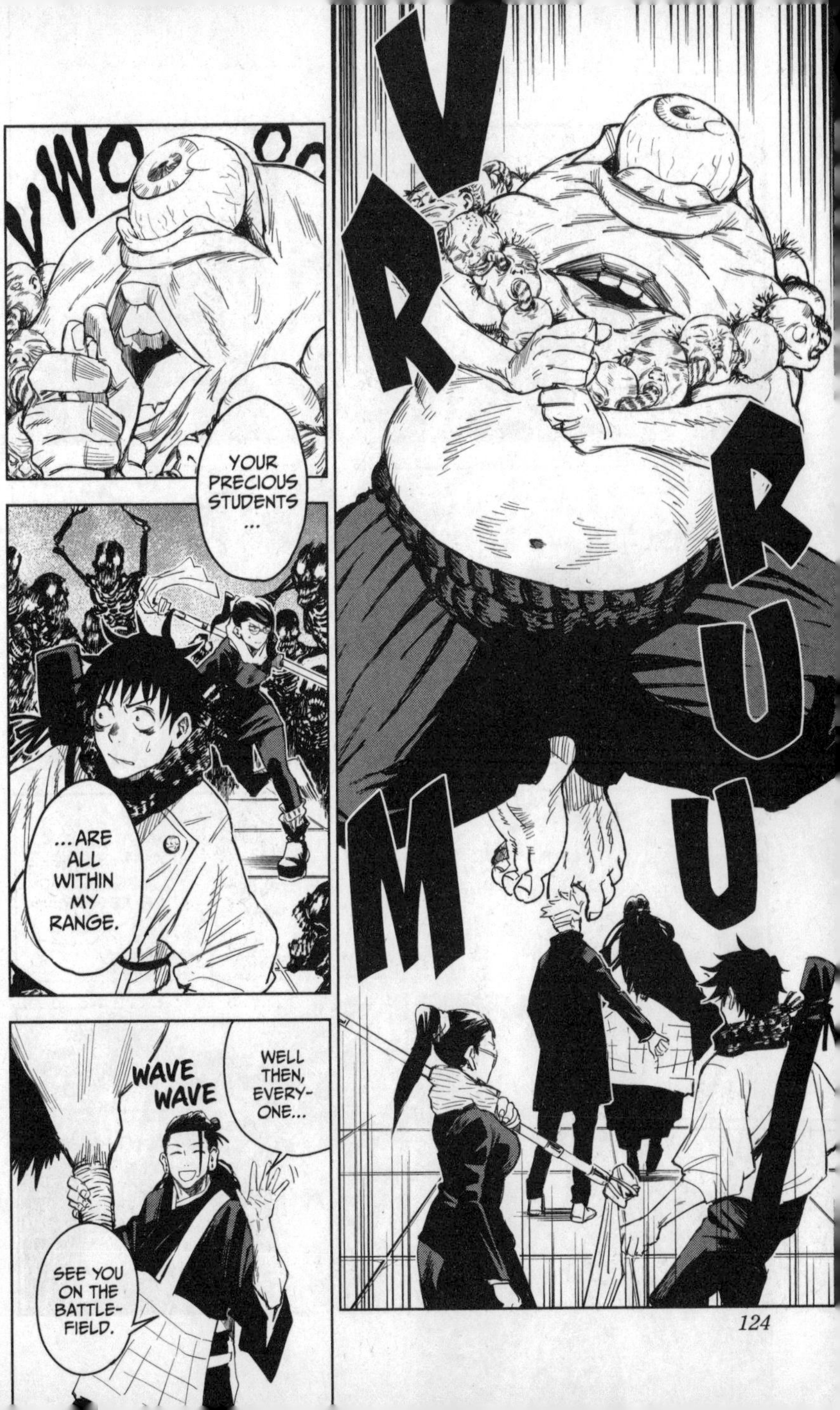
VRRUUM
VWOOO
YOUR PRECIOUS STUDENTS...
...ARE ALL WITHIN MY RANGE.
WELL THEN, EVERY-ONE...
WAVE WAVE
SEE YOU ON THE BATTLE-FIELD.

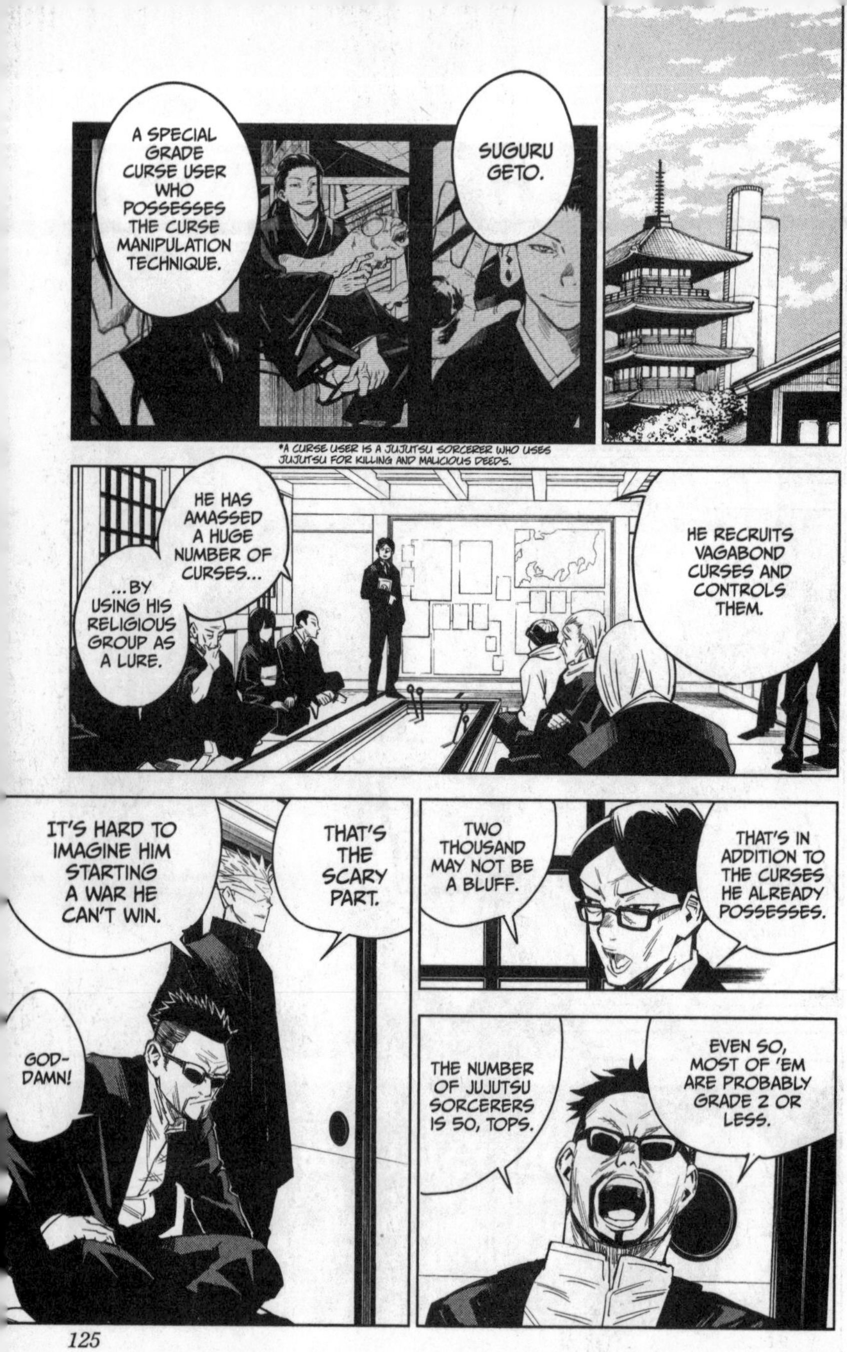
SUGURU GETO.
A SPECIAL GRADE CURSE USER WHO POSSESSES THE CURSE MANIPULATION TECHNIQUE.
HE RECRUITS VAGABOND CURSES AND CONTROLS THEM.
HE HAS AMASSED A HUGE NUMBER OF CURSES...
...BY USING HIS RELIGIOUS GROUP AS A LURE.
THAT'S IN ADDITION TO THE CURSES HE ALREADY POSSESSES.
TWO THOUSAND MAY NOT BE A BLUFF.
EVEN SO, MOST OF 'EM ARE PROBABLY GRADE 2 OR LESS.
THE NUMBER OF JUJUTSU SORCERERS IS 50, TOPS.
THAT'S THE SCARY PART.
IT'S HARD TO IMAGINE HIM STARTING A WAR HE CAN'T WIN.
GOD-DAMN!

*A CURSE USER IS A JUJUTSU SORCERER WHO USES JUJUTSU FOR KILLING AND MALICIOUS DEEDS.

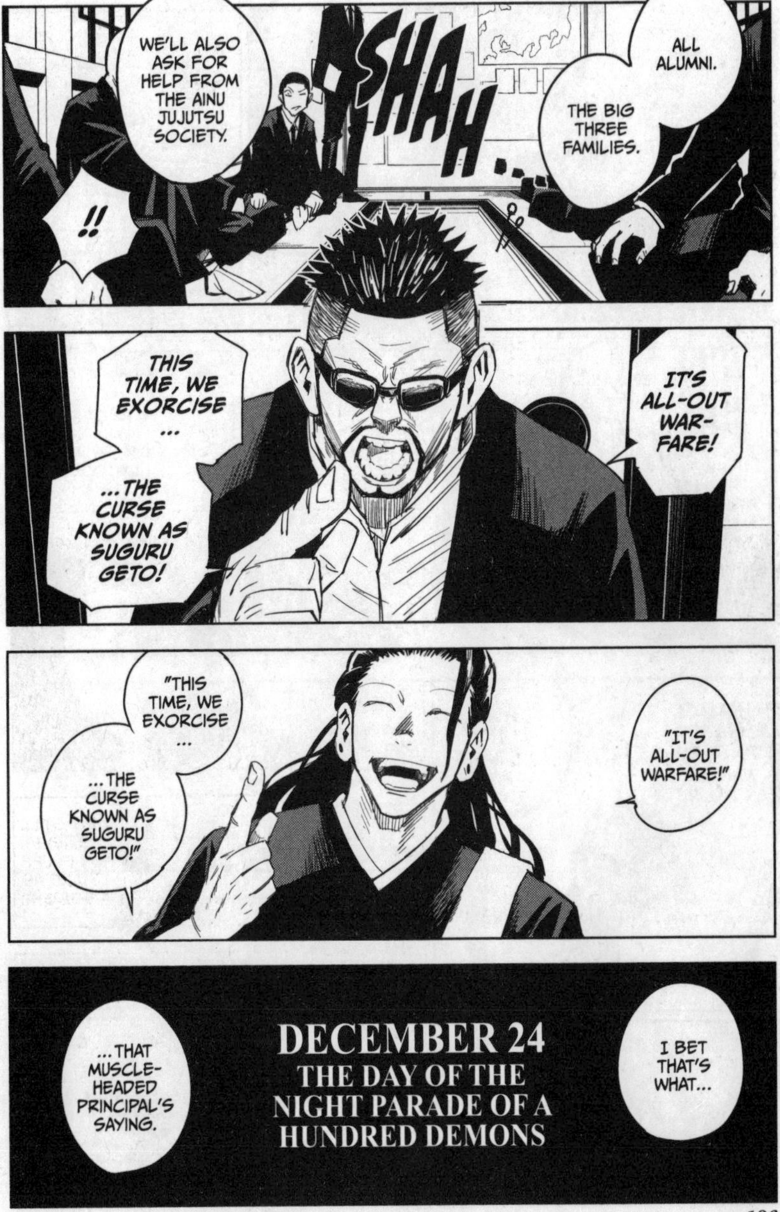
ALL ALUMNI.
THE BIG THREE FAMILIES.
SHAH...
WE'LL ALSO ASK FOR HELP FROM THE AINU JUJUTSU SOCIETY.
!!
IT'S ALL-OUT WARFARE!
THIS TIME, WE EXORCISE ...
...THE CURSE KNOWN AS SUGURU GETO!
"IT'S ALL-OUT WARFARE!"
"THIS TIME, WE EXORCISE ...
...THE CURSE KNOWN AS SUGURU GETO!"
I BET THAT'S WHAT...
DECEMBER 24
THE DAY OF THE NIGHT PARADE OF A HUNDRED DEMONS
...THAT MUSCLE-HEADED PRINCIPAL'S SAYING.

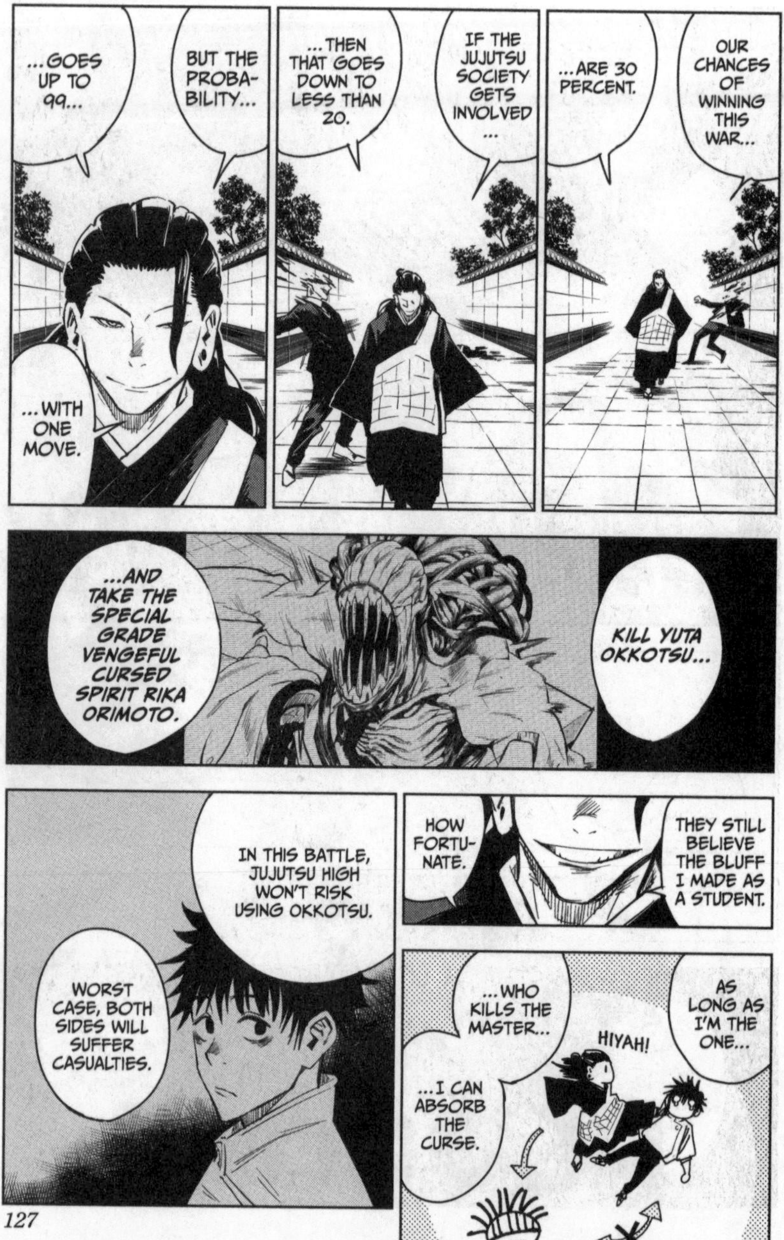
OUR CHANCES OF WINNING THIS WAR...
...ARE 30 PERCENT.
IF THE JUJUTSU SOCIETY GETS INVOLVED ...
...THEN THAT GOES DOWN TO LESS THAN 20.
BUT THE PROBABILITY...
...GOES UP TO 99...
...WITH ONE MOVE.
KILL YUTA OKKOTSU...
...AND TAKE THE SPECIAL GRADE VENGEFUL CURSED SPIRIT RIKA ORIMOTO.
THEY STILL BELIEVE THE BLUFF I MADE AS A STUDENT.
HOW FORTUNATE.
AS LONG AS I'M THE ONE...
...WHO KILLS THE MASTER...
HIYAH!
...I CAN ABSORB THE CURSE.
RIKA
IN THIS BATTLE, JUJUTSU HIGH WON'T RISK USING OKKOTSU.
WORST CASE, BOTH SIDES WILL SUFFER CASUALTIES.

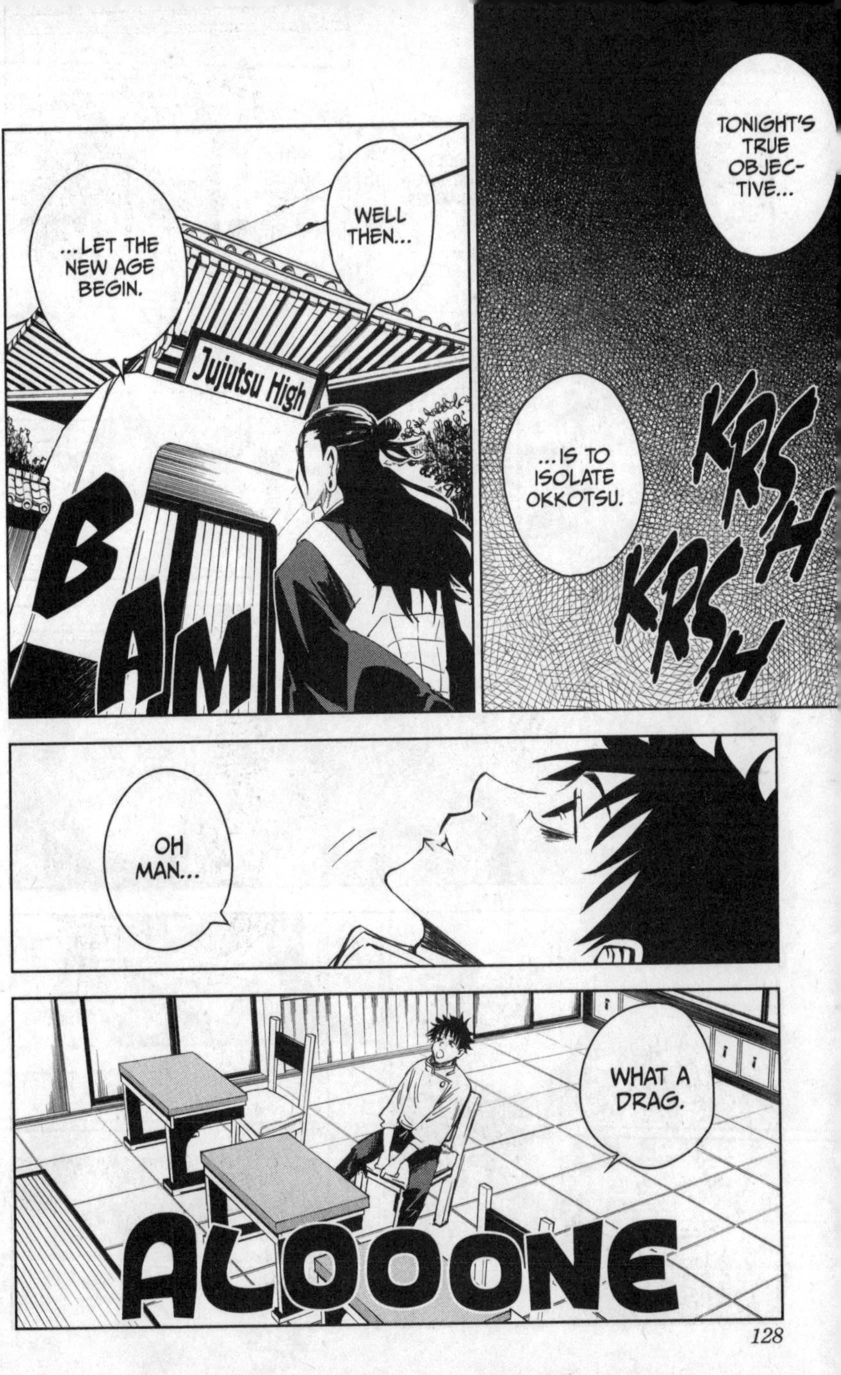
TONIGHT'S TRUE OBJECTIVE...
...IS TO ISOLATE OKKOTSU.
KRSH KRSH
WELL THEN...
...LET THE NEW AGE BEGIN.
Jujutsu High
BAM
OH MAN...
WHAT A DRAG.
ALOOONE

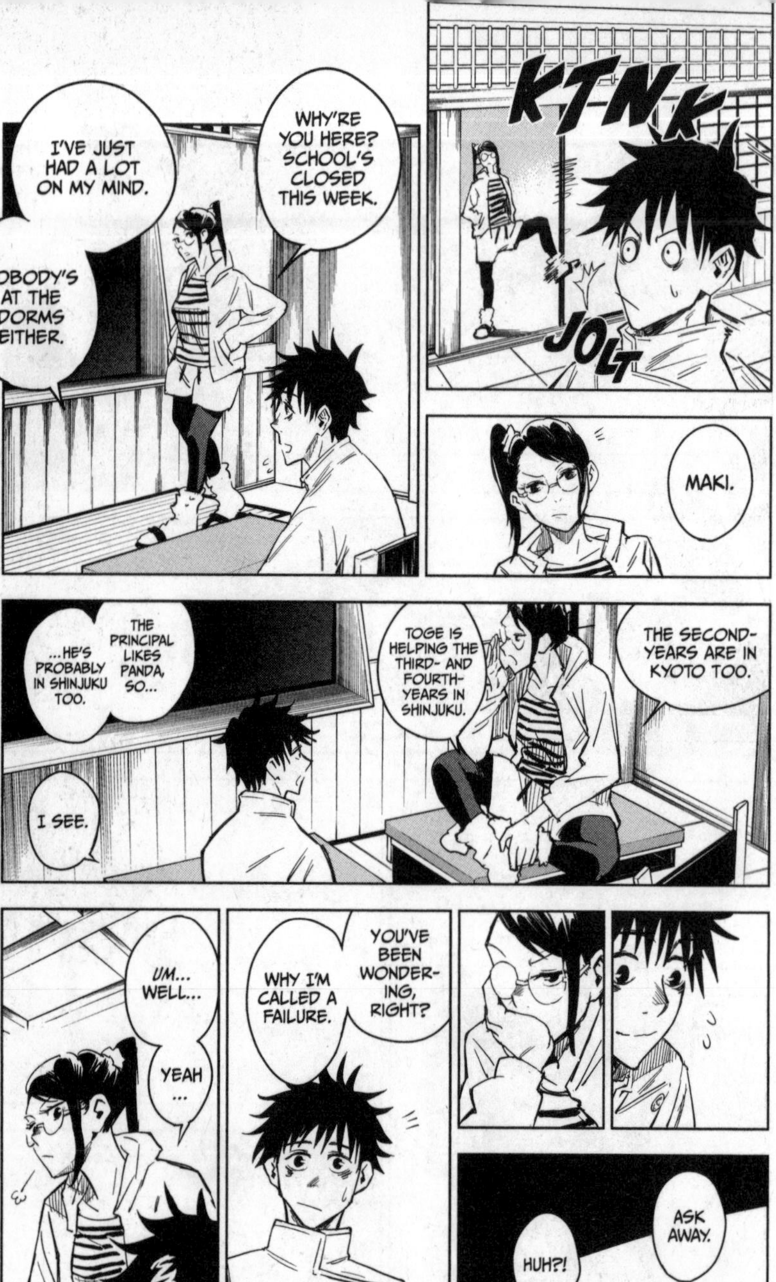
KTNK
JOLT
MAKI.
WHY'RE YOU HERE? SCHOOL'S CLOSED THIS WEEK.
I'VE JUST HAD A LOT ON MY MIND.
NOBODY'S AT THE DORMS EITHER.
THE SECOND-YEARS ARE IN KYOTO TOO.
TOGE IS HELPING THE THIRD- AND FOURTH-YEARS IN SHINJUKU.
THE PRINCIPAL LIKES PANDA, SO...
...HE'S PROBABLY IN SHINJUKU TOO.
I SEE.
ASK AWAY.
HUH?!
YOU'VE BEEN WONDER-ING, RIGHT?
WHY I'M CALLED A FAILURE.
UM... WELL...
YEAH ...

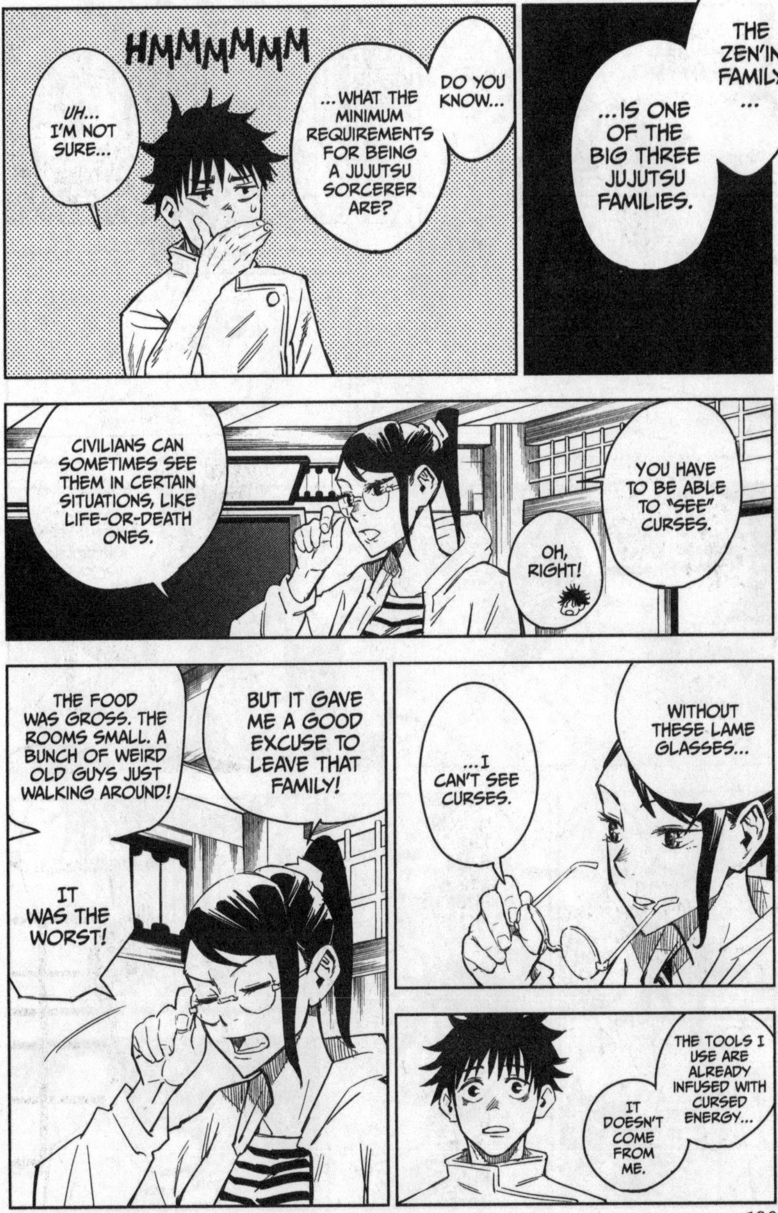
THE ZEN'IN FAMILY...
...IS ONE OF THE BIG THREE JUJUTSU FAMILIES.
DO YOU KNOW...
...WHAT THE MINIMUM REQUIREMENTS FOR BEING A JUJUTSU SORCERER ARE?
HMMMMMMM
UH... I'M NOT SURE...
YOU HAVE TO BE ABLE TO "SEE" CURSES.
OH, RIGHT!
CIVILIANS CAN SOMETIMES SEE THEM IN CERTAIN SITUATIONS, LIKE LIFE-OR-DEATH ONES.
WITHOUT THESE LAME GLASSES...
...I CAN'T SEE CURSES.
THE TOOLS I USE ARE ALREADY INFUSED WITH CURSED ENERGY...
IT DOESN'T COME FROM ME.
BUT IT GAVE ME A GOOD EXCUSE TO LEAVE THAT FAMILY!
THE FOOD WAS GROSS. THE ROOMS SMALL. A BUNCH OF WEIRD OLD GUYS JUST WALKING AROUND!
IT WAS THE WORST!

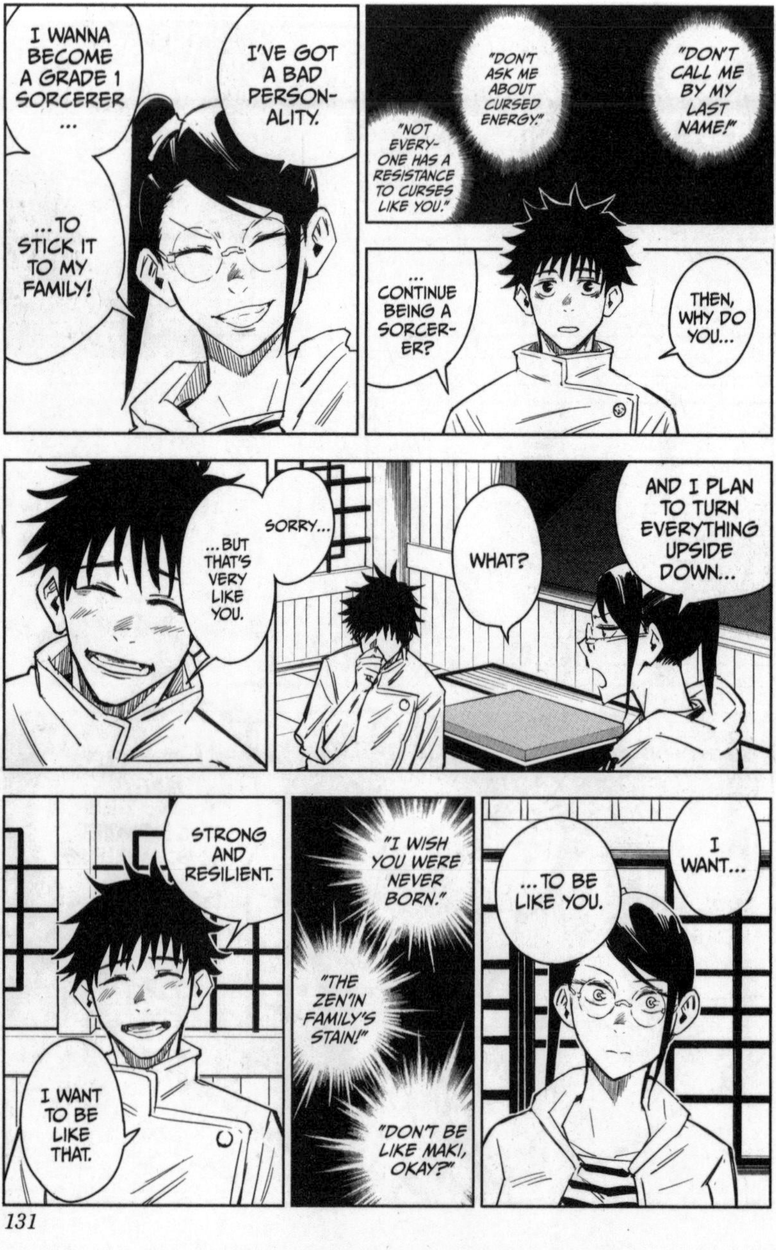
"DON'T CALL ME BY MY LAST NAME!"
"DON'T ASK ME ABOUT CURSED ENERGY."
"NOT EVERYONE HAS A RESISTANCE TO CURSES LIKE YOU."
THEN, WHY DO YOU...
...CONTINUE BEING A SORCERER?
I'VE GOT A BAD PERSONALITY.
I WANNA BECOME A GRADE 1 SORCERER...
...TO STICK IT TO MY FAMILY!
AND I PLAN TO TURN EVERYTHING UPSIDE DOWN...
WHAT?
SORRY...
...BUT THAT'S VERY LIKE YOU.
I WANT...
...TO BE LIKE YOU.
"I WISH YOU WERE NEVER BORN."
"THE ZEN'IN FAMILY'S STAIN!"
"DON'T BE LIKE MAKI, OKAY?"
STRONG AND RESILIENT.
I WANT TO BE LIKE THAT.

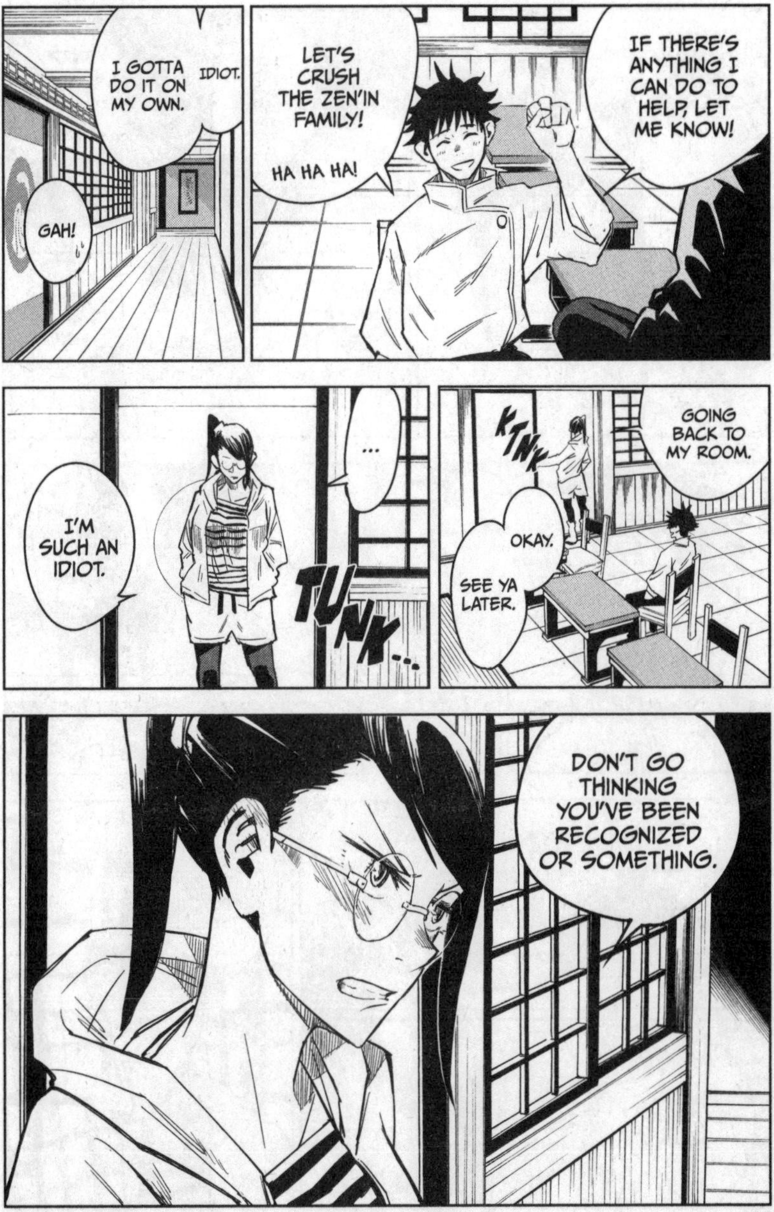
IF THERE'S ANYTHING I CAN DO TO HELP, LET ME KNOW!
LET'S CRUSH THE ZEN'IN FAMILY!
HA HA HA!
IDIOT.
I GOTTA DO IT ON MY OWN.
GAH!
GOING BACK TO MY ROOM.
KTNK
OKAY.
SEE YA LATER.
...
TUNK...
I'M SUCH AN IDIOT.
DON'T GO THINKING YOU'VE BEEN RECOGNIZED OR SOMETHING.

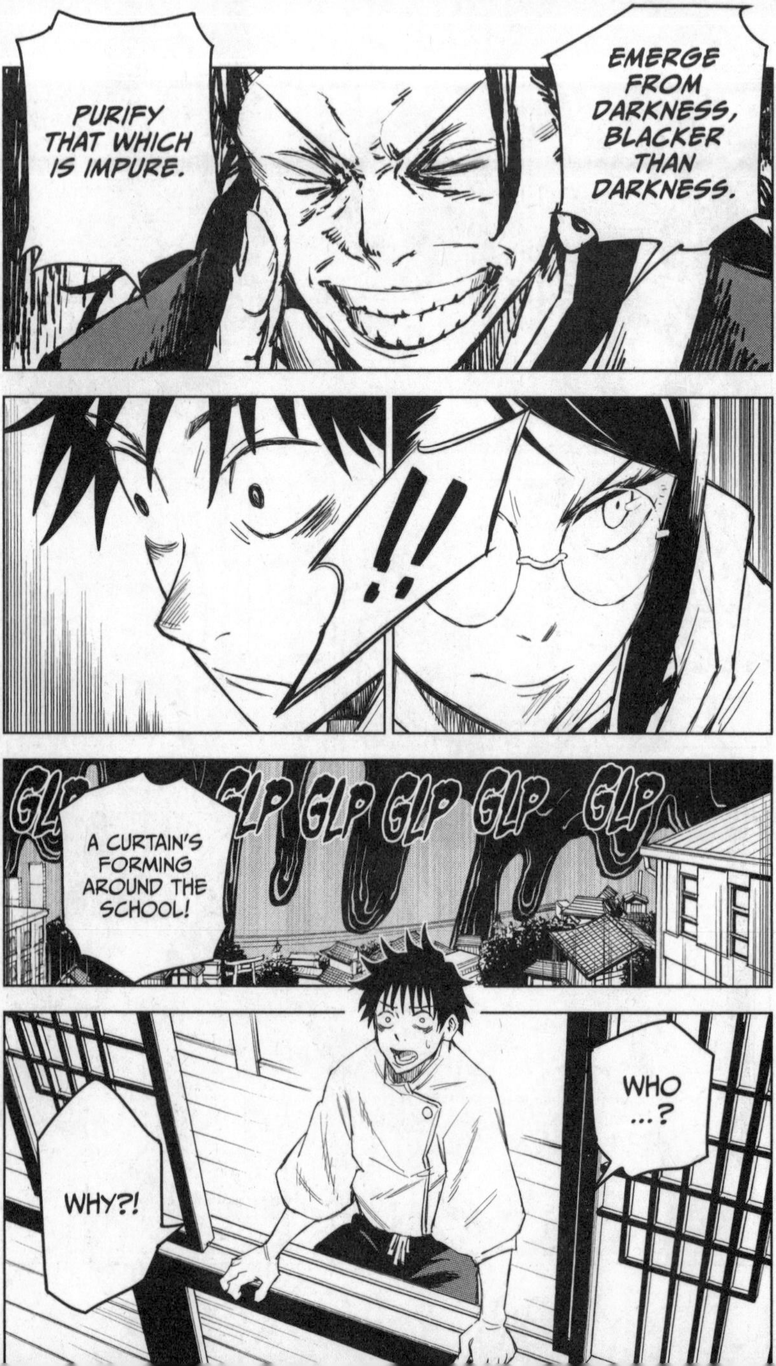
EMERGE FROM DARKNESS, BLACKER THAN DARKNESS.
PURIFY THAT WHICH IS IMPURE.
!!
GLP GLP GLP GLP GLP
A CURTAIN'S FORMING AROUND THE SCHOOL!
WHO ...?
WHY?!

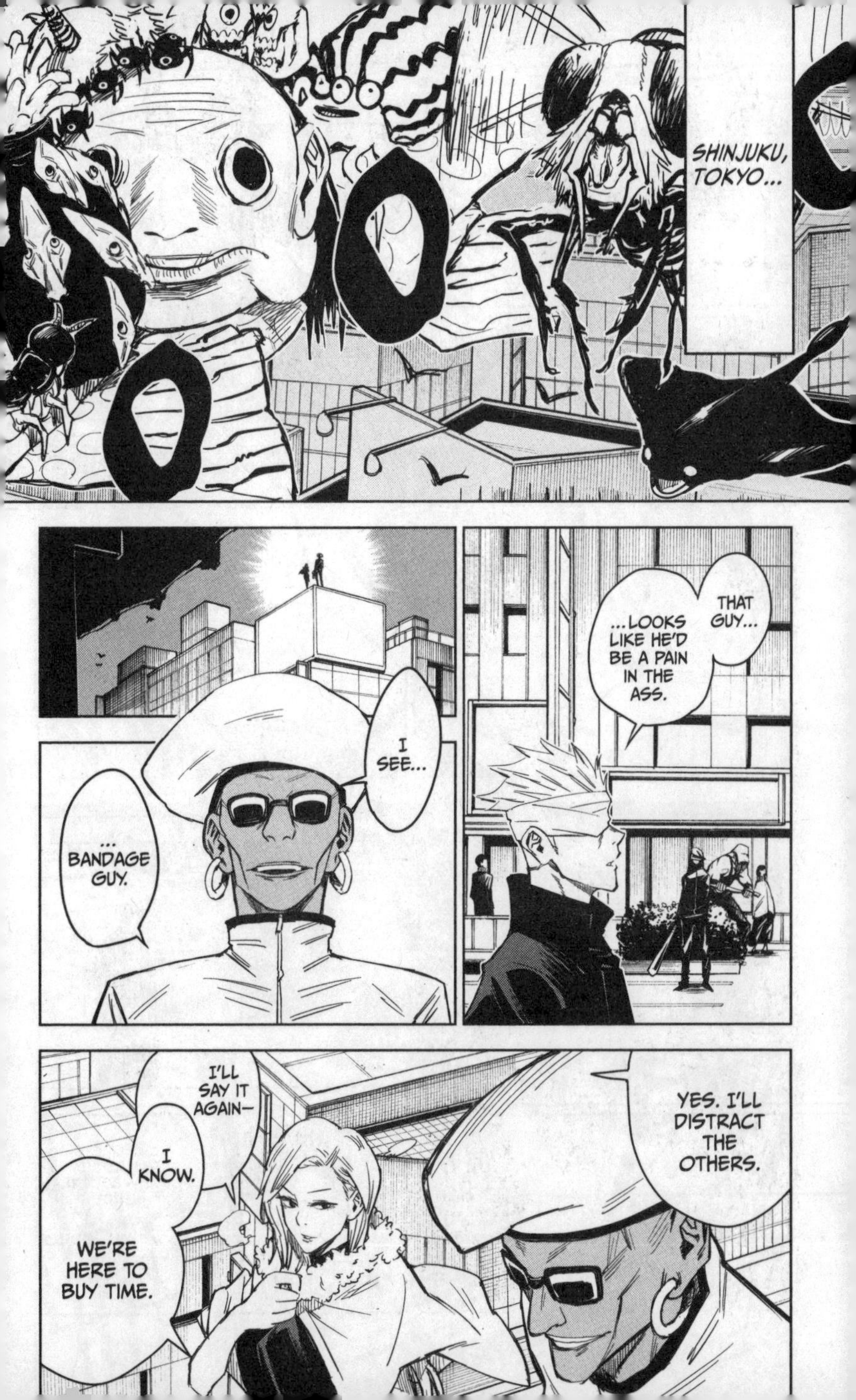
SHINJUKU, TOKYO...
THAT GUY...
...LOOKS LIKE HE'D BE A PAIN IN THE ASS.
I SEE...
...BANDAGE GUY.
YES. I'LL DISTRACT THE OTHERS.
I'LL SAY IT AGAIN—
I KNOW.
WE'RE HERE TO BUY TIME.

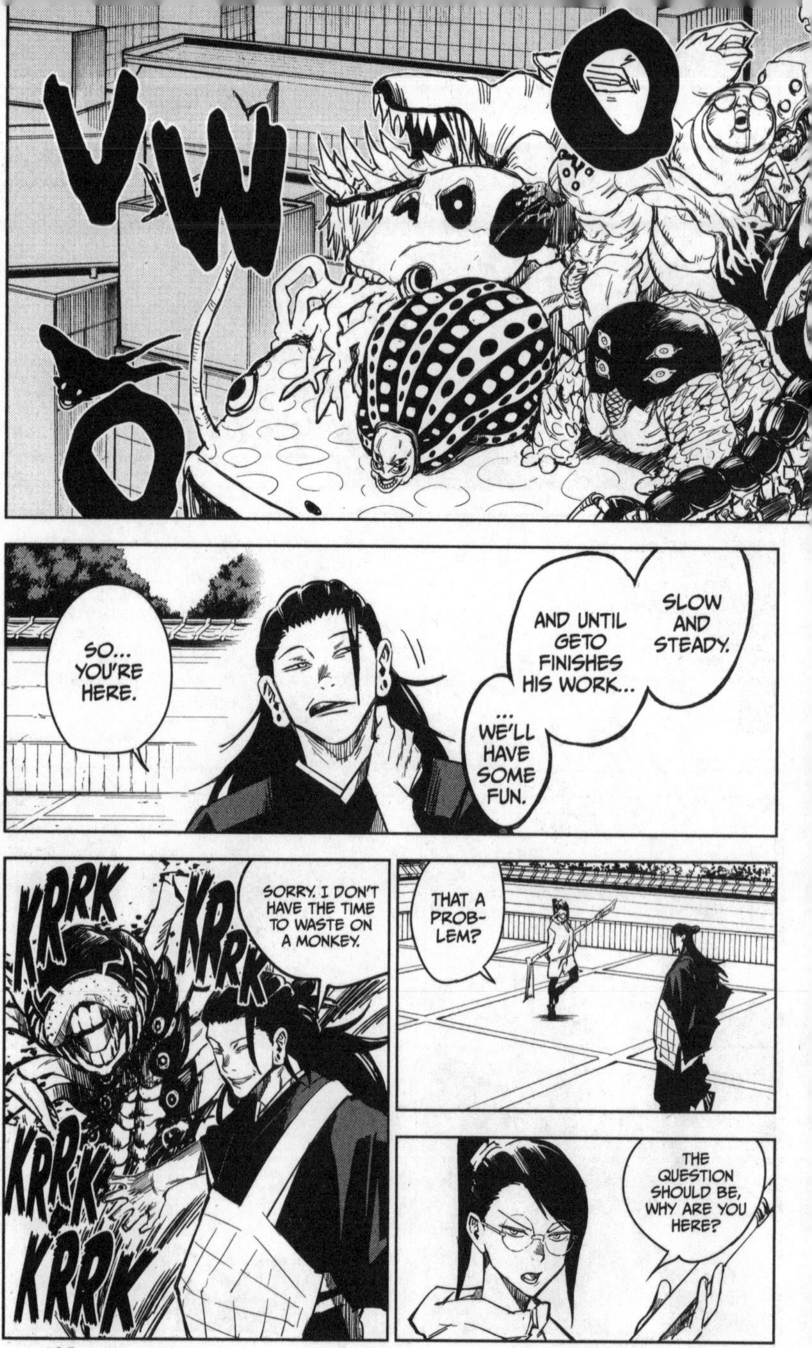
VWOO
SLOW AND STEADY.
AND UNTIL GETO FINISHES HIS WORK...
...WE'LL HAVE SOME FUN.
SO... YOU'RE HERE.
THAT A PROB-LEM?
THE QUESTION SHOULD BE, WHY ARE YOU HERE?
SORRY. I DON'T HAVE THE TIME TO WASTE ON A MONKEY.
KRRK KRRK
KRRK KRRK

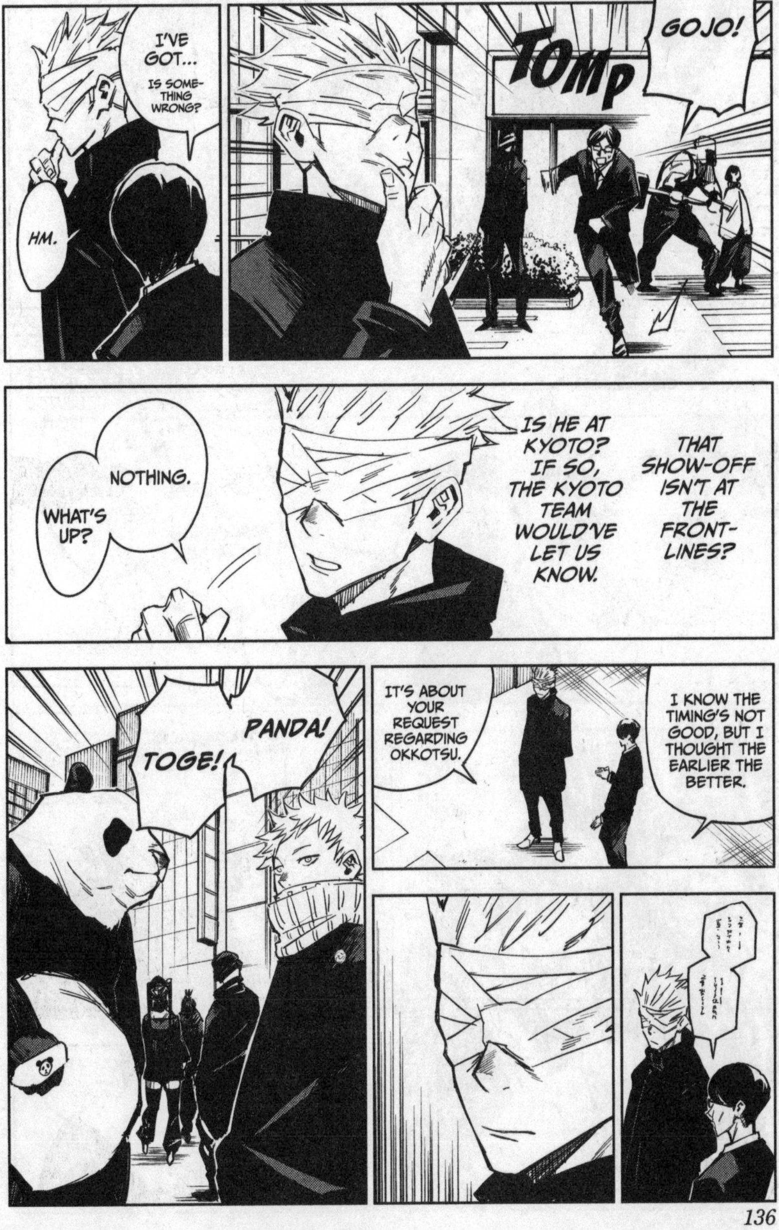
GOJO!
TOMP
I'VE GOT...
IS SOME-THING WRONG?
HM.
THAT SHOW-OFF ISN'T AT THE FRONT-LINES?
IS HE AT KYOTO? IF SO, THE KYOTO TEAM WOULD'VE LET US KNOW.
NOTHING.
WHAT'S UP?
I KNOW THE TIMING'S NOT GOOD, BUT I THOUGHT THE EARLIER THE BETTER.
IT'S ABOUT YOUR REQUEST REGARDING OKKOTSU.
PANDA!
TOGE!

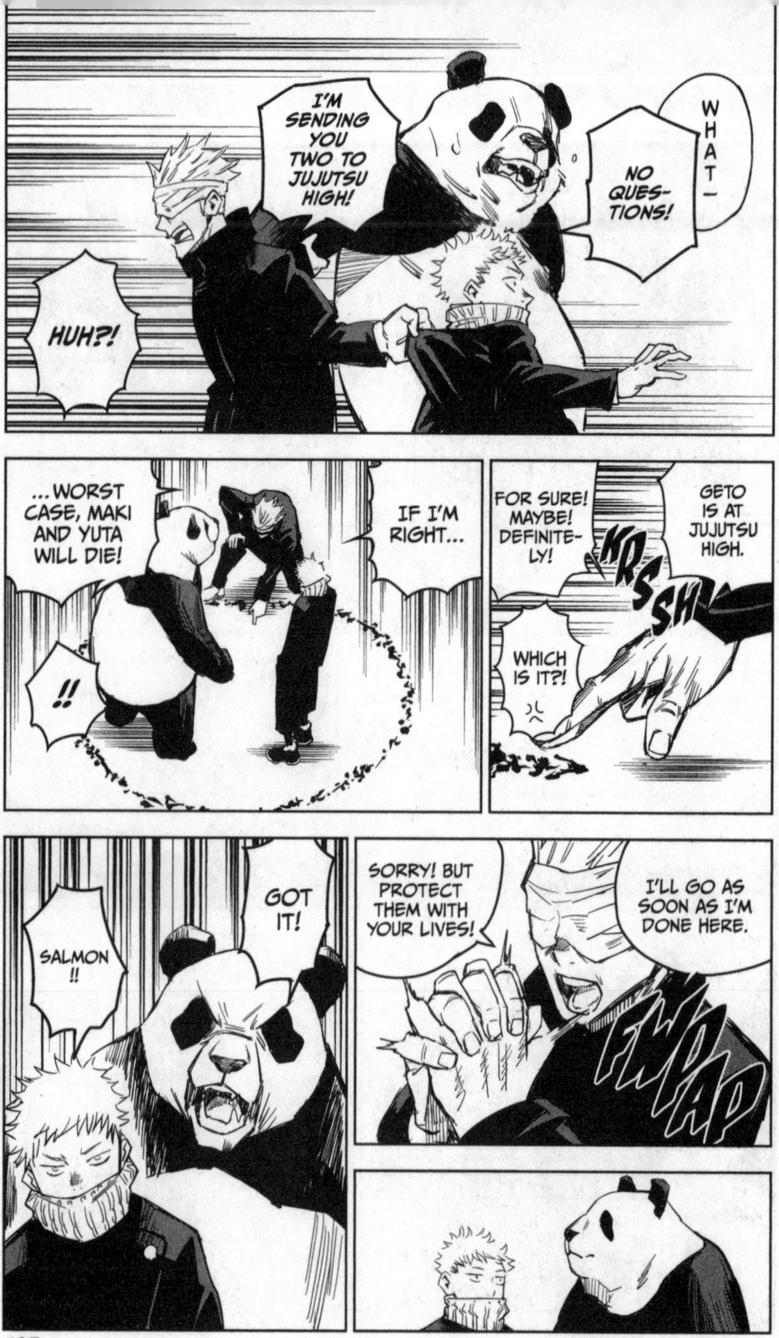
WHAT—
NO QUES-TIONS!
I'M SENDING YOU TWO TO JUJUTSU HIGH!
HUH?!
GETO IS AT JUJUTSU HIGH.
FOR SURE! MAYBE! DEFINITE-LY!
KRSSH
WHICH IS IT?!
IF I'M RIGHT...
...WORST CASE, MAKI AND YUTA WILL DIE!
!!
I'LL GO AS SOON AS I'M DONE HERE.
SORRY! BUT PROTECT THEM WITH YOUR LIVES!
FWAP
GOT IT!
SALMON !!

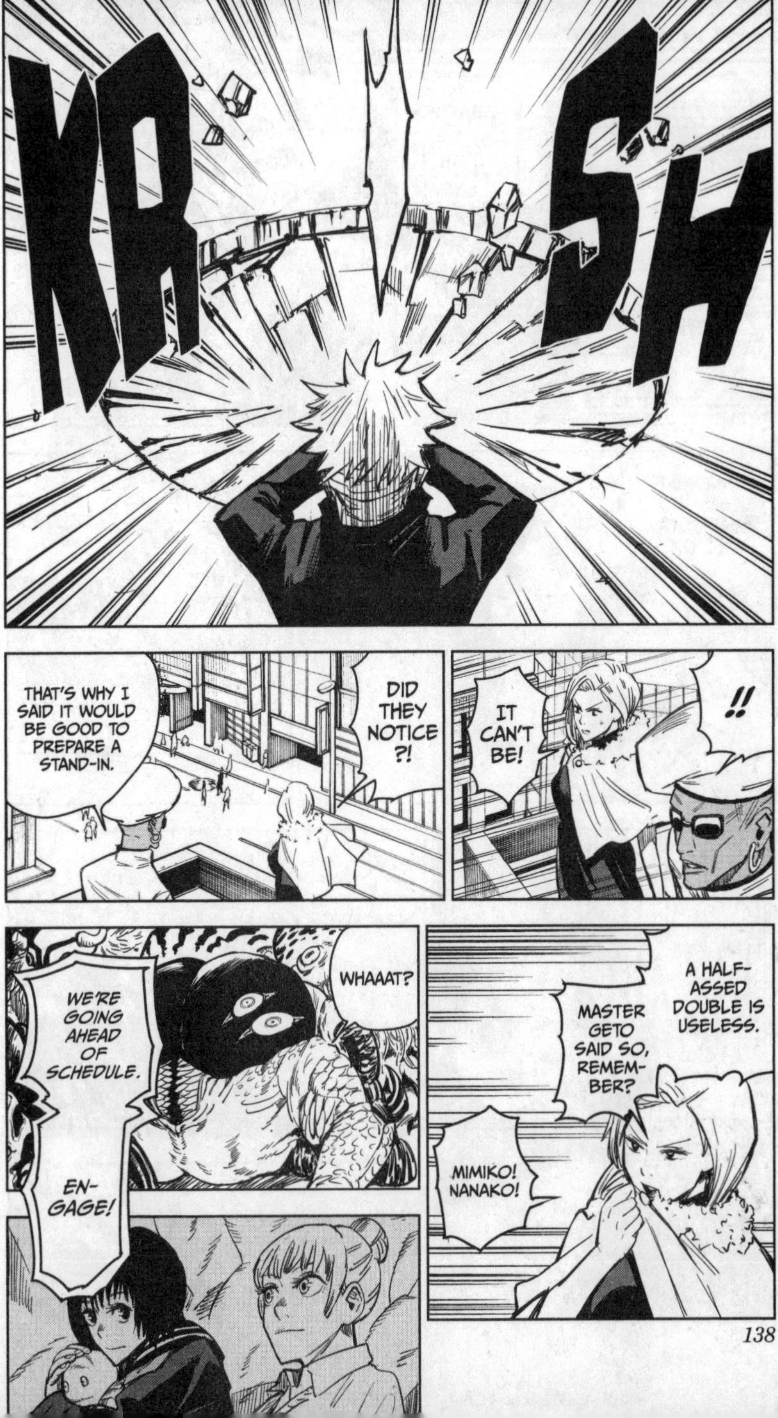
KR
SH
!!
IT CAN'T BE!
DID THEY NOTICE?!
THAT'S WHY I SAID IT WOULD BE GOOD TO PREPARE A STAND-IN.
A HALF-ASSED DOUBLE IS USELESS.
MASTER GETO SAID SO, REMEMBER?
MIMIKO! NANAKO!
WHAAAT?
WE'RE GOING AHEAD OF SCHEDULE.
EN-GAGE!

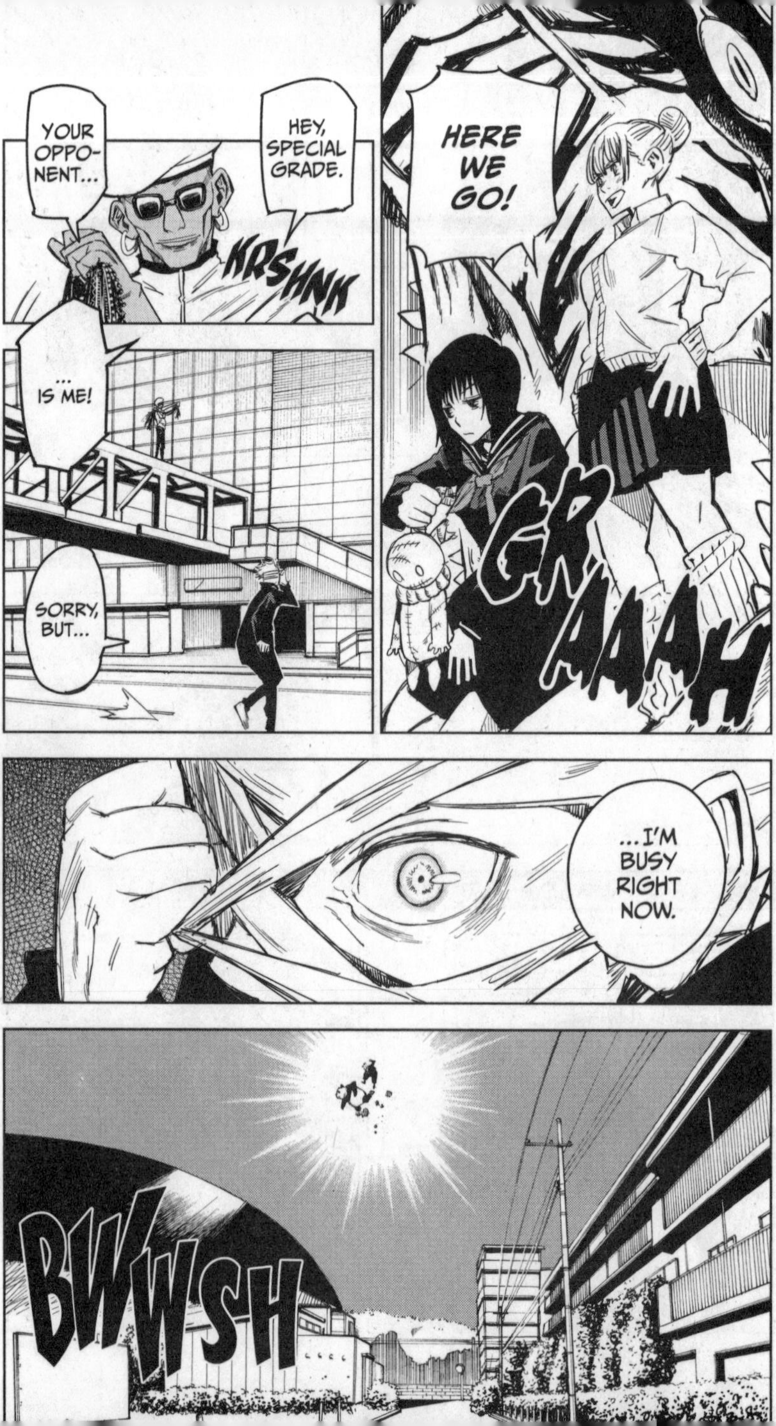
HERE WE GO!
GRAAAH
HEY, SPECIAL GRADE.
YOUR OPPONENT...
KRSHNK
... IS ME!
SORRY, BUT...
...I'M BUSY RIGHT NOW.
BWWSH

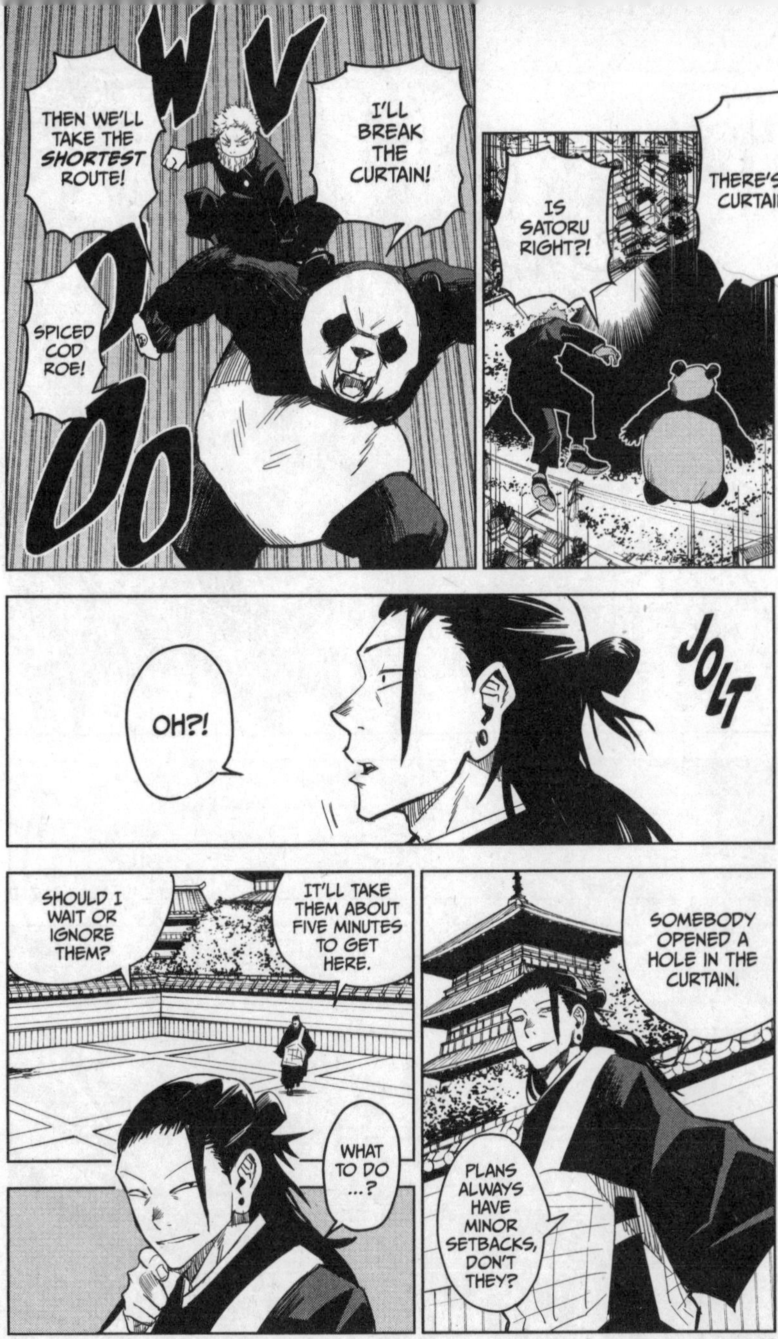
THERE'S A CURTAIN!
IS SATORU RIGHT?!
WV
I'LL BREAK THE CURTAIN!
THEN WE'LL TAKE THE SHORTEST ROUTE!
SPICED COD ROE!
DOO
JOLT
OH?!
SOMEBODY OPENED A HOLE IN THE CURTAIN.
PLANS ALWAYS HAVE MINOR SETBACKS, DON'T THEY?
IT'LL TAKE THEM ABOUT FIVE MINUTES TO GET HERE.
SHOULD I WAIT OR IGNORE THEM?
WHAT TO DO ...?

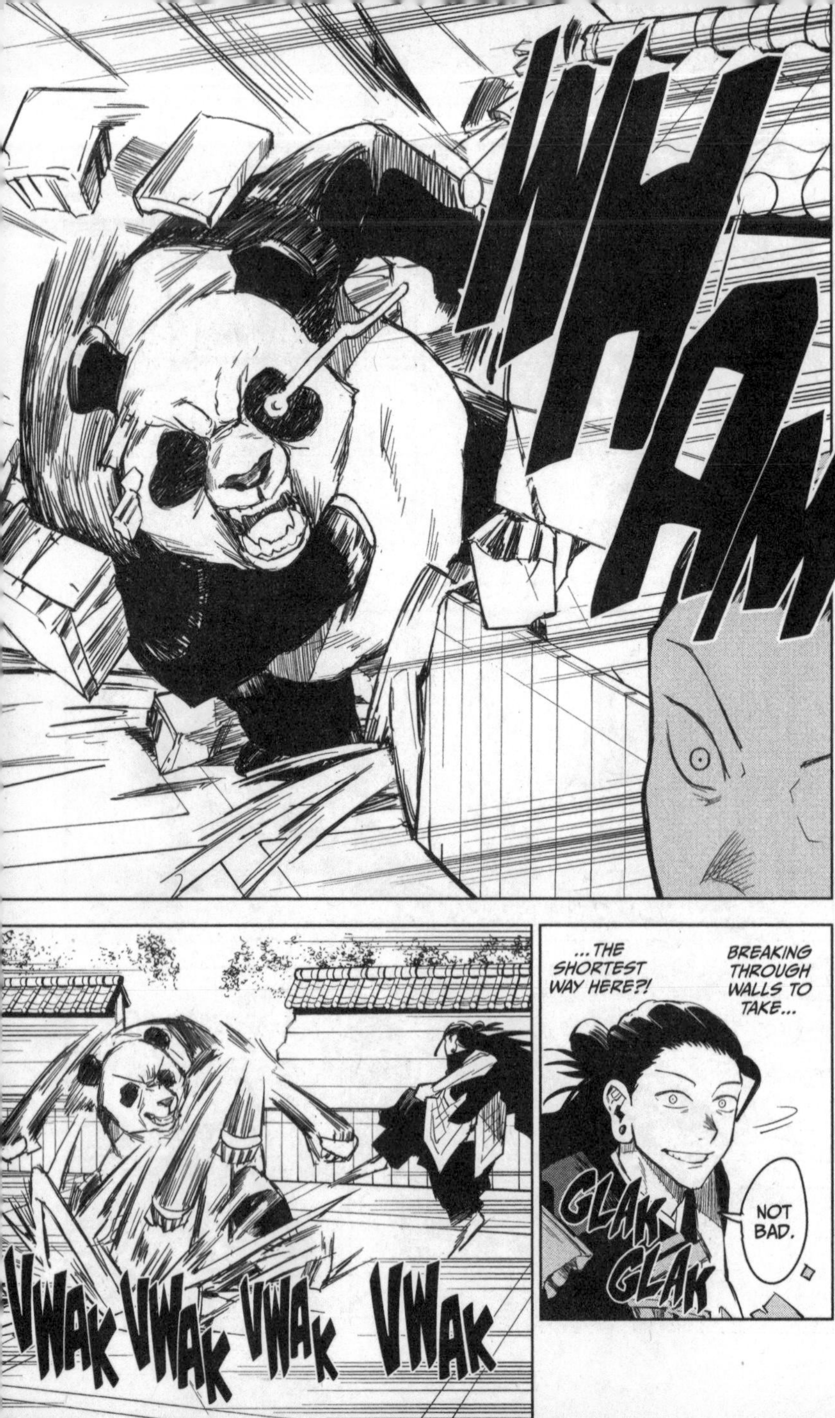
WHAM
BREAKING THROUGH WALLS TO TAKE...
...THE SHORTEST WAY HERE?!
GLAK GLAK
NOT BAD.
VWAK VWAK VWAK VWAK

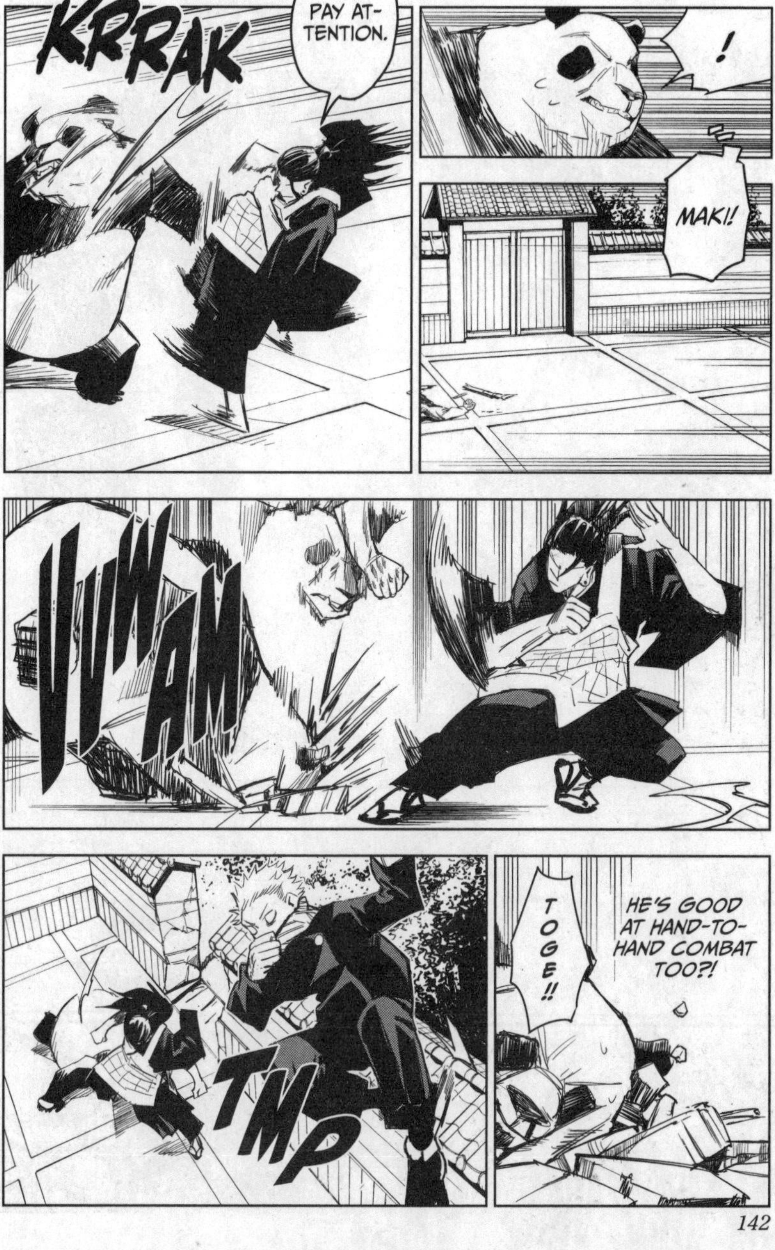
!
MAKI!
KRRAK
PAY AT-TENTION.
VWAM
HE'S GOOD AT HAND-TO-HAND COMBAT TOO?!
TOGE!!
TMP

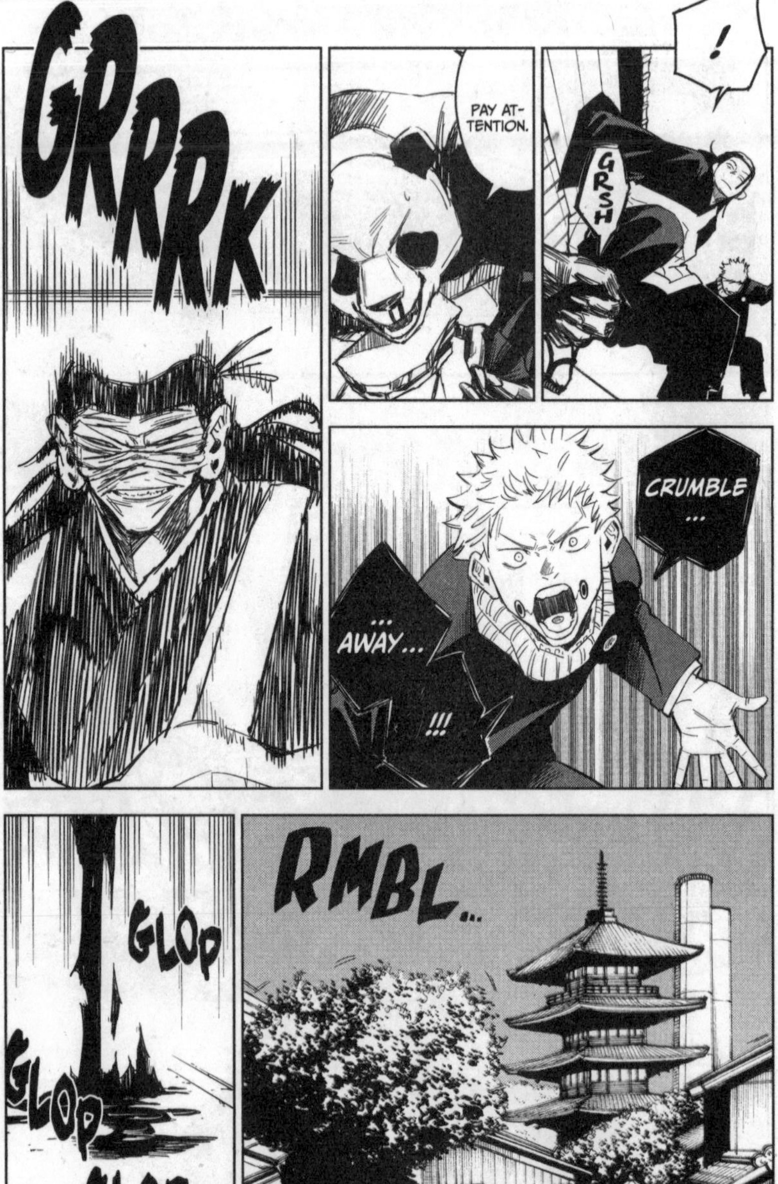
!
GRSH
PAY AT-
TENTION.
CRUMBLE
...
...
AWAY...
!!!
GRRRK
RMBL..
GLOP
GLOP
GLOP

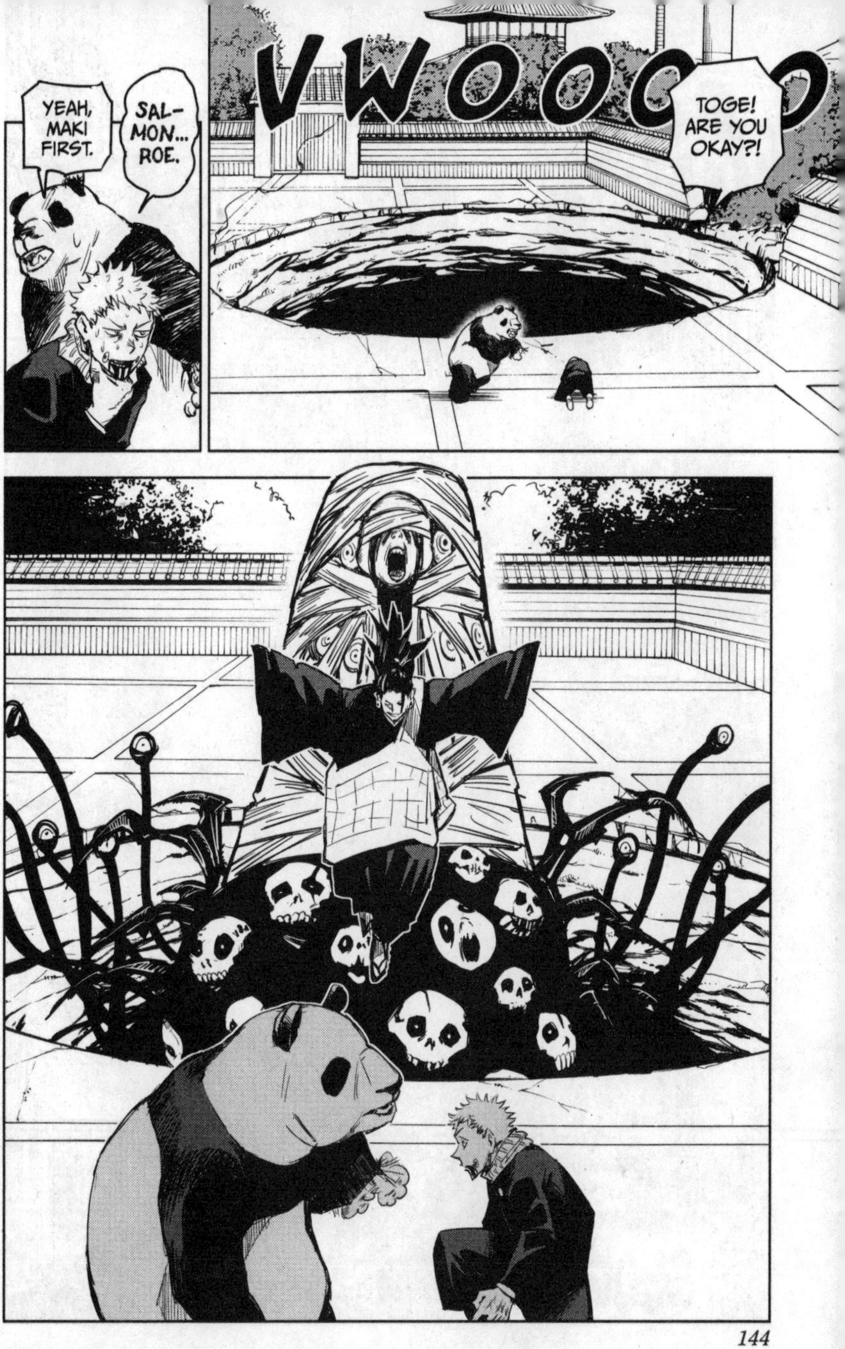
VWOOOO
TOGE! ARE YOU OKAY?!
SAL-MON... ROE.
YEAH, MAKI FIRST.

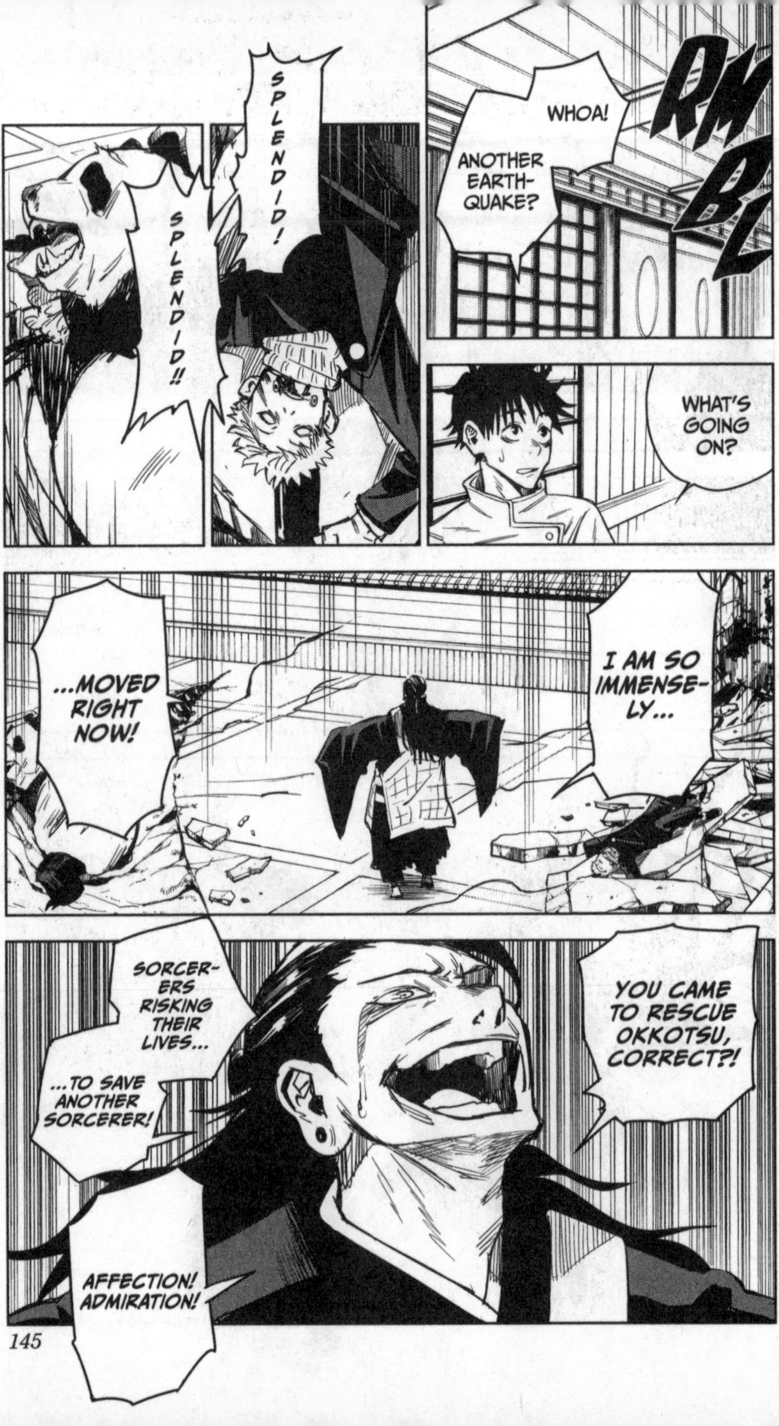
RMBL
WHOA!
ANOTHER EARTH-QUAKE?
WHAT'S GOING ON?
SPLENDID!
SPLENDID!!
I AM SO IMMENSE-LY...
...MOVED RIGHT NOW!
YOU CAME TO RESCUE OKKOTSU, CORRECT?!
SORCERERS RISKING THEIR LIVES...
...TO SAVE ANOTHER SORCERER!
AFFECTION! ADMIRATION!

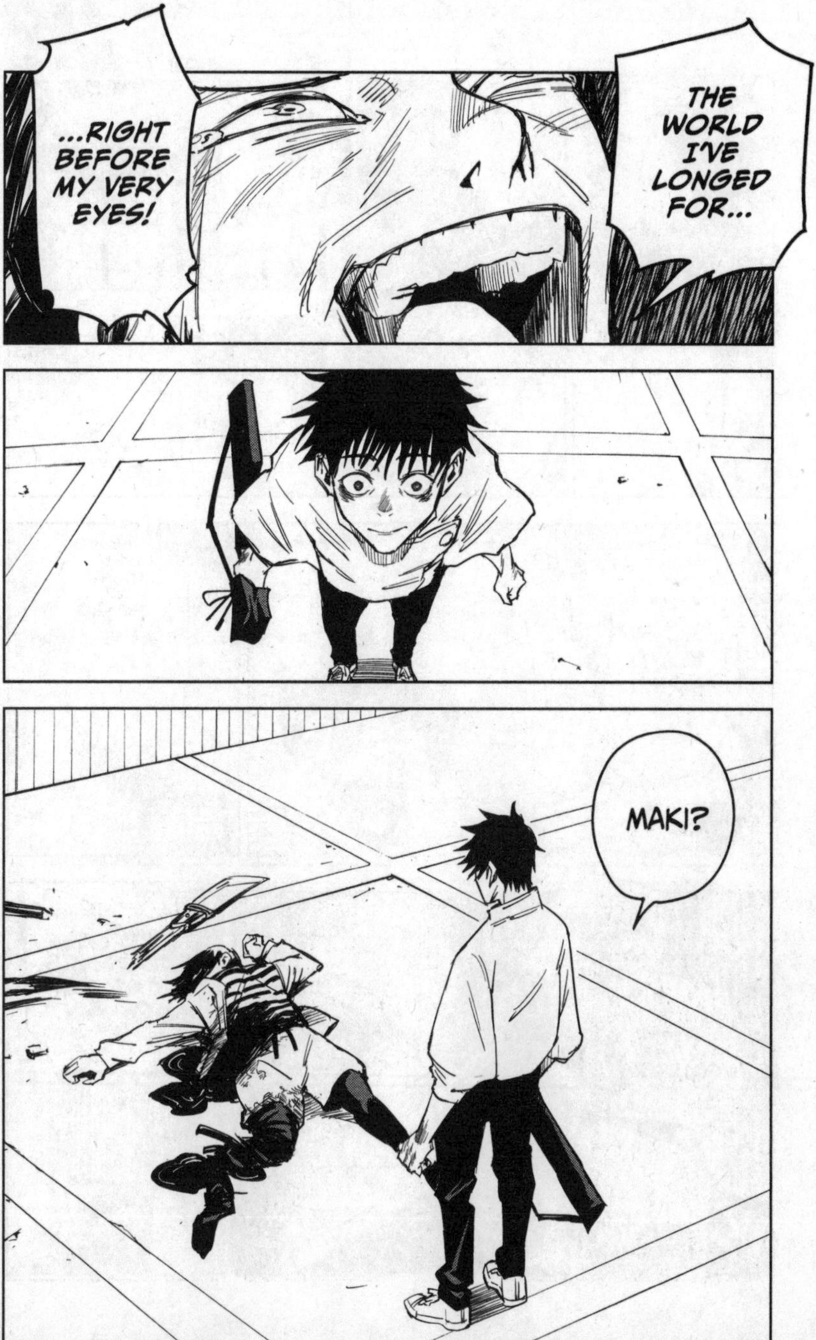
THE WORLD I'VE LONGED FOR...
...RIGHT BEFORE MY VERY EYES!
MAKI?

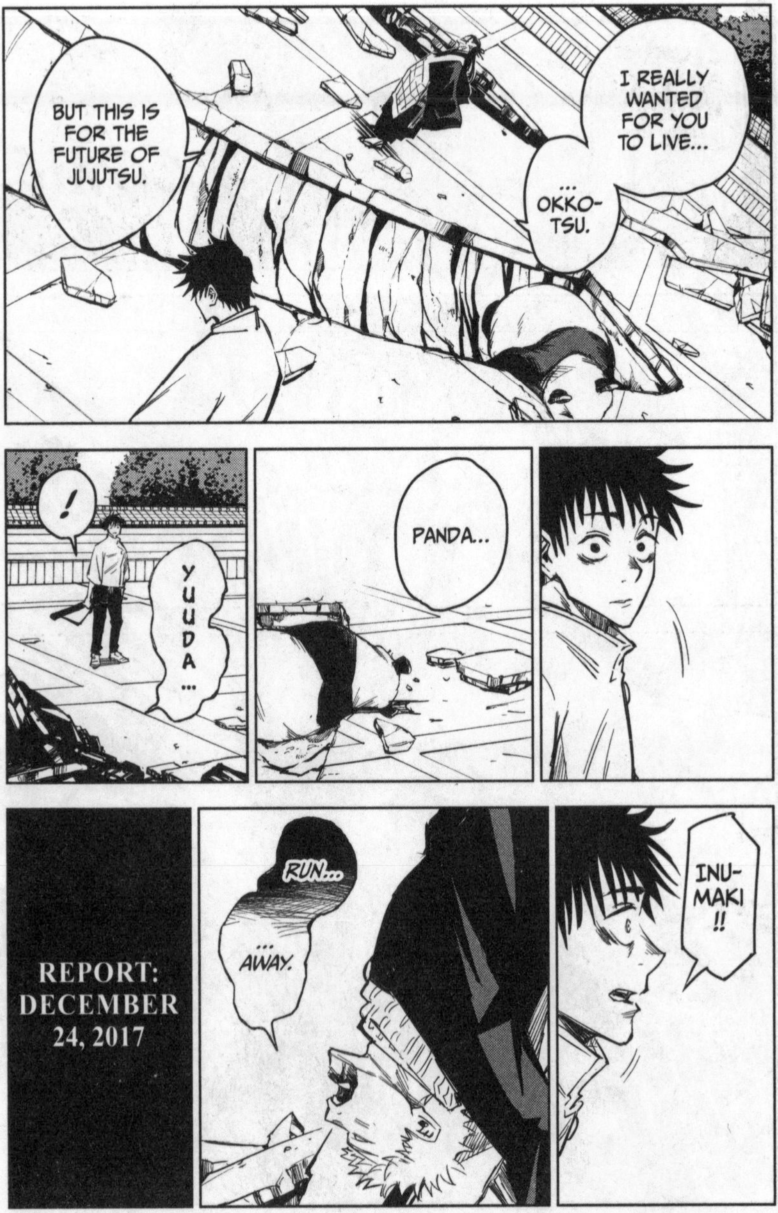
I REALLY WANTED FOR YOU TO LIVE...
...OKKOTSU.
BUT THIS IS FOR THE FUTURE OF JUJUTSU.
PANDA...
!
YUUDA...
INUMAKI!!
RUN...
...AWAY.
REPORT: DECEMBER 24, 2017

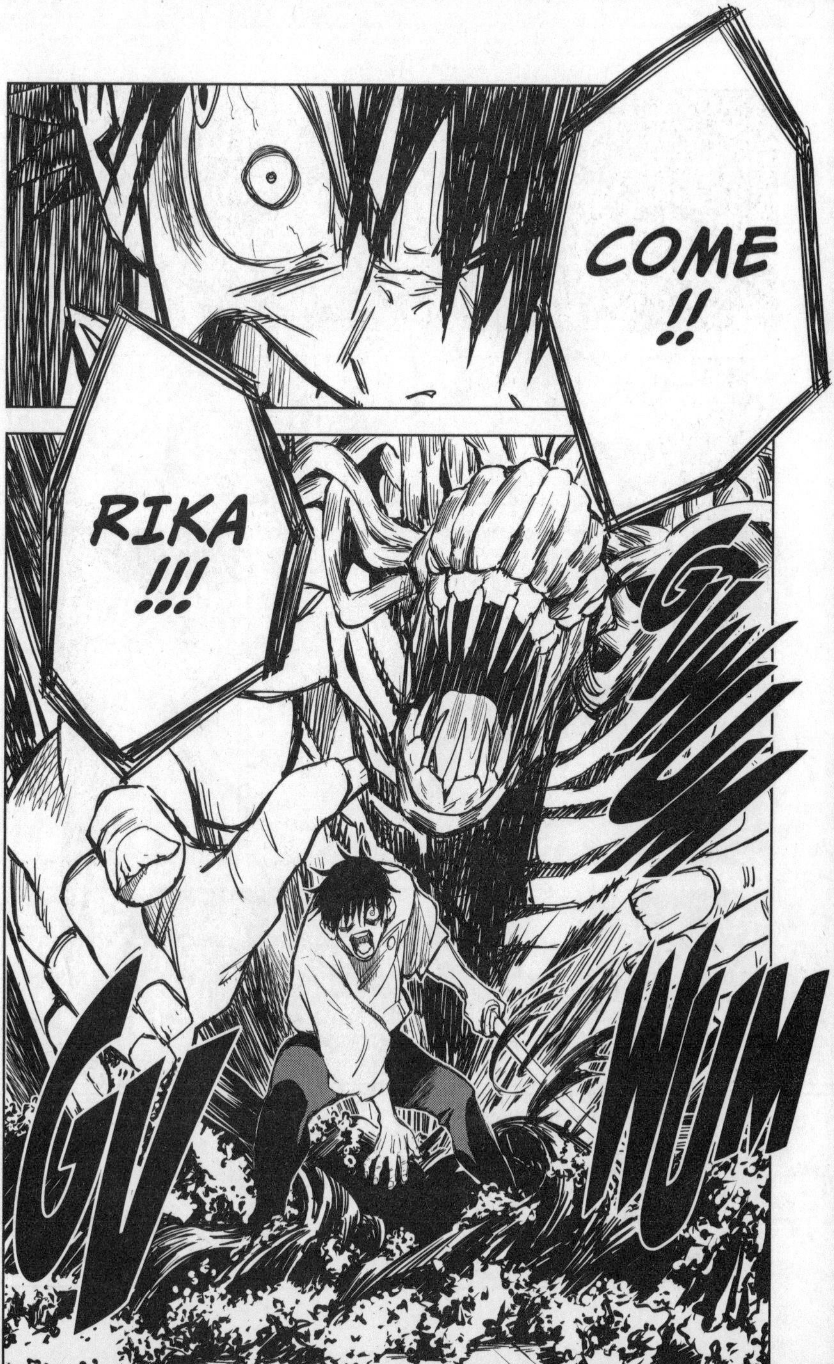
COME !!
RIKA !!!

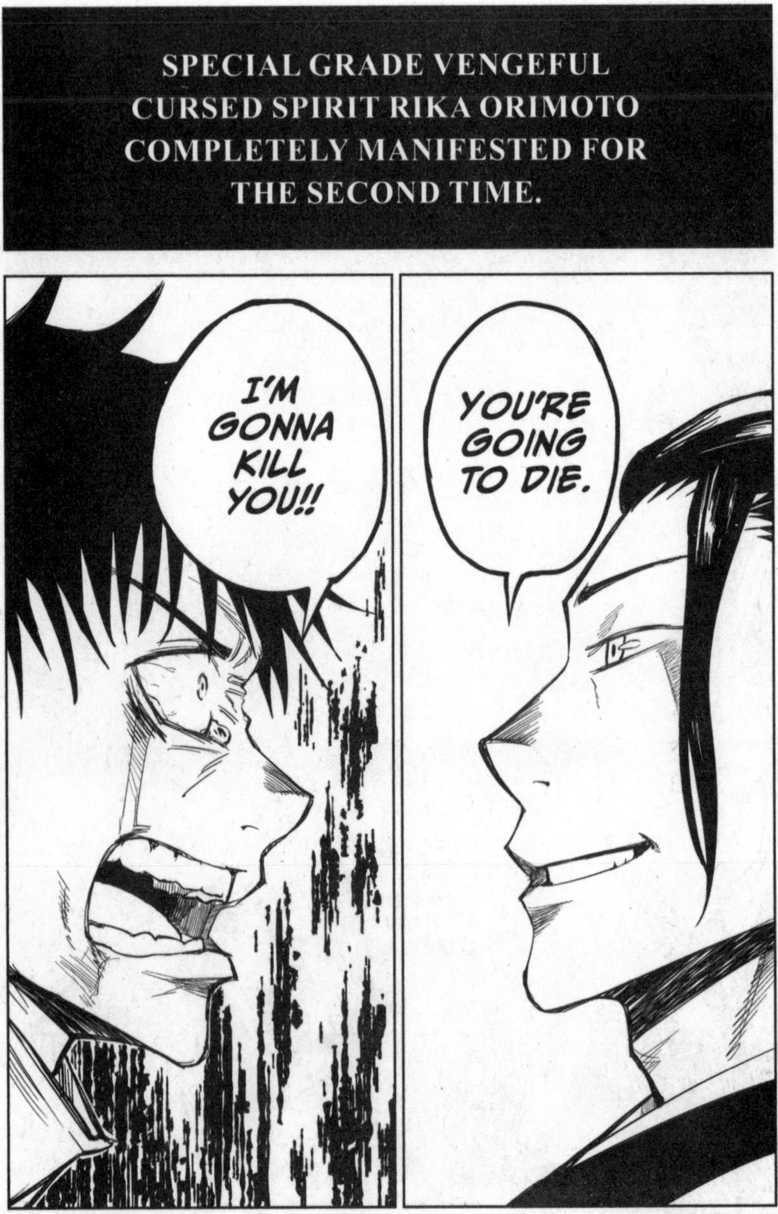
SPECIAL GRADE VENGEFUL CURSED SPIRIT RIKA ORIMOTO COMPLETELY MANIFESTED FOR THE SECOND TIME.
YOU'RE GOING TO DIE.
I'M GONNA KILL YOU!!

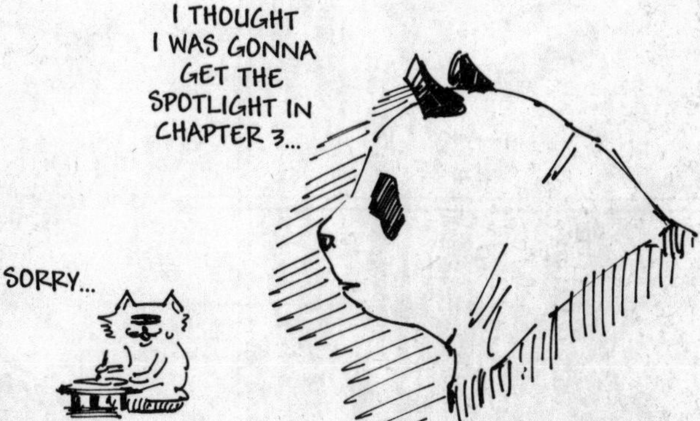
I THOUGHT I WAS GONNA GET THE SPOTLIGHT IN CHAPTER 3...
SORRY...

Final Chapter: Bright Darkness

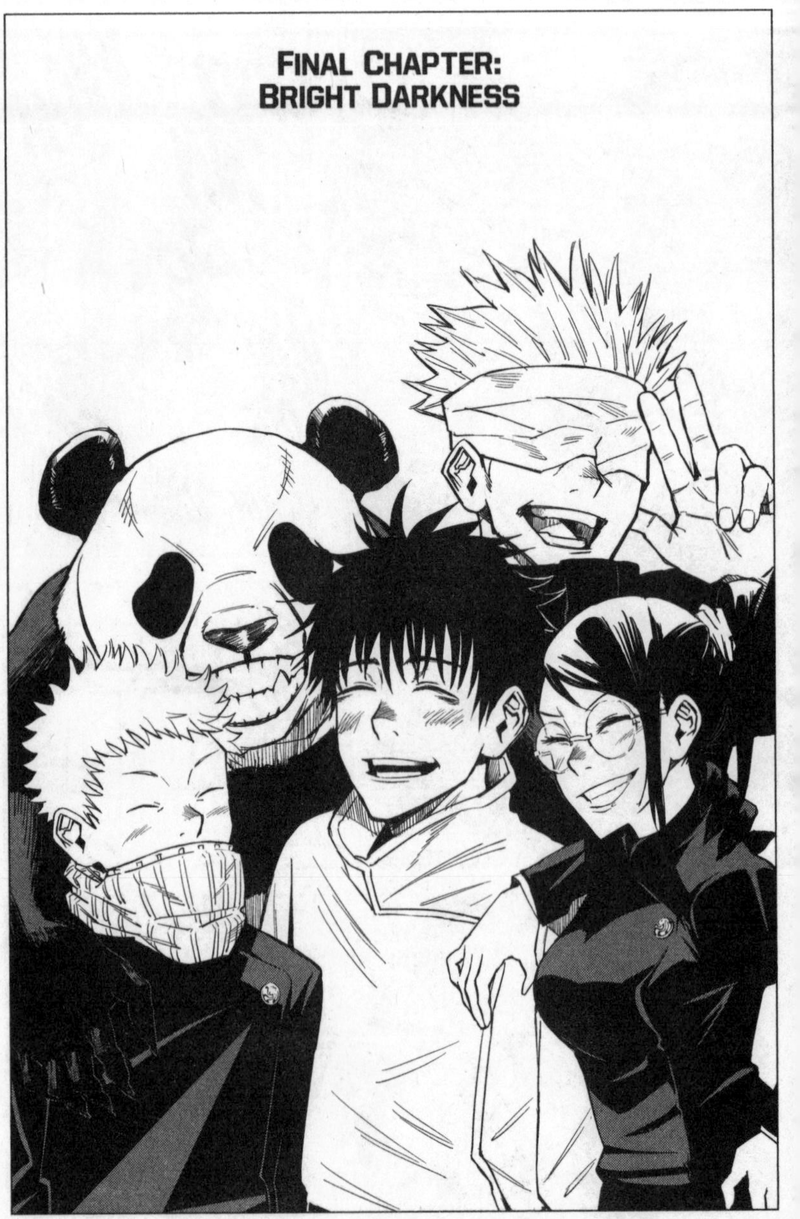

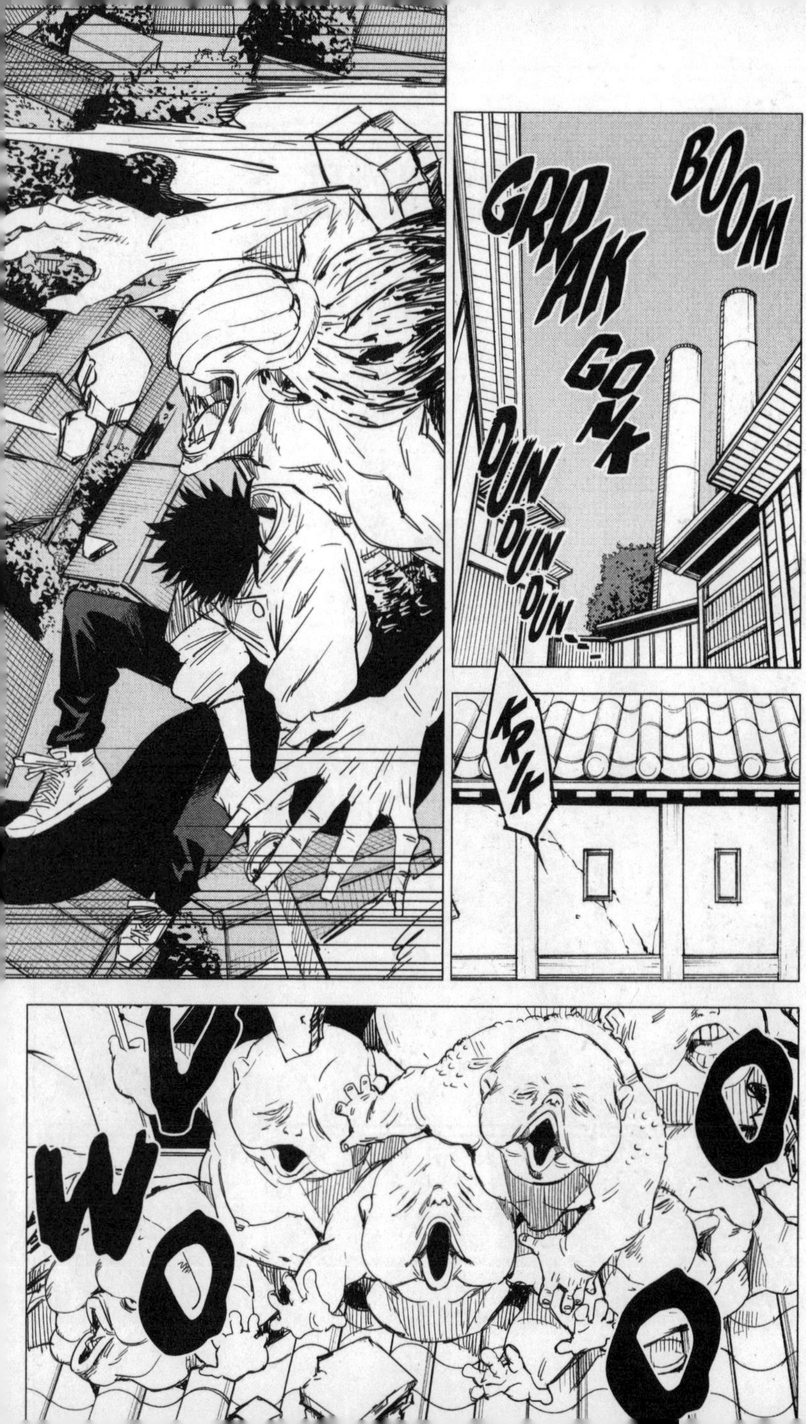
BOOM
GRRAK
GONK
DUN DUN DUN DUN...
KRIK
WOOO

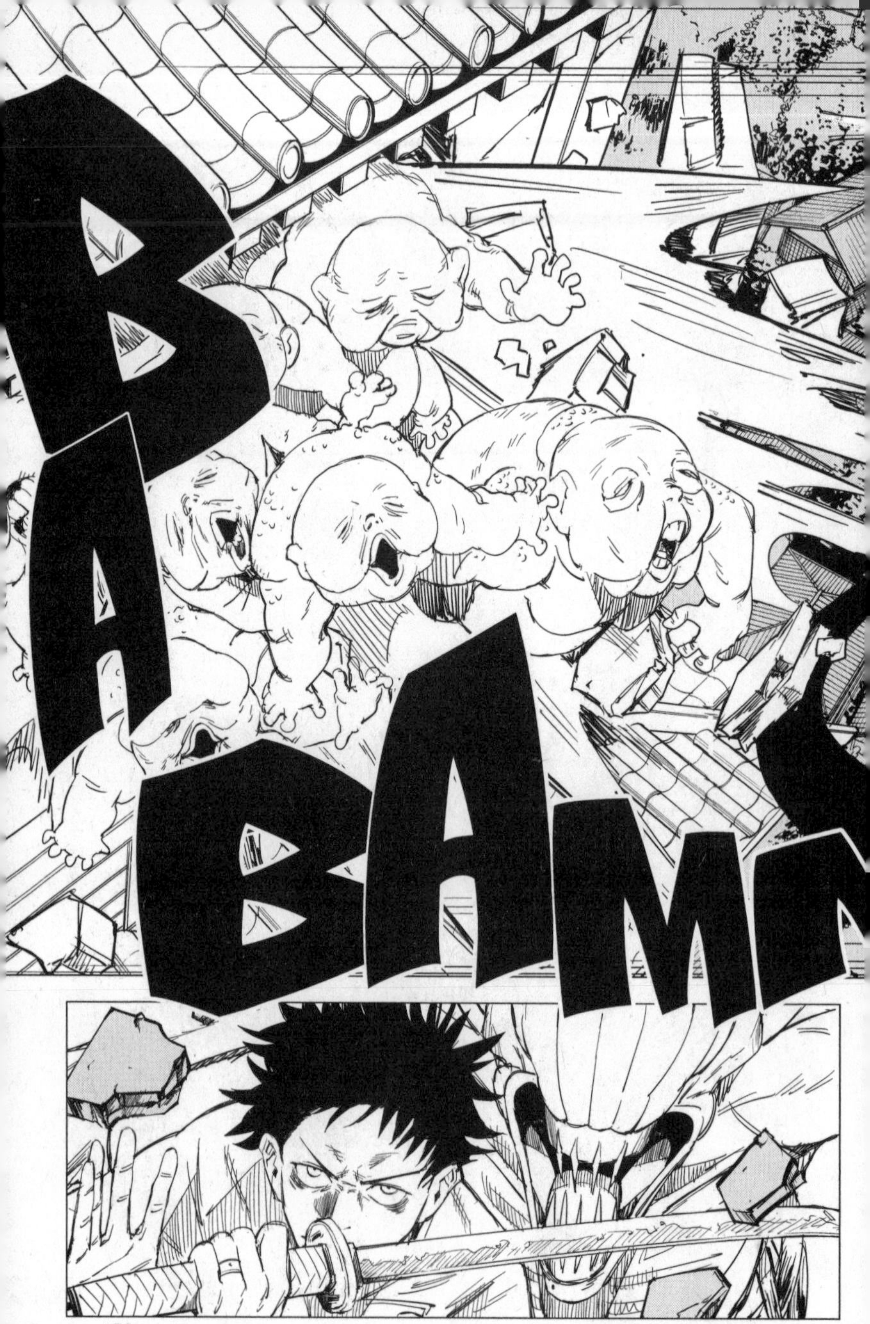
BA
BAM

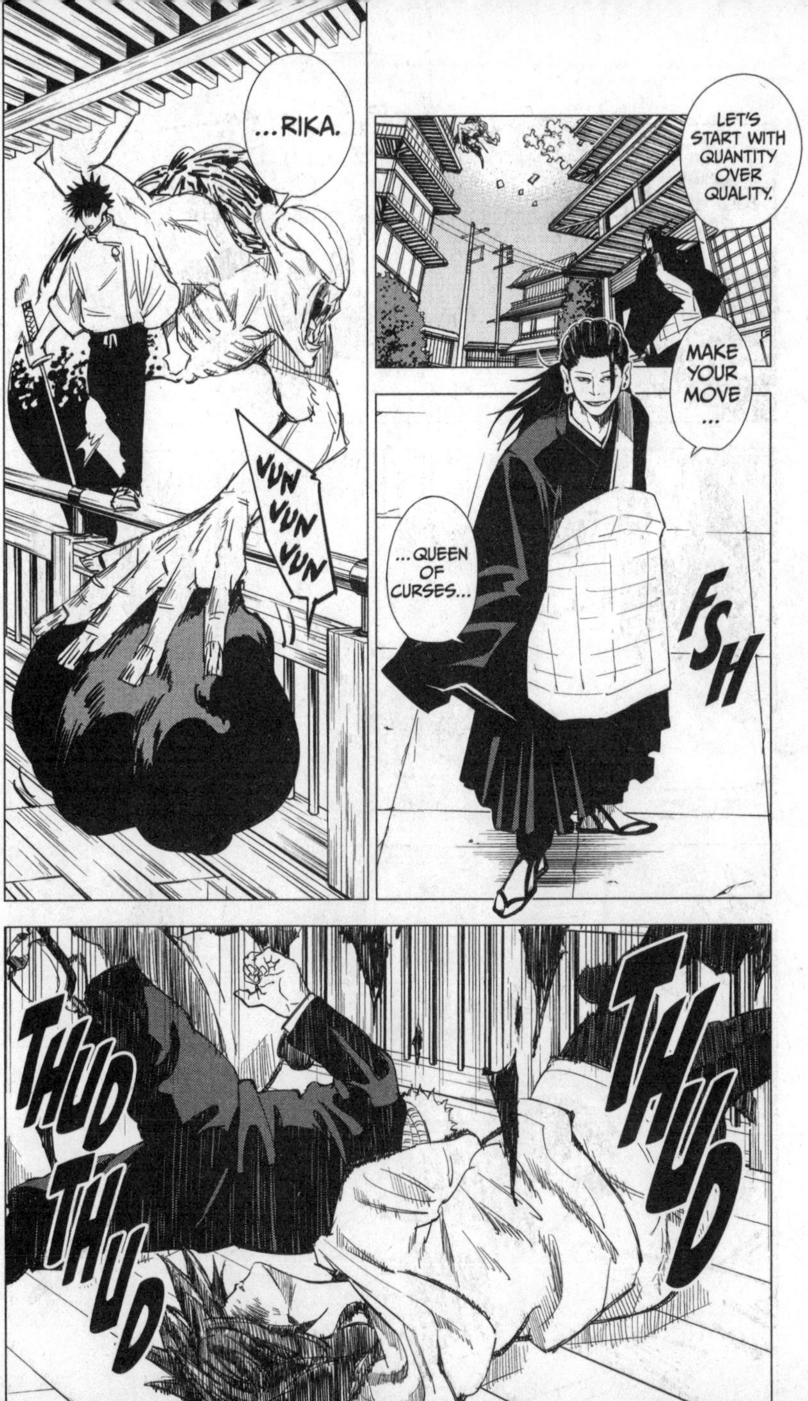
LET'S START WITH QUANTITY OVER QUALITY.
MAKE YOUR MOVE ...
...QUEEN OF CURSES...
FSH
...RIKA.
VUN VUN VUN
THUD
THUD THUD

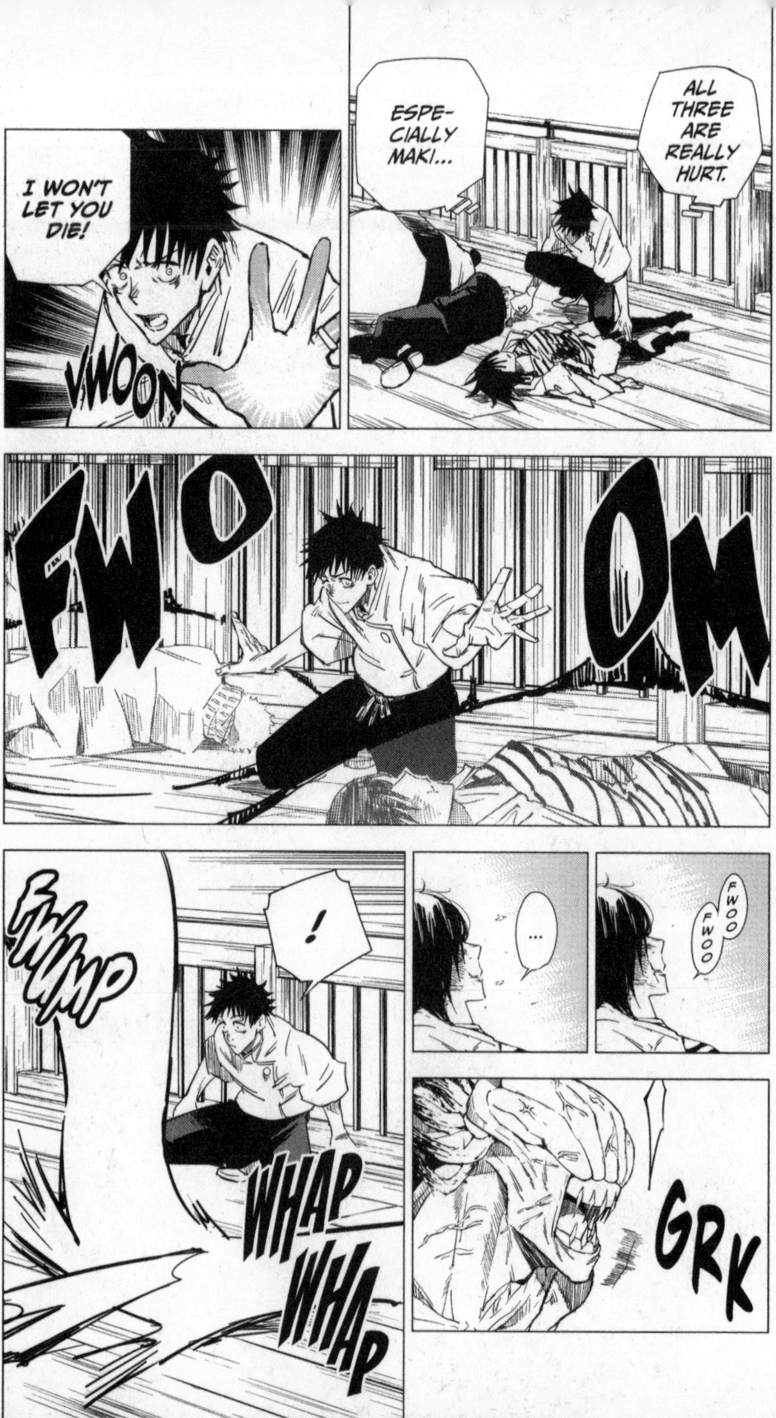
ALL THREE ARE REALLY HURT.
ESPE-CIALLY MAKI...
I WON'T LET YOU DIE!
VWOON
FWOOM
FWOO FWOO
...
GRK
!
FWUMP
WHAP WHAP

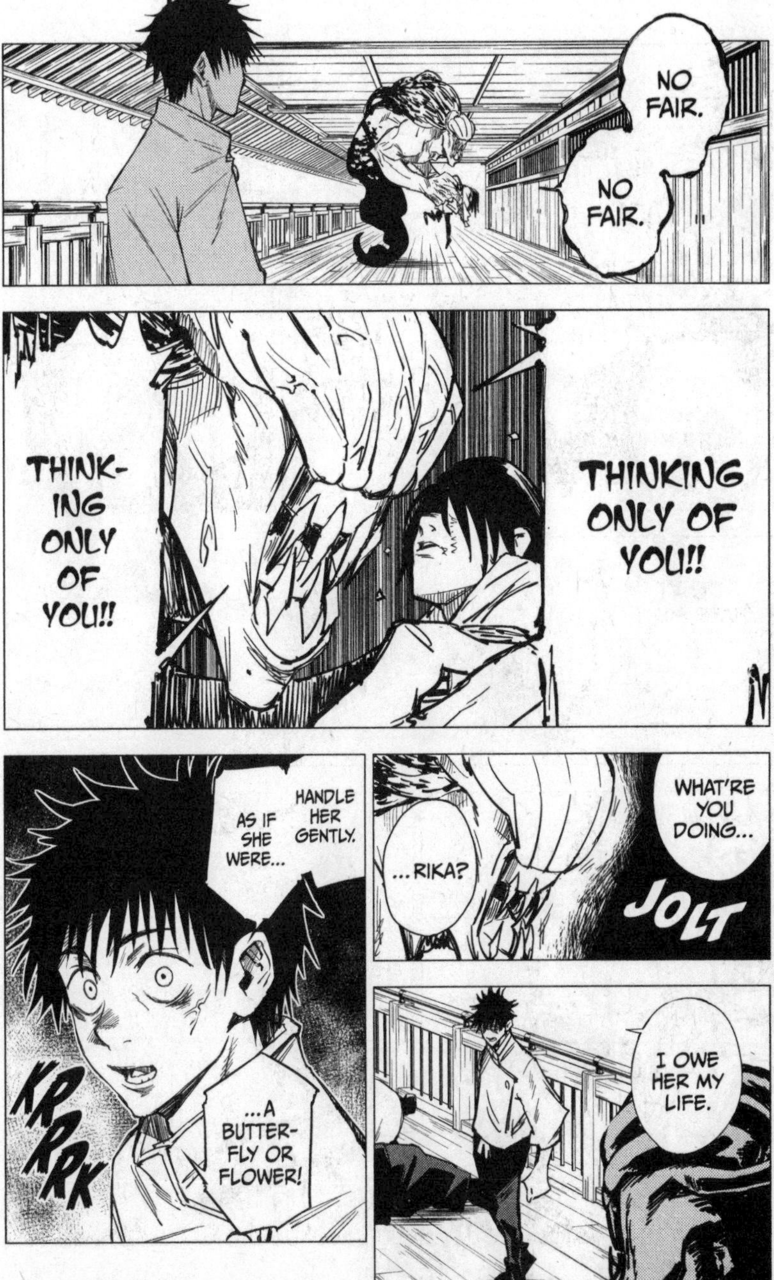
NO FAIR.
NO FAIR.
THINKING ONLY OF YOU!!
THINK-ING ONLY OF YOU!!
WHAT'RE YOU DOING...
JOLT
...RIKA?
I OWE HER MY LIFE.
HANDLE HER GENTLY.
AS IF SHE WERE...
...A BUTTER-FLY OR FLOWER!
KRRRK

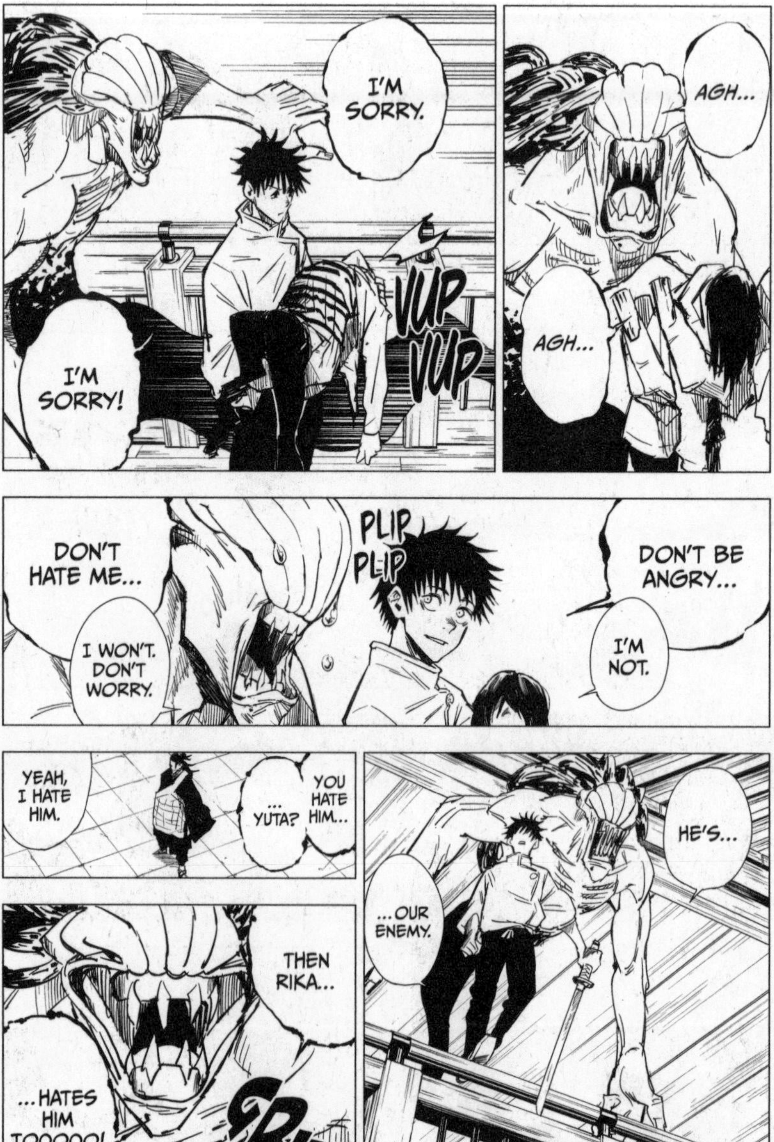
AGH...
AGH...
I'M SORRY.
VUP VUP
I'M SORRY!
DON'T BE ANGRY...
I'M NOT.
PLIP PLIP
DON'T HATE ME...
I WON'T. DON'T WORRY.
HE'S...
...OUR ENEMY.
YOU HATE HIM...
... YUTA?
YEAH, I HATE HIM.
THEN RIKA...
...HATES HIM TOOOOO!
GRIN

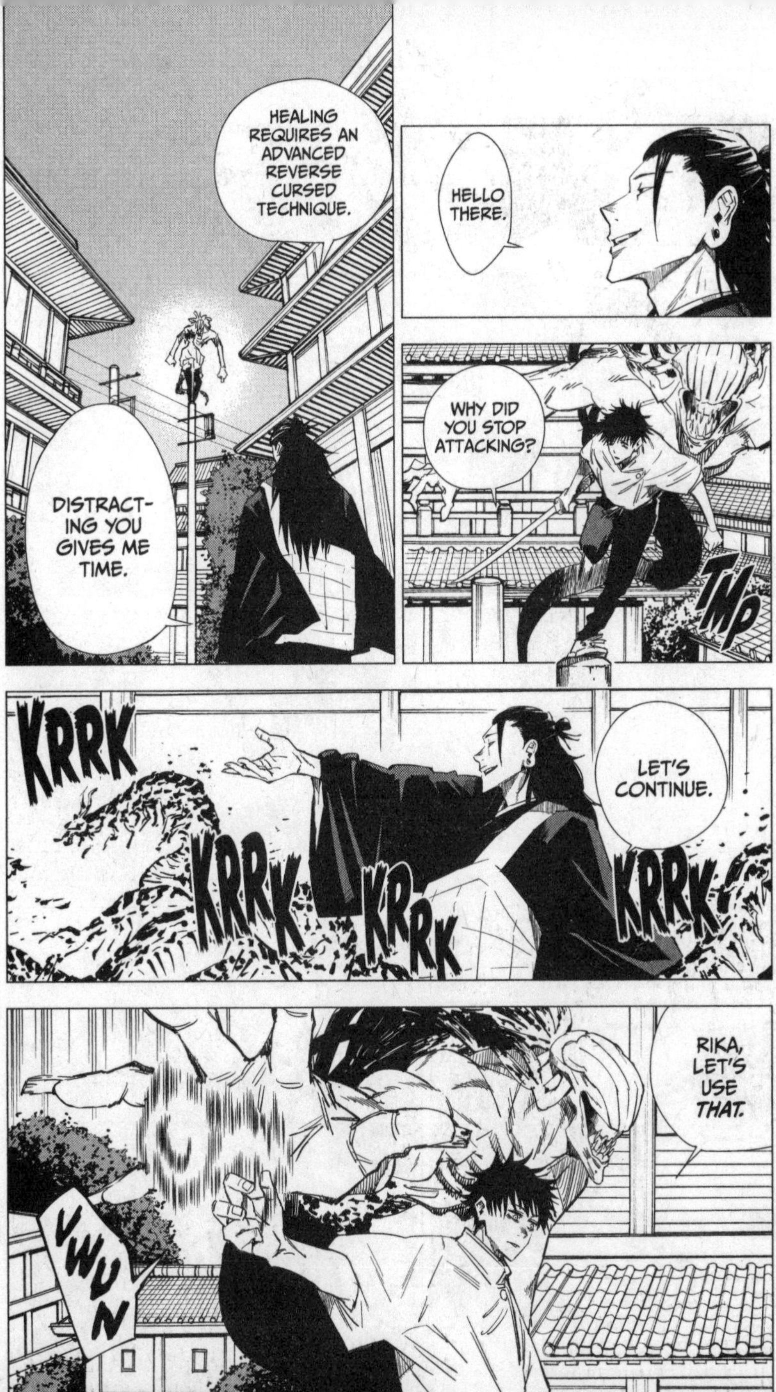
HELLO THERE.
WHY DID YOU STOP ATTACKING?
TMP
HEALING REQUIRES AN ADVANCED REVERSE CURSED TECHNIQUE.
DISTRACTING YOU GIVES ME TIME.
LET'S CONTINUE.
KRRK
KRRK
KRRK
KRRK
RIKA, LET'S USE *THAT.*
VWUN

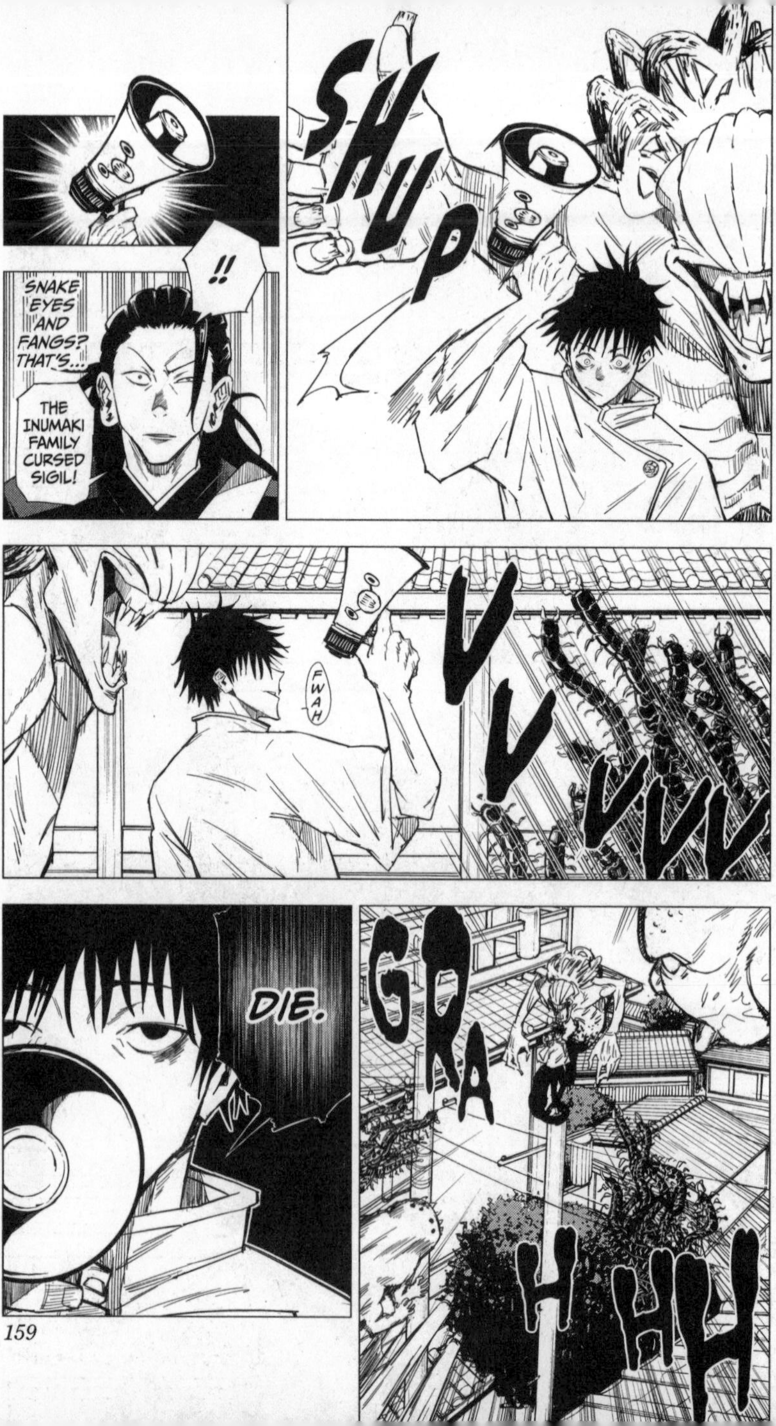
SHUP
!!
SNAKE EYES AND FANGS? THAT'S...
THE INUMAKI FAMILY CURSED SIGIL!
VVVVVV
FWAH
GRAHHHH
DIE.

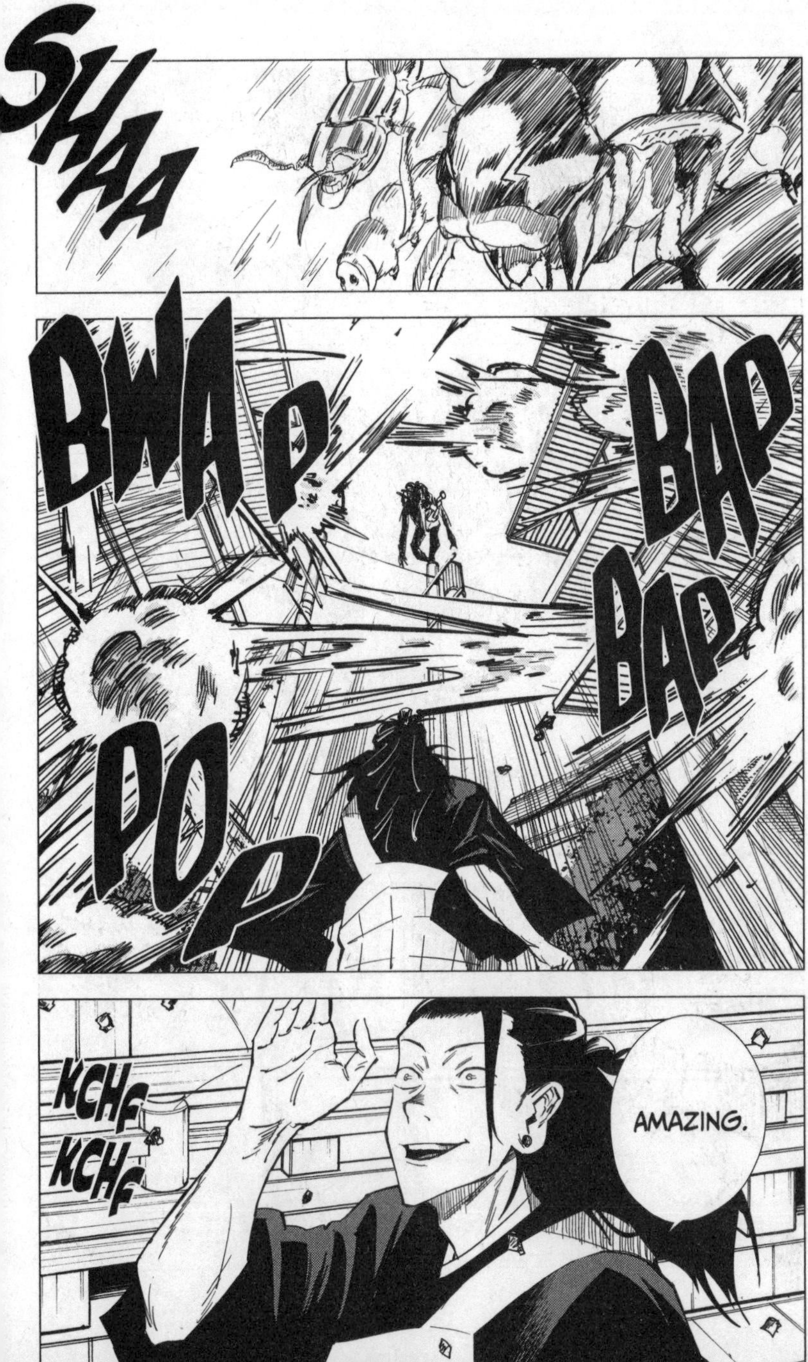
SHAA
BAP
BAP
BWAP
POP
AMAZING.
KCHF
KCHF

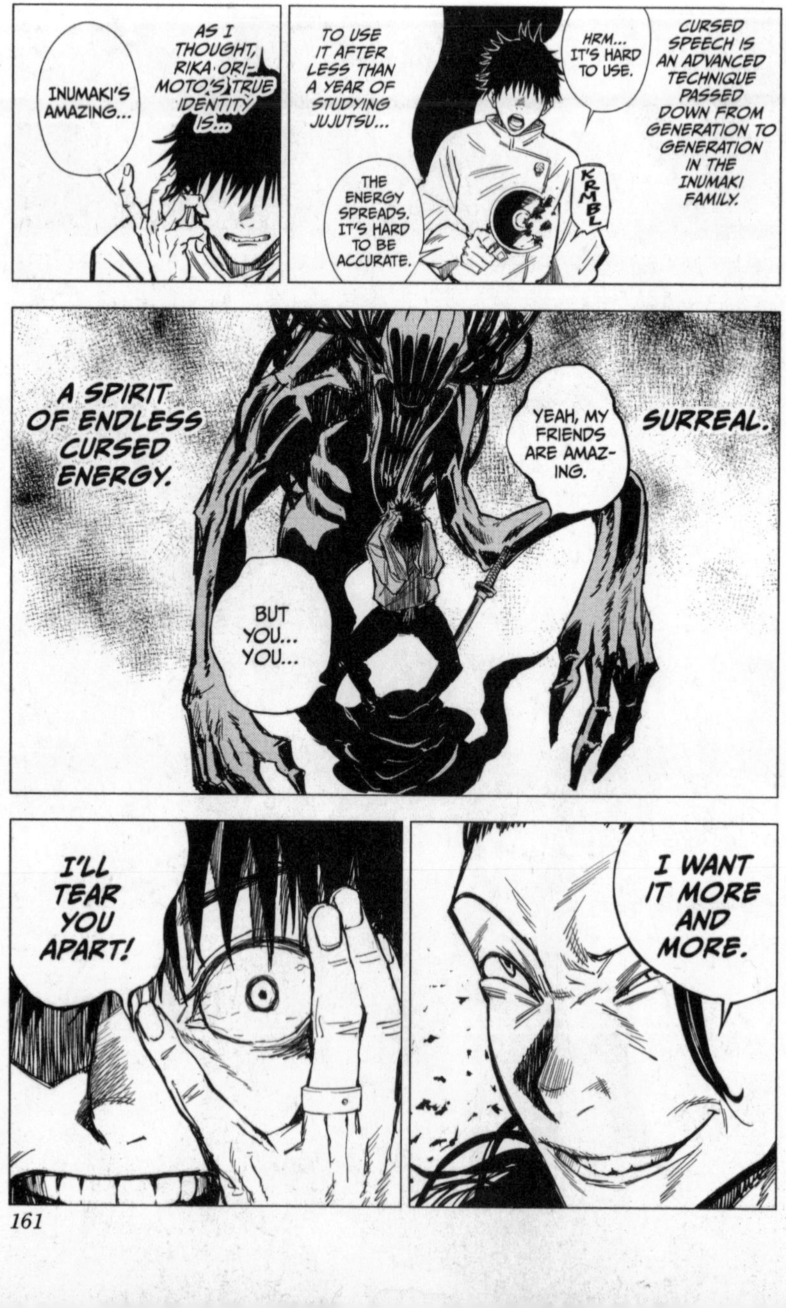
CURSED SPEECH IS AN ADVANCED TECHNIQUE PASSED DOWN FROM GENERATION TO GENERATION IN THE INUMAKI FAMILY.
HRM... IT'S HARD TO USE.
KRMBL
TO USE IT AFTER LESS THAN A YEAR OF STUDYING JUJUTSU...
THE ENERGY SPREADS. IT'S HARD TO BE ACCURATE.
AS I THOUGHT, RIKA ORI-MOTO'S TRUE IDENTITY IS...
INUMAKI'S AMAZING...
SURREAL.
YEAH, MY FRIENDS ARE AMAZ-ING.
A SPIRIT OF ENDLESS CURSED ENERGY.
BUT YOU... YOU...
I WANT IT MORE AND MORE.
I'LL TEAR YOU APART!

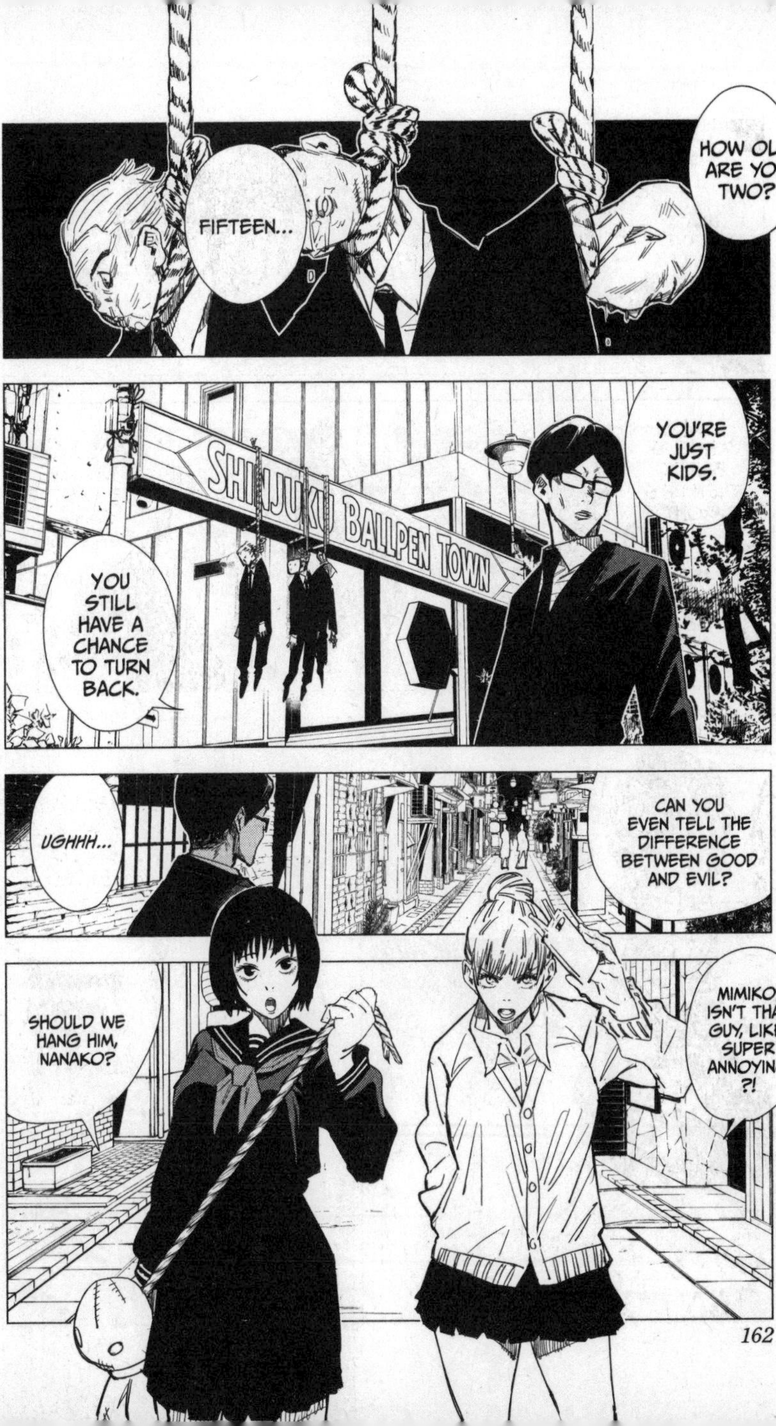
HOW OLD ARE YOU TWO?
FIFTEEN...
YOU'RE JUST KIDS.
SHINJUKU BALLPEN TOWN
YOU STILL HAVE A CHANCE TO TURN BACK.
CAN YOU EVEN TELL THE DIFFERENCE BETWEEN GOOD AND EVIL?
UGHHH...
MIMIKO, ISN'T THAT GUY, LIKE, SUPER ANNOYING?!
SHOULD WE HANG HIM, NANAKO?

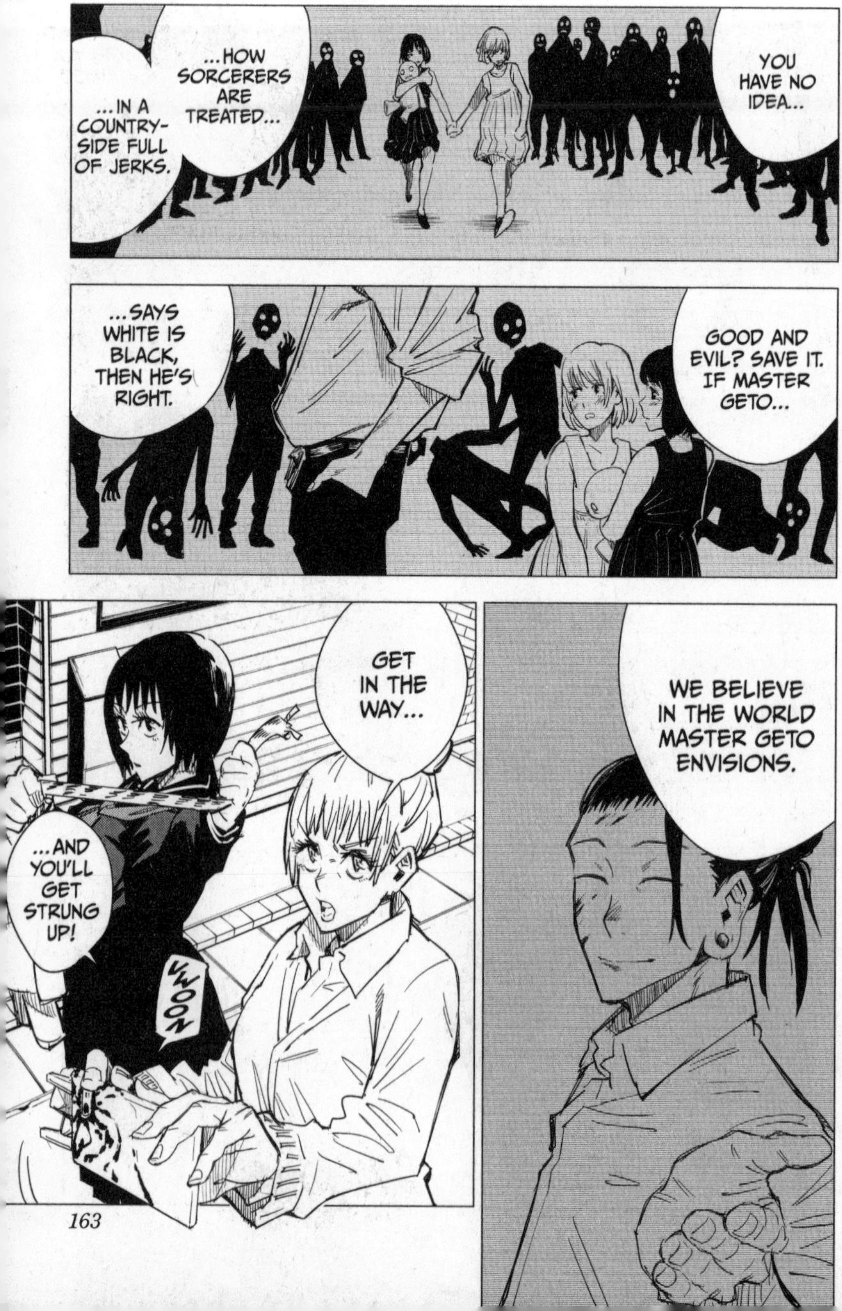
YOU HAVE NO IDEA...
...HOW SORCERERS ARE TREATED...
...IN A COUNTRY-SIDE FULL OF JERKS.
GOOD AND EVIL? SAVE IT. IF MASTER GETO...
...SAYS WHITE IS BLACK, THEN HE'S RIGHT.
WE BELIEVE IN THE WORLD MASTER GETO ENVISIONS.
GET IN THE WAY...
...AND YOU'LL GET STRUNG UP!
VWOON

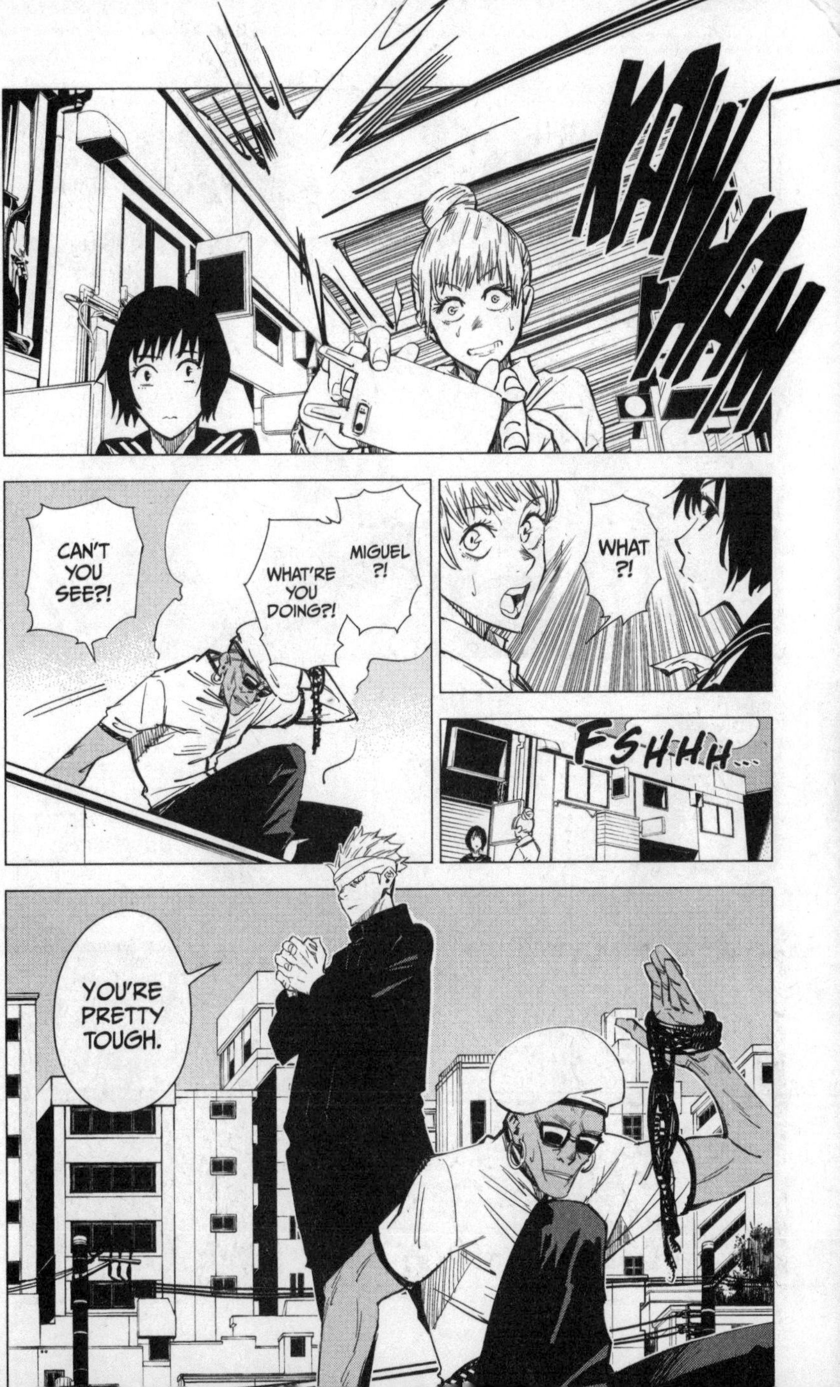
WHAT ?!
FSHHH...
MIGUEL ?!
WHAT'RE YOU DOING?!
CAN'T YOU SEE?!
YOU'RE PRETTY TOUGH.

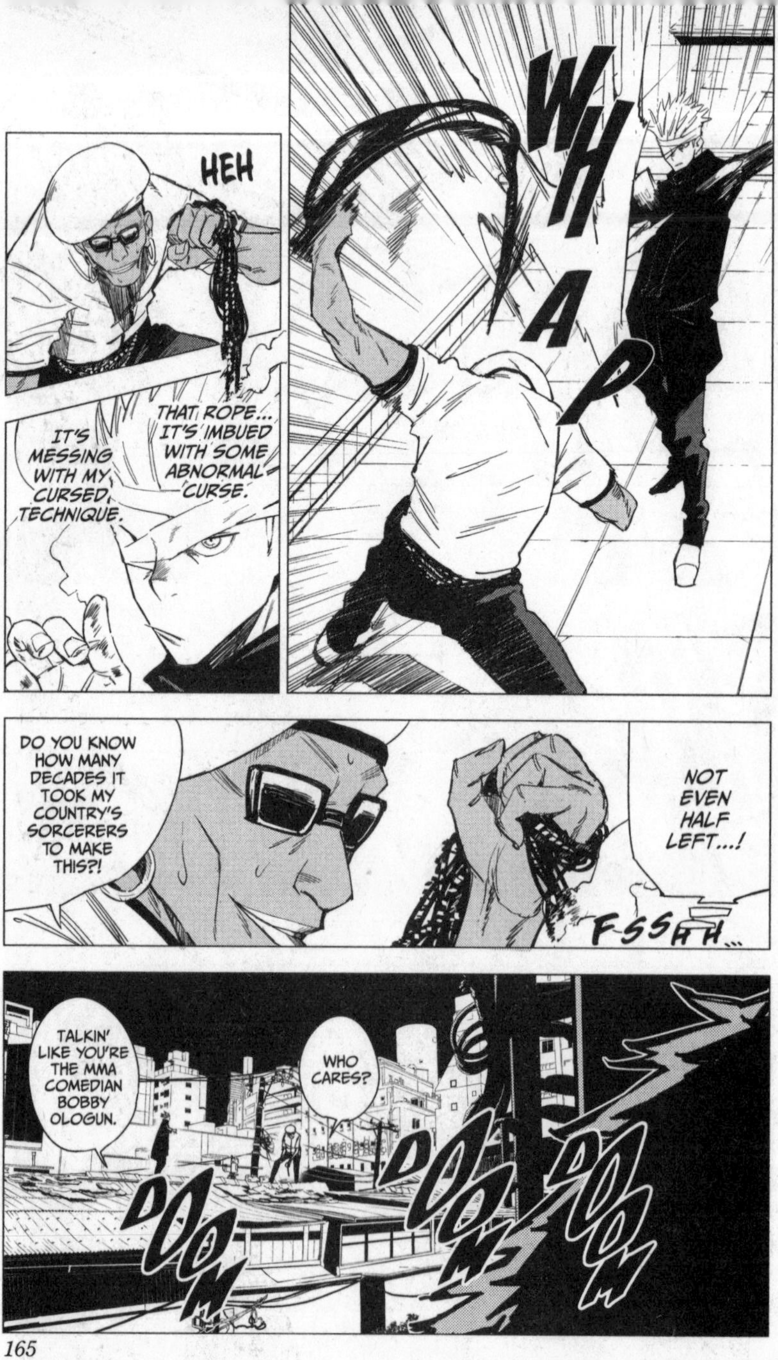
WHAP
HEH
THAT ROPE... IT'S IMBUED WITH SOME ABNORMAL CURSE.
IT'S MESSING WITH MY CURSED TECHNIQUE.
NOT EVEN HALF LEFT...!
DO YOU KNOW HOW MANY DECADES IT TOOK MY COUNTRY'S SORCERERS TO MAKE THIS?!
FSSHH...
DOOM
DOOM
WHO CARES?
TALKIN' LIKE YOU'RE THE MMA COMEDIAN BOBBY OLOGUN.
DOOM

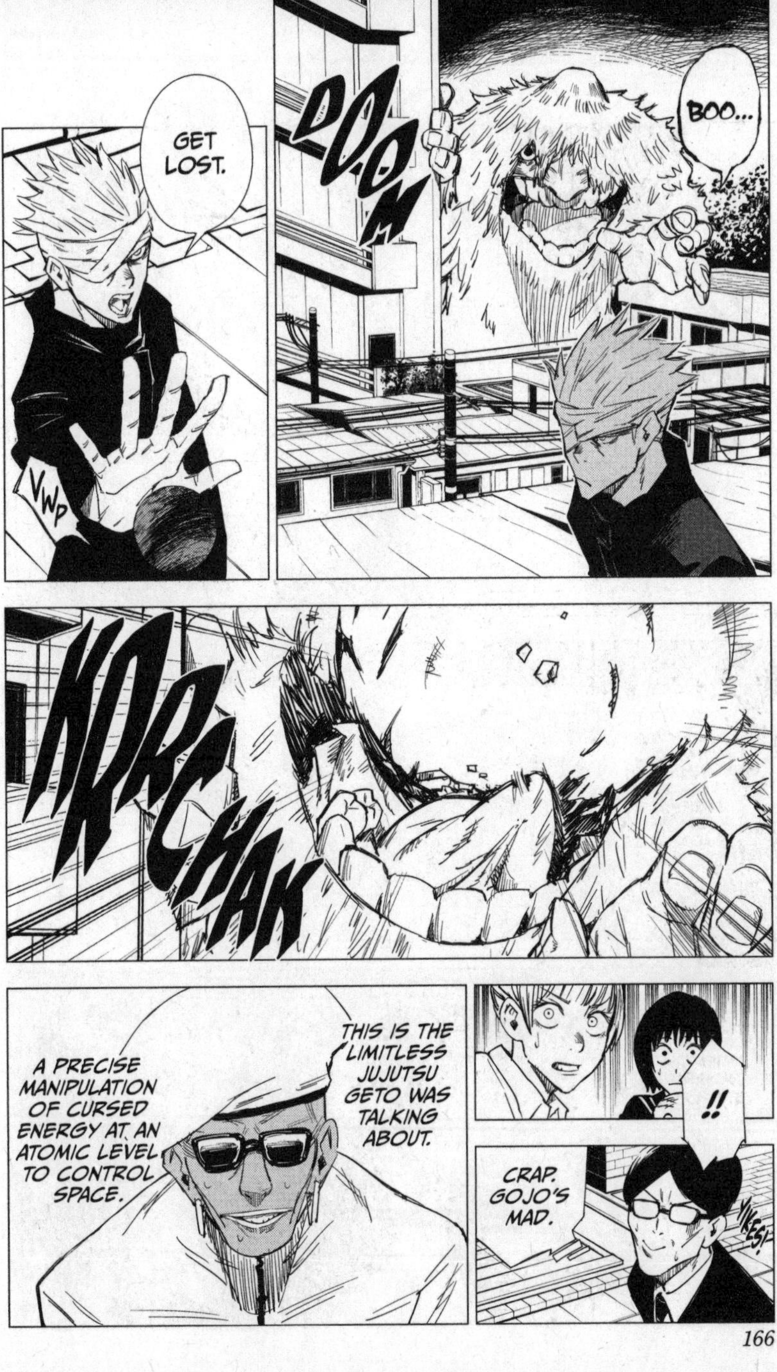
BOO...
DOOM
GET LOST.
VWP
KRCHAK
!!
CRAP. GOJO'S MAD.
YIKES!
THIS IS THE LIMITLESS JUJUTSU GETO WAS TALKING ABOUT.
A PRECISE MANIPULATION OF CURSED ENERGY AT AN ATOMIC LEVEL TO CONTROL SPACE.

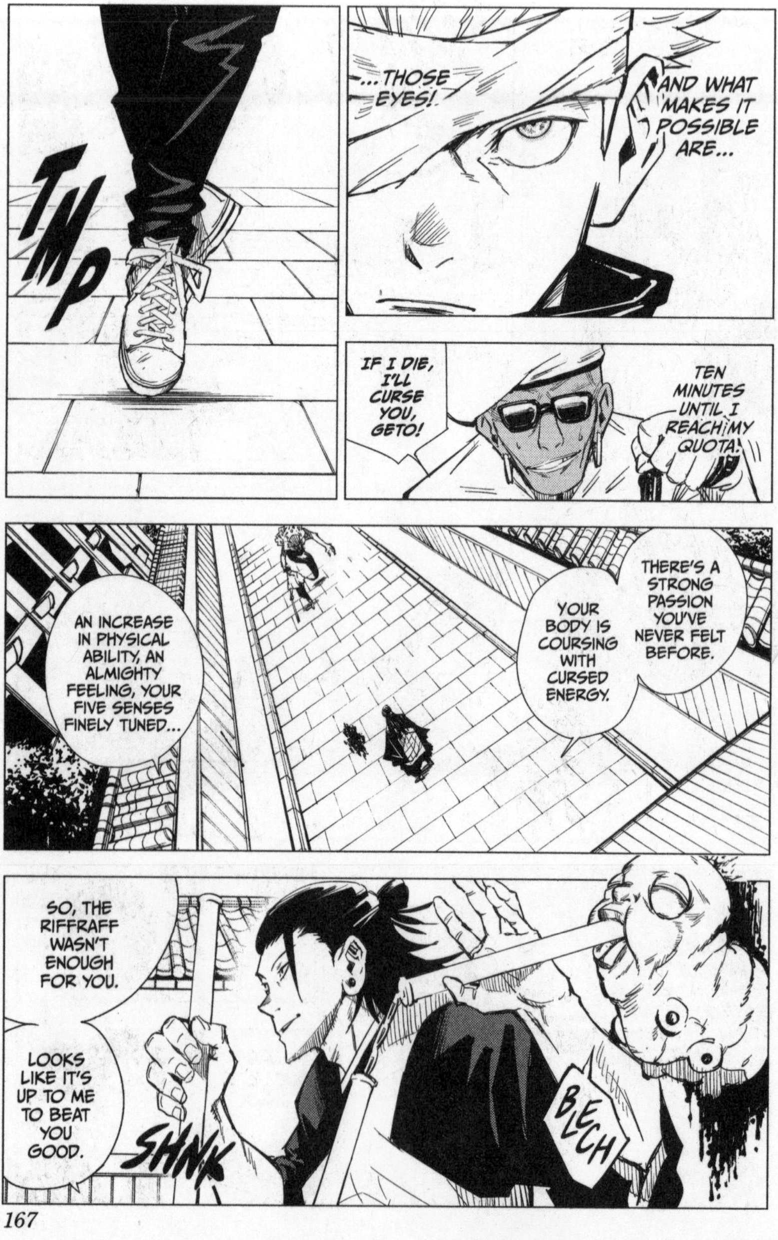
AND WHAT MAKES IT POSSIBLE ARE...
...THOSE EYES!
TEN MINUTES UNTIL I REACH MY QUOTA!
IF I DIE, I'LL CURSE YOU, GETO!
TMP
THERE'S A STRONG PASSION YOU'VE NEVER FELT BEFORE.
YOUR BODY IS COURSING WITH CURSED ENERGY.
AN INCREASE IN PHYSICAL ABILITY, AN ALMIGHTY FEELING, YOUR FIVE SENSES FINELY TUNED...
BLECH
SO, THE RIFFRAFF WASN'T ENOUGH FOR YOU.
LOOKS LIKE IT'S UP TO ME TO BEAT YOU GOOD.
SHNK

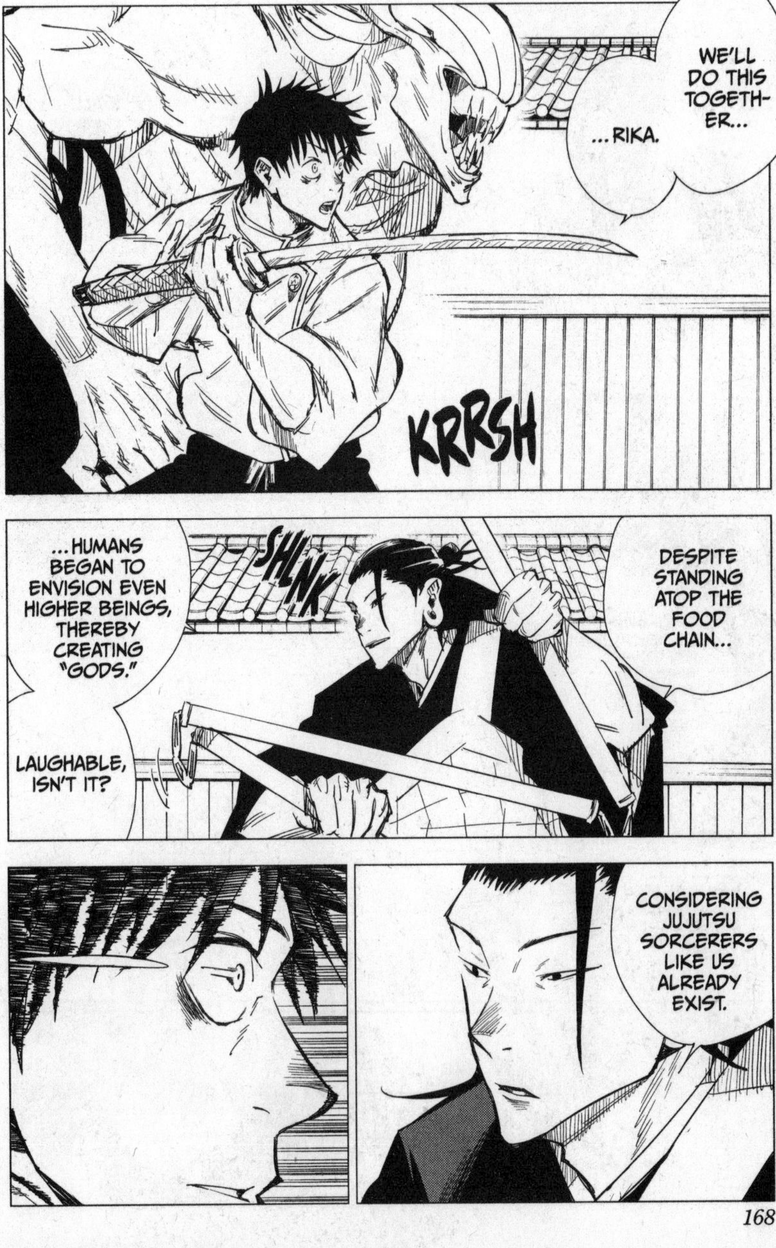
WE'LL DO THIS TOGETHER... ...RIKA.
KRRSH
DESPITE STANDING ATOP THE FOOD CHAIN...
SHLNK
...HUMANS BEGAN TO ENVISION EVEN HIGHER BEINGS, THEREBY CREATING "GODS."
LAUGHABLE, ISN'T IT?
CONSIDERING JUJUTSU SORCERERS LIKE US ALREADY EXIST.

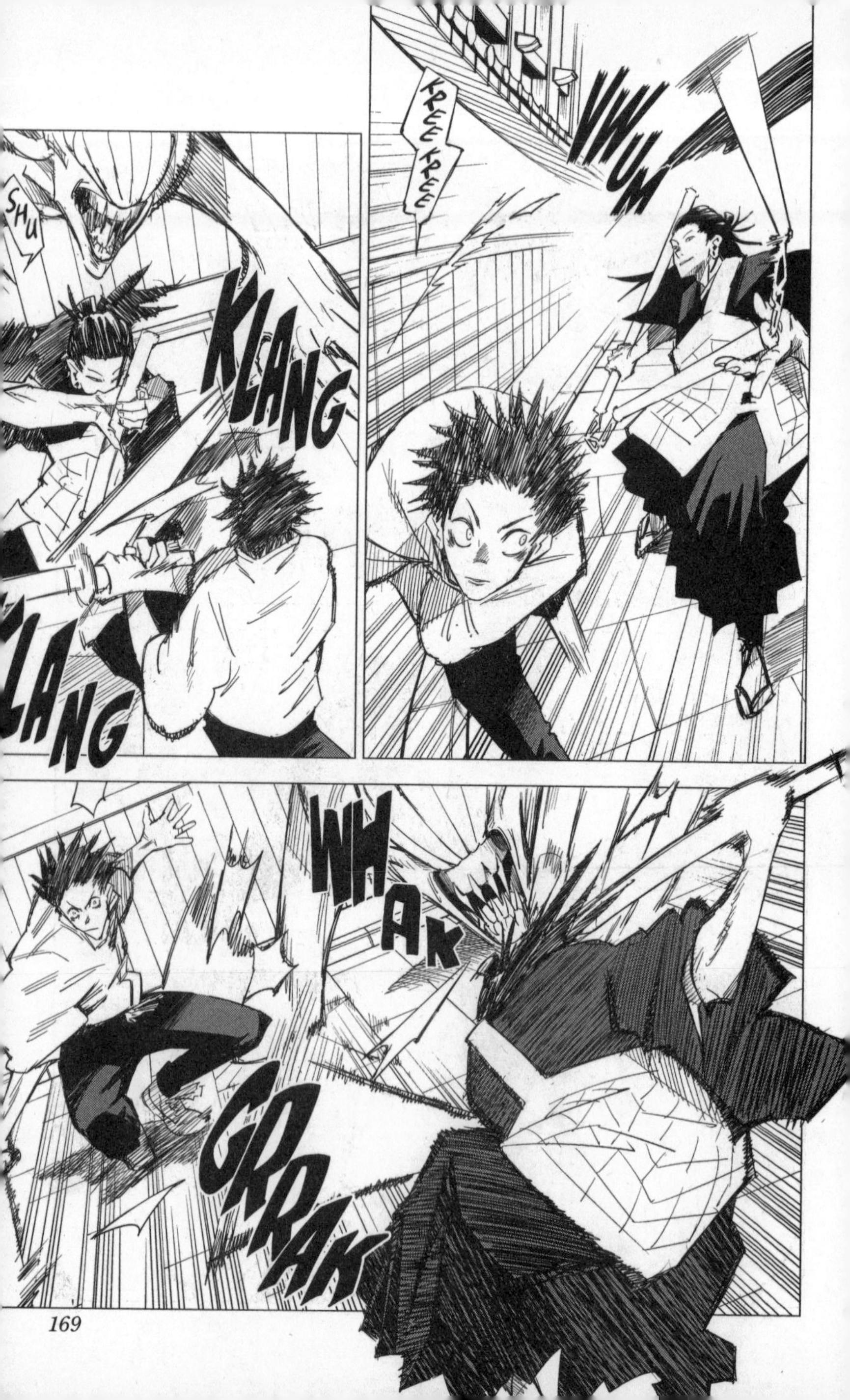
KREE KREE
VWUM
SHU
KLANG
KLANG
WHAK
GRRAK

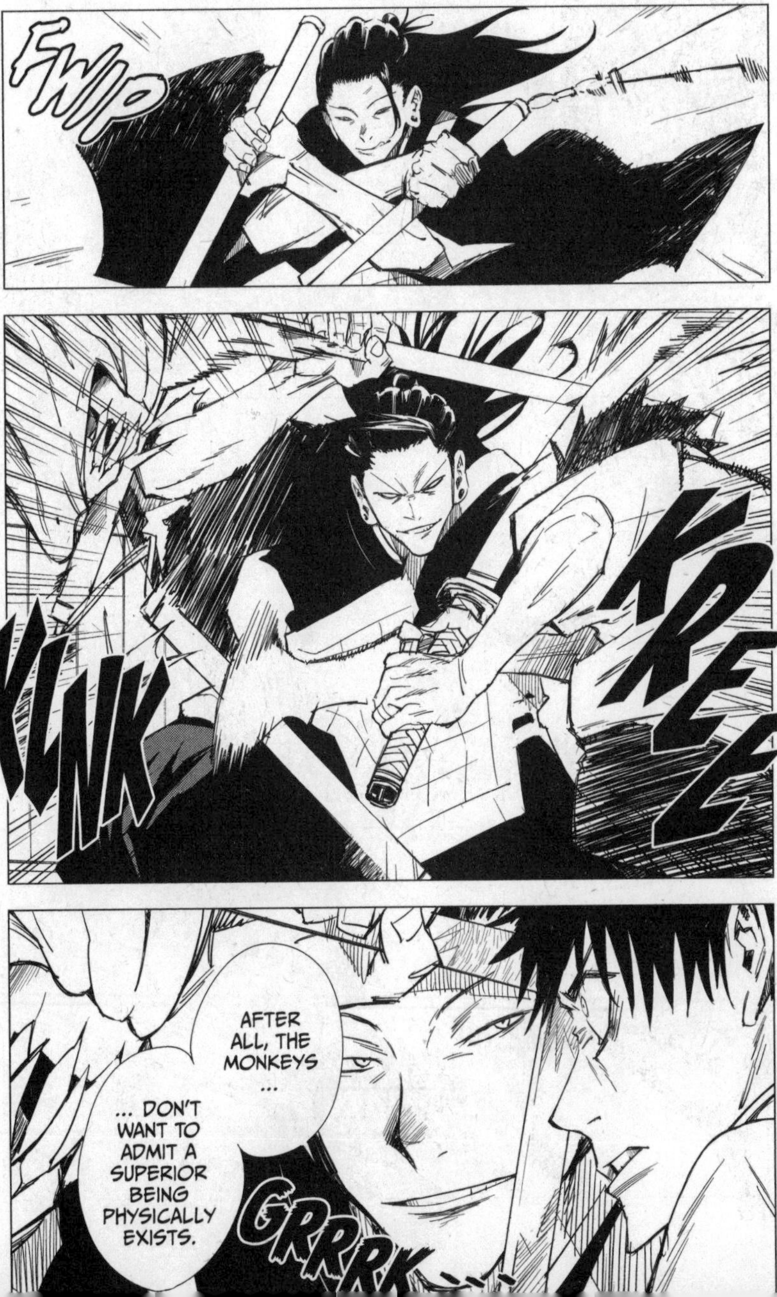
FWIP
KREE
KLINK
AFTER ALL, THE MONKEYS ...
... DON'T WANT TO ADMIT A SUPERIOR BEING PHYSICALLY EXISTS.
GRRRK...

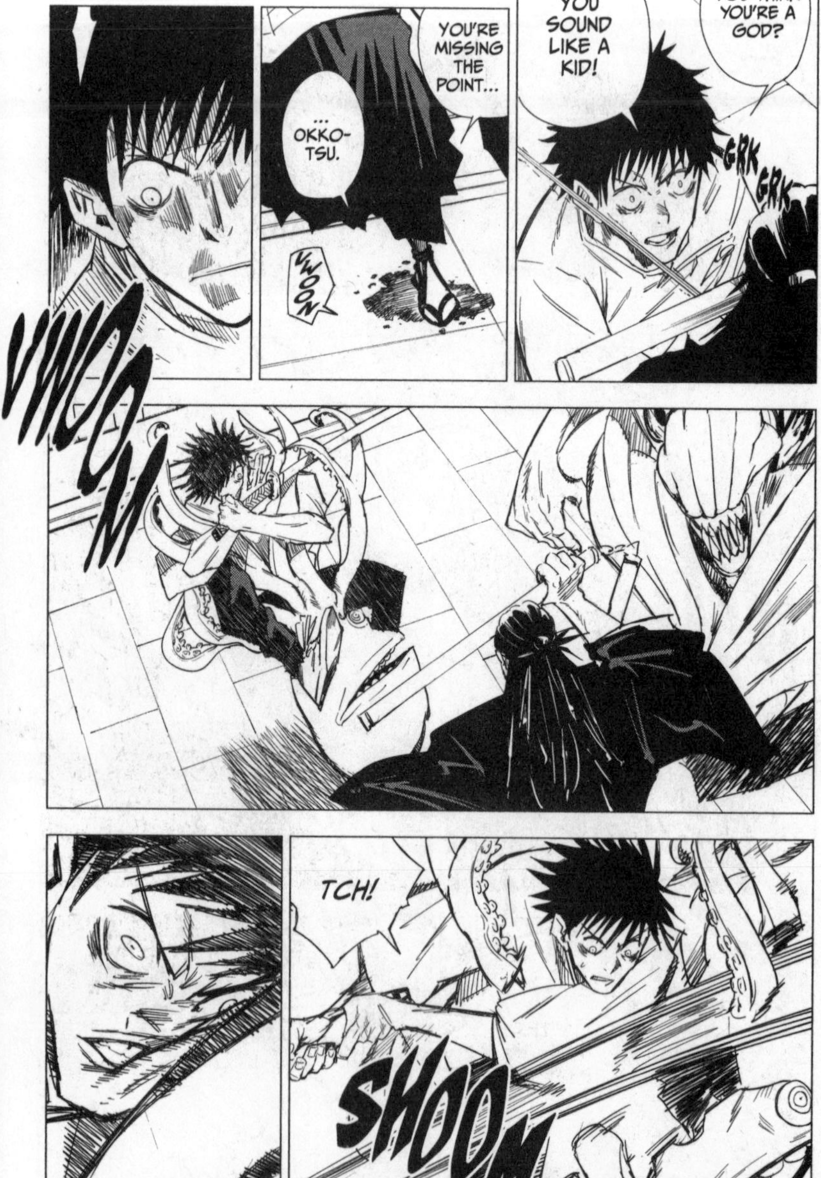
YOU THINK YOU'RE A GOD?
YOU SOUND LIKE A KID!
GRK GRK
YOU'RE MISSING THE POINT...
... OKKO-TSU.
VWOON
VWOOM
TCH!
SHOOM

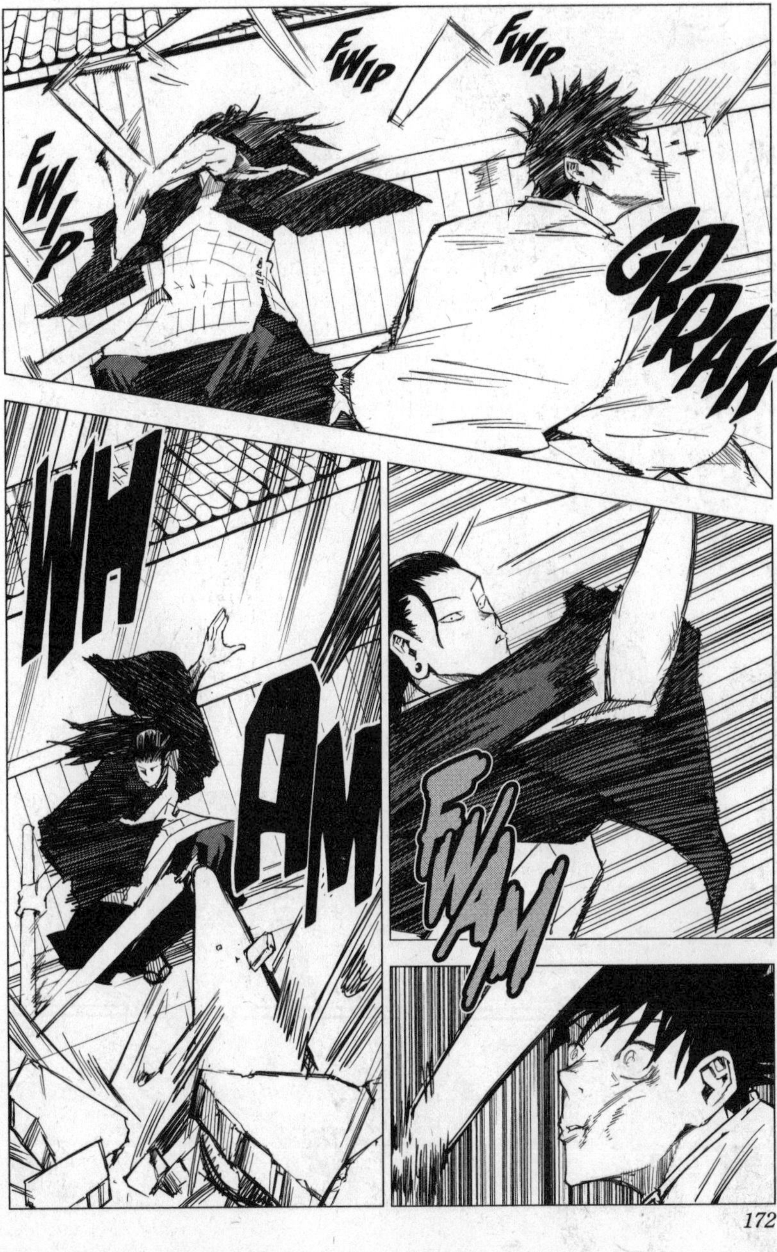
FWIP
FWIP
GRRAK
FWIP
FWAM
WHAM

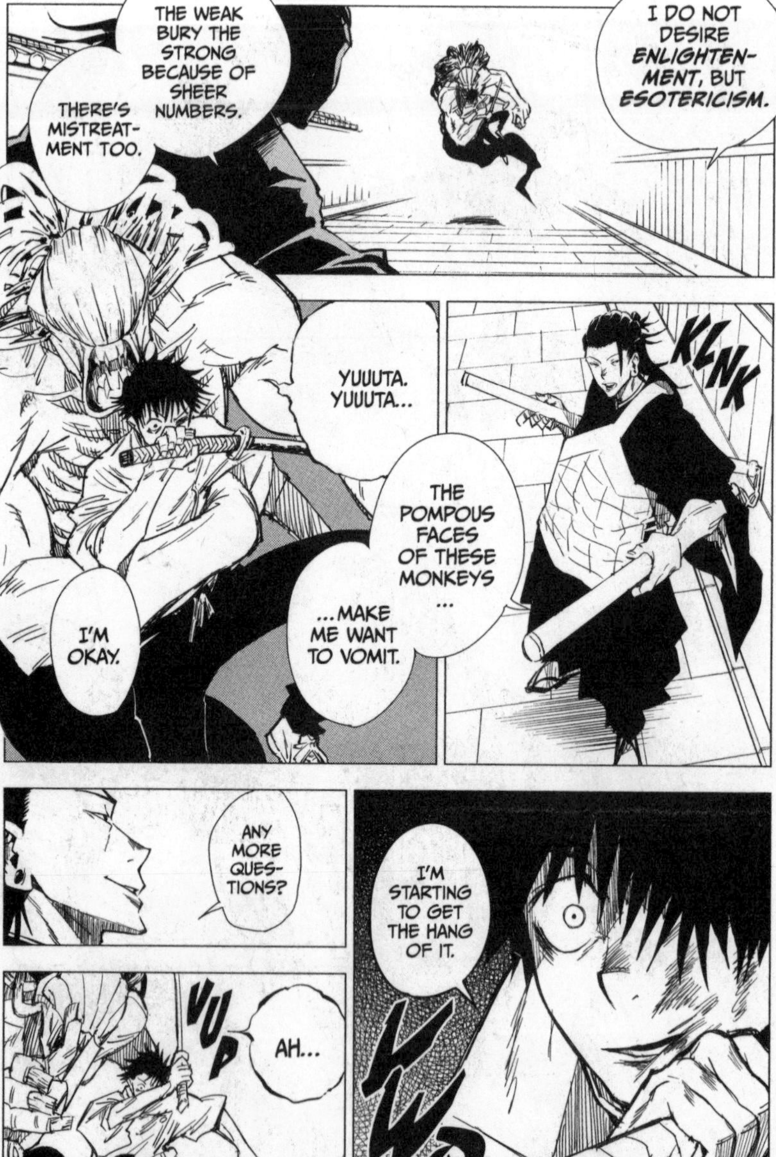
I DO NOT DESIRE ENLIGHTENMENT, BUT ESOTERICISM.
THE WEAK BURY THE STRONG BECAUSE OF SHEER NUMBERS.
THERE'S MISTREATMENT TOO.
KLNK
THE POMPOUS FACES OF THESE MONKEYS...
...MAKE ME WANT TO VOMIT.
YUUUTA. YUUUTA...
I'M OKAY.
I'M STARTING TO GET THE HANG OF IT.
VWWP
ANY MORE QUESTIONS?
VUUP
AH...

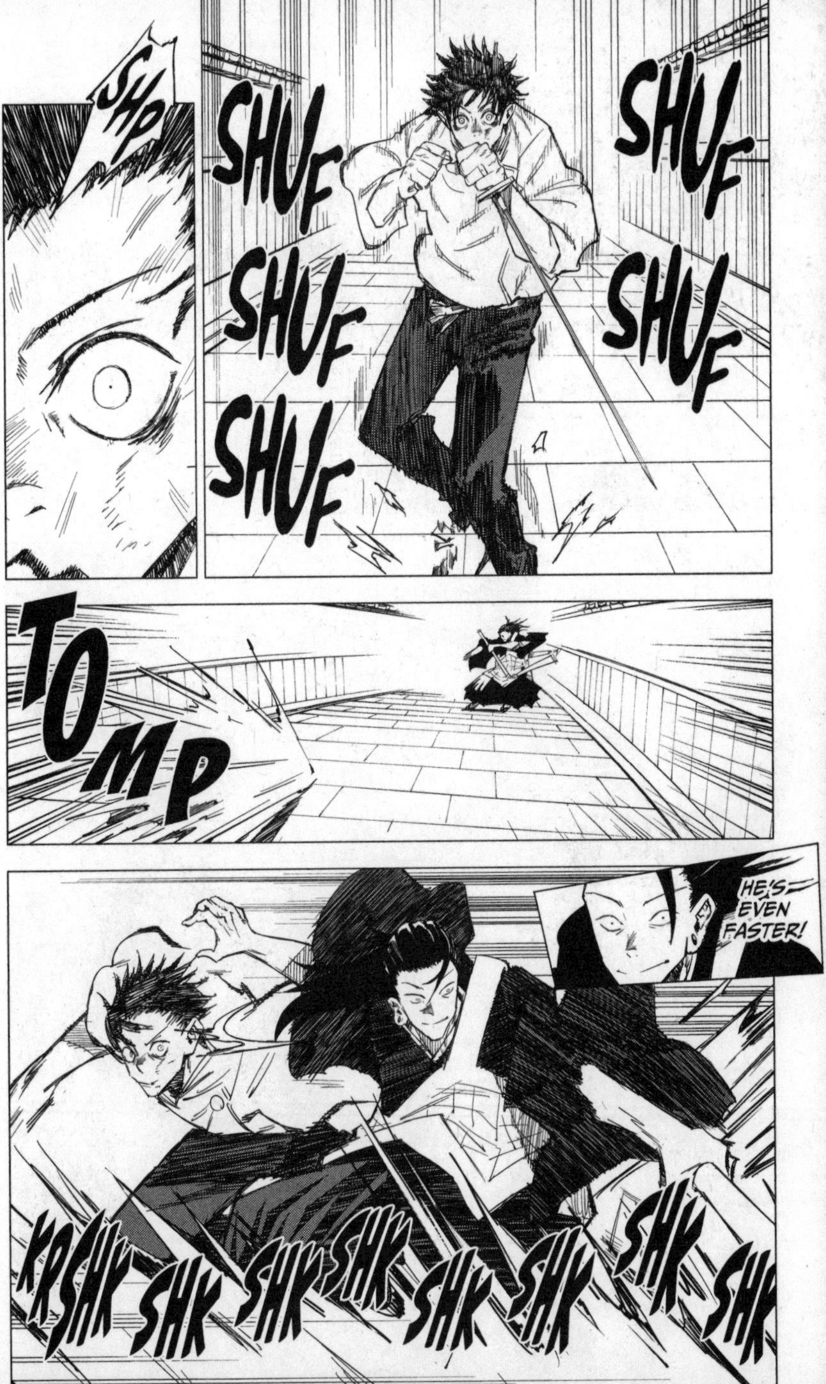
SHUF
SHUF
SHUF
SHUF
SHUF
SHP
TOMP
HE'S EVEN FASTER!
SHK
SHK
SHK
SHK
SHK
SHK
SHK
KRSHK

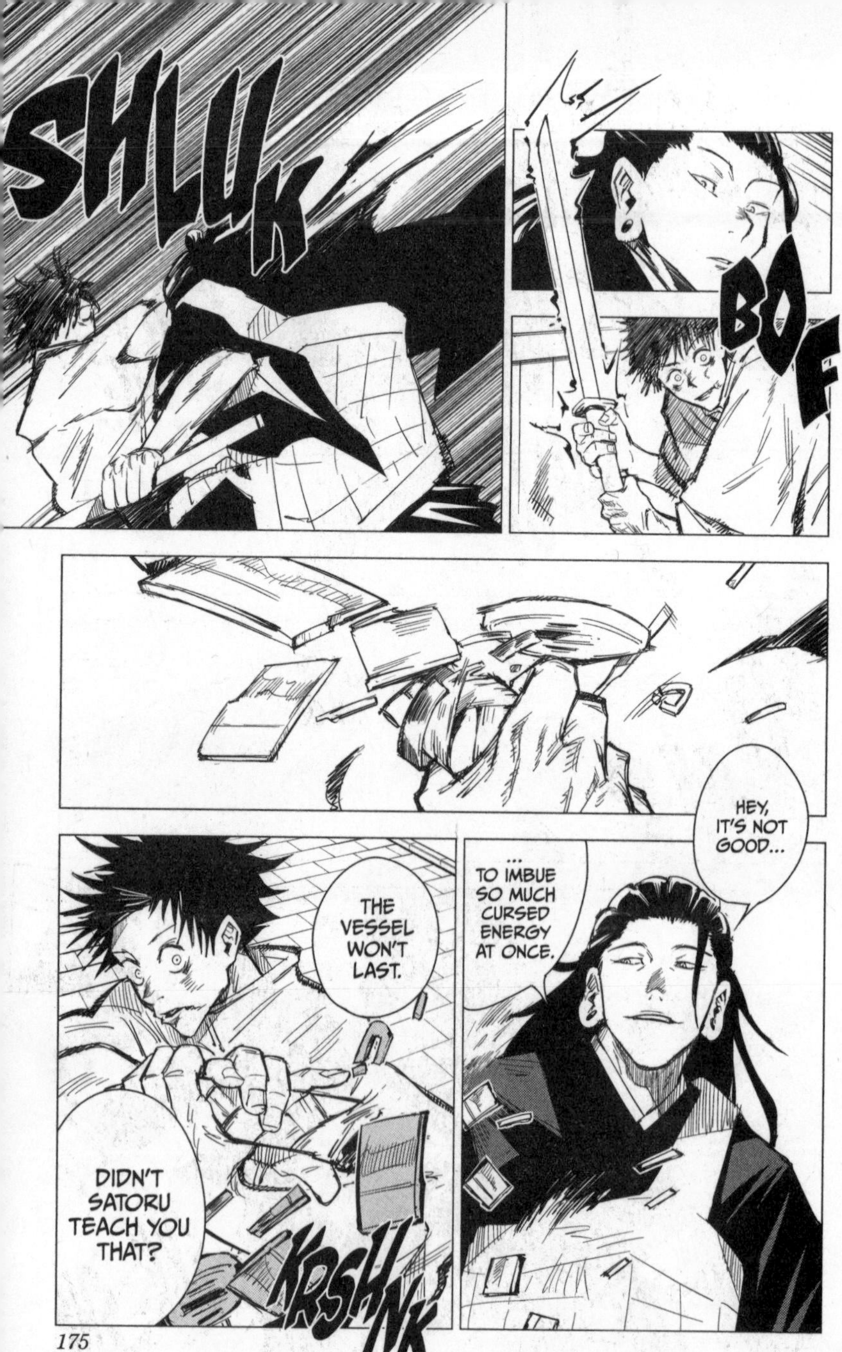
BOOF
SHLUK
HEY, IT'S NOT GOOD...
... TO IMBUE SO MUCH CURSED ENERGY AT ONCE.
THE VESSEL WON'T LAST.
DIDN'T SATORU TEACH YOU THAT?
KRSHNK

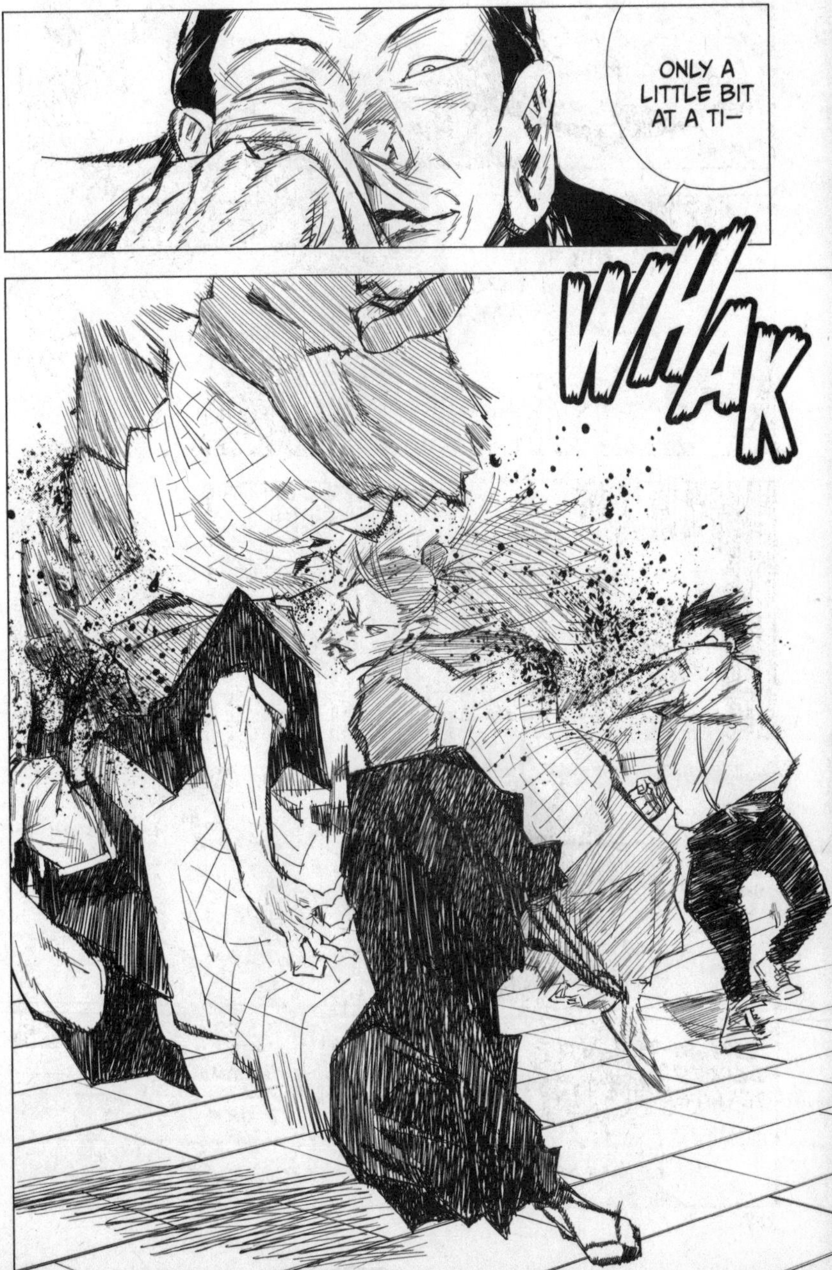
ONLY A LITTLE BIT AT A TI–
WHAK

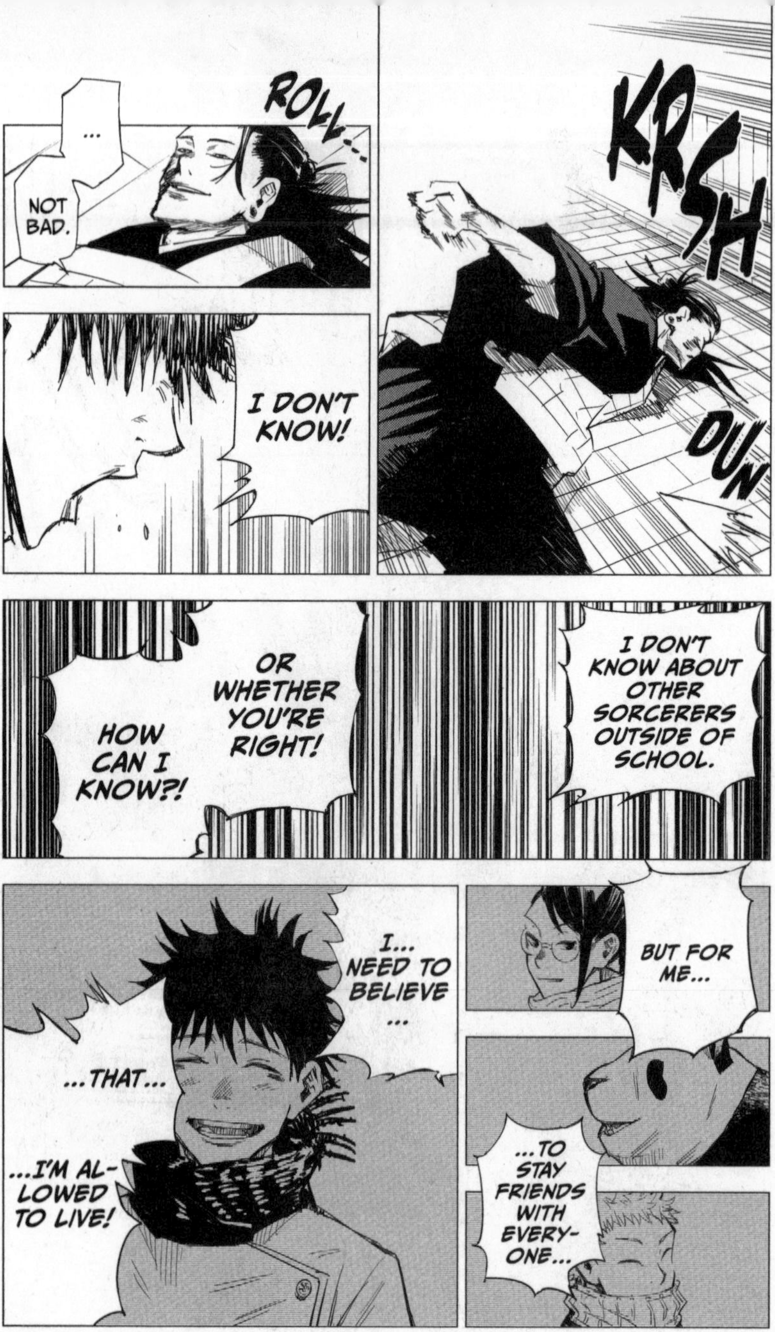
KRSH
DUN
ROLL...
...
NOT BAD.
I DON'T KNOW!
I DON'T KNOW ABOUT OTHER SORCERERS OUTSIDE OF SCHOOL.
OR WHETHER YOU'RE RIGHT!
HOW CAN I KNOW?!
BUT FOR ME...
...TO STAY FRIENDS WITH EVERY-ONE...
I... NEED TO BELIEVE ...
...THAT...
...I'M AL-LOWED TO LIVE!

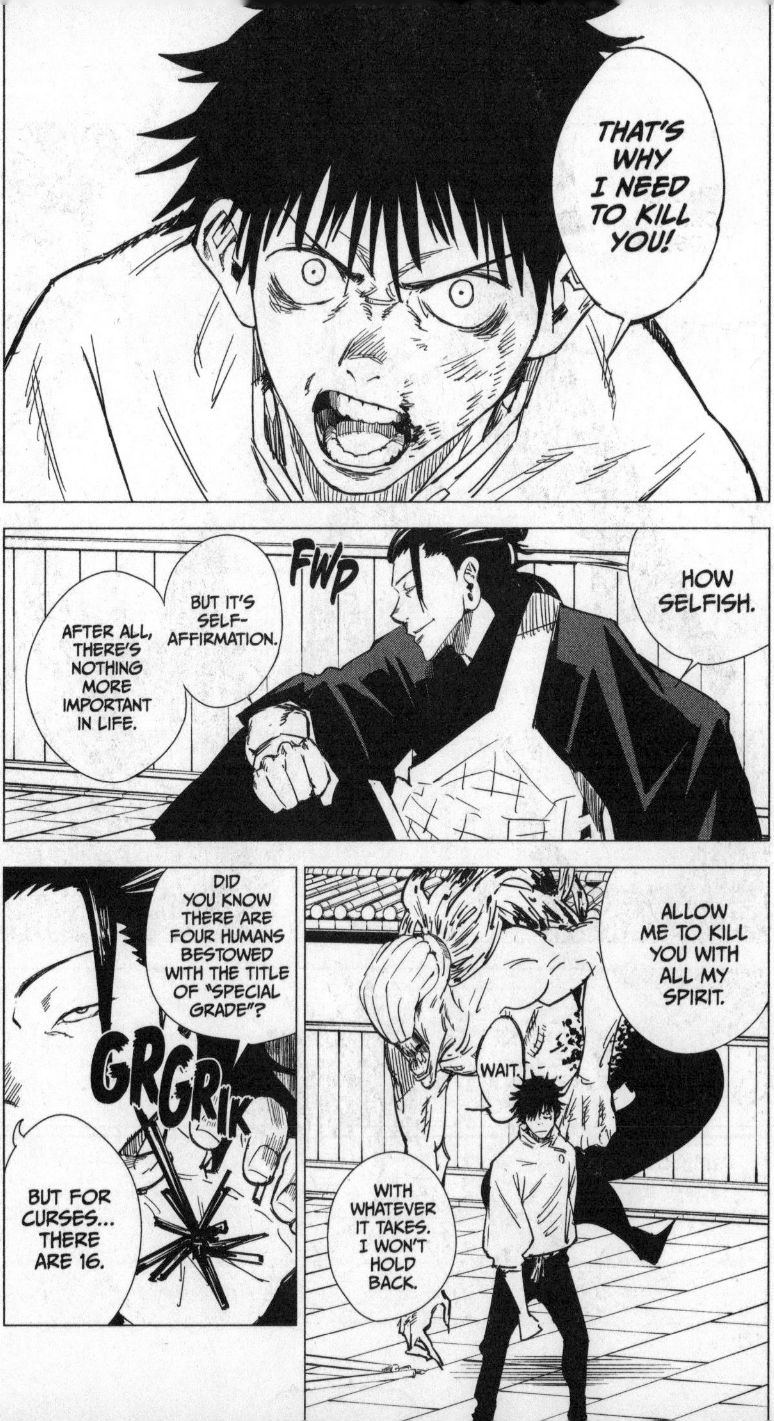
THAT'S WHY I NEED TO KILL YOU!
HOW SELFISH.
FWP
BUT IT'S SELF-AFFIRMATION.
AFTER ALL, THERE'S NOTHING MORE IMPORTANT IN LIFE.
ALLOW ME TO KILL YOU WITH ALL MY SPIRIT.
WAIT.
WITH WHATEVER IT TAKES. I WON'T HOLD BACK.
DID YOU KNOW THERE ARE FOUR HUMANS BESTOWED WITH THE TITLE OF "SPECIAL GRADE"?
GRGRIK
BUT FOR CURSES... THERE ARE 16.

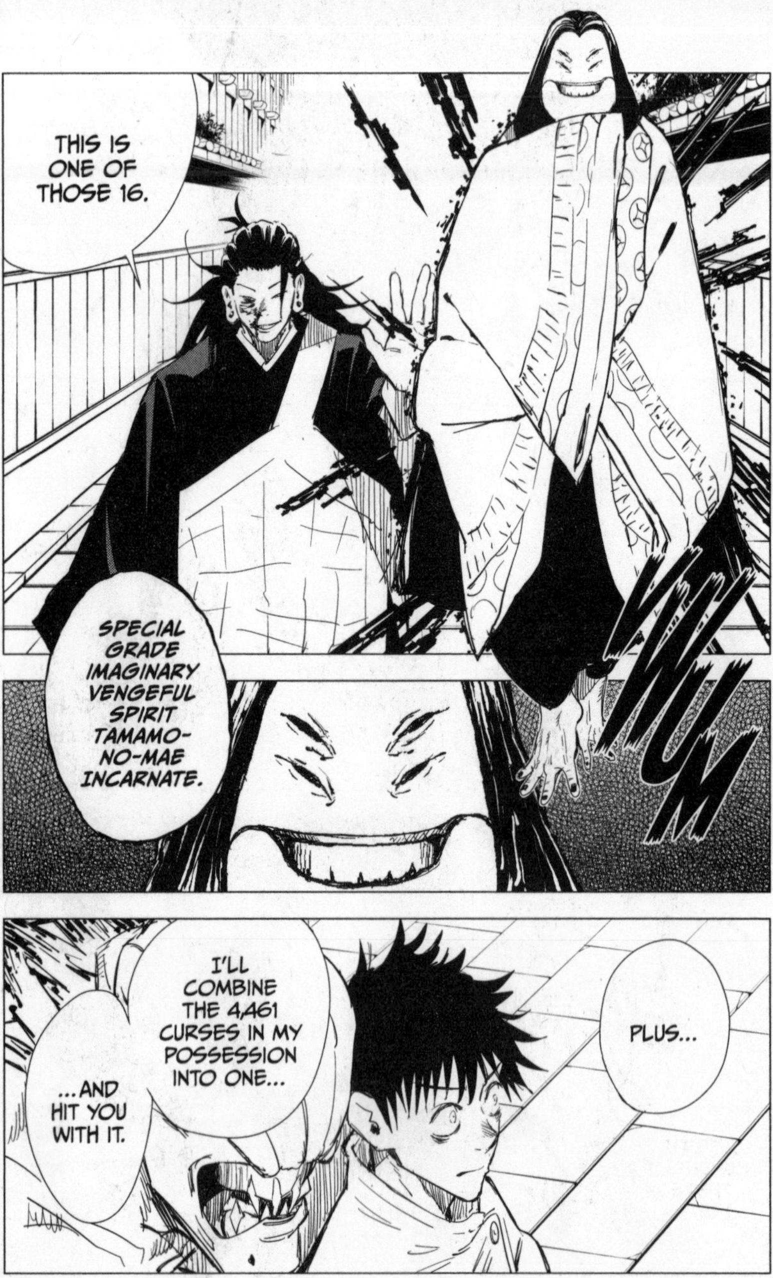
THIS IS ONE OF THOSE 16.
SPECIAL GRADE IMAGINARY VENGEFUL SPIRIT TAMAMO-NO-MAE INCARNATE.
VWUM
PLUS...
I'LL COMBINE THE 4,461 CURSES IN MY POSSESSION INTO ONE...
...AND HIT YOU WITH IT.

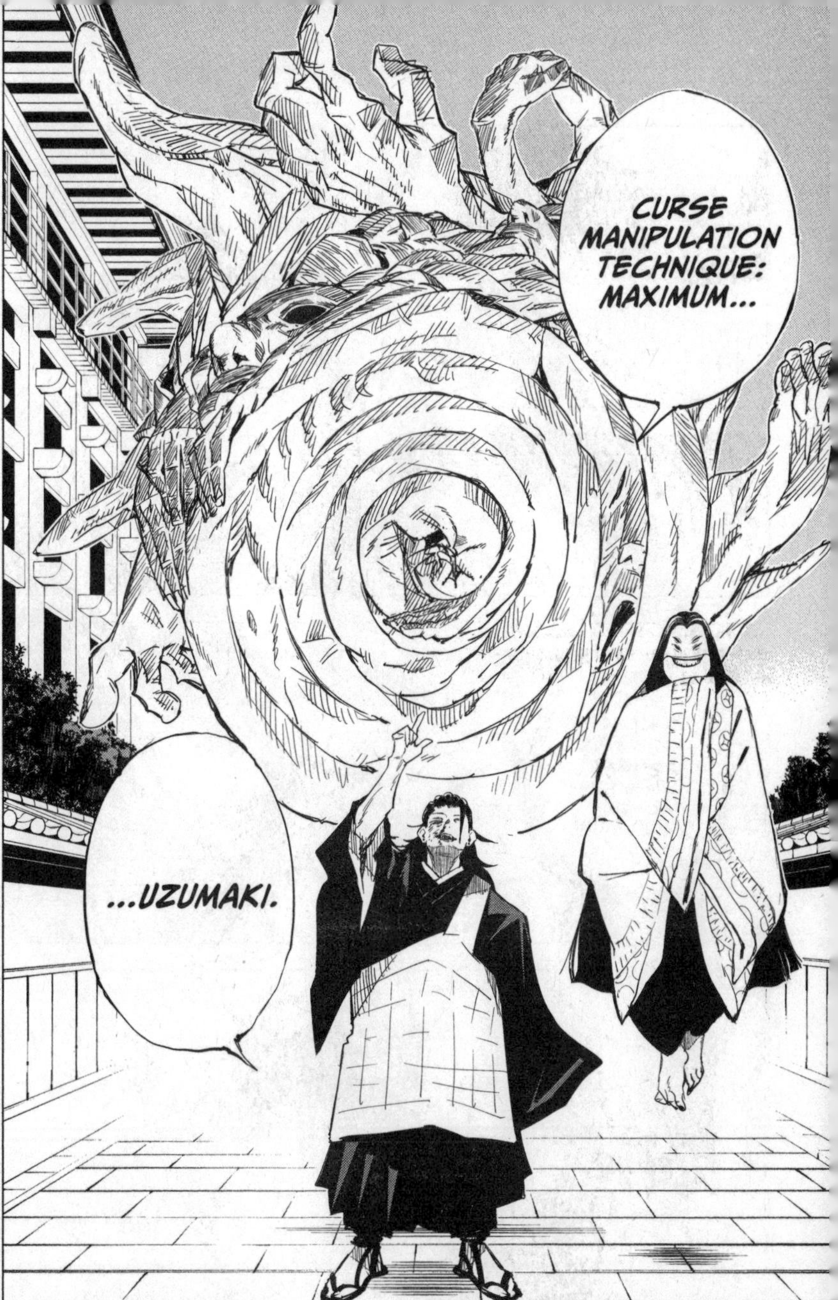
CURSE MANIPULATION TECHNIQUE: MAXIMUM...
...UZUMAKI.

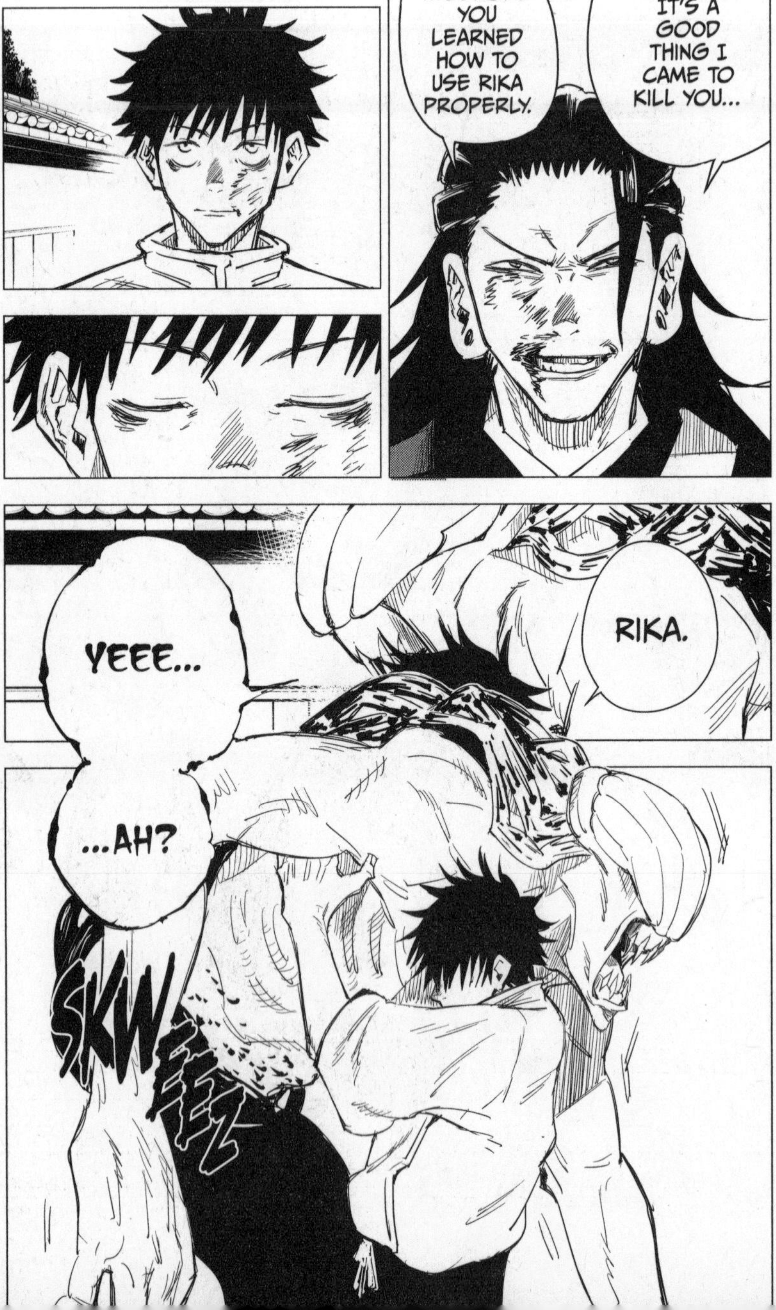
OKKOTSU. IT'S A GOOD THING I CAME TO KILL YOU...
...BEFORE YOU LEARNED HOW TO USE RIKA PROPERLY.
RIKA.
YEEE...
...AH?
SKWEEZ

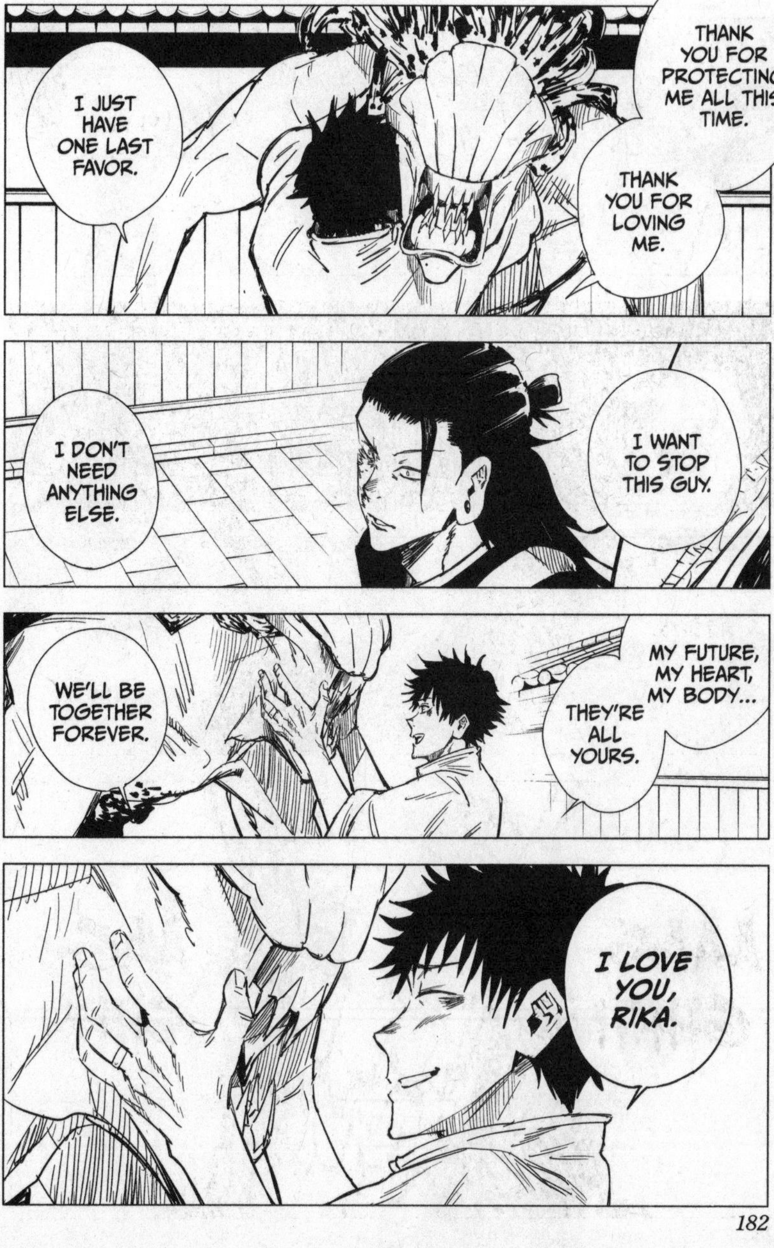
THANK YOU FOR PROTECTING ME ALL THIS TIME.
THANK YOU FOR LOVING ME.
I JUST HAVE ONE LAST FAVOR.
I WANT TO STOP THIS GUY.
I DON'T NEED ANYTHING ELSE.
MY FUTURE, MY HEART, MY BODY...
THEY'RE ALL YOURS.
WE'LL BE TOGETHER FOREVER.
I LOVE YOU, RIKA.

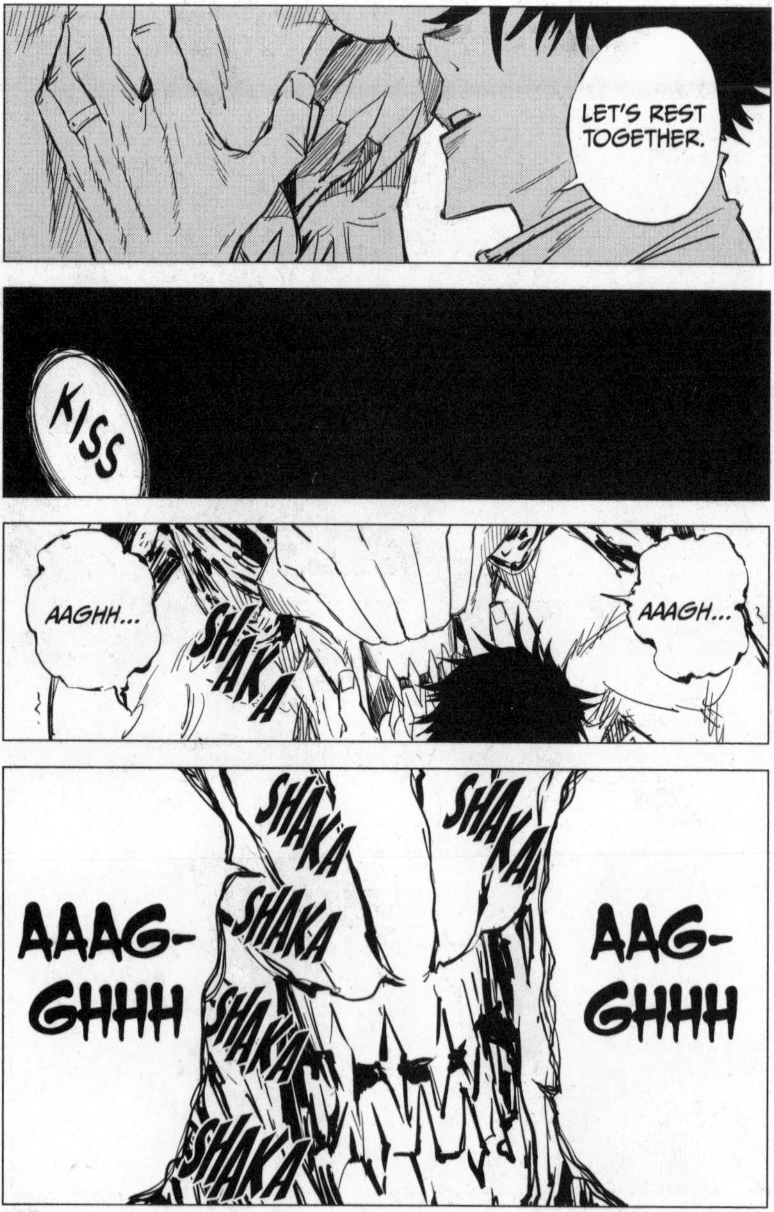
LET'S REST TOGETHER.
KISS
AAAGH...
SHAKA
AAGHH...
AAG-GHHH
SHAKA
SHAKA
SHAKA
SHAKA
SHAKA
AAAG-GHHH

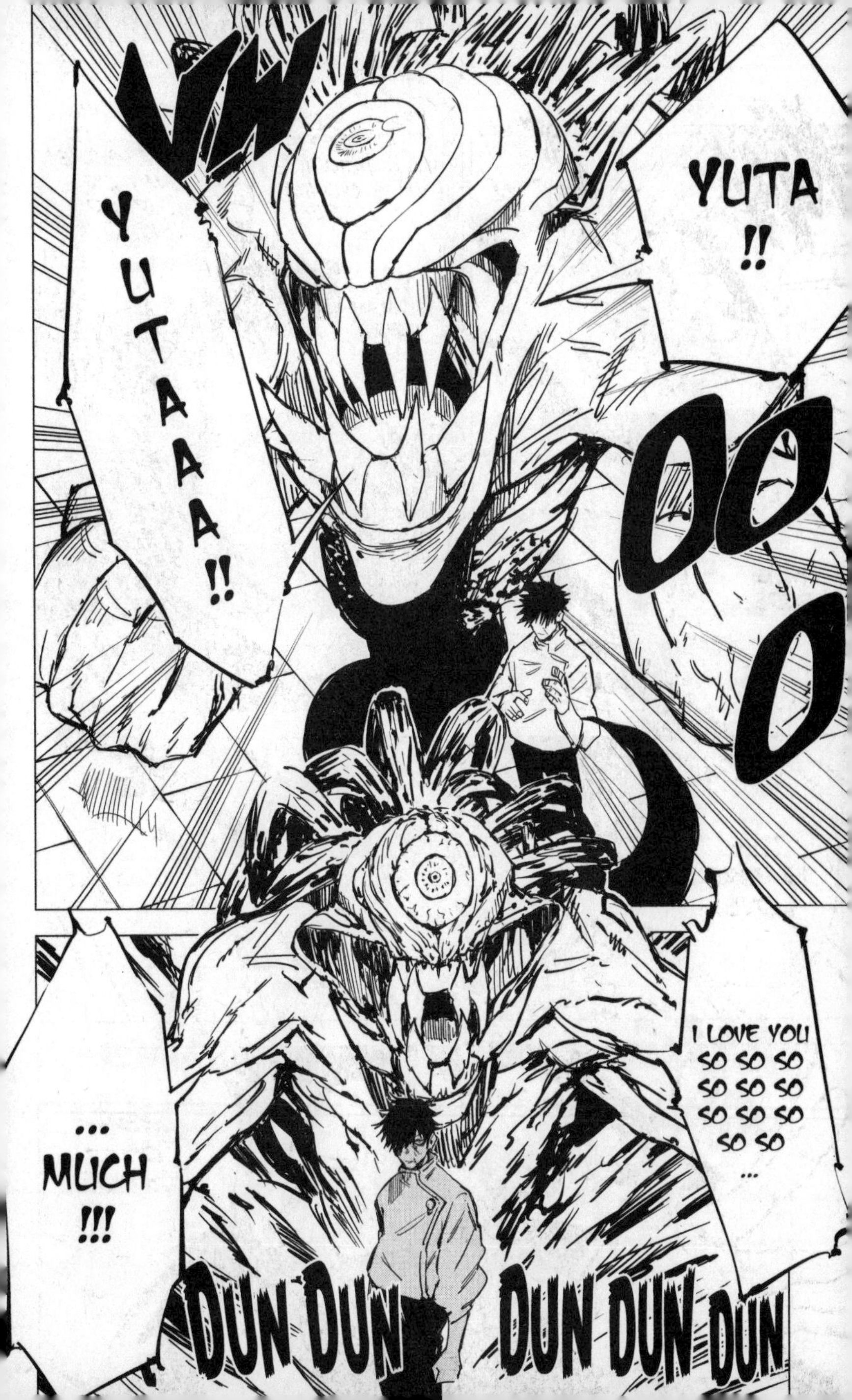
YUTA !!
VW
YUTAAA !!
OOOO
I LOVE YOU SO SO SO SO SO SO SO SO SO SO SO ...
... MUCH !!!
DUN DUN DUN DUN DUN

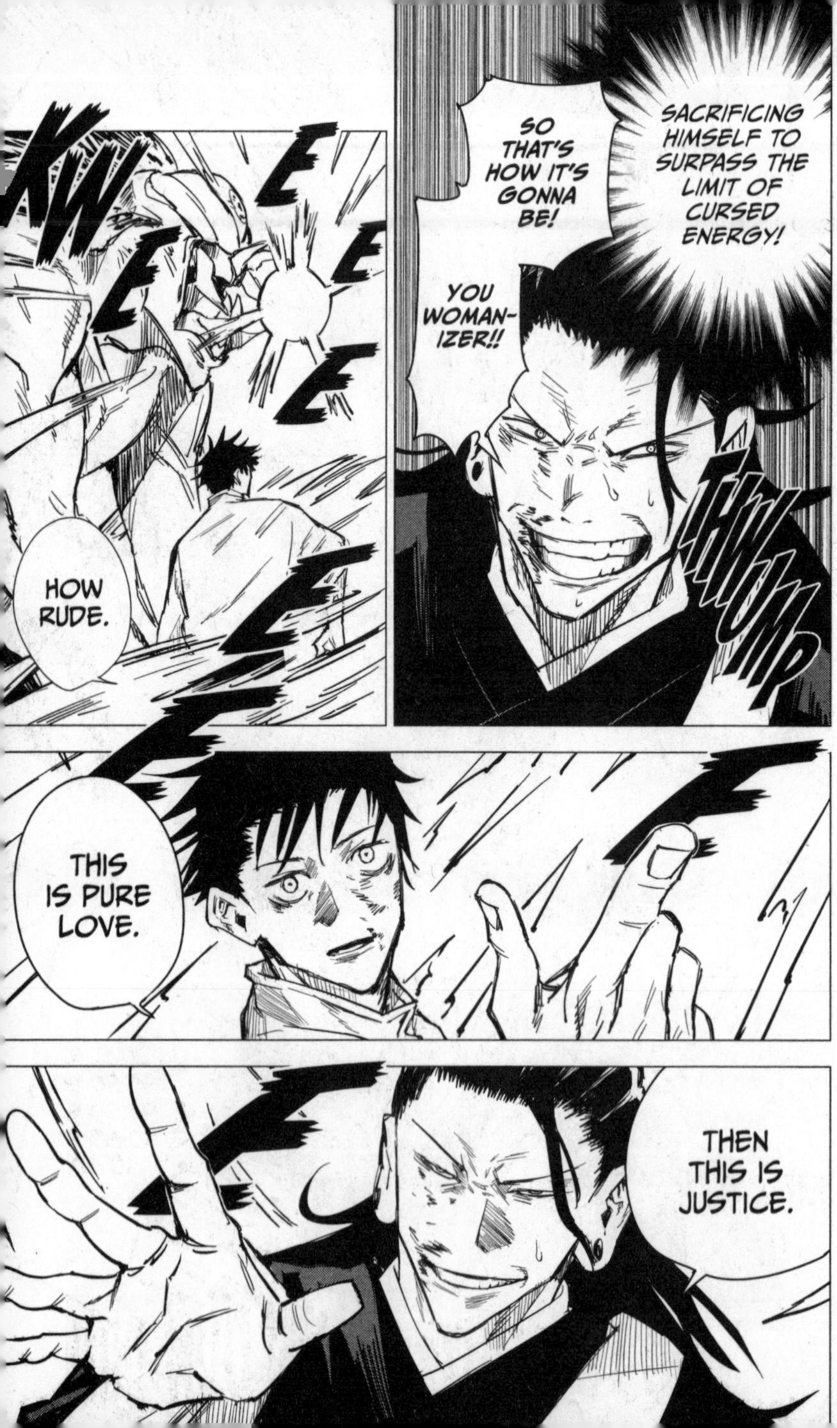
SACRIFICING HIMSELF TO SURPASS THE LIMIT OF CURSED ENERGY!
SO THAT'S HOW IT'S GONNA BE!
YOU WOMAN-IZER!!
THWUMP
KWEEEEE
HOW RUDE.
THIS IS PURE LOVE.
THEN THIS IS JUSTICE.

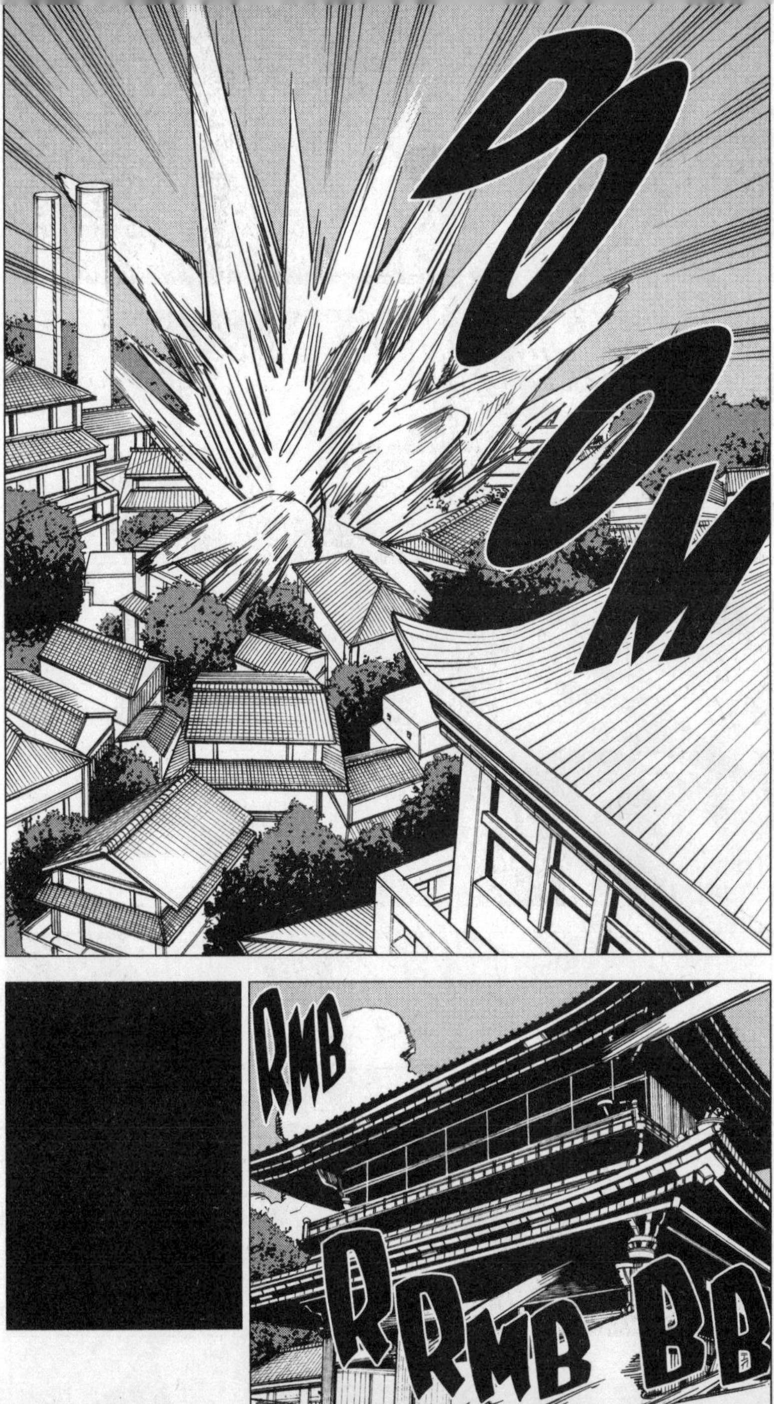
DOOOM
RMB
RRMB BB

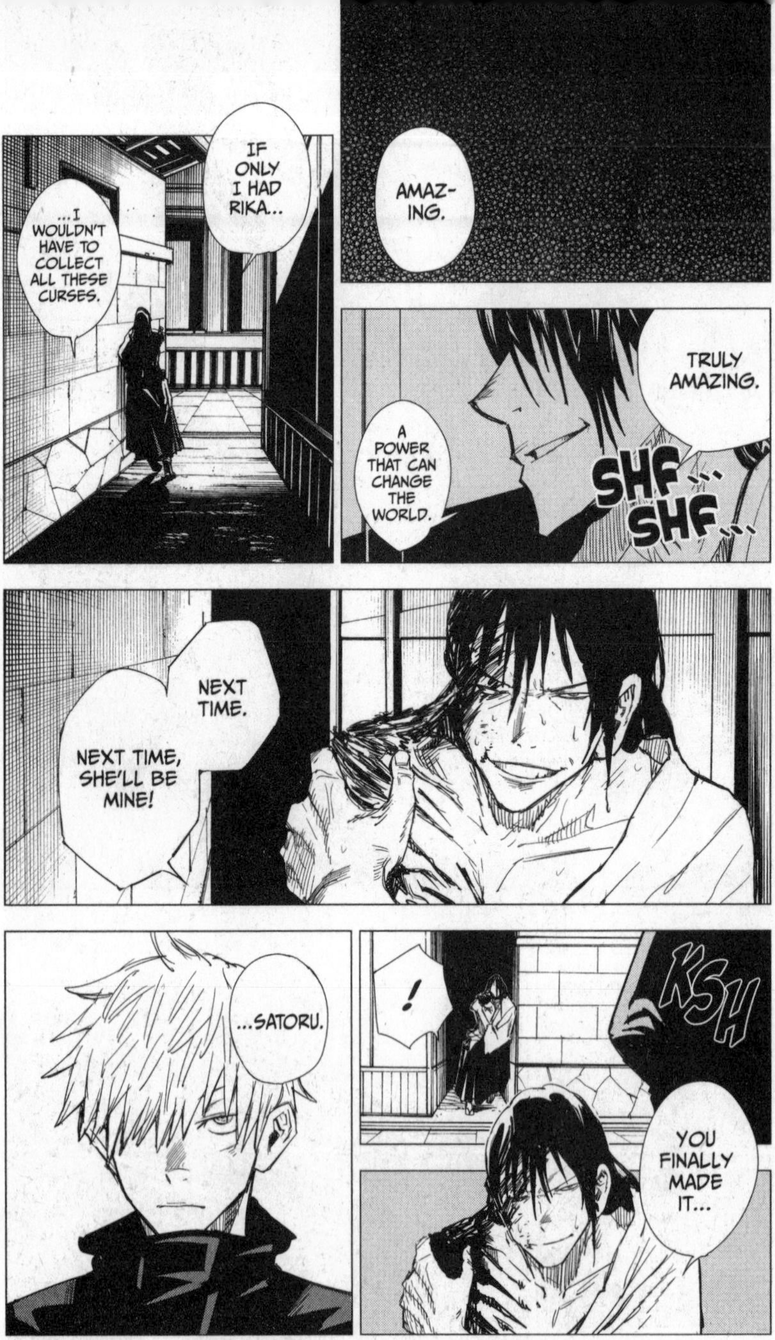
AMAZ-ING.
TRULY AMAZING.
A POWER THAT CAN CHANGE THE WORLD.
SHF... SHF...
IF ONLY I HAD RIKA...
...I WOULDN'T HAVE TO COLLECT ALL THESE CURSES.
NEXT TIME.
NEXT TIME, SHE'LL BE MINE!
KSH
!
YOU FINALLY MADE IT...
...SATORU.

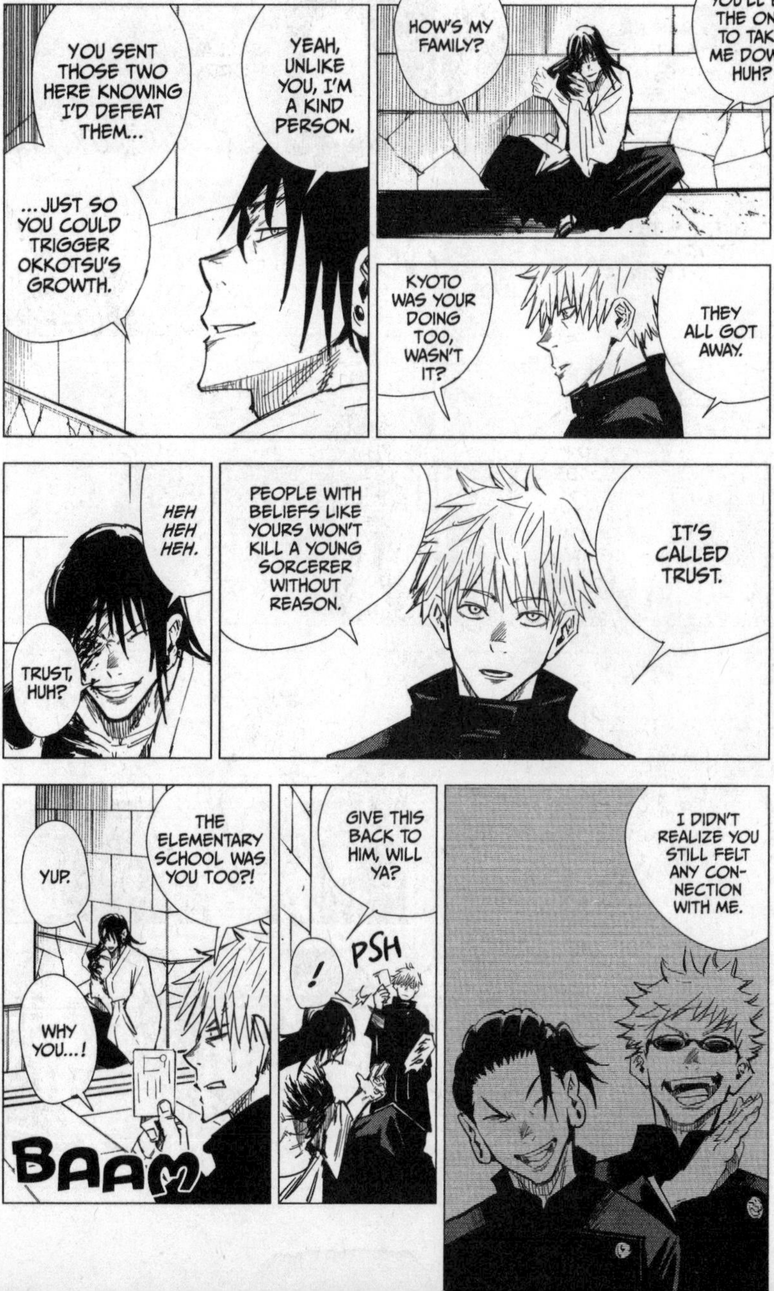
SO YOU'LL BE THE ONE TO TAKE ME DOWN, HUH?
HOW'S MY FAMILY?
THEY ALL GOT AWAY.
KYOTO WAS YOUR DOING TOO, WASN'T IT?
YEAH, UNLIKE YOU, I'M A KIND PERSON.
YOU SENT THOSE TWO HERE KNOWING I'D DEFEAT THEM...
...JUST SO YOU COULD TRIGGER OKKOTSU'S GROWTH.
IT'S CALLED TRUST.
PEOPLE WITH BELIEFS LIKE YOURS WON'T KILL A YOUNG SORCERER WITHOUT REASON.
HEH HEH HEH.
TRUST, HUH?
I DIDN'T REALIZE YOU STILL FELT ANY CONNECTION WITH ME.
GIVE THIS BACK TO HIM, WILL YA?
PSH
!
THE ELEMENTARY SCHOOL WAS YOU TOO?!
YUP.
WHY YOU...!
BAAM

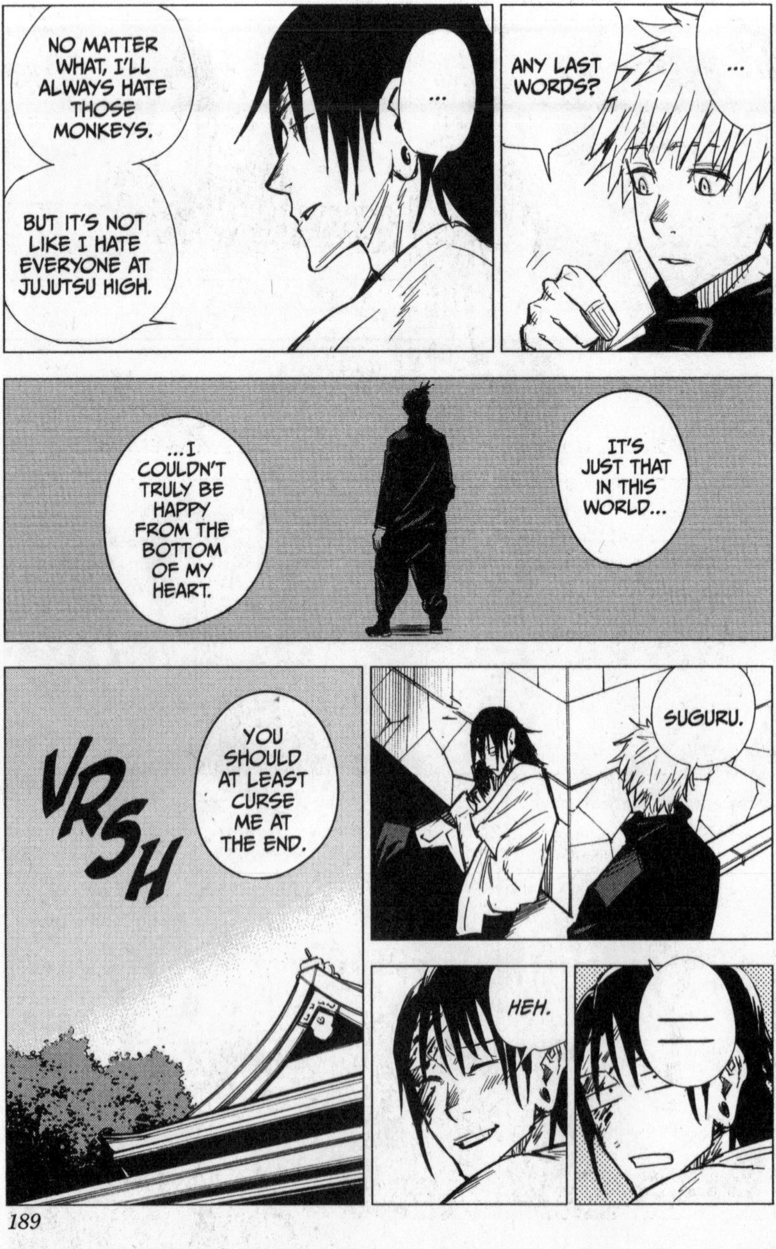
...
ANY LAST WORDS?
...
NO MATTER WHAT, I'LL ALWAYS HATE THOSE MONKEYS.
BUT IT'S NOT LIKE I HATE EVERYONE AT JUJUTSU HIGH.
IT'S JUST THAT IN THIS WORLD...
...I COULDN'T TRULY BE HAPPY FROM THE BOTTOM OF MY HEART.
SUGURU.
HEH.
YOU SHOULD AT LEAST CURSE ME AT THE END.
VRSH

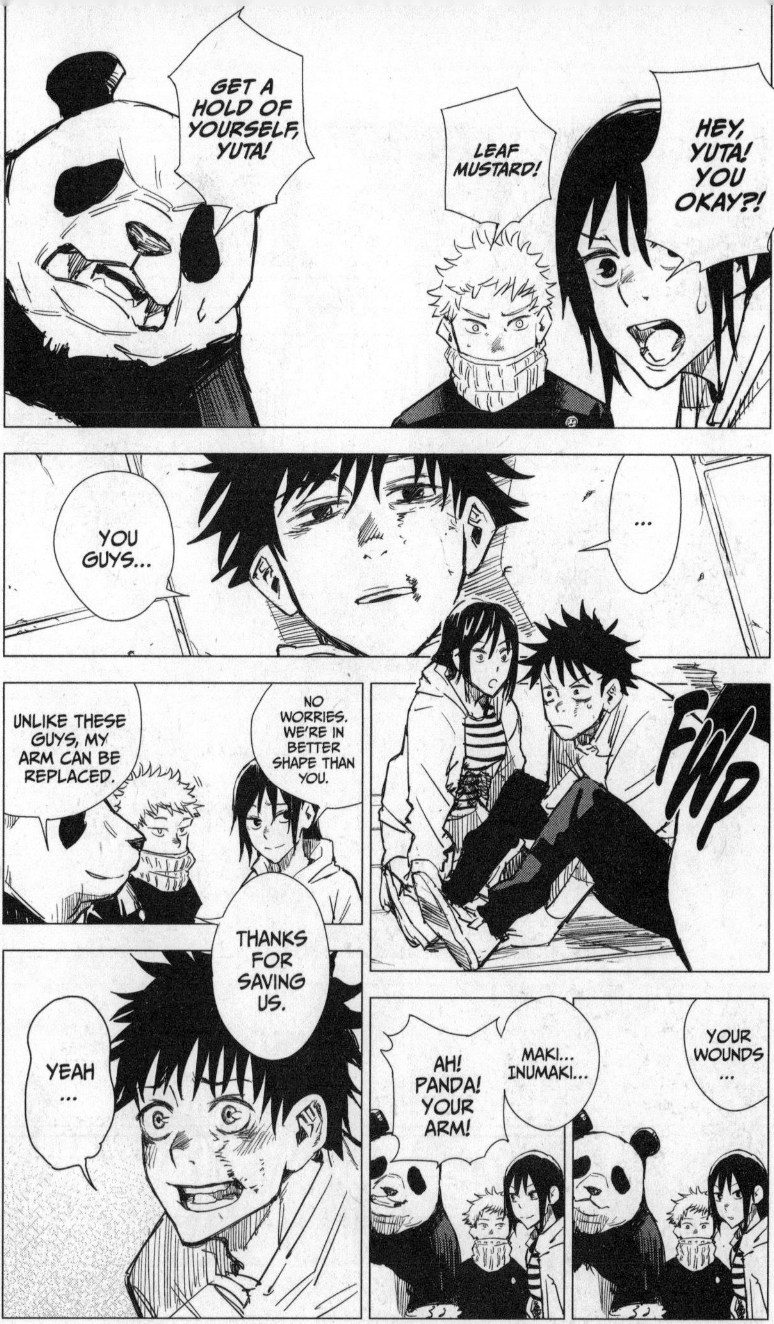
HEY, YUTA! YOU OKAY?!
LEAF MUSTARD!
GET A HOLD OF YOURSELF, YUTA!
...
YOU GUYS...
FWP
NO WORRIES. WE'RE IN BETTER SHAPE THAN YOU.
UNLIKE THESE GUYS, MY ARM CAN BE REPLACED.
YOUR WOUNDS ...
MAKI... INUMAKI...
AH! PANDA! YOUR ARM!
THANKS FOR SAVING US.
YEAH ...

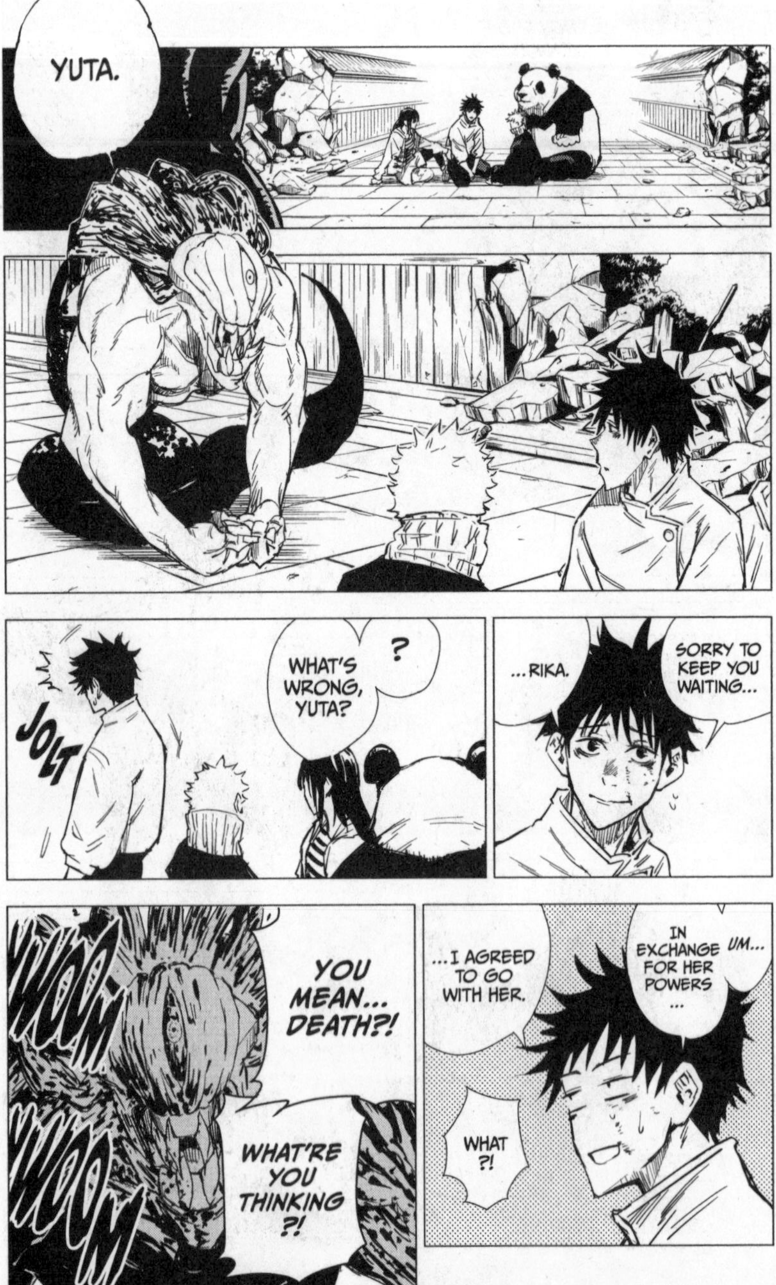
YUTA.
SORRY TO KEEP YOU WAITING...
...RIKA.
?
WHAT'S WRONG, YUTA?
JOLT
UM...
IN EXCHANGE FOR HER POWERS ...
...I AGREED TO GO WITH HER.
WHAT ?!
YOU MEAN... DEATH?!
WHAT'RE YOU THINKING ?!

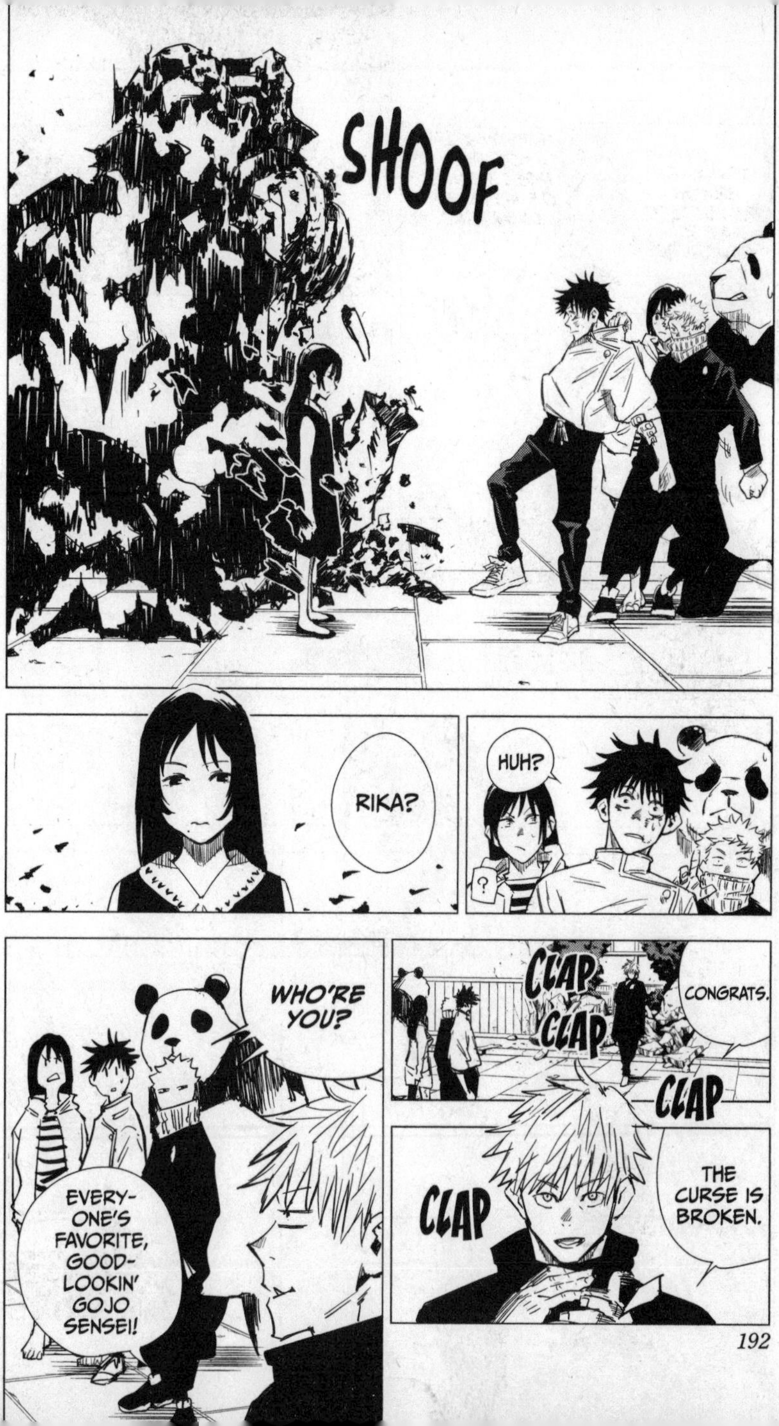
SHOOF
HUH?
RIKA?
CLAP CLAP
CONGRATS.
CLAP
CLAP
THE CURSE IS BROKEN.
WHO'RE YOU?
EVERY-ONE'S FAVORITE, GOOD-LOOKIN' GOJO SENSEI!

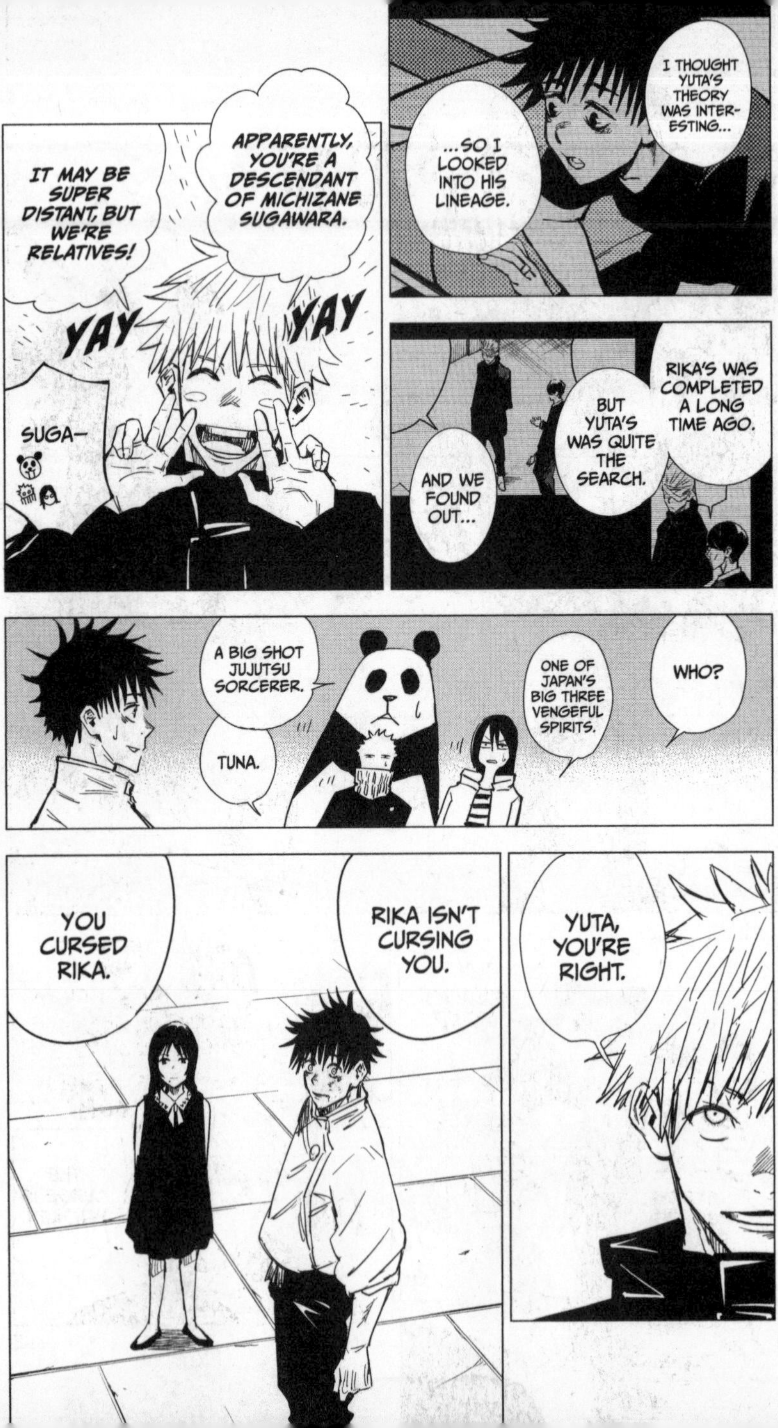
I THOUGHT YUTA'S THEORY WAS INTERESTING...
...SO I LOOKED INTO HIS LINEAGE.
RIKA'S WAS COMPLETED A LONG TIME AGO.
BUT YUTA'S WAS QUITE THE SEARCH.
AND WE FOUND OUT...
APPARENTLY, YOU'RE A DESCENDANT OF MICHIZANE SUGAWARA.
IT MAY BE SUPER DISTANT, BUT WE'RE RELATIVES!
YAY
YAY
SUGA—
WHO?
ONE OF JAPAN'S BIG THREE VENGEFUL SPIRITS.
A BIG SHOT JUJUTSU SORCERER.
TUNA.
YUTA, YOU'RE RIGHT.
RIKA ISN'T CURSING YOU.
YOU CURSED RIKA.

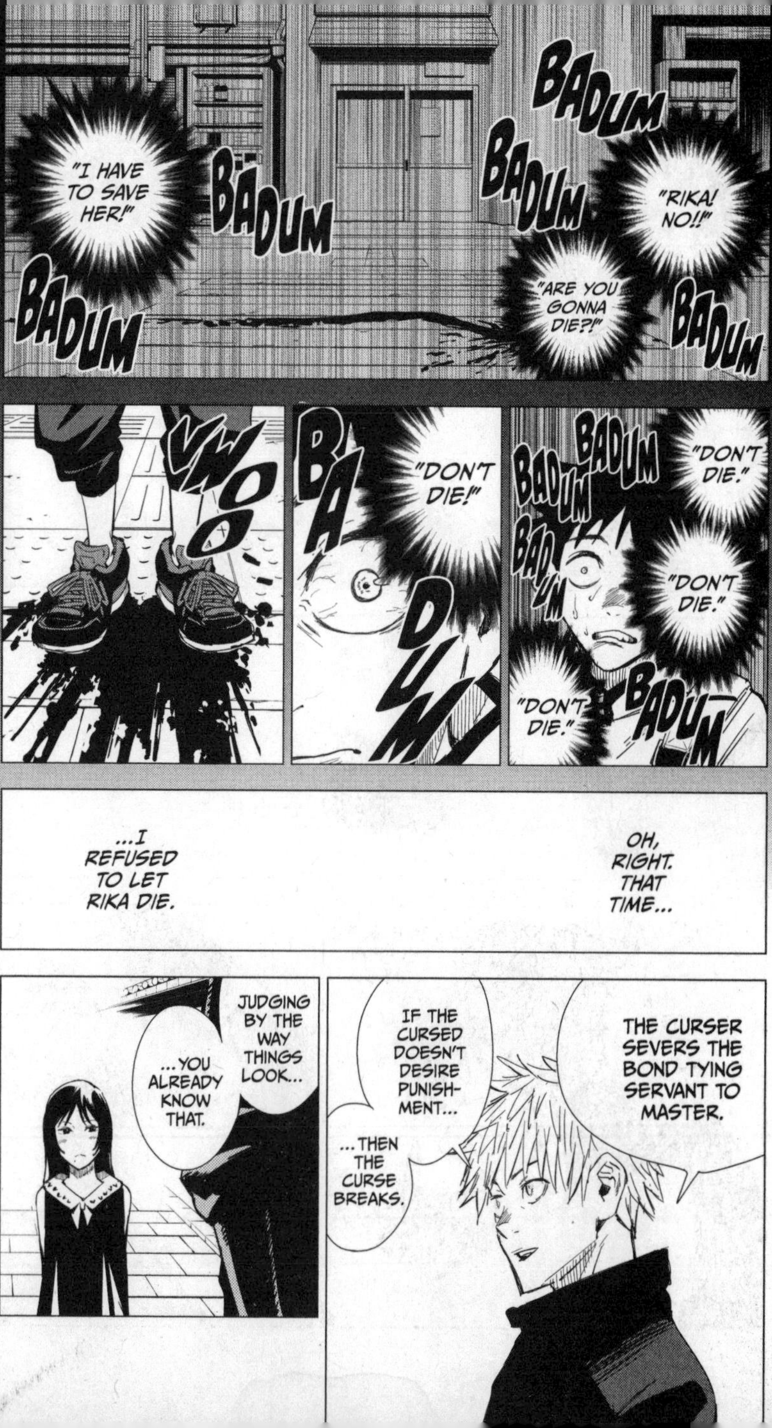
BADUM
BADUM
"RIKA! NO!!"
"ARE YOU GONNA DIE?!"
BADUM
BADUM
"I HAVE TO SAVE HER!"
BADUM
BADUM
BADUM
"DON'T DIE."
BADUM
"DON'T DIE."
"DON'T DIE."
BADUM
BA
"DON'T DIE!"
DUM
VWOO
OH, RIGHT. THAT TIME...
...I REFUSED TO LET RIKA DIE.
THE CURSER SEVERS THE BOND TYING SERVANT TO MASTER.
IF THE CURSED DOESN'T DESIRE PUNISHMENT...
...THEN THE CURSE BREAKS.
JUDGING BY THE WAY THINGS LOOK...
...YOU ALREADY KNOW THAT.

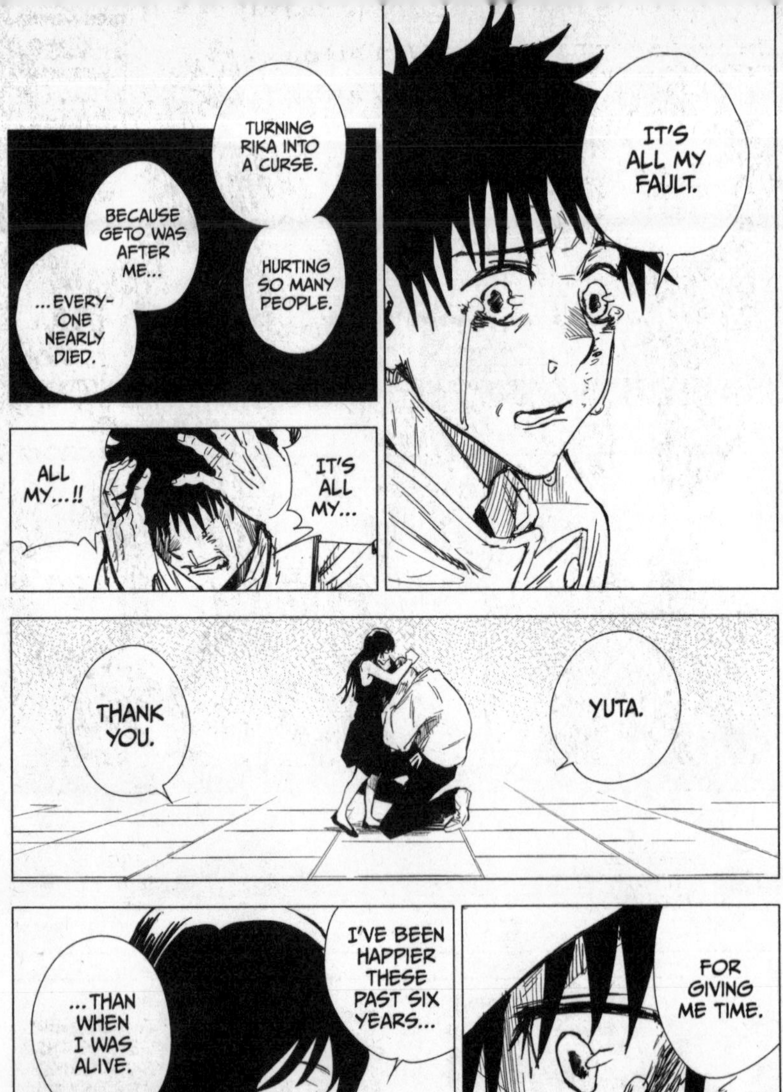
IT'S ALL MY FAULT.
TURNING RIKA INTO A CURSE.
HURTING SO MANY PEOPLE.
BECAUSE GETO WAS AFTER ME...
...EVERY-ONE NEARLY DIED.
IT'S ALL MY...
ALL MY...!!
YUTA.
THANK YOU.
FOR GIVING ME TIME.
FOR LETTING ME BE BY YOUR SIDE.
I'VE BEEN HAPPIER THESE PAST SIX YEARS...
...THAN WHEN I WAS ALIVE.

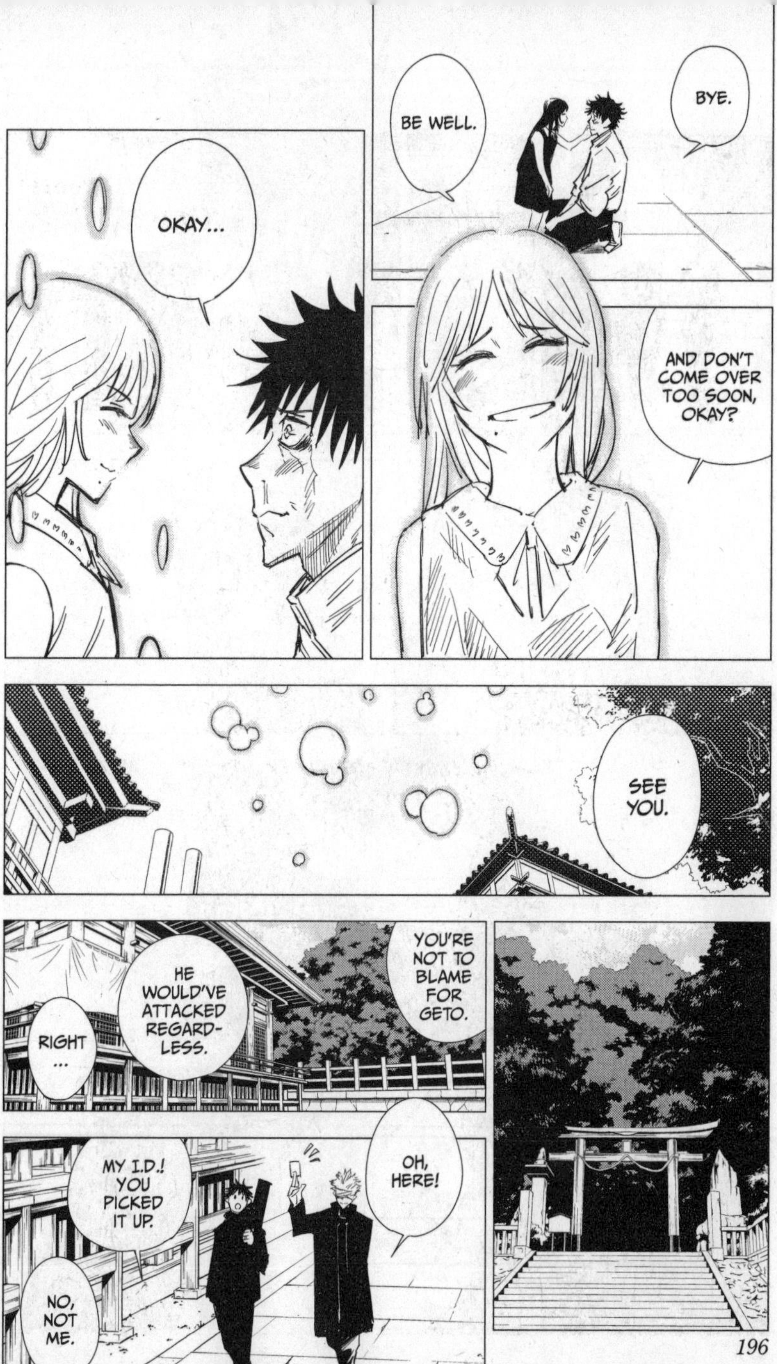
BYE.
BE WELL.
AND DON'T COME OVER TOO SOON, OKAY?
OKAY...
SEE YOU.
YOU'RE NOT TO BLAME FOR GETO.
HE WOULD'VE ATTACKED REGARD-LESS.
RIGHT ...
OH, HERE!
MY I.D.! YOU PICKED IT UP.
NO, NOT ME.

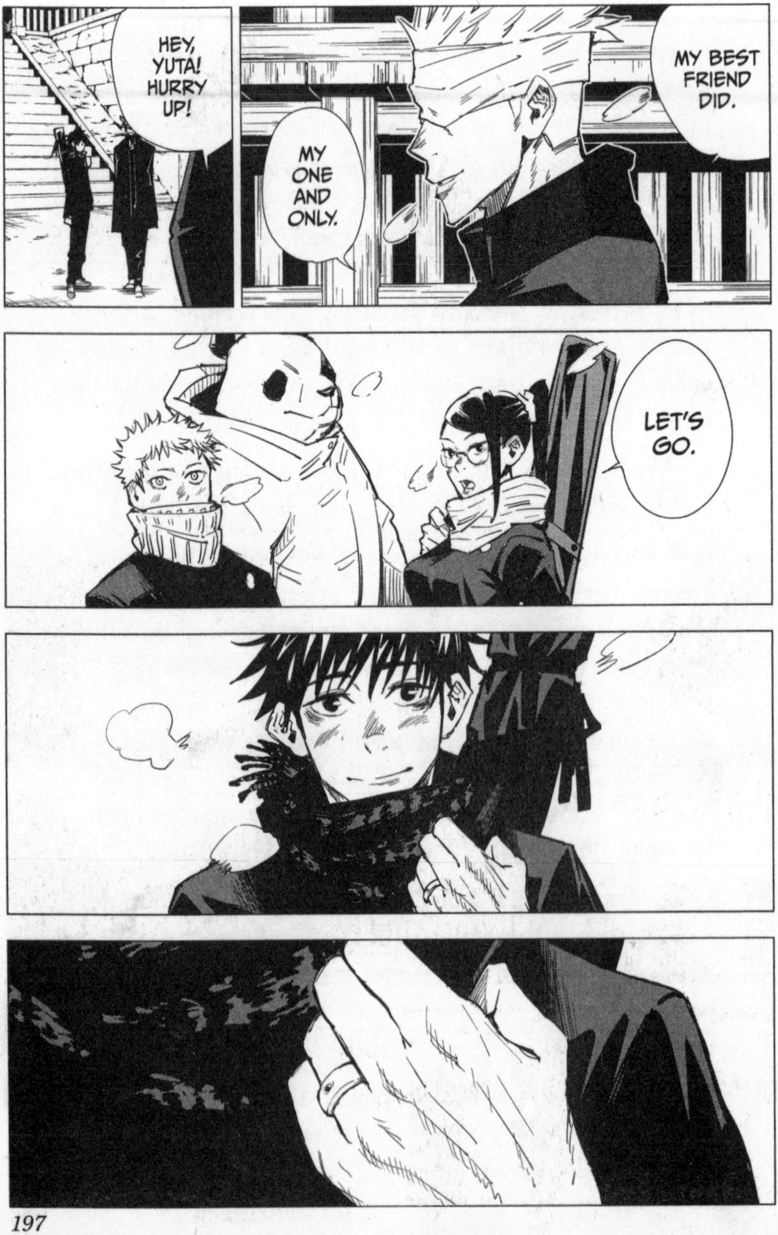
MY BEST FRIEND DID.
MY ONE AND ONLY.
HEY, YUTA! HURRY UP!
LET'S GO.

POSTSCRIPT (?)

• Truth be told, by the time volume 0's four chapters were finished for the monthly magazine, I had no intention of trying to get *Jujutsu Kaisen* serialized in *Weekly Shonen Jump*. Thankfully, the content of volume 0 was well received, so it was more convenient to get something serialized that was already made. Also, I was told that when volume 0 would be made into graphic novel format, it could be featured as a prelude to the *Weekly Shonen Jump* series and be read by a lot more people. So, I figured, "Why not?! Let's do this!" And thus, *Jujutsu Kaisen* was born!

• When I explain it like this, I make it sound as though I forced *Jujutsu Kaisen* to start, but that's not true!

• When I start a manga series, I don't really have a "theme" (principles?) in mind. I begin by thinking about things like, "These twists would be interesting" or "These characters might be cool" or "This scene would be amazing." I think in general terms when coming up with a story. (Doing it this way, I end up with a theme regardless...) For this reason, the numerous ideas I've had that didn't make the cut for other manga are being funneled into *Jujutsu Kaisen*! I'm having a blast!!

• I've already decided on the final chapter's content as well as several things that will happen along the way. However, I still don't know how the dots will connect. I hope everything will turn out okay... But will I be able to finish it...?

• To those who've read my work and support me (fan mail gives me strength), thank you for everything! I'll do my best not to let you down!

Gege Akutami

THOSE WHO'VE READ VOLUMES 1 AND 2 MIGHT HAVE NOTICED THAT THE MVP OF THE NIGHT PARADE OF A HUNDRED DEMONS IS MIGUEL.
GOOD JOB, ME!
I DID WELL!
GRK
SHORTLY THEREAFTER, MIGUEL WAS THRUST INTO A LIFE OF DIFFICULTY...
SMIRK

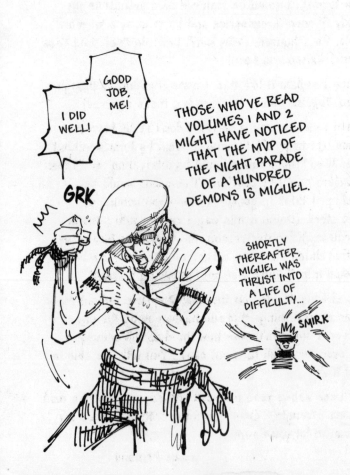

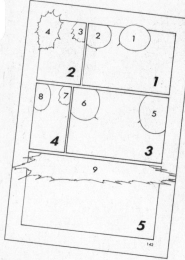

JUJUTSU KAISEN

reads from right to left, starting in the upper-right corner. Japanese is read from right to left, meaning that action, sound effects and word-balloon order are completely reversed from English order.

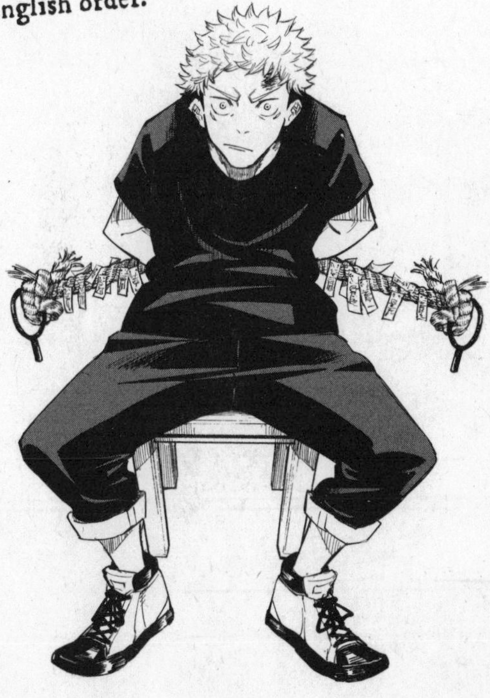